The *Real* Royal Family

The *Real* Royal Family

The Image of God in Scripture and Ethics

James E. Schultz

WIPF & STOCK · Eugene, Oregon

THE REAL ROYAL FAMILY
The Image of God in Scripture and Ethics

Wipf & Stock
An Imprint of Wipf and Stock Publishers
199 W. 8th Ave., Suite 3
Eugene, OR 97401

www.wipfandstock.com

PAPERBACK ISBN: 978-1-7252-7718-2
HARDCOVER ISBN: 978-1-7252-7719-9
EBOOK ISBN: 978-1-7252-7720-5

03/25/21

For my wife Kari
and daughters Jamie and Daphne,
with love

Contents

Acknowledgements

A LOT OF PEOPLE have shown me what it means to become more like Jesus. Though I cannot mention them all here, some had a direct or indirect bearing on this book and I would like to express my gratitude to them. My parents Larry and Sharon Schultz first introduced me to Jesus when I was young, discipled me (which was like breaking a mule), and supported me in my educational pursuits. My brother Bob, a superb drummer and even better man, has always been a reflective listener and conversation partner. My wife Kari and daughters Jamie and Daphne have supported my educational pursuits regardless of the time and expense involved. I hope to be just as supportive as they pursue their callings.

Thanks to Matthew Wimer and everyone at Wipf & Stock for your help and support. Many scholars and servants of God have shaped my perspective, methods, and values through their teaching and example over the years, including David Jones, Charles Worthington, Tim Munyon, Lavonne Larson, the late Paul Feinberg, John Feinberg, Wayne Grudem, David Howard, Andreas Köstenberger, the late James Sire, Ruth Tucker, James Hernando, Wave Nunnally, Stanley Burgess, Paul Lewis, Deborah Gill, Paige Comstock Cunningham, Scott Klusendorf, Carley Kendrick, and Debbie Lamm-Bray. The congregation of Lighthouse Assembly of God in Brookings, Oregon has been a great sounding board for the ideas expressed here, as has been my high school class at Brookings Harbor Christian School. Since this book is an adaptation of my doctoral dissertation at Assemblies of God Theological Seminary, I want to especially thank dissertation committee members Charlie Self and Doug Oss for inspiring the approach I used here and teaching me a great deal about ethics, civil dialogue, and biblical theology. My dissertation advisor James Railey Jr. deserves special recognition for his theological expertise and guidance from the beginning of this process. He meticulously combed through each chapter and helped me refine the content in many ways. My friends in the doctoral program have both inspired and amused me many times throughout the journey: Stephen Todd (go Irish!), Brian Lidbeck, Donna Bustos, Allison MacGregor, Mark Murphree, Joseph Tan, and Karissa King. My father-in-law Kerry McRoberts (the Chief) has had a great impact on me as a theology student beginning when he taught at Trinity Bible College and continuing through countless discussions right up to the present (sometimes during football games). And my mother-in-law Vicki (Scooby) has been surprisingly supportive of her incautious son-in-law!

All these faithful servants of God have helped make this book better than it would have been otherwise, but any shortcomings it possesses are on me. I thank God the Father, Son, and Holy Spirit most of all because any knowledge of truth we may have comes from God and I would be living a pointless lie if he had not drawn me into his royal family. *Soli Deo gloria.*

Abbreviations

1–2 Clem.	1–2 Clement
1–2 En.	1–2 Enoch
1QS	Rule of the Community (in the Dead Sea Scrolls)
4Q171	Pesher on Psalms (in the Dead Sea Scrolls)
4Q475	Renewed Earth (in the Dead Sea Scrolls)
Akk.	Akkadian
An.	Tertullian, *De Anima* (*The Soul*)
ANET	James Bennett Pritchard, ed. *The Ancient Near Eastern Texts Relating to the Old Testament.* 3rd ed. Edited by James B. Pritchard. Princeton: Princeton University Press, 1969.
Ant.	Josephus, *Antiquities of the Jews*
Apol.	Tertullian, *Apologeticus* (*Apology*)
Art.	Article
Barclay	Barclay New Testament
Barn.	Epistle of Barnabas
BDAG	William Arndt, Frederick W. Danker, Walter Bauer, and F. Wilbur Gingrich. *A Greek-English Lexicon of the New Testament and Other Early Christian Literature.* 3rd ed. Chicago: University of Chicago Press, 2000.
BDB	Francis Brown, Samuel Rolles Driver, and Charles Augustus Briggs. *Enhanced Brown-Driver-Briggs Hebrew and English Lexicon.* Oxford: Clarendon, 1977.

CAD	University of Chicago, and Ignace J. Gelb. *The Assyrian Dictionary of the Oriental Institute of the University of Chicago.* Chicago: Oriental Institute, 1956.
CD	Karl Barth. *Church Dogmatics.* Edited by Thomas Forsyth Torrance. Translated by Geoffrey W. Bromiley. London: T. & T. Clark, 2004.
Cf.	Compare
Conf.	Philo, *De Confusione Linguarum* (*On the Confusion of Tongues*)
Cult. fem.	Tertullian, *De Cultu Feminarum* (*The Apparel of Women*)
De Fid. Orth.	John of Damascus, *De Fide Orthodoxa* (*The Orthodox Faith*)
EDNT	Horst Balz and Gerhard Schneider, eds. *Exegetical Dictionary of the New Testament.* 3 vols. Grand Rapids, MI: Eerdmans, 1991.
E.g.	For example
Ep.	Pliny the Younger, *Epistulae* (*Epistles*)
ESV	English Standard Version
Et al.	And others
Eth. Enoch	Ethiopic Enoch
Fug.	Philo, *De Fuga et Inventione* (*On Flight and Finding*)
Gen. litt.	Augustine, *De Genesi ad Litteram* (*On Genesis Literally Interpreted*)
Gen. Man.	Augustine, *De Genesi Contra Manichaeos* (*On Genesis against the Manichaeans*)
Gen. Rab.	Genesis Rabbah (from the Talmud)
Gig.	Philo, *De Gigantibus* (*On Giants*)
GNB	Good News Bible
Haer.	Irenaeus, *Adversus Haereses* (*Against Heresies*)
HALOT	Ludwig Koehler, Walter Baumgartner, M. E. J. Richardson, and Johann Jakob Stamm. *The Hebrew and Aramaic Lexicon of the Old Testament.* 5 vols. Leiden; New York: E. J. Brill, 1999.

HCSB	Holman Christian Standard Bible
Hist. eccl.	Eusebius, *Historia Ecclesiastica* (*Ecclesiastical History*)
Hist. rom.	Dio Cassius, *Historiae Romanae* (*Roman History*)
Hom. Luc.	Origen, *Homiliae in Lucam* (*Homilies on Luke*)
I.e.	that is (in other words)
ILO	International Labor Organization
Isaac	Ambrose, *De Isaac vel anima Isaac* (*Isaac, or The Soul*)
Jub.	Jubilees
KJV	King James Version
L.A.E.	Life of Adam and Eve
L&N	Johannes P. Louw and Eugene Albert Nida. *Greek-English Lexicon of the New Testament: Based on Semantic Domains.* New York: United Bible Societies, 1996.
LEB	Lexham English Bible
Leg. 1, 2, 3	Philo, *Legum Allegoriae 1, 2, 3* (*Allegorical Interpretation 1, 2, 3*)
Legat.	Philo, *Legatio ad Gaium* (*On the Embassy to Gaius*)
LXX	The Septuagint
Marc.	Tertullian, *Adversus Marcionem* (*Against Marcion*)
N	Note (footnote or endnote)
NASB	New American Standard Version
NEB	New English Bible
NIV	New International Version
NKJV	New King James Version
NLT	New Living Translation
NT	New Testament
Op. cit.	In the work already cited
Opif.	Philo, *De Opificio Mundi* (*On the Creation of the World*)
OT	Old Testament

Phaen.	Aratus, *Phaenomena* (*Phenomena*)
Pud.	Tertullian, *De Pudicitia* (*Modesty*)
Q.	Question
Serm.	Augustine, *Sermones* (*Sermons*)
Sir	Sirach
Somn. 1, 2	Philo, *De Somnis 1, 2* (*On Dreams*)
TDNT	*Theological Dictionary of the New Testament.* 10 vols. Edited by Gerhard Kittel and Gerhard Friedrich. Translated by Geoffrey W. Bromiley. Grand Rapids: Eerdmans, 1964–76.
Test. Dan	Testament of Dan
Test. Levi	Testament of Levi
Theaet.	Plato, *Theaetetus*
TLNT	Ceslas Spicq and James D. Ernest. *Theological Lexicon of the New Testament.* 3 vols. Translated and edited by James D. Ernest. Peabody, MA: Hendrickson, 1994.
TLOT	Ernst Jenni and Claus Westermann. *Theological Lexicon of the Old Testament.* 3 vols. Translated by Mark Biddle. Peabody, MA: Hendrickson, 1997.
Trin.	Augustine, *De Trinitate* (*The Trinity*)
War	Josephus, *Wars of the Jews*

Introduction

Then God said, "Let us make mankind in our image, in our likeness,
so that they may rule over the fish in the sea and the birds in the sky,
over the livestock and all the wild animals, and over all the creatures that
move along the ground." So God created mankind in his own image,
in the image of God he created them; male and female he created them.
God blessed them and said to them, "Be fruitful and increase in number;
fill the earth and subdue it. Rule over the fish in the sea and the birds
in the sky and over every living creature that moves on the ground."

(GEN 1:26–28)[1]

CHRISTIANS BELIEVE THAT GOD created human beings in his image and likeness and that this truth grounds the value of human life (Gen 9:6). But with these points the consensus ends because several questions receive very different answers from various Christians. What exactly is the image of God? Is the likeness of God the same thing as the image, or is it different? Are unborn children and the mentally disabled made in God's image? Does sin destroy the image of God, damage it, or not have any effect on the image at all? How does the image of God relate to the blessing and mandate in Genesis 1:28? No small amount of ink has been spilled to answer these questions, but the debate continues, owing perhaps to a combination of factors including the rarity of scriptural references to the image and likeness, the lack of a straightforward definition of the

---

1. Unless otherwise noted, all verse designations are from English versions, including where they differ from the Hebrew OT.

image in Scripture itself, and the theological, philosophical, political, and cultural assumptions and agendas interpreters bring to the study.[2]

Some interpreters think the image of God refers to capacities of the soul like reason, conscience, and free will. This structural view dominated Christian thought up until the last century or so. Others think humanity's relationship to God or capacity for relationships with God, others, and creation is what the image is all about. Relational interpretations grew influential throughout the twentieth century. At the same time, others, especially Old Testament specialists, set forth a resurgent royal/functional view that exercising dominion in creation is what it means to image God.[3] Others combine some or all of these ideas into an eclectic view. "And" is sometimes better than "or," particularly when the options do not contradict each other and when Scripture seems to support all the ideas. But adherents of these views sometimes do make mutually exclusive statements so that one must choose one or another perspective. And the interpretations and applications of these texts are also mutually exclusive at times.

This debate matters. American culture has recently become more aware of the worldwide problem of human trafficking. A 2012 study by the International Labour Organization (an agency of the United Nations) estimated that there were nearly twenty-one million slaves worldwide, 55 percent of whom were women and girls. Twenty-two percent of slaves were enslaved for sexual purposes while 68 percent were for labor exploitation.[4] The last century witnessed several genocides, including those by the Nazi Regime, the Soviets, Maoist China, the Khmer Rouge in Cambodia, and the Young Turks against the Armenians.[5]

Religious persecution continues around the world. Over the last ten years, approximately nine hundred thousand Christians have been killed for their faith.[6] The Council on Foreign Relations is tracking over two dozen conflicts and potential conflicts around the world, including the civil war in Syria, Russian aggression in Ukraine, tensions over North Korean nuclear and ballistic missile development, Boko Haram militancy

---

2. See Kilner, *Dignity and Destiny*, 37–51.

3. See Middleton, *Liberating Image*, 17–29 for a brief historical survey.

4. "ILO Global Estimate," paras. 5, 4.

5. "Modern Era Genocides."

6. "Status of Global Christianity."

in Nigeria, the destabilization of Mali, and others.[7] Nine nations have nuclear weapons and another two are clearly attempting to develop them.[8]
One wonders how much longer it will be before someone else decides to
use them on a civilian population.

There have been over sixty-one million surgical abortions performed
legally in the United States since 1973 and countless chemical abortions
due to abortifacient "contraceptives" and emergency "contraceptives."[9]
Recently, investigative journalists from the Center for Medical Progress
released a number of undercover videos showing that Planned Parenthood has been selling the parts of aborted fetuses for profit.[10] Assisted
suicide is now legal in nine states plus the District of Colombia: Oregon,
Colorado, Hawaii, Maine, New Jersey, Vermont, Washington, Montana,
and California. Oregon, the first state to legalize the practice, saw 1,657
patients end their lives this way between 1997 and early 2020. Washington had nearly that many (1,622) by the time they released their 2019
annual report in spite of the fact that the practice has only been legal
since 2009.[11] Whereas biotechnology has produced welcome tools for
the diagnosis, treatment, and prevention of diseases, it has also given
rise to heated debates about the ethics of embryonic stem-cell research,
therapeutic cloning, gene therapy, genetic enhancement, and other issues

7. "Global Conflict Tracker." My point here is not that all armed conflict is necessarily wrong. War is a tragic consequence of the fall and often involves the desecration
of human beings in various horrendous ways.

8. "Nuclear Weapons: Who Has What?"

9. "Physician-Assisted Suicide Fast Facts." Quotation marks around contraceptives
appear because many such measures may allow conception but prevent implantation
of the embryo. Pro-life people acknowledge the biological fact that pregnancy begins
with conception/fertilization and thus these cases involve early abortions. Some pro-
choice people do not consider a woman to be pregnant until implantation and regard
the intentional demise of embryos before implantation as contraception even though
conception has obviously occurred and contraception refers to a means of preventing
conception. See Beckwith, *Defending Life*, 162–63.

10. See "Investigative Footage." Planned Parenthood's attempt to discredit these
videos asks us to believe that anything not included in the footage provided by the
Center for Medical Progress, if known, would somehow mean Planned Parenthood
staff members did not say what they clearly said on the videos. See the unconvincing
article by Calmes, "Planned Parenthood Videos Were Altered." For the testimony of
these same Planned Parenthood employees under oath admitting to fetal trafficking
for profit as well as infanticide, see "Fetal Trafficking Under Oath" as well as the court
documents provided by the Center for Medical Progress on the same website.

11. "Physician-Assisted Suicide Fast Facts."

involving human tissue.[12] America has recently debated the ethics of enhanced interrogation on suspected terrorists in the interests of national security.[13] And this is only a partial list of ways humans beings are being mistreated or potentially mistreated today.

The positions people hold about the image of God can have profound consequences for the actions they allow, prescribe, and proscribe. This is a key argument of John Kilner's book, *Dignity and Destiny: Humanity in the Image of God*.[14] That is, one can defend human value and thus rights for all humans using a theology of the image, or one can try to justify desecrating and abusing some human beings using a theology of the image.

My own interest in the image of God relates primarily to ethics and the purposes God has in mind for human life. I have cared deeply about the abortion debate since I watched a little girl, about twelve weeks gestation, being dismembered using a suction tip. She was shown in a film called *The Silent Scream*, in which ultrasound technology was used to provide viewers with a window into the womb during an abortion.[15] As an eleven year old boy, I was outraged that such violence was legal and thought to be morally acceptable in America. I have never gotten over that sense of the injustice of the act. I had no defined theology of the image of God, but only a sense that her life had value to the God who created her. I later based my belief in the value of her life on the image of God. Ironically, writers like Dolores Dunnett have defended the right to abortion in certain cases by appealing to the image of God that pro-lifers have appealed to in opposition to abortion.[16] Thus, there is a need for careful biblical interpretation and application on the subject of God's image.

In order to arrive at the most biblically warranted conclusion possible, chapters 1 and 2 begin with a biblical theology of the image of God (Old Testament and New Testament, respectively). Vern Poythress delineates several types of biblical theology, including the one to be used here, a single theme approach wherein "one can follow the historical

---

12. See Mitchell et al., *Biotechnology*.

13. See "Debate: Enhanced Interrogation."

14. See Kilner, *Dignity and Destiny*, 3–51 for a case that certain views of the image of God lead to devastation rather than liberation of human beings. This issue will be discussed below.

15. Nathanson, *Silent Scream*.

16. Dunnett, "Evangelicals and Abortion," 216. On her argument, see chapter 4.

development of a single theme within the whole of special revelation."[17] The theme will not be used as an organizing center for an entire Bible biblical theology. At the same time, it will be developed in conversation with biblical theologians who have developed some understanding of the image of God within such comprehensive biblical theologies. The relevant texts are Gen 1:26–27; 5:1–3; 9:6; Exod 20:4–6; Deut 5:8–10; 4:16–17; Ps 8:5; Dan 2:35; 3:1; Matt 22:20–21; Col 1:15; 2 Cor 4:4; 1 Cor 11:7; Acts 17:28–29; Col 3:9–10; Eph 4:22–24; 2 Cor 3:18; 1 Cor 15:49; Rom 8:29; Jas 3:9; Heb 2:7; and 1 John 3:2. These will be covered roughly in the order in which they were revealed in history (often but not necessarily by date of writing), except in the case of Paul, whose material is best treated according to his eschatological framework of what was, what is already, and what is not yet. Several of these passages quote or allude to other image texts and thus provide intertextual exegesis. These inspired interpretations of earlier Scripture passages will be carefully noted for their contributions to the image of God concept. The hope is that sticking to the subjects, teachings, and emphases of the biblical authors will facilitate hearing the Divine author of Scripture as he sets the agenda rather than imposing foreign agendas and categories onto the biblical material.[18]

Naturally, no interpreter is immune to biases, preconceived ideas, and interests as to the conclusions. The zeitgeist can have a powerful influence on anyone. As C. Clifton Black points out, "The interpretation of the image of God has often reflected the *Zeitgeist* and has followed whatever emphasis happened to be current in psychology, or philosophy, or sociology, or theology—to which one is tempted to add the biological sciences."[19] Broadly speaking, it was tempting to see reason as central to God's image in rationalistic times, especially for theologians and philosophers. Similarly, when existentialism reigned, freedom and personal relationship may have seemed to be the essence of the image of God. And today, when environmental concerns are paramount to so many people, ecologically responsible dominion comes to the fore in expositions of the image. The hope is to follow the image of God concept as it unfolds diachronically through biblical revelation, letting the biblical material point the way to the proper understanding of God's image and likeness.

17. Poythress, "Kinds of Biblical Theology," 135. This single theme approach is found throughout Alexander and Rosner, *New Dictionary of Biblical Theology*.

18. For a discussion of the types, methods, challenges, and promise of biblical theology, see Carson, "Current Issues in Biblical Theology," 17–41.

19. Black, "God's Promise," 2352–53.

While working with the biblical evidence, interpreters must be introspective about the influence of such cultural moods, whether one's bias tends to be for or against them. Further, it is worth remembering that one may provide biblical grounding for the value of reason, freedom, relationship, and dominion without including those things in the image of God doctrine. Such realities may relate to the image without actually constituting it.

Chapter 3 will consider the implications of the biblical theology of the image of God for systematic theology. Systematic theology synthesizes the results of exegesis and biblical theology by ordering material in a logical manner and addressing the questions of the past and present. Several views of the image will be presented, evaluated, and mined for contributions to the doctrine to be defended here.

One key test for a systematic theology is how well it comports with the results of exegesis and biblical theology. Systematic theology need not de-historicize ideas, organizing them into timeless principles, as sometimes happens. One can state ideas logically while doing justice to their historical revelation and enactment in salvation history. Such concerns are why a systematic presentation follows a redemptive-historical one here.

Systematic theologies are also tested by their internal consistency. In line with both Vosian biblical theology and evangelical systematic theology, the consistency of the biblical materials is here presupposed based on the inspiration and inerrancy of Scripture.[20] Therefore, a valid test of the doctrine of the image of God will be whether it is consistent. Internal consistency does not guarantee that the doctrine is biblical and true, but inconsistency guarantees that something in the doctrine has gone awry. It would be too much to expect such a brief treatment to answer every relevant question and to tease out all the implications of the view here defended, but hopefully it can be shown how an exegetically informed biblical theology informs a proper systematic theology of the image of God.

Chapter 4 will explore the implications of the resulting doctrine of the image of God for human value. Though there are plenty of implications of the image for ethics in other areas, human dignity will be the focus here. Kilner argues forcefully that if a theology of the image of God says the term refers to present human capacities, ones that are negatively affected by sin, then human dignity is not thereby well-founded, and

20. See Vos, *Biblical Theology*, 11–14; Geisler, *Inerrancy*.

those who would desecrate and destroy humans would have a theological justification for doing so.[21] Since Genesis 9:6 bases human value on being made in God's image, the image must be an adequate foundation. Thus, any reading of the image concept that does not found human value adequately is not the biblical view. And this is only one way a theology of the image can be wide of mark. The crucial thing is to not merely claim that a theology of God's image grounds human value, but to follow the logic of the affirmations about God's image to their conclusions and evaluate them realistically. The major views of God's image will be evaluated this way, and insights gleaned from them will be applied to providing a solid foundation for human value based on the doctrine of the image to be defended here.

Old and New Testament scholars who study the image do not always thoroughly take into account the insights and concerns of systematic theologians and ethicists, and vice versa.[22] Naturally, the order in which the doctrine should be formulated starts with exegesis and biblical theology, proceeds to systematic theology, and culminates in ethical implications, as will be done here. Yet systematic theology and ethics can and should inform the biblical scholar's analysis. As previously shown, an idea of the image may be set forth by biblical scholars and systematicians only to be shown to be inadequate as a basis of human value. And this should drive interpreters back to the text to listen more carefully, to formulate doctrine more accurately, and to choose terminology more wisely. The interaction between the text and the interpreter with all his or her assumptions and agendas is a complex one. It may go back and forth many times in the interest of sharpening one's understanding.[23] Hopefully this study can bring these approaches together and yield a concept of the image that makes sense of the biblical passages, is internally consistent and comprehensible, and guides the church and the world to virtuous, Christlike character and good work that glorifies God and benefits all of his creation.

21. Kilner, *Dignity and Destiny*, 18, 22.

22. Middleton, *Liberating Image*, 24, especially highlights the problem of systematic theologians ignoring works on the image by Old Testament scholars.

23. This is the central theme in Osborne, *Hermeneutical Spiral*.

Chapter 1

A Biblical Theology of the Image of God

(Old Testament)

Genesis 1:26–27

THE STORY BEGINS WITH Moses, writing in the fifteenth century BC.[1] Genesis 1:26 says, "Then God said, 'Let us make mankind in our image,

1. There are good reasons to believe Moses wrote Genesis through Deuteronomy. The Pentateuch repeatedly tells us Moses recorded the covenant, laws, and events about which the books were written, sometimes at God's command (Exod 17:14; 24:4–7; 34:27; Num 33:1–2; Deut 31:9–11). Since Exodus begins with "and" (1:1) and clearly carries on the story of Genesis, it is natural to think Moses also wrote Genesis. Further, the authors of other historical and prophetic books attributed the Law to Moses (Josh 1:8; 8:31; 1 Kgs 2:3; 2 Kgs 14:6; 21:8; Ezra 6:18; Neh 13:1; Dan 9:11–13; Mal 4:4). Jesus and the apostles attributed statements from the Pentateuch to Moses (Matt 19:8; Mark 12:26; John 5:46–47; 7:19; Acts 3:22; Rom 10:5). Tellingly, Jesus spoke of circumcision in fulfillment of the Law of Moses in John 7:23. The practice was introduced in Genesis 17:12 and further explained in Exodus 12:48 and Leviticus 12:13. See Archer, *Survey*, 117–18, 193. See also Archer's critique of the Documentary Hypothesis on pp. 113–16. Note especially his third criticism: "The Documentarians assume that Hebrew authors differ from any other writers known in the history of literature in that they alone were incapable of using more than one name for God; more than one style of writing, no matter what the difference in subject matter; or more than one of several possible synonyms for a single idea; or even more than one theme-type or circle of interest (114). As to the date of the Exodus, which determines when Moses wrote, the earlier date of about 1,446 BC is to be preferred over the later date of 1,290 BC. Both views have strengths and difficulties, but the former has the advantage of confirmation within the biblical accounts. In Judges 11:26, Jephthah refers to three hundred years that the Ammonites failed to challenge Israelite settlements in Gilead. This would have been before King Saul's reign, which began in 1,050 BC and would have pushed the conquest back to around 1,400 BC. Paul's timeline in Acts 13:19–20 is of the four hundred and fifty

in our likeness.'" A number of debated exegetical issues surround this foundational text. The analysis to follow will focus on in whose image humans are made, defining the terms image (ṣelem) and likeness (dəmut) in the context of Genesis, relating them to one another properly, assessing the prepositions bě (in) and kě (in) for the light they shed on the subject, relating the resulting understanding of the image and likeness to the cultural commission of Genesis 1:28,[2] and considering whether image and likeness pertain to whole human individuals, parts of human individuals, all of humanity corporately, or some combination of these options.

In Whose Image Are Humans Made?

Because God insists that he is the only God (Deut 6:4) and many of the revelations that led to the formulation of the doctrine of the Trinity came later, interpreters have long struggled with the meaning of the plurals "Let *us* make mankind in *our* image, in *our* likeness" (emphasis mine). There are several lines of interpretation, some of which could impact one's understanding of God's image.

The first possibility is that God is addressing angels in his heavenly court. This understanding has been favored by many Jewish interpreters from Philo on and benefits from a possible parallel in Isaiah 6:8: "Whom shall I send? And who will go for us?" The "us" apparently includes the seraphim of verses 2 and 6. Gordon Wenham argues for this view by pointing out that angels are sometimes portrayed as men in the OT (Gen 18:2). Though 1:27 goes on to use the singular "So God created mankind in *his* own image, in the image of God *he* created them; male and female *he* created them" (italics mine), this shows that God was announcing his climactic work of creating humans to the heavenly court. Job 38:4 and 7 similarly speak of angels (the sons of God) shouting for joy when God created the earth.[3] Gerhard von Rad also favored this view, appealing to

---

years from the beginning of the Exodus to the conquest of Jerusalem during David's reign in approximately 995 BC, which pushes the Exodus back to about 1,445 BC. See Archer, *Survey*, 239–52. On either date, Genesis is clearly our earliest text regarding the image of God.

2. Anthony Hoekema defines the cultural mandate/commission as "the command to rule the earth for God, and to develop a God-glorifying culture." Hoekema, *Created in God's Image*, 14. Beale calls it the "Adamic commission." Beale, *New Testament Biblical Theology*, 64.

3. Wenham, *Genesis 1–15*, 27–28.

Psalm 8, itself a reflection on Genesis 1: "In it Yahweh is addressed; nevertheless, man is said to be made a little lower than 'Elohim.' This means that God's image does not refer directly to Yahweh but to the 'angels.' So also in verse 26. The extraordinary plural ("Let us") prevents one from referring God's image too directly to God the Lord."[4]

With respect to this last argument, David J. A. Clines counters, "But we may ask, why an author who was too sensitive to write 'I will make man in my image' proceeded to say in the next verse 'God created man in *his* image.'"[5] Regarding the Job parallel, the analogy breaks down in that Job has the angels only witnessing creation whereas Genesis would have God inviting them to create with him. Yet God had no assistance from a created being when he created everything (Isa 44:24).[6] The argument from Psalm 8 is not convincing if *Elohim* there refers to God (as will be argued below). Finally, there is no mention of angels in the first twenty-five verses of Genesis with the result that this interpretation requires readers to think the author uses pronouns for beings that had not yet been introduced into the narrative. In fact, angels do not appear in Genesis until 3:24, just after God has again used the plural "one of us."

A second view suggests that the author was borrowing from a polytheistic account and retained the plurals unintentionally. Clines attributes this view to Hermann Gunkel. This view assumes that the Documentary Hypothesis is correct in attributing the Pentateuch to multiple authors, none of whom were Moses, whose works were then edited to form the documents in their final form. However, even those who believe Moses wrote Genesis and the rest of the Pentateuch tend to think he used earlier source material. For this reason, Clines's question concerning Gunkel's position shows that it is unconvincing for those on both sides of the authorship divide. He asks, "If the author of Genesis 1 was in every other instance able to remove all trace of polytheism from the traditional material he was handling, as he is generally agreed to have done, why did he not manage to expunge the plural of 'let us'? Did he not realize the contradiction between 'let us' and 'God created' (verse 27; וַיִּבְרָא singular verb)?"[7]

A third view is that perhaps God is including the earth in *us*, for it had been mentioned in verse 24. Maimonides and some other Jewish

4. Rad, *Genesis*, 58.

5. Clines, "Image of God," 67. I am indebted to Clines's excellent analysis throughout this section.

6. Clines, "Image of God," 67.

7. Clines, "Image of God," 64.

interpreters held this view. But again, verse 27 attributes human creation to God alone.[8] For God to make humans from the ground is not the same as considering the ground a cocreator with God.

A fourth possibility is that they are plurals of self-deliberation similar to when one says, "Let's see." Possible parallels can be found in Genesis 11:7 ("let us go down"), Song of Solomon 1:11 ("we will make;" cf. v. 9 singular), and 2 Samuel 24:14 ("Let us fall"). This view has no difficulty with the singular of verse 27 since God is only referring to himself. In fact, as Clines points out, the comparative lack of difficulties for this view may be the best thing one can say in its favor.[9]

Fifth, they could be plurals of majesty. *Elohim* is the most notable example of this intensification that magnifies the fullness of God and his attributes by using the plural. The plural form could be used of many gods (e.g., Exod 12:12) or the emphatically singular God, Yahweh (Deut 6:4). According to Jack Scott, *Elohim* only occurs in Hebrew and uniquely conveys both unity and plurality. When plurals of majesty have a singular referent, the noun is usually accompanied by singular verbs, pronouns, and adjectives.[10] But the pronouns "us" and "our" in verse 26 would have to be exceptions to this rule. W. H. Schmidt shows that there is some flexibility in this regard.

> As a designation for Israel's God, ʾelōhîm is grammatically construed to be sg. generally (Gen 1:1; Ps 7:10; 2 Kgs 19:4), but can also be accompanied by a pl. attribute or predicate with no recognizable difference in meaning. Often both possibilities are found in the same body of literature: ʾelōhîm ḥayyîm "living God" (Deut 5:26; 1 Sam 17:26, 36; Jer 10:10; 23:36) and ʾelōhîm ḥay (2 Kgs 19:4, 16; cf. 2 Sam 2:27), ʾelōhîm qədōšîm "holy God" (Josh 24:19) and hā ʾelōhîm haqqādôš (1 Sam 6:20); cf. also . . . 1 Sam . . . 28:13; Ps 58:12.[11]

Clines rejects this view, pointing to the lack of just such exceptions.[12] This view has no difficulty with the singulars in verse 27. As E. A. Speiser

8. Clines, "Image of God," 65.

9. Clines, "Image of God," 68.

10. Scott, "אלה," 44; Gesenius, *Hebrew Grammar*, 398–99.

11. Schmidt, "אֱלֹהִים," 117–18. He cites some of the same examples as Gesenius, *Hebrew Grammar*, 428–29.

12. Clines, "Image of God," 65.

points out, if the pronouns are plural simply to match *Elohim*, then the issue is purely grammatical and does not affect the meaning of the passage.[13]

A sixth option is that the plural is an early intimation of plurality
in the one God. If one translates *ruaḥ* in verse 2 "the *Spirit* of God was
hovering over the waters," as many modern translations rightly do,[14] then
that provides a being in the previous verses for Elohim to include in the
"us" and "our" of verse 26. Then, too, there is no problem with the singulars in verse 27 if the Spirit is in a real sense one with the Father. John
Peter Lange set forth this view over one-hundred and fifty years ago.[15]
Clines defends it by referencing a few passages that attribute creative
work to the Holy Spirit, such as Job 33:4 ("The Spirit of God has made
me; the breath of the Almighty gives me life"), Psalm 104:30 ("When you
send your Spirit, they are created, and you renew the face of the ground"),
and Ezekiel 37 (God puts his Spirit into Israel and brings them to life).
Anticipating the objection that such a thought would not have occurred
to the monotheistic author of Genesis, Clines counters,

> If one compares the vivid personification of Yahweh's wisdom in
> Proverbs 8 as His partner in creation, it is perhaps not inconceiv-
> able that the Spirit could have been similarly thought of by the
> author of Genesis 1 as another 'person' within the Divine Being.
> Certainly the Spirit is in a number of places depicted as distinct
> from Yahweh (e.g., the Spirit of Yahweh in Judges), though no-
> where so obviously personal as in the New Testament.[16]

Wenham will not rule this out as the *sensus plenior* (fuller sense) of
the passage (in his case, building on the notion that "us" includes the angels). He says, "Certainly the NT sees Christ as active in creation with the
Father, and this provided the foundation for the Early Church to develop
a Trinitarian interpretation. But such insights were certainly beyond the
horizon of the editor of Genesis."[17] But this may not be an all-or-nothing
issue, as Victor Hamilton points out: "It is one thing to say that the author
of Gen. 1 was not schooled in the intricacies of Christian dogma. It is

---

13. Speiser, *Genesis*, 7.

14. NIV (quoted), KJV, LEB, NLT, ESV, NASB, NKJV. Cf. NRSV's "a wind from God."

15. Lange, *Genesis*, 173.

16. Clines, "Image of God," 69.

17. Wenham, *Genesis 1–15*, 28.

another thing to say he was theologically too primitive or naïve to handle such ideas as plurality within unity."[18]

As to the specific role of Christ in creation, Colossians 1 calls Jesus the image of God (v. 15), alluding to and interpreting Genesis 1:26. Then in 3:10, Colossians says the new humanity is "being renewed in knowledge in the image of its Creator." This means Christ is the pattern in which we humans were made (and are being remade) and should logically be included in the "our" and "us" of Genesis 1:26. Colossians 1:16 also says all things (which includes humans) were created "through him and for him" (v. 16; see also John 1:1–3). This means Christ should also be included in the statement, "So God created mankind in his own image" (Gen 1:27). There is an argument, then, from the context of Genesis 1 for the Holy Spirit's inclusion in the "us" and an argument from inspired intertextual interpretation of Genesis 1 in Colossians for the inclusion of Christ in the "us."[19] Christ fits into the creation story as its agent, pattern (for humanity), and purpose. Many interpreters and theologians ancient and modern have seen this verse as an early hint of the Trinity.[20]

Of course, on this view Moses would have had the Holy Spirit in mind and not Christ. What Moses wrote contained more truth than he knew about the majestic God of Israel. Over time, God revealed more and more about himself until his people had enough information to formulate the doctrine of the Trinity. Without being dogmatic about the matter, this explanation does justice to both the original audience's likely understanding of the passage and the concern to read the Old Testament with the light shed on it by the coming of Christ (see Luke 24:25–27), and to understand the latter as consistent with and organically related to the former. As Douglas Oss puts it, "any 'fuller' meaning of a text must also account for the human level of meaning."[21] The impact of this interpretation on the doctrine of the image of God will later be considered.

---

18. Hamilton, *Genesis*, 134.

19. William Dumbrell lays out a similar, though brief, argument to the same conclusion. Dumbrell, *End of the Beginning*, 175.

20. E.g., Augustine, *Gen. litt.* 3, 19, 29; Calvin, *Genesis*, 92. Ross, *Creation and Blessing*, 112; Horton, *Genesis*, 26; McRoberts, "Holy Trinity," 3105.

21. Oss, "Canon as Context," 111.

Image

"Image" (*ṣelem*) occurs seventeen times in the Hebrew OT, five of which are in image of God passages (Gen 1:26, 27 [twice]; 9:6, and 5:3). Six times it refers to idols, statues of false gods (Num 33:52; 2 Kgs 11:18; 2 Chr 23:17; Ezek 7:20; 16:17; Amos 5:26). Once it refers to wall carvings of Babylonian soldiers (Ezek 23:14). Three times it means models of rats and tumors (1 Sam 6:5, 11 [twice]). An unusual sense arises in Psalms 39:7 and 73:20, the latter of which speaks of the wicked this way: "They are like a dream when one awakes; when you arise, Lord, you will despise them as fantasies" (*ṣelem*). This compares the destruction of the wicked with the transience of a dream (vv. 18–19). Unlike two and three-dimensional objects, the fantasy is not physical, but only a mental image. Clines says that, outside of Genesis 1 (which is at issue in the debate) these are the only two passages in the OT that use the term of a non-physical thing, though the Akkadian cognate *ṣalmu* is used metaphorically several times.[22] This shows a certain flexibility in what is typically a more concrete term.[23] J. Richard Middleton is probably correct in his judgment that the common denominator in these meanings of *ṣelem* is "(visible) form (whether solid or unsubstantial)."[24]

The etymology of the word is uncertain. Some scholars think it derives from *ṣēl* (shadow). Avivah Gottlieb Zornberg explains the significance on this theory: "there is the sense that the human being is a shadow that God casts into the world. One of the primary functions of shadows is to say something about the reality of what is casting a shadow."[25] Hans Wildberger finds this etymology untenable, preferring the Semitic *ṣlm*, which means "to cut off, hew, cut, carve," in part because this option illuminates the uses seen above and partly because the Akkadian *ṣlmu* means "statue."[26] It is easy to see such a verbal idea behind idols and carvings, but one would probably have to consider the phantoms of Psalms 39:7 and 73:20 as extensions of the root idea.

More helpful than etymology are the connotations of "image." Scholars have studied the term in the ancient Near East for its potential relevance to the doctrine of the image of God. Images could be things

22. Clines, "Image of God," 74.
23. Wildberger, "צֶלֶם," 1081.
24. Middleton, *Liberating Image*, 45.
25. In Moyers, *Genesis*, 19–20.
26. Wildberger, "צֶלֶם," 1080.

people made from various materials or could actually be people made by a god. In either case the image was thought to be filled with the divine breath or fluid.[27] There are two different types of parallels cited by scholars. Rad explains manufactured images this way: "Just as powerful earthly kings, to indicate their claim to dominion, erect an image of themselves in the provinces of their empire where they do not personally appear, so man is placed upon earth in God's image as God's sovereign emblem. He is really only God's representative, summoned to maintain and enforce God's claim to dominion over the earth. The decisive thing about man's similarity to God, therefore, is his function in the non-human world."[28]

But how close is the parallel to Genesis? One can readily see why the distant subjects of the king would need a reminder of who is boss, but why would the earth and animal kingdom need such an emblem? Could they understand it? Is it the ruled in this case who must understand the authority of the image or is it the rulers made in the image? Though Middleton does not spell out such reasons, he favors the second type of parallel over this one.[29] Nevertheless, the connotation of authority is there, which explains much in the context of Genesis, even if it takes an additional step to get from symbol of authority to executor of authority.

The second type sees certain people or even all people as images. In his discussion of the meaning of ṣelem in *Theological Lexicon of the Old Testament*, Wildberger explains that kings and occasionally others were said to be made in the image of a god or to actually be the image of a god. After saying that Genesis 1:26 and 28 and Psalm 8 portray humans as rulers of creation, he writes,

> This perspective finds further support in the fact that the *king* was described as the image of god among Israel's neighbors. Yet a few texts do speak of the creation of humanity in general in the image of the deity . . . The king or pharaoh is described as the "image" of the deity much more often, however. In the Akk. realm, the king is praised as the image of the deity Bel or Shamash (e.g., "the father of the king, my lord, was the very image of Bēl, and the king, my lord, is likewise the very image of Bēl ," *CAD* Ṣ:85b; cf. Wildberger, op. cit. 253ff.). The title occurs even more frequently in Egypt, esp. in the 18th Dynasty: the pharaoh is the "image of Re," "holy image of Re," "my living

27. Clines, "Image of God," 81.

28. Rad, *Genesis*, 60.

29. Middleton, *Liberating Image*, 25.

image on earth," etc. Two aspects of this usage are significant in view of Gen 1:26f.: (1) such contexts discuss the dominion of Pharaoh in terms similar to the manner in which Gen 1 speaks of the dominion of humanity, e.g., "the king, bodily (son of Re) . . . the good god, image of Re, son of Amun, who tramples down the foreigners" (W. Helck, *Urkunden der 18. Dynastie: Überset-zung zu den Heften 17–22* [1961], 176) or "the earth is subject to you because of your prowess" (op. cit. 385); (2) the *creation* of the king is discussed (cf. also Psa 2:7), e.g., "splendid image of Atum, which Harakhti himself created; divine king, lord of the great dual crown; with beautiful face, when he has appeared with the *3tf*-crown; whose might is broad" (op. cit. 213). One may determine, then, that the origins of the concept of human-ity's divine image are associated with ancient Near Eastern con-cepts of the king as the son, the representative, viceroy, proxy of God on earth.[30]

Kenneth Mathews provides one example of a text that speaks of all humans as images of Re, *The Instruction for King Meri-ka-Re* (a twenty-second century BC Egyptian text). It reads, "He made the breath of life (for) their nostrils. They who have issued from his body are his images."[31] There is a tension here between humanity's humble position as "well di-rected . . . cattle of the god" on the one hand and their more honorable position as those for whom Re conquered the water-monster, designed the universe "according to their desire," provided flora and fauna as food, built a shrine for them, and acts to help those who weep.[32]

The ideological similarity to Genesis 1 (as well as Gen 2:7) seems clear, though literary dependence is not certain. As one who is skeptical of the Documentary Hypothesis and who believes Moses, the educated Egyptian prince, wrote Genesis, this Egyptian background for the be-liefs that humanity was made in God's image and that the image involves authority is quite impressive to me. This is not to suggest that Moses im-ported all of Egyptian royal theology but that he may have employed the terminology and concepts he had learned in Egypt where they matched

---

30. Wildberger, "צֶלֶם," 1083. The common denominator between the two types of parallels (things and people), namely dominion, is enough to prompt some scholars to cite both types as support for a functional view of God's image (without distinguishing them). See, e.g., Rad, *Genesis*, 58, 60; Beale, *New Testament Biblical Theology*, 31–32.

31. Mathews, *Genesis*, 168n206. The quotation from *The Instruction for King Meri-ka-Re* can be found in Pritchard, *ANET*, 417.

32. Pritchard, *ANET*, 417.

what God had revealed to him about human origins and purposes. Genesis emphatically does not share the ancient Egyptian belief in the divinity of its kings or the notion that creation came at the end of a conflict with a water-monster.[33] But it clearly shares a royal concept of human responsibility in creation. It may be that the truth about humans being made in God's image was passed from Adam down to future generations and was retained in Egypt to some extent. This is much like how Greg Beale explains the similarities between ancient pagan temples and that of Israel.[34]

Many Old Testament scholars and other theologians throughout the last century have also been impressed with such ancient Near Eastern parallels and have correspondingly found the image of God to be tied in some way to the God-given authority to rule over the creation and animals. Middleton, whose study of the image of God attempts to bring together Old Testament scholars with systematic theologians in forging the proper doctrine of the image of God, says that, beginning with the early twentieth century, the royal interpretation of the image gradually became the dominant view among OT scholars, enjoying a virtual monopoly by century's end.[35]

Perhaps the most powerful reason this is the case is found in the connection between image and rule in Genesis 1:26–28. On the heels of God's decision to make humans in his image and likeness, he says, "and let them rule over the fish of the sea, and over the birds of heaven, and over the cattle, and over all the earth, and over every moving thing that moves upon the earth" (LEB). After verse 27 says God did just that, it says, "And God blessed them, and God said to them, "Be fruitful and multiply, and fill the earth and subdue it, and rule over the fish of the sea and the birds of heaven, and over every animal that moves upon the earth" (LEB). It is clear that there is some connection between the image and the activities of multiplying, filling the earth, ruling over the animals and earth, and subduing the earth. Christopher Wright comments, "The two affirmations are so closely linked in the text that there can be no doubt that they are meant to be related. Human beings are made to be like God; human beings are made to rule over the rest of creation."[36]

---

33. On the Egyptian belief in the divinity of their kings, see Middleton, *Liberating Image*, 109–10.

34. Beale, *Temple*, 29.

35. Middleton, *Liberating Image*, 29.

36. Wright, *Old Testament Ethics*, 119. It is true that the animals are also told to

But just what is the connection between image and rule? Does being made in God's image consist in ruling? Is ruling a result of being made in the image? Or is human rule God's purpose, or at least one of God's purposes, for creating people in his image?

The grammar of the text supports the idea of purpose: God created humans in his image not least so that we might rule the creation, thereby representing him. The conjunction *wĕ* between "likeness" and "rule" is rendered "and" in many translations (KJV, NRSV, LEB, ESV, NASB), left untranslated in a couple (NLT, NKJV), and translated "so that" they may rule in the NIV. The NIV rightly provides this more interpretive translation because the Hebrew construction clearly points to the purpose behind creating people in the Divine image. As Christopher Wright explains, "Exegetically, when two 'jussive' clauses (clauses like 'Let something happen' or 'Let us do something') follow one another with a simple conjunction, the overall sense can be to make the second the intended result of the first, or what the first enables to happen . . . [T]he thrust of God's two statements could be taken as 'Let us make human beings in our own image and likeness so that they may exercise dominion over the rest of creation.' The two are not identical, but the first intentionally enables the second."[37]

The same thing happens in English. If you were to say to your teenager, "Please go to the store and get some milk," it would be clear to anyone that getting milk is the purpose for which the youth is to go to the store. Many interpreters agree that ruling is a/the purpose of creating people in God's image.[38] John Kilner cites the same grammatical reason as Wright in support of the ruling purpose[39] yet downplays the importance of rule in the overall doctrine, in part because the idea of ruling creation does not appear in all of the texts that discuss the image of God.[40] One might wonder if it is really necessary to see rule in all of the passages,

---

multiply in v. 22, yet that was not for the purpose of ruling. Rather, God wanted his creation to teem with living beings (Isa 45:18). While this is surely one purpose for the command to multiply for both animals and humans, the latter group has an additional purpose for multiplying: to rule more effectively.

37. Wright, *Old Testament Ethics*, 119n21. So also Clines, "Image of God," 96.

38. Rad, *Genesis*, 59; Wenham, *Genesis 1–15*, 33; Ross, *Creation and Blessing*, 112; Hamilton, *Genesis*, 138; Cohen, *Be Fertile and Increase*, 22; Brueggemann, *Theology of the Old Testament*, 452; Flender, "Εἰκών," 287.

39. Kilner, *Dignity and Destiny*, 207. See also Clines, "Image of God," 96.

40. Kilner, *Dignity and Destiny*, 202.

though the emphasis on rule in Genesis 1 would lead one to expect to see it as a recurring theme in image texts.

Though rule is the purpose of God for making humans in his image in Genesis 1:26, the notion of dominion appears to be inherent in the meaning of "image" (*ṣelem*) itself. Clines presses the point:

> Man is here described in royal terms, not only in the command to have dominion, but in the image of God phrase itself. The term 'image of God' in itself indicates the regal character of man, it seems to us, just as it does in Egypt, where only the king is image of God, and where his rulership is often specifically associated with his being the image. Hence the command to have dominion (Gen. 1:26, 28) does not advertise some function of man which may or may not devolve from his being the image; he has dominion only because he is the image, and his being the image means, without any further addition, that he is already ruler.[41]

The Egyptian texts which said all humans are images of the deity do not weaken Clines's point by demoting kings, but rather support his point by promoting the non-royal population. Wenham and Hamilton call this the "democratization" of the image, giving every human royal responsibility and status.[42] Rule is implied in *ṣelem* and is the purpose for which God made people in his image. He made people rulers in order to rule.

The context supports this understanding. Having planted his garden, God "rested" (*nuaḥ*) Adam in it "to work [*ābad*] it and take care of [*shāmar*] it" (Gen 2:15). Rest will be considered further below. Clearly, working and taking care of Eden refer to cultivation and stewardship, but something more seems to be implied as well. According to Beale, when used together, the two terms sometimes refer to "priests who 'keep' the service' (or 'charge') of the tabernacle (see Num 3:7–8; 8:25–26; 18:5–6; 1 Chr 23:32; Ezek 44:14)."[43] Numbers 18 is especially instructive. The priests are responsible for "offenses connected with the sanctuary, and ... with the priesthood" (v. 1). The Levites are to assist the priests but are not allowed to go near the furnishings in the tent of meeting on pain of death to themselves and the priests as well, since they were responsible for the care (*mishmeret*, a cognate of *shāmar*) of the sanctuary and its contents. This was to be the service (*ābad*) God gave the priests as a gift. This was not demeaning slave labor; the responsibility came with privilege and honor. Similarly, in Ezekiel's vision of the end-time restored temple, the priests who allowed the uncircumcised into the temple and served God amidst idols "must bear the consequences of their sin" (vv. 10 and 12). God would appoint priests "to guard *shāmar*, the temple for all the work that is to be done in it" (v. 14). That Moses wrote both Genesis and Numbers and paired these two terms referring to Adam and priests suggests that he thought of Adam as serving in a priestly role in the garden of Eden and that this is similar to the role priests had in the temple: to execute the designated responsibilities and to deny access to anything and anyone who does not belong there. After the fall, when Adam and Eve failed to overcome the serpent's temptation and keep him at bay, God banished them from the garden and "placed on the east side of the Garden of Eden cherubim and a flaming sword flashing back and forth to guard (*shāmar*) the way to the tree of life" (Gen 3:24)—an image later evoked by the cherubim overshadowing the ark of the covenant in the temple (Exod 25:20; 37:9; 1 Kgs 8:7; 1 Chr 28:18; Heb 9:5). Such considerations lead Beale to refer to Adam as a "'priest-king', since it is only after the 'fall' that priesthood is separated from kingship, though Israel's eschatological expectation is of a messianic priest-king (e.g., see Zech 6:12–13)."[44] The later writings (Chronicles and Ezekiel) suggest that biblical authors picked up on this connection.

The case for such a job description becomes more convincing the more parallels there are between the tabernacle/temple and Eden, and Beale argues for a number of these parallels. To be more precise, Beale argues that God instructed the Israelites to build the tabernacle and temple according to the pattern God showed them (Exod 25:9, 40; 1 Chr 28:19), resulting in a structure that would serve as a microcosm of the cosmos. Psalm 78:69 seems to indicate this when it says, "He built his sanctuary like the heights, like the earth that he established forever." There would be three parts of the tabernacle/temple: "(1) The outer court represented the habitable world where humanity dwelt; (2) the holy place was emblematic of the visible heavens and its light sources; (3) the holy of holies symbolized the invisible dimension of the cosmos where God and his heavenly hosts dwelt."[45]

---

44. Beale, *Temple*, 70. Further support for the notion that Adam's responsibilities were priestly comes from Wenham, *Genesis 1–15*, 67; Dumbrell, *End of the Beginning*, 42.

45. Beale, *Temple*, 33.

Space forbids a detailed defense of this thesis. Readers are advised to consult especially Beale's *The Temple and the Church's Mission* and the literature there cited. But briefly in support of (1), the outer court of the temple had within it a sea of cast metal held up by twelve bulls, three facing in each of the four directions (2 Chr 4:4). The sea's lip was like that of a lily blossom (2 Chr 4:5). Before the tabernacle and temple, God instructed Moses to "make an altar of earth" (Exod 20:24).[46] The representations of earth, sea, and animals in the temple's outer court suggest that the outer court is a microcosm of the earth and all it contains. In support of (2), the holy place had a lampstand with seven lamps on it (Exod 37:17–24), which may have represented the light from the sun, moon, planets, and/ or stars. These sources of light govern day and night and thus time (Gen 1:14–19) so that there may be symbolism here of both time and space.[47] Finally, in support of (3), a pair of cherubim guard the holy of holies (1 Kgs 6:23–28), which is also true of God's heavenly sanctuary (Rev 4:7–9). The ark of the covenant was understood as God's footstool. God sat enthroned in heaven with his feet, figuratively speaking, on the ark of the covenant (1 Chr 28:2; Ps 99:5; 132:7–8).[48] God reigned from the temple, the holy of holies in particular, the connecting point between heaven and earth, the place where humans could have access to God.

Now some other connections between the temple and Eden must be traced in addition to the cherubim guarding both Eden and the ark of the covenant in the temple. Leviticus 26:1–13 contains a series of blessings God promised Israel if they would obey the Mosaic Covenant. Among them are rain and agricultural abundance reminiscent of Eden (vv. 3–5). Verse 9 then says, "I will look on you with favor and make you fruitful and increase your numbers, and I will keep my covenant with you." This is a clear restatement of the cultural commission, involving both blessings and responsibilities. Then God makes this promise: "I will put my dwelling place among you, and I will not abhor you. I will walk among you and be your God, and you will be my people" (vv. 11–12). The dwelling place here is the tabernacle, the precursor of the Jerusalem temple and symbol of God's presence with and reign over Israel (Exod 25:8; Ps 74:7). The verb for "walk" is a form of *hālak*, the same verb used of God

---

46. Beale, *Temple*, 33–34.

47. Beale, *Temple*, 34–35.

48. Beale, *Temple*, 35–36. Beale provides further arguments for these connections from Scripture, Judaism, and ancient Near Eastern parallels. See pp. 36–60.

walking in the garden of Eden (Gen 3:8).[49] The personal relationship God extended to Adam and Eve in the garden has been offered to Abraham and his descendants (Gen 17:7) and would be the central feature of his covenants from then on (Exod 6:7; Jer 7:23; 11:4; 24:7; 30:22; 31:1; Zech 13:9; 2 Cor 6:16; Rev 21:3). Psalm 36:8–9 links Eden with the temple through a reference to the water flowing from each. Beale provides some helpful commentary: "They drink their fill of the abundance of your house [temple]; And Thou dost give them to drink of the river of Thy delights [literally, 'the river of your Edens'!]. For with Thee is the fountain of life; In Thy light we see light [perhaps a play of words on the light from the lampstand in the Holy Place]."[50]

Adam and Eve had responsibilities in Eden that were spiritual as well as physical, responsibilities that could be described as both royal and priestly, responsibilities that were passed on to Israel (Exod 19:5–6) and then to the church (1 Pet 2:9). The image of God pertains to the royal responsibilities, so it is possible that it also pertains in some way to the priestly ones as well, especially since the two seem to be closely tied together. The garden of Eden was God's sacred place where he invited the first couple to commune with him and share in his joyous presence and reign even as he later invited Israel to do in his land. As Exodus 15:17–18 says, "You will bring them in and plant them on the mountain of your inheritance—the place, Lord, you made for your dwelling, the sanctuary, Lord, your hands established. The Lord reigns for ever and ever." The temple in the midst of Israel meant that God intended to dwell with and reign over Israel in the same way he did in Eden.

One final point must be established. God did not intend for Adam and Eve's progeny to stay in the confines of the original Eden, but to fill the earth. Beale writes, "Genesis 1:27 provides the means by which the commission and goal of verse 28 was to be accomplished: humanity will fulfill the commission by means of being in God's image. They were to reflect God's kingship by being his vice-regents on earth. Because Adam and Eve were to subdue and rule 'over all the earth', it is plausible

---

49. Beale, "Eden," 334. Note the similar view in Dumbrell, *End of the Beginning*, 41–42: "If it is the presence of God in Eden which permits the garden to function as a sanctuary, then tabernacle/temple theology is designed to enable the promised land as a whole to serve as a sacred shrine."

50. Beale, "Eden," 9. The translation here is apparently a precursor to the NASB (the only differences between them are the archaic versus modern pronouns).

to suggest that they were to extend the geographical boundaries of the garden until Eden covered the whole earth."[51]

What can be said in support of this idea? Isaiah 45:18 says God "fashioned and made the earth, he founded it; he did not create it to be empty, but formed it to be inhabited." This expands on verse 17, where God spoke of saving Israel eternally, which includes both gathering Israel back to her land after the Babylonian exile (v. 13) and bringing in gentiles as well (vv. 13–15), promises not fulfilled in the sixth century BC return (see Ezra 9:8–9), setting the stage for fulfillment through the ministry of Jesus. Jesus announced the end of the exile in his hometown synagogue in Nazareth (Luke 4:18–19, quoting Isa 61:1–2) and later sent his followers to all the nations to gather Jews and gentiles into his kingdom (Acts 1:8). Paul viewed this mission as a fulfillment of Isaiah's prophecy of the centrifugal mission that would result in a centripetal gathering of God's people to God's holy mountain. "He gave me the priestly duty of proclaiming the gospel of God, so that the Gentiles might become an offering acceptable to God, sanctified by the Holy Spirit" (Rom 15:16). When Paul called his gentile converts an offering, he was probably alluding to Isaiah 66:20. In this passage, Isaiah prophesied that God would send his emissaries to the nations and proclaim God's glory there (v. 19)—the centrifugal aspect of God's mission. The result would be a gathering of God's people to Zion—the centripetal aspect of mission that Isaiah had spoken of in 2:1–5.[52] The offerings themselves would be bodies, given freely to God (Rom 12:1). The setting of this gathering in Isaiah 65 and 66 is the new heavens and new earth (see 65:17 and 66:22). This location would be able to accommodate the vast throng of multiplying people (Isa 54:2–3). This shows that eternal salvation is associated with both humanity accomplishing the cultural commission to fill the earth and Israel's return from exile, leading to her fulfillment of her responsibility as a kingdom of priests to spread knowledge of God and thereby bless the nations (Exod 19:5–6; Gen 12:3). It would appear that multiplication by both procreation and evangelization are crucial to this plan.

But what about the connection with Eden? Isaiah 51:3 says, "The Lord will surely comfort Zion and will look with compassion on all her ruins; he will make her deserts like Eden, her wastelands like the garden

51. Beale, *Temple*, 28.

52. Moo, *Romans*, 890n35; Wright, *Mission of God*, 523–26. The overlapping geographical references in Isaiah 66:19 and Romans 15:19–29 suggest that Paul saw Isaiah 66:19–21 as programmatic for his ministry, right down to where he planned to preach.

of the Lord. Joy and gladness will be found in her, thanksgiving and the sound of singing." One could argue that this and similar references (Gen 13:10; Ezek 36:35) are only comparisons between the lushness of Eden and Israel. But because of the allusions to Eden in prophecies about the new creation, the connection must be stronger. The New Jerusalem will have the tree of life for healing and health (Rev 22:2; cf. Ezek 47:1–12; Gen 2:9), a river of life (Rev 22:1–2; cf. Ezek 47:1–12; Gen 2:10–14), no curse on the ground to make work painful and less productive (Rev 22:3; cf. Gen 3:17–19), and great blessing on all who are there (Rev 22:7, 14; cf. Gen 1:28).[53] Israel and the portions of the earth required for the expanded community of God's people will be part of an expanded Eden, which corresponds to the notion of an expanded temple.[54] In sum, this is the new heavens and new earth. Other evidence for this notion will be discussed below.

Likeness and How it Relates to Image

But what does *dəmut* (likeness) mean and how does it relate to *ṣelem*? *Dəmut* is a noun related to the verb *dmh*, which means "be like, resemble."[55] The noun form has three general meanings, according to *HALOT*, namely "model," "likeness," and "shape."[56] An example of "model" is in 2 Kings 16:10, when it is used of a sketch of an altar King Ahaz wanted to have built. Under "likeness," it is used to compare the venom of wicked rulers to that of a snake in Psalm 58:4.[57] Under "shape," it refers to the "figures of bulls" encircling the cast metal sea in the temple area (2 Chr 4:3). In the visions of Ezekiel, *dəmut* often refers to things he saw. For example, he saw "the likeness (*dəmut*) of four living creatures, and this *was* their appearance: a human form" (*dəmut*; Ezek 1:5 LEB). This is the most frequent way

---

53. See Beale, *Revelation*, 1103–8. Much of Judaism along with early Christianity looked forward to an eternal end like the beginning in Eden. See *Barn.* 6:13; *Test. Dan.* 5; *Test. Levi* 18; *1 En.* 25:4–6; *2 En.* 8–9; 4 Ezra 2:12–45, 6:38–59; 4Q171; 4Q475; *Gen. Rab.* 12. On the views of intertestamental authors, see Nickelsburg, *Resurrection*; Nickelsburg, "Salvation," 299–314. For the Rabbinic writings, see Neusner, "Restoration of Israel," 285–96. On this theme and relevant ancient and modern literature, see Wright, *Resurrection*.

54. Beale, *Temple*, 129–33.

55. BDB, 197.

56. *HALOT* 226.

57. *HALOT* 226.

Ezekiel used *dəmut* (1:5 [twice], 10, 13, 16, 26 [twice], 28; 10:1, 10, 21–22).
As Ernst Jenni points out, it can be "distanced from the related word: 1:22;
followed by *kəmar' ēh* "like the appearance of": 1:26; 8:2)."[58] Without such
qualification, the word need not be thought to convey diminished similarity, but rather "the word in and of itself refers to total comparability and
not to a perceptibly lesser degree of mere similarity, but that the need to
refer to comparability exists only if similarity is not self-evident."[59]

Allen Ross believes *dəmut* "further explains the meaning of 'image.'
It describes 'similarity.'"[60] Clines makes a distinction between *ṣelem* and
dəmut, saying that they do not refer to separate aspects of a person, but
that *demut* "specifies what kind of an image it is: it is a 'likeness'-image,
not simply an image; representational, not simply representative."[61] Similarly, Hoekema says, "the image is also a likeness, 'an image which is like
us. The two words together tell us that man is a representation of God
who is like God in certain respects."[62]

Some of the church fathers made more of the distinction between
"image" and "likeness." In part, this was based on the Septuagint's unwar-
ranted insertion of *kai* between the two terms (*eikōna* and *homoiōsin*,
respectively), which then influenced the Vulgate. For roughly fifteen
hundred years of readers and hearers, this left the impression that the
two conveyed separate ideas.[63] Irenaeus says, "But if the Spirit be wanting
to the soul, he who is such is indeed of an animal nature, and being left
carnal, shall be an imperfect being, possessing indeed the image [of God]
in his formation, but not receiving the similitude through the Spirit; and
thus is this being imperfect."[64] The image itself refers to the human capacity for reason and free will.[65] This feature cannot be lost by a human
being, for it is what makes one human. The similitude (likeness), one's
actual moral resemblance to God, however, can be lost due to sin and
regained by salvation. Irenaeus spoke of the full extent of human restoration this way: "For we cast blame upon him, because we have not been

---

58. Jenni, "דמה," 340.

59. Jenni, "דמה," 340.

60. Ross, *Creation and Blessing*, 112.

61. Clines, "Image of God," 91.

62. Clines, "Image of God," 90–98.

63. Hoekema, *Created in God's Image*, 13.

64. Irenaeus, *Haer.* 5.6.1.

65. Irenaeus, *Haer.* 4.4.3.

made gods from the beginning, but at first merely men, then at length gods . . . He declares, "I have said, Ye are gods; and ye are all sons of the Highest."[66] As Irenaeus famously puts it, "our Lord Jesus Christ, who did, through his transcendent love, become what we are, that he might bring us to be even what he is himself."[67] This concept of salvation, known as *theosis* or deification, came to profoundly shape Greek patristic and Eastern Orthodox theology.[68] It conformed rather well with Plato's formulation: "Therefore we ought to try to escape from earth to the dwelling of the gods as quickly as we can; and to escape is to become like God, so far as this is possible; and to become like God is to become righteous and holy and wise."[69] The fundamental idea that the image consisted in rational abilities (with or without additional attributes like conscience, free will, etc.) and was different from the likeness, actually referring to different aspects of a person, became the dominant way of seeing the image until the Reformation and continues to enjoy significant support today.[70]

But several factors militate against this way of seeing the distinction between ṣelem and dəmut. Both terms appear together in Ezekiel 23:14–15 with the same referent. Here again, LEB offers a literal rendering that illuminates the parallel: "And she increased her whorings, and she saw men carved on the wall, images (ṣelem) of Chaldeans carved in red, belted with a belt at their waist with turbans on their heads, all of them *giving the* appearance of adjutants, the image (dəmut) of the Babylonians." As a number of scholars point out, the two terms are used interchangeably here.[71] In addition, a statue of King Had-yisi was found at Tell Fakhariyeh (Syria) dating from the ninth century BC. On it the two terms (in Aramaic) are used interchangeably to refer to the statue itself.[72] Jeremy Cohen, who has meticulously tracked the interpretation of

---

66. Irenaeus, *Haer.* 4.38.4, citing Ps 82:6–7.

67. Irenaeus, *Haer.* 5, Preface.

68. Cross and Livingstone, "Deification," 467.

69. Plato, *Theaet.* 176a–b. Note that Irenaeus did not share Plato's hope for an escape from earth, but rather looked forward to the renewal of all things. "For neither is the substance nor the essence of the creation annihilated (for faithful and true is he who has established it), but 'the *fashion* of the world passeth away'" (*Haer.* 5.36.1).

70. Kilner, *Dignity and Destiny*, 127.

71. Wenham, *Genesis 1–15*, 30. Mathews, *Genesis*, 167n197; Kilner, *Dignity and Destiny*, 125. Westermann, *Genesis 1–11*, 146.

72. Wenham, *Genesis 1–15*, 29. Mathews, *Genesis 1–11*, 167. Mathews cites Millard and Bordreuil, "Statue from Syria," 135–41.

Genesis 1:28 throughout Jewish and Christian interpreters in the ancient and medieval periods, points out that the Yavnean Rabbis saw no distinction between the image and likeness. Indeed, the Septuagint translators used *eikōn* to translate both ṣelem (Gen 1:26; 5:3; 9:6) and *dəmut* (Gen 5:1). Distinguishing between image and likeness, along with locating the image in the soul or intellect, only enter Rabbinic thought later as a result of Hellenistic influence.[73]

But the strongest argument for taking ṣelem and *dəmut* as interchangeable is how Genesis itself uses them. Mathews sets out the evidence this way.

> "Image" and "likeness" occur in tandem only in 1:26 and 5:3, but the order of the words differs in 5:3. The two terms are found essentially the same in use and are interchangeable. "Image" alone, for example, in v. 27 is adequate for the sense of v. 26, and "likeness" is sufficient by itself in 5:1. There is no special significance to their order since as we noted they have a transposed order in 5:3, a passage that certainly echoes v. 26. This would question the legitimacy of attributing to *dəmut* a special feature in the tandem; some have recommended that it clarifies or heightens the meaning of ṣelem. Others have argued oppositely that it tempers the word "image" by assuring that mankind is not divine but only has a "likeness" (correspondence) to the divine. The LXX translation distinguished between ṣelem (*eikōn*) and *dəmut* (*homoiōsis*) at both 1:26 and 5:3, where the tandem of terms occur, but used the same term "image" *(eikōn)* for both Hebrew words at 1:27 *(ṣelem)* and 5:1 *(dəmut)*, indicating that the words have the same force.[74]

Thus, "image" and "likeness" are interchangeable and do not refer to separate parts of a person. As will become clear below, the biblical writers tended to portray humans as whole beings rather than dividing them into their constituent parts. There is nothing in Genesis 1 to suggest God had different aspects of people in mind with the two terms. As for the notion

73. Cohen, *Be Fertile and Increase*, 111–12. Yavnean Rabbis were instrumental in adapting Judaism to the new situation after AD 70, when the temple in Jerusalem was destroyed by the Romans, making centralized worship around the animal sacrificial system, led by the Levitical priests, impossible. They shifted the focus towards the Torah, writing down and building upon the Pharisaic traditions in what would begin to form the Mishnah. On this transition from Second Temple to Rabbinic Judaism, see Cohen, *From the Maccabees to the Mishnah*, 214–32.

74. Mathews, *Genesis*, 166–67. For some of the same arguments, see Calvin, *Genesis*, 93–94.

of Clines, Hoekema, and Ross that "likeness" clarifies or adds the notion of similarity to the representation implied by *ṣelem* (of a whole being in his/her entirety), it seems that similarity is implied in *ṣelem* to begin with, so *dəmut* is not really adding anything new, but rather giving a parallel term with overlapping meaning, in agreement with Mathews. That is not to say that *dəmut* carries all the connotations of *ṣelem*, but that similarity is within the overlap of the two terms.

The Prepositions *Bə* and *Kə*

Here the meaning of the prepositions used with "image" and "likeness" will be examined. *Bə* precedes *ṣelem* and often means "in, at," but can also mean "among," "upon," "at, on, within" (in a temporal sense), "according to" [Gen 1:27 is listed under this meaning in *HALOT* with the note that it is "often the same as and alternating with → כְּ"], "into," "with," "away from," "by."[75] *Kə* can mean "as," "as many as," "according to" [the sense Gen 1:26 is listed under, designating "conformity of kind"], "on," or "in."[76] One can readily see the overlap between the two terms, particularly "in" and "according to." Moses used the prepositions interchangeably, *bə* with *ṣelem* and *kə* with *dəmut* in Genesis 1:26, but switching to *kə* with *ṣelem* and *bə* with *dəmut* in 5:3, so one should refrain from drawing conclusions based on which preposition prefixed which noun.[77]

Clines argues that *bə* in Genesis 1:26 is a *beth essentiae*, and he thus advocates translating it "'Let us make man as our image' or 'to be our image', and the other references to the image are to be interpreted similarly. Thus one may say that according to Genesis 1 man does not have the image of God, nor is he made *in* the image of God, but is himself the image of God."[78] According to *Gesenius' Hebrew Grammar* §119.i, which Clines cites in support, this is a possibility (e.g., Exod 6:3, "I appeared to Abraham, to Isaac and to Jacob *as* God Almighty").[79] Paul will later say "man is the image and glory of God" (1 Cor 11:7), perhaps reading *bə* the same way.

---

75. *HALOT* 103–5.

76. *HALOT* 453–54.

77. Keil and Delitzsch, *Commentary*, 1:39; Rad, *Genesis*, 58.

78. Clines, "Image of God," 80. See also Ross, *Creation and Blessing*, 112; Wildberger, "צֶלֶם," 1082.

79. Gesenius, *Gesenius' Hebrew Grammar*, 379.

But Clines's argument is not persuasive. Kilner points out that "*kə* is much less likely to have that meaning (and *kata* in the New Testament even less so). In other words, regardless of how one translates *bə*, the meaning throughout the Bible hardly can be that people 'are' God's image."[80] Wenham also argues against Clines, noting both the interchangeable uses in 1:26 and 5:3 and the closely parallel Exodus 25:40, where Moses was to make the items used in the tabernacle "according to the pattern" (*bətabənîtām*) shown on the mountain.[81] This is in line with a different meaning of *bə* that Clines calls *beth* of the norm.[82] According to *Gesenius' Hebrew Grammar*, it designates "close connexion with something (also in a metaphorical sense, following some kind of pattern . . . or in a comparison, as in Gn 1:26)."[83] It seems that "following some kind of pattern" is the nature of the comparison in Genesis 1:26. If this is correct, then humans are not images of God, but beings created in the pattern of God. The NRSV's "*in* our image, *according to* our likeness" may reflect this understanding. In addition to the arguments above, Jesus himself is called the image of God in Colossians 1:15 and 2 Corinthians 4:4. Paul speaks in both books about believers being transformed into the Divine image (Col 3:10 and 2 Cor 3:18), which sets forth Christ as the pattern, the model, the paradigm for all believers. Intertextual biblical interpretation by Paul seems to support the notion that the image is the pattern according to which people are formed.

Souls, Whole Persons, and/or the Whole of Humanity?

In Genesis 2:7, some interpreters find reference to a soul that distinguishes humans from the other creatures. The King James Version translates it, "And the Lord God formed man *of* the dust of the ground, and breathed into his nostrils the breath of life; and man became a living soul." Philo wrote that God breathed the image of God into Adam here, also taking *nepeš* as "soul." Thus, he thought the image of God was imparted at this time and consisted of Adam's soul, which gave him spiritual and

---

80. Kilner, *Dignity and Destiny*, 90. Kilner also points out that most exegetes ancient and modern have argued against identifying human beings (as we presently are) as the image of God, 1 Cor 11:7 notwithstanding (on which, see below).

81. Wenham, *Genesis 1–15*, 29.

82. Clines, "Image of God," 70.

83. Gesenius, *Gesenius' Hebrew Grammar*, 379.

intellectual capacities, a view many of the church fathers followed.[84] But *nepeš ḥayyāh* ("living soul" in the KJV) is the same phrase used of the land and sea creatures in 1:20, 21, 24, and 2:19. If the phrase refers to the image of God in humans, it would also have to refer to the image of God in clownfish. The King James Version translators must have seen the difficulty because they translated 1:20 "the moving creature that hath life" and 1:21, 24, and 2:19 "living creature." This is why many modern translators properly avoid a reference to the soul and translate the phrase in these verses "living beings/creatures" and the like.[85] Bruce Waltke explains,

> In its most synthetic use *nepeš* stands for the entire person. In Gen 2:7 "man became a living creature" [*nepeš*]—the substantive must not be taken in the metaphysical, theological sense in which we tend to use the term "soul" today. Precisely the same Hebrew expression (*nepeš ḥayyāh*)—traditionally rendered "living soul" occurs also in Gen 1:20, 21, and 24. In other words, man is here being associated with the other creatures as sharing in the passionate experience of life and is not being defined as distinct from them. It is true, however, as Oehler points out that the source of the *nepeš* of animals is the ground, whereas the source of the *nepeš* of Adam is God.[86]

This is supported by Kittel's, a fact that will become important when we consider New Testament references to Genesis 2:7.

> נֶפֶשׁ is the usual term for a man's total nature, for what he is and not just what he has. This gives the term priority in the anthropological vocabulary, for the same cannot be said of either spirit, heart, or flesh. The classical text in Gn. 2:7 clearly expresses this truth when it calls man in his totality a נֶפֶשׁ חַיָּה . . . It should be noted that it expresses the external aspect of a man rather than the modalities of his life. The word נֶפֶשׁ developed in two main directions which correspond more to structures of thought than to a chronological sequence. The two directions might be

---

84. Philo, *Opif.* 134–35. See Gregory of Nazianzus (*Dogmatic Hymns* 7), Tertullian (*An.* 3.4), Augustine (*Gen. Man.* 2.8.10) and Ambrose (*Isaac* 2.4).

85. E.g., NIV, NRSV, LEB, ESV, NASB, and even the NKJV.

86. Waltke, "נֶפֶשׁ," 590. In support of the idea that the OT teaches a holistic anthropology, see also Wright, *Old Testament Ethics*, 119; Niebuhr, *Nature and Destiny*, 1:151. None of this, however, negates the fact that *nepeš* sometimes refers to "soul as the centre and transmitter of feelings and perceptions." Examples include Exod 23:9; Job 23:13; and Prov 23:2. Yet it can also refer to a corpse (e.g., Lev 19:28), demonstrating the flexibility of the term. See *HALOT* 713.

defined in terms of form and movement. The נֶפֶשׁ is almost always connected with a form. It has no existence apart from the
body. Hence the best translation in many instances is "person"
comprised in corporeal reality.[87]

One consequence of this interpretation is that humans should not
be thought of as mostly transcendent, detached from creation, but rather
deeply bound up with creation. All creatures are made of the same basic stuff and exist in a symbiotic relationship. According to Clines, this
holistic emphasis in Hebraic anthropology has been recognized almost
unanimously in recent scholarship. This led him to reflect, "When this
insight is applied to the doctrine of the image, it is difficult to resist the
conclusion that the whole man is in the image of God."[88] Indeed, it is
hard to see why taking the life of a person made in God's image would
be wrong if the whole self, including the body, was not considered to be
made in the image (see Gen 9:6). Matthews chides the majority of commentators on the image of God for dividing people into their constituent
parts in reference to the image of God. "This dichotomy, however, is at
odds with Hebrew anthropology; as 2:7 bears out, a person is viewed as
a unified whole. The whole person, even all human life collectively, is in
mind in 1:26."[89]

This does not imply that God has a body. He does not. He is able to
create, see, know, hear, act, and carry out his plans in creation without a
body. But humans cannot carry out analogous actions without bodies.
People visibly image the invisible God. This does justice to the OT uses of
ṣelem, most of which refer to physical objects. As with the uses that refer
to images of gods, when used of humans made in God's image, *ṣelem*
assumes that the created one, not the one creating, is physical.

Verse 27 reads "in the image of God he created them; male and female he created them." This should make it crystal clear that women and
men are equal in being made in God's image and likeness. But, disturb-
ingly, Kilner lists a number of influential theologians and leaders of the
church who taught that either women are not made in God's image or
they are made only partially in his image (whereas men are made fully
in his image), including Tertullian, Ambrosiaster, Diodore of Tarsus,

---

87. Schweizer et al., "Ψυχή," 620.

88. Clines, "Image of God," 57. See also VanGemeren, *Progress of Redemption*, 63.

89. Mathews, *Genesis*, 167–68. See also Calvin, *Genesis*, 95; Piper, "Image of God";
Hoekema, *Created in God's Image*, 94.

Chrysostom, Augustine, Thomas Aquinas, Gratian, Peter Abelard, Ern-aud of Bonneval, John Donne, and John Calvin. Some men have then used this idea to justify mistreating women.[90] If this were so, one might wonder why the prohibition of murder in Genesis 9:6, grounded explic-itly in our creation in God's image, makes no distinction between killing a male and killing a female in ascribing blame and assigning the proper penalty for the crime. Susan Niditch is right to point out that "human-kind is found in two varieties, the male and female, and this humanity in its complementarity is a reflection of the Deity."[91] It is important to note that God created only two genders, and it would seem he himself is responsible for which gender a person is born. The gender of one's em-bodied self is part of the gift of life and the image in which he created people. Nor is there anything here to support the idea that some races or nationalities are more in God's image than others, as some have tried to argue.[92] Rather, as Paul said in Acts 17:26, all nations came from one man. The image and likeness of God are passed on through procreation from Adam to the last person to be born (see below), which leaves no grounds for ranking the degrees to which the various nations or races image God. The image of God thus provides the foundation for the equal value of each and every human being.

It is not just the individual person that is made in God's image, it is the human race as a whole. The NRSV brings this corporate sense out clearly, and with gender-inclusive language: "Let us make humankind in our image, according to our likeness; and let them have dominion."[93] All human beings collectively are in view, suggesting that it will require the whole human race of both genders to image God.[94] In fact, this collec-tive/corporate sense of the image of God underlies the biblical teaching that one individual, Adam, represented all of humanity when he re-belled against God. The result was not only death to Adam, but to all. This opened up the possibility of another Adamic figure, Jesus Christ,

---

90. See Kilner, *Dignity and Destiny*, 32–35.

91. Niditch, "Genesis," 30.

92. See Kilner, *Dignity and Destiny*, 20–28 for several examples of people twisting Scripture to justify the subjugation of Jews, Native Americans from North, Central, and South America, and African Americans.

93. See also LEB. NLT is similar with "human beings." NIV has "mankind." Many translations read "man" (KJV, NKJV, ESV, NASB).

94. Kilner, *Dignity and Destiny*, 85–87; Hoekema, *Created in God's Image*, 99–101.

representing all humanity with an act of righteousness that brings life to his people (Rom 5:12–21).

Such considerations suggest that human beings are relational by nature. God made people male and female and instituted the marriage relationship that makes the two one (Gen 2:23–25). He addressed them from the beginning of their existence (Gen 1:28; 2:16–17; 3:9–19). These earliest chapters of Genesis do not say that relationship is the purpose or essence of the image of God. But the door is certainly left open for subsequent canonical development of the connection between relationships and image.

The Image, the Cultural Commission, and Covenant

There are two related issues to work through here. First, what does Genesis 1 authorize humans to do to and in creation? Can people waste, pollute, abuse, drive to extinction, and destroy with impunity? Second, is human dominion part of a covenant, and if so, what sort of covenant? The first is an ecological concern that has become increasingly important to many people in the last half century, and the second is about fundamental human purposes.

In his enormously influential 1967 article, "The Historical Roots of our Ecologic Crisis," Lynn White Jr. argued that the Western Christian reading of the Genesis narrative bears the lion's share of the blame for humanity's exploitation of nature. People are made in God's image and thus share, to a significant degree, God's transcendence of nature. People can thus exploit a natural world that is distinct from them to their own ends. Believers' citizenship is in heaven, and nature is not sacred in any sense, contra the paganism Christianity vanquished, leaving no spiritual powers to protect nature from humanity. This attitude of dualistic disconnectedness and dominance is ubiquitous among both Christians and post-Christians of the West. The result is human-caused erosion from mining, deforestation, hydrogen bombs, atmospheric change from fossil fuels, vast amounts of garbage and sewage caused by the population explosion, the extinction and endangerment of various animal species, etc. In place of these attitudes, White suggested people imitate the humility of Saint Francis of Assisi, who deposed humans and thought in terms of a democracy, with humans taking their place alongside the rest of God's creatures.[95]

95. White, "Historical Roots," 1203–7.

Contemporary ecologists have a term for this democratization: biocentrism (in contrast to anthropocentrism), the notion that "natural things other than human beings are intrinsically valuable and have, therefore, moral standing."[96] White, like many today, believed there should be fewer human beings for the sake of the planet and other animals.[97]

It may be true that the West has read human dominion in the sinful, exploitative way White describes, but there are features of the Genesis account that do not sit well with this reading. In fact, White himself did not claim that Genesis, rightly understood, supports this reading. The proper approach to human dominion over nature is enumerated in the text. The Genesis narrative portrays God as humanity's ruler, giving them purposes and commands (1:28; 2:15, 17). Yet he also gives them gifts (1:29; 2:9, 16) and blesses them (1:28), resulting in well-being. It is not hard to see here the roots of the servant-leader concept Jesus later taught (Matt 20:25–28). If people take their cues from their Father, they will act to benefit what is under their care. The human responsibility before God to rule and subdue creation results, when done properly, in the well-being of creation.

At a few points in the narrative of Genesis, Adam is seen following in God's footsteps. God planted a garden, then put Adam there "to work (*ābad*) it and take care of (*shāmar*) it" (2:15). Walter Brueggemann says "the verbs suggest not exploitative, self-aggrandizing use of the earth, but gentle care for and enhancement of the earth and all its creatures."[98] God created everything, then gave procreative powers to humans (which is also true of animals, of course). God created animals, then "He brought them to the man to see what he would name them; and whatever the man called each living creature, that was its name. So the man gave names to all the livestock, the birds in the sky and all the wild animals" (2:19–20). Keil and Delitzsch point out that "calling or naming presupposes acquaintance. Adam is to become acquainted with the creatures, to learn their relation to him, and by giving them names to prove himself their lord."[99] Perhaps it is more like exercising godly lordship than proving

---

96. Hoffman, "Business and Environmental Ethics," 399. Of course, there are varieties of biocentrism that adjudicate various apparent conflicts between humans and animals or ecosystems differently.

97. White, "Future of Compassion," 108.

98. Brueggemann, *Theology of the Old Testament*, 461.

99. Keil and Delitzsch, *Commentary*, 1:55.

lordship (to whom is this proving lordship?), but naming seems to be a way humans rule the animals here.[100]

First Kings 4:33 describes the wisdom and understanding of Solomon (see v. 29), including his understanding of nature. "He spoke about plant life, from the cedar of Lebanon to the hyssop that grows out of walls. He also spoke about animals and birds, reptiles and fish." This listing of animals echoes that in Genesis 1:26 and 2:19–20, which suggests that the writer of 1 Kings 4 saw a similarity between Adam's and Solomon's wisdom. A king of Israel was thus doing his part in the commission of Genesis 1:26–28 by discovering what he could about the various species and passing on his knowledge to others, in addition to his political responsibilities.[101]

One of the first things one learns about God's nature in Genesis is that he creates. The book shows some interest in human productivity and creativity (4:20–22): "Adah gave birth to Jabal; he was the father of those who live in tents and raise livestock. His brother's name was Jubal; he was the father of all who play stringed instruments and pipes. Zillah also had a son, Tubal-Cain, who forged all kinds of tools out of bronze and iron." All of these innovations could be used for good or evil. Raising livestock to eat the animals at that stage, when humans and animals had been given the trees and plants rather than each other for food (Gen 1:29–30), would have been wrong. The Genesis narrative does not say for what purpose the livestock were raised. Tools and musical instruments were invented, which seem to be mentioned as positive developments of culture. Tools could be used to subdue the ground (Gen 1:28). As for musical instruments, there is nothing in Genesis 1–3 about music, but it would become important in the history of God's people as can be seen in Israel's organized worship reflected in the Psalms. The context of Genesis 4:19–24 sounds a note of alarm about Lamech, who had more than one wife, whom he then bragged to about his outdoing the violence of his ancestor Cain in the "Song of the Sword."[102] At the very least, the words show poetic rhythm and that art could be used for evil as well as good, such as when Adam gratefully waxed poetic about his newly created wife, Eve (Gen 3:23). In any case, this record of cultural development shows

---

100. Middleton, *Liberating Image*, 293–94.

101. See Beale, *New Testament Biblical Theology*, 69–70.

102. Beale, *New Testament Biblical Theology*, 285–86.

that humans were generally to create rather than to destroy, to build rather than to tear down.

All of this underscores a point Middleton makes about the manner in which God rules creation and therefore the manner in which human dominion must be exercised.

> Given the portrayal or rendering of God's power disclosed by a careful reading of Genesis 1, I suggest that the sort of power or rule that humans are to exercise is generous, loving power. It is power used to nurture, enhance, and empower others, non-coercively, for their benefit, not for the self-aggrandizement of the one exercising power. In its canonical place in the book of Genesis, the creation story in 1:1–2:3 thus serves as a normative limit and judgment on the violence that pervades the primeval history, indeed the rest of the Bible and human history generally.[103]

God invites people to share in his rule, giving them significant power to affect the course of history, as Genesis 2 and 3 show. Yet the overarching message of Genesis is that God both makes generous covenant promises and is faithful and powerful to fulfill them in spite of seemingly overwhelming obstacles—including those set out by the free actions of people.[104] And he often used people with free will (even though they were deeply flawed) to accomplish all of this.

This generous and loving servant-leadership, established from the context of Genesis 1 and 2, sets up the proper framework within which to understand the command to subdue (*kābas*) the earth and rule over (*rāda*) the animals. These terms, as Christopher Wright explains, "entail benevolent care for the rest of creation as entrusted into human custodianship."[105] *Kābas*, considered the harsher of the two terms, means "to subdue somebody, to subjugate," whether people (Jer 34:16) or earth, as in Genesis 2.[106] The fact that it can be used of rape (Esth 7:8) may

---

103. Middleton, *Liberating Image*, 295. Middleton goes too far when he speaks of God "stepping back, withdrawing, to allow humans to exercise this newly granted power, *to see what develops*" (italics mine). In n70, he acknowledges the significant similarity of his view to Clark Pinnock's Open Theism. This view denies God's omniscience and weakens the doctrine of God's sovereignty. However, the basic insight that God has entrusted humans with responsibility and freedom to affect various consequences in the world is compatible with other views of God's foreknowledge, such as Middle Knowledge. See Craig, "Middle Knowledge," 141–64.

104. See Hill and Walton, *Survey*, 82–90.

105. Wright, *Mission of God*, 425.

106. *HALOT* 460.

raise eyebrows. But Wright says that in Genesis 1 it probably just refers to the task of agriculture.[107] That God commanded Israel to let the land rest every seven years and every fiftieth year shows that Israel was to use the land, not to abuse it (Lev 25:1–12).[108] These laws are in line with the dominion of Genesis 1:28.[109]

God created human beings on the same day he created land animals, the sixth day. God had commanded that the land (*āreṣ*) produce those animals (v. 24), an event summarized in 2:9 as forming the animals "out of the ground" (*adāmāh*). In Genesis 2:7, God took some dust (*āpār*) from the ground (*adāmāh*) and formed it into the man (*ādaām*). This fact should humble humanity, though not in a Platonic sense that forgets the foundational truth that the ground and everything that comes from it are very good (1:31). Rather, as Mathews says, this fact shows that human beings are closely related to nature by bodily constitution and purpose.[110] That God breathed life into humanity bespeaks human dependence on him for the foundational gift of life, for which people owe him thanks, praise, and obedience (see Isa 29:16; 45:9; 64:8; Jer 18:1–14).[111] God clearly wanted human beings to be mindful that they came from the same ground the animals and trees of Eden came from (2:8–9), the very ground they were called to work and take care of in Eden (2:15). Unfortunately, after Adam and Eve sinned, their punishment included a curse on the ground that would result in pain as they worked and banishment from Eden's ground until they died and returned to the dust (*āpār*) of the ground (*adāmāh*; 3:17–19). Leonard J. Coppes notes that "he was driven to it rather than it being given to him. He was to go down rather than up. His life moved in and toward death rather than in and toward life . . . Thus, we see that *ādām/adāmāh* are deeply involved in the pattern creation-fall-redemption."[112]

107. Wright, *Old Testament Ethics*, 120.

108. For an explanation of the significance of the Jubilee for land and the family as a self-sustaining economic unit, see Wright, *Mission of God*, 289–323.

109. For an extended discussion of biblical texts that teach creation care in the context of human stewardship under God, see Wright, *Mission of God*, 103–44. A more critical interaction with Scripture that nevertheless acknowledges the rich biblical resources for creation care is Horrell, "Ecological Ethics," 255–60.

110. Mathews, *Genesis 1–11*, 196. See also Wright, *Old Testament Ethics*, 117.

111. Allen, "עָפָר," 687.

112. Coppes, "אדם," 11.

White spoke against human transcendence from nature because he thought it would justify abusing creation according to human whims. But White's article has at its heart a false dichotomy: people are either part of nature or transcend nature. On the contrary, people are a part of nature *and* transcend it with the ability to choose among moral options and know about good and evil (Gen 2:15–17; 3:22). God gave humans authority to rule (transcendence), thus representing him in creation (as part of nature). In fact, he made people in his image and likeness (transcendence, but including the body, which is part of nature) in order that they would exercise dominion (as part of nature). One must hold these realities in tension. As so often in dealing with complex theological issues, "and" is better than "either/or."

The second question in this section concerns whether or not one should think of human dominion as part of a covenant God made with Adam and Eve before the fall. Dumbrell describes the somewhat flexible term for covenant (*bərît*) this way: "Covenants presupposed a set of existing relationships to which by formal ceremony they gave binding expression. They operated between two parties, though the status of the parties varied considerably. The language of covenant was carefully prescribed by convention. One 'cut a covenant', oath and witnesses were moreover involved, and often there was an associated sign."[113]

The Westminster Confession of Faith teaches that there was a covenant with Adam and calls it a covenant of works (VII.2). Hoekema points out that the term "covenant" (*bərît*) does not occur in Genesis 1–3, nor is there any trace of a covenant ratification ceremony or oath.[114] There is some debate on whether or not Hosea 6:7 supports the idea that there was a covenant in Eden. It reads, "As at Adam, they have broken the covenant; they were unfaithful to me there." But the NIV footnote provides the alternatives, "Or *Like Adam*; or *Like human beings*." "Adam" can refer to the first man, human beings in general or the town of Adam (Josh 3:16) or even, if emended, Admah (as in Hos 11:8; see Gen 19:29). "There" (*shām*) usually means "there," but *HALOT* also says it can be used with a temporal significance: "then, at that time, just then Ps 14:5 132:17."[115] Yet both uses in the Psalms seem to read better in the local sense, "there." There is a question whether the locative translation does not fit "as" (*kə*)

---

113. Dumbrell, *Covenant and Creation*, 20.

114. Hoekema, *Created in God's Image*, 119–20.

115. *HALOT* 1547.

in verse 7a or if it should be emended to *bə* ("at"). The most natural translation of *Adam* is the first man, yet the most natural reading of *shām* is local. Dumbrell may be right that the city Adam is mentioned to make the point that ever since Israel crossed the Jordan they had been unfaithful to the Mosaic covenant,[116] but the narrative in Joshua gives no support for this, since nothing negative happened at Adam and the first defiant behavior recorded after Israel crossed the Jordan was the sin of Achan in Joshua 7. Perhaps the first clause is about Adam and the second about the sins of the people who live in Ephraim and Judah (v. 4), Gilead (v. 8), Shechem (v. 9), and Israel/Ephraim (v. 10; note especially "there" [*shām*] before "Ephraim"). But since the evidence is so ambiguous, the text will not bolster nor weaken the case for an Adamic covenant.[117]

A clear reference to a *bərît* with Adam is not the only way to detect a covenant, though such a reference would raise the degree of certainty. Beale summarized the components of a covenant that are present in the earliest chapters of Genesis: "(1) two parties are named; (2) a condition of obedience is set forth; (3) a curse for transgression is threatened; (4) a clear implication of a blessing is promised for obedience."[118] The curse is death (Gen 2:17), a sentence pronounced immediately (3:19), though carried out an unspecified amount of time later (5:5).[119] Geerhardus Vos points out that a deeper connection should be made here between death and separation from God, the latter of which happened immediately, as God banished Adam and Eve from the "Garden of God" (3:23–24; see Ezek 28:13). "In other words, expulsion from the garden (i.e., from God's presence) means expulsion to death. The root of death is in having been sent forth from God."[120] The reverse is also true: Enoch "walked with God"

---

116. Dumbrell, *Covenant and Creation*, 45.

117. In agreement with Dumbrell, *Covenant and Creation*, 46; Hoekema, *Created in God's Image*, 120. In support of the idea that Hosea 6:7 refers to a covenant with Adam and Eve, see Beale, *New Testament Biblical Theology*, 43–44.

118. Beale, *New Testament Biblical Theology*, 43. Beale cites support for the covenant with Adam and Eve from several intertestamental Jewish sources, including *2 En* 31:1; *L.A.E.* 8:1–2; Sir 17:11–12; 1QS 4:22–23; and Philo, *Leg.* 3:246. Cohen sees substantial agreement among Jewish and Christian interpreters on this point. See Cohen, *Be Fertile and Increase*, 47, 63–66.

119. Vos sees the phrase "in the day that thou eatest thereof" (KJV) as a Hebrew idiom he renders, "as surely as thou eatest thereof," emphasizing inevitability (similar to 1 Kgs 2:37). See Vos, *Biblical Theology*, 38.

120. Vos, *Biblical Theology*, 39–40.

and was later spared from death (Gen 5:24), a strong clue that fellowship with God and life are meant to be tied closely together (see John 17:3).

This may not mean that Adam was immortal by nature (incapable of dying), however, for blessings are the other side of curses. If the first humans were cursed with death, it would seem that life was the promised blessing. When God banished Adam and Eve from Eden, it was so that they would not eat the fruit of the tree of life and live forever. This was punishment, yet it also meant they would not have to live forever in their fearful, ashamed, rebellious, pain-filled, and evil-knowing (in a disadvantageous way) state.[121] Had they not sinned, they would not have been blocked from eating this fruit and living forever. Whether Adam and Eve were immortal by nature, conceived apart from the test of obedience, is a speculative question the author of Genesis did not care to answer. The important thing in this connection was what humans would do regarding the tree of the knowledge of good and evil.

Nor was eternal life (bodily, as there is no hope here of disembodied souls in heaven) the only possible blessing that the first couple might have received if they had passed the test. There were other "escalated blessings" (Beale's term): they would have filled the earth; they would have experienced successful dominion in an earth devoid of pain, evil, and violence; they would have filled the earth with God's glory as his image-reflecting children; they would have received knowledge of good and evil in the proper way (see below); and they would have ultimately experienced the goal of creation, Sabbath rest, in imitation of God who, after working six days, rested on the seventh.[122] This rest would become an eschatological goal (see Heb 3–4).

The rest of God was in fact an active rest. What God rested from in Genesis 2:3 was "all the work of creating he had done." This leaves open the possibility of doing other sorts of work, as Jesus said the Father was doing in John 5:17.[123] Beale makes a good case that "resting is best understood as the enjoyment of a position of sovereign rule in a cosmic temple, after the quelling of chaotic forces" similar to when a candidate for US president wins an election and comes to settle in the White House

---

121. Rad, *Genesis*, 97.

122. On such escalated blessings, see Beale, *New Testament Biblical Theology*, 33–46.

123. Shead, "Sabbath," 745–46.

to begin his job of governing the country.[124] This is much like Dumbrell's point concerning 2 Samuel 6 and 7:

> We note that the impulse for the building of a house for Yahweh arose from the fact that Yahweh "gave rest to David from all his enemies round about" (v. 1). Just as building the tabernacle was the fitting climax to the Exodus redemption and pointed to its meaning, so here the question of building a temple comes as the consummation of the conquest now finalized by David's defeat of the Philistines in chapter 5. We may also note by way of anticipation that in Ezekiel 40–48 the building of the temple comes as the consummation of all things, the goal of eschatology and follows the final eschatological battle (chaps. 38–39).[125]

Something like this active sense of rest also seems to be true of humans made in God's image. People exercise a ruling function in God's ordered creation as Adam did in the garden of Eden in which God rested/settled (*nuah*) him so that he could "work and take care of it." Deuteronomy 5:15 explains a key reason Israel was to do no work on the Sabbath: "Remember that you were slaves in Egypt and that the Lord your God brought you out of there with a mighty hand and an outstretched arm. Therefore the Lord your God has commanded you to observe the Sabbath day." An analogy is set up between God laboring the six days of creation and Israel laboring in Egypt. As God rested and began to reign over his land, so would Israel. They could now be fruitful and multiply (now to fulfill God's promises to and through Abraham built on the cultural commission; see Gen 12:1–3; 17:2–8; 22:17–18; 26:3–4; 28:3–4; 35:11–12), exercise godly dominion, guard the land from evil intrusion, and enjoy a relationship with God, who would walk and dwell among them as God had done with Adam and Eve in Eden (see Lev 26:9–13). In Psalm 95, God urges Israel not to again harden their hearts as they did at Meribah (Exod 17:7), a typical example of the rebellion of the Exodus generation that explains why God declared on oath, "They shall never enter my rest." This oath is an apparent echo of Numbers 14:30, which says, "Not one of you will enter the land." It was true that Israel had to cease from work on the Sabbath to commemorate both God's cessation of creation and their own redemption from Egypt, yet the goal of Sabbath rest in the promised land included the accomplishment of the cultural commission—work!

124. Beale, *New Testament Biblical Theology*, 796–97. God's resting as King over Israel from his temple is spoken of in 1 Chr 28:2; 2 Chr 6:41; Ps 132:7–8, 13–14; Isa 66:1.

125. Dumbrell, *End of the Beginning*, 47.

This makes sense of the fact that New Testament believers also enter their rest (already in Heb 4:3, 9–11; not yet in Rev 14:13) and look forward to both serving God (Rev 22:3) and reigning with God (Dan 7:27; Rev 2:26–27; 3:21; 22:5). This sounds like active rest, ruling and enjoying the new promised land of the new creation with fruitful work unopposed by the powers of evil and enjoying the everlasting presence of God forever. Sabbath rest will be ours at last (see Isa 66, esp. v. 23).[126]

But what was the test and what does it say about the image of God? The command is straightforward: do not eat the fruit of the tree of the knowledge of good and evil. The text does not say how eating would lead to such knowledge. The fruit is not said to contain magical power. Vos is right to say that God chose to grant knowledge to them, but they could receive it from him after one of two choices: disobedience or obedience. This is why the covenant has often been called the "covenant of works" rather than of grace. Grace pertains to God giving salvific gifts one does not deserve, yet Adam and Eve were not undeserving until the fall. Hoekema argues that the term "covenant" was not used of an arrangement of any kind before the fall and therefore only pertains to saving grace. Perhaps, yet his admission of many of the central points of significance in the Adamic covenant suggests that this is an argument that is more about terms than substance. He affirms Adam's headship and representation of the human race, the probationary command that tested his obedience, the sin and death that came through his disobedience, and Adam's being a type of the last Adam, Christ (as in 1 Cor 15:45–49).[127]

The fact that Adam and Eve would gain moral knowledge that they did not already possess meant that their knowledge would be somewhat fuller than it had been, resulting in more similarity to God in that way (see Gen 3:22). A probation condition was needed, the meeting or not meeting of which would lead to blessings or curses. The condition could have been anything God chose. Eating was not the point in and of itself, but rather trust and obedience. God was not holding back a blessing from them at all, nor was he motivated by envy or lack of generosity.[128] Satan

---

126. Space does not permit a full defense and explanation of this notion of Sabbath. See Shead, "Sabbath"; Beale, *New Testament Biblical Theology*, 777–801.

127. Hoekema, *Created in God's Image*, 121.

128. Following Vos, *Biblical Theology*, 29–36. Some interpreters see the knowledge of good and evil as autonomy-related knowledge so that the temptation is to determine their own right and wrong, thus presuming to take on a prerogative of God, a grasp at deification. See Hamilton, *Genesis*, 190; Hoekema, *Created in God's Image*, 104. There

tempted Adam and Eve to doubt that God prohibited the eating (v. 1), doubt God's generous provision of all the other food from all the other trees (v. 1; cf. 2:16–17), doubt that death would result from eating the forbidden fruit (v. 4), believe God is withholding the benefit of knowledge (v. 5), and this out of envy (v. 5).[129] Had Eve accurately remembered and quoted God's command concerning the tree, the door to deception would not have been opened. Yet perhaps the grain of truth Satan used here was that Adam and Eve would and could never match God's omniscience, a quantitative limitation on humanity by virtue of their contingency and finiteness. Satan may have been trying to use the power of suggestion to get Adam and Eve to want divinity rather than creatureliness. Human pride and the presumption of divine prerogatives certainly has plenty of history to illustrate it. Apparently fooled and failing to trust God about these matters and wanting that knowledge (and to satisfy their taste buds—see v. 6), they ate the fruit. They did gain an experiential knowledge of evil and the contrast between it and good—albeit a knowledge fit for humans and well short of Divine omniscience. Yet they could have had an even greater knowledge of good and evil without such an experience of evil in that they would have both understood Satan's temptation strategies and retained the knowledge of God's prohibition, generous provision, the consequences of disobedience, and the experiential understanding that God withholds no good thing from his people who do his will. This would have been full knowledge, which Paul says God gives humans he renews in his image (a clear echo of Gen 1:26 and 2:17 in Col 3:10). This clearly implies that the image of God involves knowledge in some way. This link will be developed and related to the unfolding concept of the image.

In sum, the image and likeness together mean that humanity as a whole and each human being individually represents God in dominion

---

is evidence of people grasping at such prerogatives (e.g., Isa 5:20) and divine worship (Acts 12:21–23) and this is clearly part of the sin problem. The New Age movement's appropriation of pantheistic monism certainly embodies such pretensions—see McRoberts, *New Age or Old Lie?*, 77–79. But this interpretation of the tree requires us to take God's statement that Adam and Eve had become like himself, knowing good and evil (3:22) as ironic, whereas it seems to be a straightforward statement of the result of their act: similarity to God in that one respect, namely knowing about good and evil. It requires "know" to mean "choose" instead, which is not well-attested. And Paul's intertextual biblical interpretation of the passage in Col 3:10 promises knowledge as a part of the renewal of God's image. Thus, however we construe the knowledge of good and evil, it must be something God wanted us to have. And God did not want us to have autonomy.

129. See Ross, *Creation and Blessing*, 133–37.

and reflects the sort of being God is, to some extent. In Genesis, this is the basis for the mandate to rule over creation, the one purpose Genesis mentions for God making humanity in his image. This purpose is clearly carried forward beyond the fall, finding its way into further covenants God made with people, showing that God intends to accomplish his original creational purposes in spite of the fall of humanity.

Genesis 5:1–3

The next mention of the image is in Genesis 5:1–3.

> This is the written account of Adam's family line. When God created mankind, he made them in the likeness of God. He created them male and female and blessed them. And he named them "Mankind" when they were created. When Adam had lived 130 years, he had a son in his own likeness, in his own image; and he named him Seth.

Verses 1 and 2 recapitulate several aspects of Genesis 1:26–28, including the image and likeness, the corporate unity of humanity, the making of human beings as male and female, and the blessing that would enable the rain to come and the land to produce food and would enable the people in Adam's line to live, multiply, and enjoy life and fellowship with God. To bless means "to endue with power for success, prosperity, fecundity, longevity, etc."[130] Adam and Eve had fallen into sin in Genesis 3, and the consequences came crashing down upon them, eventually including death, which 5:5 records. Death becomes a constant refrain throughout the chapter and forms a startling contrast to the blessing mentioned in verse 2.[131] But one of those consequences was not losing God's image and likeness, as its repetition in the introduction to the account of Adam's line suggests and as Genesis 9:6 makes crystal clear.[132]

But granted this, why would verse 3 say that Seth was in Adam's image and likeness? Clines thinks this is simply saying that Seth looked like Adam and has nothing to do with the image of God.[133] Other scholars have taken this as a suggestion that the fall of Genesis 3 had yet another

130. Oswalt, "בָּרַךְ," 132.

131. Ross, *Creation and Blessing*, 173–74.

132. Ross, *Creation and Blessing*, 174; Kilner, *Dignity and Destiny*, 151. Wenham, *Genesis 1–15*, 126–27; Hamilton, *Genesis*, 255–56.

133. Clines, "Image of God," 78n117.

consequence beyond those narrated throughout chapters 3 and 4, namely weakness or sinful corruption.[134] One way to put it is that the same person can bear more than one likeness, and those the person resembles may be different in important ways, as here. It is not clear why the author of Genesis would care if Seth looked like his father, but it is clear why he would care if Seth bore a resemblance to Adam's corrupted character. In addition, in 1 Corinthians 15:49, Paul will develop the rest of the human race's similarity to Adam, making it obvious that this is a problem that transformation into the image of Christ will solve. In the light of such reasons, this text implies that moral corruption was spreading from the first human generation on to the second.

One other issue deserves comment. The possibility was left open above that there is a paradigm, Christ, who is the image of God after which the rest of humanity was patterned. Christ is the image; humans are made according to the image. But there is a difficulty if one applies that thought here. As John Piper points out, "obviously the author does not mean that there was an image of Adam according to which Seth was fashioned."[135] Does this mean one should abandon the idea that Jesus is the image and thus paradigm? Not if there is a certain amount of flexibility in how image language is used. First Corinthians 11:7 calls man the image of God, the only exception to the rule of saying humans are made in/according to the image of God. This flexibility suggests one should not make too much of the exceptions and allow for the formulation of a theology of the image according to the rule.

Genesis 9:6

The next mention of the image of God is in Genesis 9:6, after God had sent a flood to punish people for their wickedness ("every inclination of the thoughts of the human heart was only evil all the time," Gen 6:5) and violence (Gen 6:11). Here God made a covenant with creation (v. 8) and gave direction and blessings to Noah and his family so that they could carry the creation project forward. God considered the earth and animals and especially human beings valuable. In the flood story, God was willing to kill all but a handful of people in a process that was destructive to the

---

134. Mathews, *Genesis*, 310; Lange, *Genesis*, 270; Kilner, *Dignity and Destiny*, 151–52; Hoekema, *Created in God's Image*, 15–16; Horton, *Genesis*, 45–46.

135. Piper, "Image of God."

earth and animals, too. Does this mean God did not really value human (or animal) life after all? Or does it suggest the seriousness of the sins of his viceroys? The narrative from Genesis 3–11 shows how consequential the free choices of people could be and how much harm they could bring to each other and the creation. Perhaps one should ponder at this point how much good could have been done by their ongoing obedient actions. But in time evil and violence became commonplace. The contrast between what should have been done by the stewards of creation and what actually was being done and contemplated was vast. If one accepts the original death penalty for sin (Gen 2:17) as just in principle, one has no legitimate grounds to reject it in practice in the flood story. If human rule over nature and animals could be a benefit to them, as was argued above, then their failure to rule could be a detriment to them. And when a ruler is punished, it tends to affect those under his/her authority. Thus, God's punishment in the flood narrative, severe though it may seem to human beings (who have a penchant for seeing their own sin as far less of a problem than it is), does not undermine the value of human beings taught in Genesis 1–2. It underlines the importance of human beings fulfilling the cultural commission rather than setting up contrary commissions of their own.

This chapter has close connections to Genesis 1:26–28. "Then God blessed Noah and his sons, saying to them, "Be fruitful and increase in number and fill the earth" (Gen 9:1, repeated in v. 7). As in Genesis 1:28, the multiplying would enable the ruling. And God's blessing would enable the multiplying. The intended result would be well-being and happiness.

This similarity to Genesis 1 heightens the sense of contrast when God grants humans permission to eat animals, turning human rule into something to fear (vv. 2–3). Clearly this is less than the ideal of Genesis 1–2. It certainly shows that one sort of living being is significantly more valued than another kind of living being. Both have the *nepeš ḥayyāh* of Genesis 1:30 (7:22 uses *rûaḥ ḥayyîm* with the same meaning, again of people and animals), but only one is made in God's image. Yet the covenant to never again use a flood to kill all life on earth is made with not only humans, but with every living creature (*nepeš ḥayyāh*) and earth itself. The importance of this is seen in that it is stated repeatedly throughout verses 12–17, God makes the rainbow a sign to remind himself of his promise (vv. 14–16), and it is an everlasting covenant (vv. 12

and 16). To make such a covenant with all of creation, God must value creation highly.[136]

In order to discourage violence from becoming the widespread problem it had been before the flood, God authorized a new penalty for murder and pointed to its basis: "And for your lifeblood I will surely demand an accounting. I will demand an accounting from every animal. And from each human being, too, I will demand an accounting for the life of another human being. 'Whoever sheds human blood, by humans shall their blood be shed; for in the image of God has God made mankind'" (Gen 9:5–6). Here again, human beings after the fall were still said to be made in the image of God. Their value based on the Divine image becomes even clearer as it grounds the penalty for murdering one made in that image. Here it seems that the only thing of equal value that can be taken from one who has taken the life of a being made in God's image is his/her own life. Money would be no substitute (Num 35:31–34).[137] This notion of retributive justice found expression in the *lex talionis* of the Mosaic Law (Exod 21:23–25).

Hoekema sees further significance of murdering a person made in God's image. "The man who has been murdered is someone who imaged God, reflected God, was like God, and represented God. Therefore, when one kills a human being, not only does he take that person's life, but he hurts God himself—the God who was reflected in that individual. To touch the image of God is to touch God himself; to kill the image of God is to do violence to God himself."[138]

One does not necessarily get this idea from an exegesis of the passage by itself, but by how Jesus and James will later draw an equivalence between how people treat other people and how they treat God (Matt 25:31–46; James 3:9). In James's case, this equivalence is tied to the image of God. But Genesis shows that God values human life very highly, considerably more than animals, which he also does value. Genesis 9 is the first clear statement that the image of God is why people must be treated in a certain way—a nonviolent way. That is, humans enjoy a negative right to not be murdered, a right to live. Christian ethicists have summed up the value of human life with several terms, including sanctity, sacredness,

---

136. Horrell, "Ecological Ethics," 257.

137. Wright, *Old Testament Ethics*, 308.

138. Hoekema, *Created in God's Image*, 16.

dignity, worth, value, and others. This value is based on the fact that God created people in his image and therefore values them and so should we.[139]

Kilner does not think that ruling over creation is the point of the reference to God's image in Genesis 9:6, saying that the subject of dominion over the animals in verses 1–4 is left behind when the image is introduced in verse 6.[140] But that is an overly narrow concept of context. And animals are to be held accountable for killing people in verse 5. Plus, human political authorities are authorized to take the lives of murderers here, and human authority structures are obviously relevant to the rule of humans.

The Noahic covenant seems to build a bridge between the Adamic and Abrahamic covenants. We have already noted that in Genesis, bearing children is necessary for accomplishing the cultural commission (though this does not mean everyone is required to have children). It was crucial for the sake of repopulating the earth after the flood. And it would also be essential in order to accomplish God's purpose of raising up a new nation from Abraham in order that God may bless all nations through it. In Genesis 12:1–3, God promised Abraham, "I will make you into a great nation, and I will bless you; I will make your name great, and you will be a blessing. I will bless those who bless you, and whoever curses you I will curse; and all peoples on earth will be blessed through you." This passage uses the blessing terminology of Genesis 1:28 and the conceptual parallel of fruitful multiplying in "I will make you into a great nation." The cultural commission is passed on to the patriarchs of Israel repeatedly, in whole or in part, throughout Genesis (17:2–8; 22:17–18; 26:3–4, 24; 28:3–4, 13–14), sometimes in the form of promises and other times in the form of commands, such as "be fruitful and multiply" (as in Gen 35:11–12).[141] These promises and their fulfillments figure prominently in the rest of the books of the Pentateuch as well (Exod 1:7; Num 23:10–11; Lev 26:9; Deut 7:13; 15:4–6, et al.). The significance of this is captured by Beale. "Thus, in the repetition of the commission to the patriarchs noted above, the mention of 'all the nations of the earth' being 'blessed' by Abraham's 'seed' alludes to a renewed human community bearing God's image and 'filling the earth' with regenerated progeny who also reflect

---

139. For a lucid discussion of the meaning of the various terms used to describe the value of human life, see Gushee, *Sacredness of Human Life*, 16–36.

140. Kilner, *Dignity and Destiny*, 202.

141. On God's covenant with Abraham involving both promise and command, both unconditional and conditional elements, see Wright, *Mission of God*, 205–8.

God's image and shine out its luminosity to others in the 'city of man' who do not rebel and also come to reflect God. Thus, these new converts are 'blessed' with the favor of God's glorious presence and become a part of God's ever-increasing kingdom and rule."[142]

To Beale's point, God let the soon-to-be leader of his covenant people, Abraham, in on what he was about to do in Sodom and Gomorrah, apparently to draw him into a teachable moment about justice. "Shall I hide from Abraham what I am about to do? Abraham will surely become a great and powerful nation, and all nations on earth will be blessed through him. For I have chosen him, so that he will direct his children and his household after him to keep the way of the Lord by doing what is right and just, so that the Lord will bring about for Abraham what he has promised him" (Gen 18:17–19). This text provides a means by which Israel would be used by God to bless the nations. As Abraham and his descendants directed their children to walk uprightly and justly, God would bless them and they would influence the nations, who would then also be blessed by God. Building upon this, God later designated Israel "a kingdom of priests and a holy nation" (Exod 19:6), a means through which God would bless all nations on earth.[143] This priestly moral and spiritual influence, closely tied to royal responsibility, is helped along by the procreation and proper raising of children in the Abrahamic Covenant, showing that spiritual and physical interests are not mutually exclusive, but intertwined.[144] It would seem that a holistic anthropology fits with a holistic concept of God's purposes in the world.

Exodus 20:4–6//Deuteronomy 5:8–10; 4:16–17

> You shall not make for yourself an image in the form of anything in heaven above or on the earth beneath or in the waters below. You shall not bow down to them or worship them; for I, the Lord your God, am a jealous God, punishing the children for the sin of the parents to the third and fourth generation of those who hate me, but showing love to a thousand generations of those who love me and keep my commandments.

142. Beale, *New Testament Biblical Theology*, 53.

143. Stuart, *Exodus*, 423. According to the Apostle Paul, blessing the nations through Israel was accomplished through justifying the nations by faith (Gal 3:8–9).

144. See Malachi 2:13–15 on the raising of godly offspring as a reason God generally wants spouses to remain married (though cf. Matt 19:4–9 and 1 Cor 7:12–16).

These passages do not use the term *ṣelem*, which sometimes refers to idols, but do use parallel terms for idols. What they teach will have an important bearing on the image of God theme as it unfolds. The first commandment forbids the worship of any god other than Yahweh (Exod 20:3). The second commandment forbids worshiping God using an image (Exod 20:4). God's stated reason for the second commandment is that he is a jealous God, part of a metaphor for the relationship between God and his people, which is similar to the relationship between husband and wife. Both relationships require an exclusive, faithful love for the other that brooks no rivals or substitutes. For this reason, Scripture frequently refers to idolatry metaphorically as adultery (e.g., Exod 34:13; Deut 31:16; Jer 3:14; Hos 1:2; Ezek 23:3–21; Jas 4:4–5). This is intolerable to God because he is a jealous God (Exod 20:5), wanting the devotion that is rightfully his.[145]

But there is another primary aspect of idolatry, one that carries strong implications for our study of the image of God. Deuteronomy 4:15–20 explains why an image is not be used in the worship of God.

> You saw no form of any kind the day the LORD spoke to you at Horeb out of the fire. Therefore watch yourselves very carefully, so that you do not become corrupt and make for yourselves an idol, an image of any shape, whether formed like a man or a woman, or like any animal on earth or any bird that flies in the air, or like any creature that moves along the ground or any fish in the waters below. And when you look up to the sky and see the sun, the moon and the stars—all the heavenly array—do not be enticed into bowing down to them and worshiping things the LORD your God has apportioned to all the nations under heaven. But as for you, the LORD took you and brought you out of the iron-smelting furnace, out of Egypt, to be the people of his inheritance, as you now are.

When using an idol, the worshiper will inevitably come to think of God in terms of this created thing that he himself made and a human craftsman then copied. The result would be a distorted understanding of who God is and what he is like.[146] This is why Deuteronomy 4:15 provides an explanatory preface for the prohibition of making an idol: "You saw no form of any kind the day the Lord spoke to you at Horeb out of the fire." To violate this prohibition would destroy/corrupt them (v. 16). On

---

145. On this theme in Scripture, see Ortlund, *Whoredom*.

146. Calvin, *Moses*, 2:107.

more than one occasion, once Israel worshiped God using an idol, their understanding of God, his nature, his ethical character, and his requirements soon changed for the worse (Exod 32; 1 Kgs 12:28–33). At some point, the result was worshiping a god other than Yahweh, a making of God in the person/nation's image, an ironic reversal of God having made people in his image. This is the reversal inherent in idolatry.

This is not an honest mistake, but rather a symptom of human depravity. Douglas Stuart sums up the lure of idolatry in the ancient world with several terms: guaranteed (the god/goddess would surely be with them if the idol carried the essence of him/her within it), selfish (the idolater was trying to buy the favors of the god/goddess in a sort of *quid pro quo* that made the worshipers' desires primary and the deity someone to be used as a means rather than an end, in contrast to how God presented himself in the first commandment), easy (there were few ethical obligations in ancient paganism), convenient (you could worship your deity at the local high places rather than going all the way to Jerusalem a few times a year), normal (everybody's doing it), logical (why go to a general practitioner when you can see a specialist?), pleasing to the senses (idols are art), indulgent (worship involved frequently gluttonous feasts), and erotic (cult prostitution, or the use of sympathetic magic, encouraged the deity to respond to sexual practices with their own gifts of fertility, granting children, multiplication of animal offspring, and rain for crops).[147] Idolatry and depravity went together. The desire for the latter could lead to the former, though the former could also lead to deeper states of the latter too, as we will see.

There is a related result of idolatry that is especially relevant to the image of God theme and is juxtaposed with a happier reality. Beale puts it succinctly: "What people revere, they resemble, either for ruin or restoration."[148] If one reveres and trusts in God, one becomes more like him. If one reveres and trusts a golden calf, one becomes like the golden calf.

This truth is expressed in a number of biblical texts. A brief treatment will have to suffice here. The paradigmatic example is when Israel had Aaron make a golden calf for them to worship in Exodus 32. Though the calf idol may have been an imitation of an Egyptian god (Ptah or Amon-Re), Canaanite deity (Baal), or other ancient deities,[149] the deity (or deities)

---

147. Stuart, *Exodus*, 450–54.

148. Beale, *We Become What We Worship*, 16.

149. Beale, *We Become What We Worship*, 84n37.

thus represented was said to have brought Israel out of Egypt (vv. 4 and 8) so that this was a violation of the second commandment.[150] The text does not directly say that Israel became like this calf, but rather suggests this in the description of the people. In addition to saying these Israelites had become corrupt (v. 7), God calls them "stiff-necked people" (v. 9). "They are being portrayed as wild calves or untrained cows: they became (1) 'stiff-necked' (Ex 32:9; 33:3, 5; 34:9) and would not obey, but (2) they 'were let loose' because 'Aaron had let them go loose' (Ex 32:25), (3) so that 'they had quickly turned aside from the way,' (Ex 32:8) and they needed to be (4) 'gathered together' again 'in the gate' (Ex 32:26), (5) so that Moses could 'lead the people where' God had told him to go (Ex 32:34)."[151]

Moses seems to have been mocking the Israelites for becoming like a calf, stubborn and rebellious. Calvin says the description, "stiff-necked" is based on oxen who refuse to submit under the yoke.[152] Hosea 4:16–18 similarly describes Israel, and in reference to Israel's idolatrous ways. "The Israelites are stubborn, like a stubborn heifer. How then can the Lord pasture them like lambs in a meadow? Ephraim is joined to idols; leave him alone! Even when their drinks are gone, they continue their prostitution." Because they revered a heifer, they became like the heifer and would not be led by the Lord they should have revered. Once Israel worshiped the golden calf at Horeb, as Richard Lints points out, "from this point forward in Israel's history acts of rebellion are characterized by appeal to the calf's attributes—a stiff neck, a hard heart, ears that cannot hear and eyes that cannot see."[153]

The themes of reversal and becoming what we worship carry over in Deuteronomy.

> Therefore watch yourselves very carefully, so that you do not become corrupt and make for yourselves an idol, an image of any shape, whether formed like a man or a woman, or like any animal on earth or any bird that flies in the air, or like any creature that moves along the ground or any fish in the waters below. And when you look up to the sky and see the sun, the moon and the stars—all the heavenly array—do not be enticed into bowing down to them and worshiping things the Lord your God has apportioned to all the nations under heaven. (Deut 4:15b–19)

150. Keil and Delitzsch, *Commentary*, 1:466.

151. Beale, *We Become What We Worship*, 77–78.

152. Calvin, *Moses*, 3:341.

153. Lints, *Identity and Idolatry*, 92.

As Christopher Wright notes, the creatures listed appear in almost exactly the opposite order when compared to Genesis 1. "The rhetorical effect matches the theological implication: When people worship creation instead of the Creator, everything is turned upside down. Idolatry produces disorder in all our fundamental relationships."[154] Instead of God over humans, who are over animals, humans reduce God to less than animals by making God out to be like animals. Then they worship the resulting god, moving themselves lower than animals and becoming like the animal-like supposed god. Or they make God in their own image rather than the reverse. Psalm 106:19–20 reflects on the episode: "At Horeb they made a calf and worshiped an idol cast from metal. They exchanged their glorious God for an image of a bull, which eats grass." As has already been pointed out, the serpent leading humans to rebel against God was an attempt to flip the order of creation on its head. Here it is clear that idolatry is an accessory to that process.

In Deuteronomy, Moses speaks of the moral character of Israel and the likelihood that they will rebel against God after he dies using the same language as that used of the golden calf worshipers. They are stiff-necked (9:13 and 31:27; cf. Exod 32:9) and corrupt (9:12 and 31:29; cf. Exod 32:7) and have turned aside from the commandments of God (9:12 and 31:29; cf. Exod 32:8). Beale argues that "the point of the comparison between the first generation's idolatry and that of future generations is that the golden calf idolatry was seen to be paradigmatic of Israel's future idolatry, so that the latter was to be patterned after the former."[155] Further, 29:4 says, "But to this day the Lord has not given you a mind that understands or eyes that see or ears that hear."

We see similar sensory organ malfunction language in Isaiah, which is profoundly influenced by Deuteronomy.[156] Indeed, Isaiah begins his

---

154. Wright, *Mission of God*, 143.

155. Beale, *We Become What We Worship*, 77.

156. On the Mosaic authorship of the Pentateuch, see chapter 2, note 1 above. In defense of the eighth-century BC prophet Isaiah's authorship of Isaiah 1–66, see Motyer, *Prophecy of Isaiah*, 23–30; Archer, *Survey*, 365–90. The view of John the Baptist and the apostles holds great weight. In John 12:38–40, John quotes both Isaiah 53:1 and 6:10. He introduces the first quotation with "the word of Isaiah the prophet," then links the second quotation with "as Isaiah says elsewhere" (v. 39). He concludes with a brief explanation prefaced by "Isaiah said this" (v. 41). Clearly, John was not merely citing the name of a book, but what he understood to be the inspired words of the eighth-century BC prophet Isaiah, words from what is often considered Isaiah and Deutero-Isaiah, demonstrating that this distinction would have been foreign to him.

first oracle with "Hear me, you heavens! Listen, earth!" (1:2), a clear echo of "Listen, you heavens, and I will speak; hear, you earth, the words of my mouth" in Deuteronomy 32:1. There follow a number of parallels between the two chapters: God having brought up children, who then rebelled against him (Deut 32:5–6; Isa 1:2); their condition is now like Sodom and Gomorrah (Deut 32:32; Isa 1:9–10); they are idolatrous (Deut 32:17, 21, 37–38, and Isa 1:21, 29); they do not know or understand (Deut 32:6 and Isa 1:3); and God will avenge himself by punishing them (Deut 32:43 and Isa 1:24–25).

Their lack of spiritual understanding is famously revisited in the sensory-organ malfunction language of Isaiah 6:9–10.

> He said, "Go and tell this people: 'Be ever hearing, but never understanding; be ever seeing, but never perceiving.' Make the heart of this people calloused; make their ears dull and close their eyes. Otherwise they might see with their eyes, hear with their ears, understand with their hearts, and turn and be healed.'"

Scholars have long puzzled over what this means for human freedom and the justice of God. Brevard Childs insists that this callousing of Israel's hearts was God's doing (not following the Septuagint's transference of responsibility to Israel) but that this occurred in a particular moment of Israel's history and should not be applied to the world in general. It marks a turning point for Israel wherein God has decreed judgment, a judgment announced in the parable of the vineyard and woes of chapter 5 and based on Israel's failure to produce the fruit of righteousness and justice (see 5:7).[157] Gary Smith adds a helpful metaphor regarding the decreed and therefore inevitable judgment: "If one were to compare this to a parent punishing a disobedient child, one would say that once the stubborn child is over the knee and the hand is swinging, it is too late to offer repentance to avoid punishment."[158] But then why send Isaiah to preach to them? Beale notes that, first of all, the punishment is for idolatry (citing the indictments of this unfaithfulness in 1:29–31; 2:8, 18–20), along with the other sins that accompany it, which are listed throughout the first five chapters of Isaiah. Second, Israel becoming like her idols is

---

Nor is this the only instance of these men attributing various parts of Isaiah to this prophet (see Matt 12:17–18, quoting Isa 42:1; Matt 3:3, quoting Isa 40:3; Luke 3:4, quoting Isa 40:3–5; Acts 8:28, quoting Isa 53:7–8; Rom 10:16, quoting Isa 53:1; Rom 10:20, quoting Isa 65:1).

157. Childs, *Isaiah*, 56–57.

158. Smith, *Isaiah 1–39*, 195n222.

the *talionic* punishment for idolatry. "People are punished by means of their own sin."[159] What goes around comes around, and in pretty much the same form in which they sent it around. Eyes and ears do not help idols see either literally or spiritually. Israel's idolaters also will have the necessary organs but be unable to perceive the truth about God and the idols. This type of punishment is analogous to people turning away from God and, as the appropriate consequence, being deprived of his presence for all eternity. The punishment is felt in that what a rebel wants is never as good as he thinks it will be, a fact he would know had he listened to the warnings and promises of God. Isaiah was called to tell Israel to become like their idols as punishment for their idolatry.[160] The New Testament will make use of this concept as well, showing that this situation is not entirely unique. Contra Childs, some general principle seems to be in play that is applicable in other situations, yet the persistent idolatry and refusal to repent must surely be present in order for such irreversible, *talionic* judgment to be decreed. On the other side, the idolaters assume that it is God who does not see and know, a point Isaiah brings up in 29:15c–16b. "'Who sees us? Who will know?' You turn things upside down, as if the potter were thought to be like the clay!" Here again is the reversal, illustrative of the spiritual dullness that is the appropriate judgment for revering idols rather than God. Isaiah's most sustained critique of idolatry in 44:8–20 uses this same language of failure to see, know, understand, and comprehend (vv. 9, 18–19), which is caused by God in apparent judgment. Significantly, Isaiah speaks of the craftsman making an idol that is like a man in verse 13, which brings out layers of irony. A man crafts a man-like god and bows to what he has made, which is less than the craftsman is himself since it is a lifeless image of a man, whereas he himself is an actual man. The image sits in the house, unable to move, whereas the craftsman can move freely. Yet the craftsman becomes as spiritually dense as the block of wood he worships. One could add something Isaiah may or may not have had in mind: the craftsman who is made in God's image made an image that was supposed to represent God, but did not, and, in so doing, became more like the non-image he made rather than the person made in God's image that he actually is.

---

159. Beale, *We Become What We Worship*, 47.

160. Beale notes passages in which Israel is ironically commanded to continue serving idols (Ezek 20:39; Jer 44:25; Amos 4:4). See *We Become What We Worship*, 47n16.

Isaiah's sensory-organ malfunction language is picked up and its point made explicit in Psalm 115:4–8 (= 135:15–18).[161]

> But their idols are silver and gold,
> made by human hands.
> They have mouths, but cannot speak,
> eyes, but cannot see.
> They have ears, but cannot hear,
> noses, but cannot smell.
> They have hands, but cannot feel,
> feet, but cannot walk,
> nor can they utter a sound with their throats.
> Those who make them will be like them,
> and so will all who trust in them.

Objects of silver and gold cannot speak or perceive anything in a literal sense. Analogously, those who revere these objects cannot perceive spiritual realities because those who make and trust in idols end up like them. These devotees of idols cannot even perceive God (v. 3). In contrast to the idols, God "does whatever pleases him" (v. 3), is the help and shield of those who trust in Him (vv. 9–11), blesses his people and causes them to flourish (vv. 12–15), owns the heavens (v. 16), and gives the earth to humanity (v. 16). Though the emphasis lies on God's greatness in contrast to the idols, the psalm also seems to carry an implied contrast between the well-being of those who trust in God and those who trust in idols. The latter experience spiritual sensory malfunction; the former flourish and possess the earth. A major incentive to worship is the desire for safety and security. People revere and pursue whatever/whoever they think will provide these, making the ability to identify the source of Divine power vital to human well-being. Lints adds that making idols more like themselves bespoke a desire to control their own destiny, since a god like themselves would be easier to manipulate than one who was transcendent and free. Here again, "idolatry was not in the first instance a cognitive error (believing in other gods), but a fallacy of the heart (yearning for control/autonomy).[162]

Thus far, only the negative part of the equation has been emphasized. People become what they revere. Too often, ancient Israel revered

---

161. Psalm 115 seems to be either late preexilic or postexilic and Psalm 135 seems to be postexilic. Thus, both psalms would have been written after Isaiah. See Beale, *We Become What We Worship*, 46n13.

162. Lints, *Identity and Idolatry*, 86.

idols and became like them to their detriment. It remains to be seen how the New Testament will develop the positive hope of people revering God and becoming like him to their benefit.

Psalm 8:5

Next up are David's words in Psalm 8:[163]

> O Lord, our Sovereign,
> how majestic is your name in all the earth!
> You have set your glory above the heavens.
> Out of the mouths of babes and infants
> you have founded a bulwark because of your foes,
> to silence the enemy and the avenger.
> When I look at your heavens, the work of your fingers,
> the moon and the stars that you have established;
> what are human beings that you are mindful of them,
> mortals that you care for them?
> Yet you have made them a little lower than God,
> and crowned them with glory and honor.
> You have given them dominion over the works of your hands;
> you have put all things under their feet,
> all sheep and oxen,
> and also the beasts of the field,
> the birds of the air, and the fish of the sea,
> whatever passes along the paths of the seas.
> O Lord, our Sovereign,
> how majestic is your name in all the earth! (NRSV)

Verses 1 and 9 form an *inclusio*, beginning and ending the psalm with the majesty of "*Yahweh* our *Adonai*," Israel's covenant God and King.

---

163. The psalm title calls this "a psalm of David." While the psalm titles are probably not divinely inspired, one need not be skeptical of their historical reliability. Though neither Jesus nor the Apostles specifically attributed Psalm 8 to David, they did attribute several other psalms to David, in agreement with their psalm titles. E.g., Psalms 2 (Acts 4:24–25), 16 (Acts 2:25–28), 32 (Rom 4:6–8), 69 (Acts 1:20), and 110 (Matt 22:45; Mark 12:36; Luke 20:42–44; Acts 2:34). There is no good reason to doubt that David wrote Psalm 8. If he did, this would mean it dates from between 1020–975 BC. For a defense of the Davidic authorship of the psalms attributed to David, see Archer, *Survey*, 488–93. But even apart from such a conclusion, it is certain that Psalm 8 was written after Genesis (since it is a meditation on Genesis 1) and predates the epistles that quote from it in the NT, and that is the important point for our survey of the redemptive-historical development of the image of God.

A contrast is set up between the grandeur of the Creator and the vast universe, which is puny in comparison with the "fingers" with which God formed it. This in turn leads to the contrast between the vast universe and puny humanity.[164] God established his glory (*hôd*; v. 1) in the heavens in which he set the moon and stars (v. 3), a clear reference to Genesis 1:16: "God made two great lights—the greater light to govern the day and the lesser light to govern the night. He also made the stars." Analogous to the role of the moon and stars in governing the night and day and displaying the glory of God throughout its realm, humanity also has the role of governing and displaying the honor/glory/splendor (*hādār*, a cognate of *hôd* that is often juxtaposed with it[165]) with which the Lord has crowned people throughout creation. Humans' is not an inherent glory, but a glory given by God so that he may be glorified by all creation—a central goal of God in creation. As Psalm 72:19 says, "Praise be to his glorious name forever; may the whole earth be filled with his glory." Glory translates *kābôd*, which means "heaviness" when used literally, "distinction, honor" when used of people, and "power, authority, and honor of God," often accompanied by "manifestations of light" in the latter case.[166] Something of the way the metaphor works can be seen in the expression, "She is not to be taken lightly." Such a person may be considered too powerful or smart to be overlooked. God should be taken very seriously and, secondarily, the rulers he has crowned should, too. In God's case, he ought to be worshiped, served, and obeyed, all activities that may cause other people to glorify him. Beale is probably right that "The goal of divine splendor is to be achieved 'in all the earth' by humanity, whom God has crowned 'with glory and majesty' by making him in his image (v. 5). In particular, Psalm 8 says that God's glory is to be spread throughout the earth by humanity 'ruling' over all 'the works of Your hands' (vv. 6–8)."[167] In Psalm 72, the key means to this goal is the reign of the Davidic, end-time king. Verse 8 says, "May he rule from sea to sea and from the River to the ends of the earth," a passage quoted in Zechariah 9:10, clearly a Messianic context (see v. 9 quoted in Matt 21:5 and John 12:15 of Christ). Psalm 72:17 says, "Then all nations will be blessed through him, and they will call him blessed," echoing Genesis 22:18. Genesis 22:17 had looked forward to

---

164. VanGemeren, *Psalms*, under Ps 8:3. "Puny" is the language of Keil and Delitzsch, *Commentary*, 5:90.

165. Hamilton, "הוד," 209.

166. *HALOT* 457.

167. Beale, *New Testament Biblical Theology*, 37.

Abraham's descendants possessing the gates of their enemies, a theme echoed in Psalm 72:8–15. The implication is that God's covenant promises to Abraham would be accomplished through the reign of the Davidic king in fulfillment of the covenant to David. The parallel between Psalms 8 and 72 seems clear: God's glorious reign is advanced through glorious human dominion, whether the humans be political royalty or caretakers of creation. Psalm 8 clearly is a reflection on Genesis 1:26–28 (along with 1:14–19). To wit, the animals over which humans have been given authority to rule include those on the earth, in the sea, and in the air in both Genesis 1 and Psalm 8.

A *crown* of glory and honor has to do with dominion. N. T. Wright says,

> "Glory" is a standard biblical way of referring to the wise rule of humans over creation. Glory isn't simply a quality that individuals might or might not possess in and for themselves—a splendor, a status, a condition to be admired. Glory is an active quality. It is the glorious human rule through which humans themselves come to their own intended flourishing. It is, in fact, the "glory of God"—the effective rank and status which shows that humans are indeed the God-reflectors, the ones through whom the loving, wise sovereignty of the creator God is brought into powerful, life-giving presence within creation.[168]

Whether *Elohim* in verse 5 should be translated "God" (NRSV, NASB, Greek translations by Aquila, Symmachus, and Theodotion[169]), "angels" (LXX, NIV, KJV, NKJV), or the ambiguous "heavenly beings" (LEB, ESV) is debated. All three are within the range of meaning.[170] Rolf Jacobson is not alone in seeing this as a reference to a counsel of heavenly beings surrounding God's throne (citing parallels in Isa 6 and 1 Kgs 22). Whereas ancient Near Eastern parallels saw these beings as divine, the psalmist sees them as cherubim and seraphim. Even so, Jacobson says the psalm "asserts that we are like God in some ways."[171] Peter Craigie notes that some ancient translations rendered it "angels" such as the Greek OT, Syriac OT, Targums, and the Vulgate. Yet he wonders if this was prompted by modesty, "for it may have seemed rather extravagant

---

168. Wright, *After You Believe*, 89–90.

169. Bratcher and Reyburn, *Psalms*, 82.

170. *HALOT* 52–54.

171. DeClaissé-Walford et al., *Psalms*, 122n11, 124–27.

to claim that mankind was only a little less than God."[172] Hebrews 2:7 follows the Septuagint in translating it "angels," which leads to a theological point about Christ's humiliation (being made "a little lower than the angels"), death, and resulting exaltation over the angels (vv. 5 and 9).[173] Kilner is among those who do not see a reference to the image and likeness of God in Psalm 8.[174]

Psalm 8:5 should be translated "a little lower than God" and the phrase ought to be taken as a conceptual parallel of the image of God. The Psalm is a clear reflection on Genesis 1, as Kilner acknowledges.[175] Verse 3 is an allusion to Genesis 1:16. Verses 6–8 are a clear allusion to Genesis 1:26 and 28 about human authority over animals. Whatever "a little lower than *Elohim*" means, it is about the status of human beings. The language of "lower" than *Elohim* here and "over" the animals in verses 6–8 clearly has to do with the status that accompanies authority. Genesis 1 addresses that status by comparing humans to God, saying they are made in his image and likeness, so it makes sense to think that the reflection on this passage in Psalm 8:5 would also compare humans with God. The image of God in Genesis 1:26 and 28, then, is the necessary background to understand the phrase "a little lower than *Elohim*." As John Goldingay points out, "the psalm goes on like Genesis to note how they take up God's sovereignty in the world."[176] That is, they are lower than God but over the animals, which are under their feet. Plus, there is no reference to angels in the creation account. These contextual comparisons point to "God" being the proper translation here. Besides, as Hoekema points out, this is the most frequent use of "Elohim" and Scripture never teaches that angels were made in God's image.[177]

That leaves the problem of Hebrews 2. If angels manifest some sort of similarity to God (which is not stated in Scripture) and have authority (which is stated in a few biblical and extra-biblical, intertestamental passages such as Dan 10:13–14 and 12:1; Sir. 17:17; 1 En. 60:15–21; 89:70–76; Jub. 35:17; Col 1:16; Eph 6:12), the rendering "angels" in both the Septuagint and Hebrews 2 does not contradict the rendering "God."

---

172. Craigie and Tate, *Psalms 1–50*, 108.

173. See Heb 1:5–14 for the context of the argument for Jesus's superiority to angels.

174. Kilner, *Dignity and Destiny*, 203.

175. Kilner, *Dignity and Destiny*, 202.

176. Goldingay, *Psalms*, 159.

177. Hoekema, *Created in God's Image*, 18.

Humanity would be below both God and angels (who would be below God and above people), so David could have meant "God" while the writer of Hebrews could have used the lexically possible and theologically sound translation "angels" to make his argument that Christ is superior to angels, particularly since his exaltation.[178] In either case, the doctrine of the image of God and human dominion is still in view.

An important implication of Psalm 8 is the unexpectedly great honor and dignity of human beings in spite of the fall into sin. Sin does not take away God's image nor change God's purposes for human dominion nor his profound concern for people. God has graciously granted human beings great honor and responsibility to the praise of his glory. As Jacobson puts it, "God has placed all things under our feet not so that we may walk all over them, but so that we might tend and care for them, as Adam was instructed to do in the garden. The laws that govern royal behavior in Deuteronomy 17:14–20 make it clear that . . . the authority was for the sake of responsibility."[179]

Daniel 2:35 and 3:1

In Daniel 2:31–45, the prophet tells King Nebuchadnezzar of Babylon what he dreamed and what the dream meant.[180]

> "Your Majesty looked, and there before you stood a large statue—an enormous, dazzling statue, awesome in appearance. The head of the statue was made of pure gold, its chest and arms of silver, its belly and thighs of bronze, its legs of iron, its feet partly of iron and partly of baked clay. While you were watching, a rock was cut out, but not by human hands. It struck the statue on its

178. See Guthrie, "Hebrews," 946 on the use of Ps 8 in the argument of Hebrews.

179. DeClaissé-Walford, *Psalms*, 127.

180. Most critical scholars regard Daniel as a pseudepigraphic work composed around 167 BC to encourage Jews to oppose Antiochus IV Epiphanes. Yet Jesus attributed at least one of the prophecies to the sixth century BC prophet Daniel. In Matt 24:15, he refers to "'the abomination that causes desolation,' spoken of through the prophet Daniel" (Dan 9:27; 11:31; 12:11). None of the reasons adduced for pushing the book back to the second century BC seems persuasive if one grants the possibility of predictive prophecy, even if it is with impressive detail. For arguments for Daniel's authorship in the sixth century BC and against the many arguments for a Maccabean date and author, see Archer, *Survey*, 423–48. But even on the critical assumption, the book comes after Genesis and the books of Samuel and before the NT references, and that is the pertinent chronological point for the redemptive-historical approach here.

feet of iron and clay and smashed them. Then the iron, the clay, the bronze, the silver and the gold were all broken to pieces and became like chaff on a threshing floor in the summer. The wind swept them away without leaving a trace. But the rock that struck the statue became a huge mountain and filled the whole earth.

"This was the dream, and now we will interpret it to the king. Your Majesty, you are the king of kings. The God of heaven has given you dominion and power and might and glory; in your hands he has placed all mankind and the beasts of the field and the birds in the sky. Wherever they live, he has made you ruler over them all. You are that head of gold.

"After you, another kingdom will arise, inferior to yours. Next, a third kingdom, one of bronze, will rule over the whole earth. Finally, there will be a fourth kingdom, strong as iron—for iron breaks and smashes everything—and as iron breaks things to pieces, so it will crush and break all the others. Just as you saw that the feet and toes were partly of baked clay and partly of iron, so this will be a divided kingdom; yet it will have some of the strength of iron in it, even as you saw iron mixed with clay. As the toes were partly iron and partly clay, so this kingdom will be partly strong and partly brittle. And just as you saw the iron mixed with baked clay, so the people will be a mixture and will not remain united, any more than iron mixes with clay.

"In the time of those kings, the God of heaven will set up a kingdom that will never be destroyed, nor will it be left to another people. It will crush all those kingdoms and bring them to an end, but it will itself endure forever. This is the meaning of the vision of the rock cut out of a mountain, but not by human hands—a rock that broke the iron, the bronze, the clay, the silver and the gold to pieces.

"The great God has shown the king what will take place in the future. The dream is true and its interpretation is trustworthy."

"Statue" here is the Aramaic cognate of ṣelem. This image/statue represents four kingdoms (vv. 39–40), represented by their kings (as in the case of Nebuchadnezzar, who represented the Babylonian empire in v. 38).[181] Stephen Dempster is probably right to call this "a parody of the divine creation in Genesis 1, where God makes humans in the divine likeness to rule the world."[182] The final kingdom filling the whole earth

---

181. This assumes the following identification of the four empires: Babylon, Medo-Persia, Greece, and Rome. For a defense of this position, see Miller, *Daniel*, 92–97; Archer, *Survey*, 439–44.

182. Dempster, *Dominion and Dynasty*, 214.

(vv. 35, 44) is probably an echo of Genesis 1:26 and 28, where it says humans are to rule the animals and fill and rule over all the earth.[183] That God gave these kingdoms dominion (as it explicitly says of Nebuchadnezzar in vv. 37–38; see Jer 27:5–6) means that God appoints kingdoms to play a part in accomplishing the cultural commission, particularly the part that pertains to establishing order and justice (see Rom 13:1–7). The authorities may do this well or badly or any degree in between because humans, including rulers, were made free to choose good or evil.

The issue, then, concerns who will rule the earth and how, both important issues in the image of God concept in Genesis 1. The statue's ostentatious appearance probably points to hubris, starting with the Babylonian kingdom that was noted for this vice throughout its history (Gen 11:4; Isa 13:11, 19; Dan 4:30).[184] Gleason Archer Jr. notes that whatever distinctions are made between the human kingdoms, we must keep firmly in mind that this is one statue, suggesting one rebellion of humans against God.[185] Still, the jockeying for land and power between these kingdoms will be real and consequential for the people involved. The subsequent kingdoms would prove inferior to Babylon and the fourth would be noted for its destructiveness and lack of unity (vv. 40–41). Stephen Miller points out that the text suggests these empires "are not moving toward utopia but in the opposite direction."[186] Pride, destructiveness, and disunity stem from human fallenness and have no place in proper human dominion under God, which should be marked by humble service, peace, and unity.

In order to set things right, God destroys these kingdoms to set up a new kingdom that will rule properly forever. This is a Davidic kingdom, as a few facts make clear. The rock that destroys the giant statue probably alludes to David slaying Goliath with God's enablement (1 Sam 17, esp. v. 37).[187] Second Temple Judaism saw the "stone" metaphor as a symbol of the Messiah.[188] Knowing this, Jesus made creative use of this metaphor, stringing together a few "stone" texts to explain how the parable of the

---

183. Beale, *Temple*, 144; Duguid, *Daniel*, 36.

184. Dempster, *Dominion and Dynasty*, 214.

185. Archer, "Daniel," note on v. 44. Archer notes that Babylon typifies such rebellion from Gen 11 through Rev 18, where God overthrows an end-time iteration of Babylon the Great to establish the consummated kingdom of God on earth.

186. Miller, *Daniel*, 94. So also Calvin, *Daniel*, 1:164.

187. Dempster, *Dominion and Dynasty*, 214.

188. Pao and Schnabel, "Luke," 364.

vineyard in Isaiah 5:1–7 was unfolding before His contemporaries' very eyes. He told a more detailed version of the story, the parable of the tenants in Luke 20:9–16 that illuminated the nature of their leaders' response to himself, the son of the farmer in his parable. They would kill him and in response the farmer would destroy and replace them with those who would bear fruit (justice and righteousness in Is 5:6–7). Because of his hearers' horrified reaction, "May this never happen!" (v. 16), Jesus added some prophetic support. "Then what is the meaning of that which is written: 'The stone the builders rejected has become the cornerstone'? Everyone who falls on that stone will be broken to pieces; anyone on whom it falls will be crushed" (Luke 20:17b–18). Verse 17 is a quotation of Psalm 118:22, which Jesus used of his rejection by Israel's leaders (= the vineyard tenants in vv. 9–17) and forthcoming vindication as the "cornerstone." His resurrection would vindicate him by showing that he is the cornerstone of the new temple that would replace the temple of his day.[189]

But not only is that "stone" going to be rejected and then vindicated, but people are going to stumble over it to their own demise. Isaiah 8:14–15 says Yahweh "will be a holy place; for both Israel and Judah he will be a stone that causes people to stumble and a rock that makes them fall. And for the people of Jerusalem he will be a trap and a snare. Many of them will stumble; they will fall and be broken, they will be snared and captured." In the context of the Immanuel prophecy (see 7:14 and 8:8), the notion that Yahweh would be a sanctuary/holy place reads like a beautiful pointer to the incarnate Christ, who can be called the temple because it had always been his presence and reign the temple pointed towards typologically. But the emphasis in these verses is on the fact that many reject the stone and stumble over it and are broken, a reference to judgment.

But not only is the stone rejected and vindicated (Ps 118:22) as well as stumbled over, resulting in the stumblers' falling and being broken (Is 8:14–15), but it also falls on people. "Anyone on whom it falls will be crushed" (Luke 20:18b). No such metaphor was in Psalm 118:22 or Isaiah

189. Jesus, speaking in the temple, had just pre-enacted the temple's destruction (Luke 19:45–46 and par.) and was about to prophesy the temple's destruction in these words: "As for what you see here, the time will come when not one stone (*lithos*, as in 20:17) will be left on another; every one of them will be thrown down" (Luke 21:6). Calling himself the cornerstone, then, was probably a subtle way of saying what he said not so subtly in John 2:19 (interpreted in vv. 20–22): Jesus will replace the temple, as his forthcoming resurrection would show (hinted at with the vindication of the stone as the cornerstone in Luke 20:17). For more on this, see Pao and Schnabel, "Luke," 364; Beale, *Temple*, 183–84; Wright, *Jesus and the Victory*, 497–501.

8:14–15. Even if the latter text had spoken of stumblers being broken to pieces, it was a result of their tripping over a stone below rather than being crushed by a stone from above, as in Daniel 2:34, 44–45.[190] Those who were leading Israel in rejecting Jesus should count themselves, not as God's people who would defeat the pagan kingdoms and reign with Christ, but as those in league with the pagan kingdoms in opposing God's kingdom and therefore fit to be punished with them. This was shocking and offensive to say the least, which explains why the teachers of the law and chief priests immediately tried to figure out a way to arrest him (v. 19).[191]

In addition, this kingdom Daniel prophesied will last forever, just as God said David's dynasty would (2 Sam 7:11–16). God had promised the anointed, Davidic king the nations, the ends of the earth as his possession in Psalm 2:8. This is a Davidic kingdom designed to finally fulfill God's intention to fill the earth with humans exercising godly dominion, led by his anointed King.

But Nebuchadnezzar seems to have taken the dream as a personal challenge to figure out how to keep his kingdom permanently rather than allow it to be set aside by another kingdom. He ran with the head of gold idea and made an image completely of gold to represent either himself or a god—it makes little difference which since the text repeatedly emphasizes that it was Nebuchadnezzar that set up the image in 3:1–3, 5, 7, 12, 15, and 18.[192] The king set up a god rather than acknowledging that God sets up kings and removes them (2:21), in spite of the homage he paid God in 2:47. And the means he used to try to secure his permanent kingdom was to unify people in the worship of one god. Unity is a vital purpose of God, of course, but the basis of humanity's unity is to be God's kingdom, God's Spirit, and humanity's common human nature and family as those made in God's image and likeness, not some idolatrous unity that amounts to an organized coup against God's rightful rule (as was the case with the Tower of Babel in Genesis 11. See esp. vv. 4–7). Here again, image is associated with royal power and leadership in the world. Rather than common people having any sort of royal significance themselves, they are simply made to worship Nebuchadnezzar and/or his

---

190. In support of the idea that Jesus alluded to not only Ps 118:22 and Is 8:14–15 but also Dan 2:34, 44–45 here, see Pao and Schnabel, "Luke," 362–66 and Beale, *Temple*, 183–84.

191. See Wright, *Jesus and the Victory*, 500–501.

192. Following Duguid, *Daniel*, 46–47.

god, willingly or not. It would seem that many did (v. 7), but the faithful Shadrach, Meshach, and Abednego refuse to bow down and explain
that though God is able to save them, it is his decision. Either way, they
will not bow (vv. 17–18). Nebuchadnezzar thought no deity would have
enough power to save anyone from his hand (v. 15), as if he were more
powerful than a god, yet he ends up being humbled by one that "looks
like a son of the gods" (v. 25).

Though Nebuchadnezzar seems to grasp the point by the end of chapter 3 (see vv. 28–30), chapter 4 makes clear he did not, at least not fully or
permanently. In 4:30, he was admiring his handiwork, the capital city of his
empire, saying, "Is not this the great Babylon I have built as the royal resi-
dence, by my mighty power and for the glory of my majesty?" This comes
right on the heels of Daniel's advice: "Renounce your sins by doing what is
right, and your wickedness by being kind to the oppressed." The result of
his pride, wickedness, and unjust rule was a reversal: a human (a royal one
at that!) was temporarily reduced to living like a beast (vv. 25 and 33). He
ruled like a beast and ended up like a beast and, of course, lost his power.
He aspired to be above God, yet was not godly, but rather beastly. Instead
of moving up the chain of command, he moved down it.

Daniel 7 narrates a dream about the same four kingdoms in chapter
2, only this time they are portrayed not as a human image, but as beasts
with human traits (e.g., the lion with eagle's wings and a human mind in
v. 4), a metaphor for humans who behave in beastly, violent ways (e.g.,
vv. 5–7). This suggests that in addition to being able to resemble God
and other humans, people can resemble beasts as well in a sort of moral
devolution (which coincides with the movement away from utopia and
towards disorder in chapter 2). Dempster calls this "a parody of creation,
an anti-creation. As in Genesis, at the beginning the Spirit or wind blows
over the sea. But instead of the creation of light and land, culminating
in the divine image, there emerges from the chaotic sea four beasts in
succession, each more horrifying than the previous one, until the last one
emerges—a macabre spectacle, the embodiment of evil."[193]

The last beast had a proud and boastful horn (v. 8), picking up one
of the vices in the four kingdoms of chapter 2. Thus, God puts an end to
their kingdoms (vv. 9–12) and establishes a final, eternal kingdom. "In
my vision at night I looked, and there before me was one like a son of
man, coming with the clouds of heaven. He approached the Ancient of

---

193. Dempster, *Dominion and Dynasty*, 215.

Days and was led into his presence. He was given authority, glory, and sovereign power; all nations and peoples of every language worshiped him. His dominion is an everlasting dominion that will not pass away, and his kingdom is one that will never be destroyed" (Dan 7:13–14).

The ruler is called the "son of man" ('ĕnāš), which appears to echo Psalm 8:4, where David reflected on the apparent weakness and smallness of humanity: "what is mankind ('ĕnāš) that you are mindful of them?" before going on to say that people were made a little lower than God and given dominion over the animals (vv. 5–8). Does this son of man, then, replace all of humanity as ruler of creation? No. Verses 17 and 18 interpret the dream, "The four great beasts are four kings that will rise from the earth. But the holy people of the Most High will receive the kingdom and will possess it forever—yes, for ever and ever." The king and the saints are closely identified, just as the beastly kingdoms and their kings are closely identified in chapter 2. As Dempster puts it, "the son of man is a distinct individual, yet intimately associated with the saints of the Most High in the same way that the Israelite king is related to his people. It is obvious that they are closely identified, but this need not exclude the individuality of the former. His destiny is linked to that of the suffering people of God and *vice versa*."[194]

The fact that God takes the kingdom away from human-like beasts (representing humans who behave like beasts) and gives it to a man and his people (the saints) shows that he is putting creation back in proper order: God over all, humans under him (led by the son of man), and animals and everything else under them. Beastly humans have had their day and it is time for godly ones to reign. The son of man is both fully human and yet comes on the clouds of heaven, pointing to a heavenly origin.[195]

---

194. Dempster, *Dominion and Dynasty*, 216. This is similar to how Isaiah portrays the servant as both Israel (49:3) and an individual who restores Israel (49:5; 52:13—53:12). Such corporate solidarity/representation becomes crucial in understanding how NT authors interpret the OT. The NT portrays Jesus as the representative of Israel/New Israel in accomplishing what Israel was intended to accomplish and leading them in His wake (e.g., overcoming temptation in the wilderness in Matthew 4:1–11; dying in Israel's place, even on Caiaphas's interpretation in John 11:47–53; see 18:14). Paul portrays Jesus as the antitype of Adam, climactically representing the whole human race (Rom 5:12–21; 1 Cor 15:45–49). Thus, corporate representation is not an *ad hoc* explanation designed to harmonize supposedly contradictory notions in Daniel 2 and 7, but a crucial principle in biblical interpretation. On this principle, see Snodgrass, "Use of the Old Testament," 416–18.

195. Dempster, *Dominion and Dynasty*, 217; Keil and Delitzsch, *Commentary*, 9:647.

This seems to imply that the solution to humanity's problems must come from outside the fallen world and its devolving kingdoms, the utopian pretensions of socialists notwithstanding. Jesus identified himself as the son of man when he quoted Daniel 7:13 concerning his second coming and then at his trial (Matt 24:30 and par.; 26:64 and par.), an interpretation John adopted as well (Rev 1:7; 14:14).

Concluding Reflections on the Image of God in the Old Testament

By the end of the Old Testament period, the purposes of God for creation had surely not come about in full. Israel, called to carry out Adam and Eve's commission, sunk into idolatry, worshiping images as gods rather than serving God as those made in his image. The punishment and cure for this was exile in Assyria and Babylon. But God promised a restoration of Israel that sounded like nothing short of a new creation (Isa 65:17; 66:22) in which there would be justice (Isa 25:2), universal reverence for God (Isa 25:3), deliverance for the oppressed people of God (Isa 25:4–5), a feast on Zion celebrating God's arrival, victory (Isa 25:6, 9), and defeat of death (Isa 25:7–8), the resurrection of his people's bodies (Isa 26:19), and the wiping away of all disgrace and tears from his people (Isa 25:8–9). This is salvation (Isa 25:9), a salvation that will go to the ends of the earth through his servant, Israel (Isa 49:1–8), and will last for eternity. Isaiah 45:17–18 says that one goal of this salvation is to accomplish the cultural commission to fill the earth. God will save his people for eternity for (*kî* in v. 18) he did not create the world to be empty, but to be inhabited. God's purposes from the beginning set the agenda for the end.[196] It remains for the New Testament to explain how this will come about. But one thing is clear: a new exodus/return from exile will need to happen first, for Israel had only partially been restored in the sixth century BC (Isa 52:1–12; 61:1–2; cf. Ezra 9:6–9).

To review, the Old Testament tells the story of God creating human beings in his image and likeness, that is, as representatives that reflect some measure of his glory. The stated, though not necessarily exclusive, purpose for creating people in his image is so that they may rule over creation beneficently, following in God's gracious footsteps and so spreading

---

196. See Dumbrell, *End of the Beginning* for the ways God's eschatological purposes fulfill his original creational purposes.

his glory all throughout the creation. This involves procreation, agriculture, horticulture, animal husbandry, political justice, resistance to evil, training future generations obedience to God, the development of the arts, the building of civilizations, and so forth. All of this is to be carried out in close connection with God relationally and in submission to his leadership as the world's King. Since Israel was given the same responsibilities Adam, Eve, and their offspring were but stopped short of fully carrying them out, there was still a need for these ultimate purposes to be fulfilled, which seemed closely connected with Israel's restoration promises and the new creation.

It has seemed necessary to not only trace the specific references to the image of God, but also to summarize key developments in the cultural commission that is the stated purpose for which God made humans in his image. Lose track of this and one risks disregarding some of God's intended outcomes of instructing humanity about the image.

Not only that, but the approach pursued here acknowledges that theology is not merely to be construed as a series of timeless principles. God revealed his truth by telling the story of his creation past, present, and future. It seems that each person is called to find his/her part in the great narrative and play it in a way consistent with the script. The study of the image of God appears at this point to be the study of God's purposes for human life and all creation. In this creation, humans are the only ones who can intentionally and freely do his will or not, hence the reason God would reveal his will to us. Though the Old Testament does not often refer to the image of God, the concept is the foundation of other themes that do appear often, including the kingdom of God, the moral law, the responsibilities of being a kingdom of priests, the restoration of nature in the new creation, and others. Because of this, it has been necessary to weave back and forth between the forest of these larger themes and the trees of specific details in the image texts. The same process may illuminate how the New Testament continues to unfold the image motif.

Chapter 2

A Biblical Theology of the Image of God

(New Testament)

MOST OF THE NEW Testament references to the image of God are found in the Pauline and General Epistles. There is one passage in the Synoptic Gospels, one in Acts, and one in Revelation to examine, but first, it would be worthwhile to see how a few passages in the Gospels and Acts connect the cultural commission, which had been passed on to Israel, with the mission of the church. As stated above, the responsibility of multiplying, filling the earth, and ruling over creation as God's image bearers in Genesis 1:28 was passed on to Noah (Gen 9) and eventually Abraham (Gen 12:1–3; 17:2–8; 22:17–18; 26:3–4, 24; 28:3–4, 13–14) and Israel (Exod 1:7; Num 23:10–11; Lev 26:9; Deut 7:13, 15:4–6). God also involved gentile kingdoms in this (Dan 2 and 7). Is this responsibility in any sense given to the church? Paul makes that connection, and so, too, do the gospel writers.

Matthew's Gospel is particularly concerned to make such a connection. It begins with the phrase, *biblos geneseōs* ("The book of the genealogy"; Matt 1:1a ESV) of Jesus Christ. Genesis 2:4 introduces the creation of heaven and earth with this same phrase. A more significant parallel is Genesis 5:1. "This is the book of the generations (*biblos geneseōs*) of Adam. When God created man, he made him in the likeness of God" (ESV). What follows is the genealogy of Adam down to Shem, Ham, and Japheth. The parallel to Matthew seems significant. If Genesis 2 and 5 gave an account of creation and specifically humans from Adam, Matthew is signaling that he is likewise giving an account of another creation, a new creation, beginning with the last Adam. In Beale's words, "Matthew is narrating the record of the new age, the new creation, launched by the coming, death, and resurrection of Jesus Christ."[1] This implies that Jesus is also the image of God, though it will be Paul who makes that explicit. The parallel between Jesus and Adam is even more obvious in Luke, whose genealogy of Jesus goes back to "Adam, the son of God" (3:38). Luke calls Jesus the Son of God on several occasions (1:35; 4:3, 9, 41; 22:70). With this implicit Adam-Christ typology in place, Luke immediately launches into the narrative of Jesus's temptations (4:4–13), which recalls both Adam and Eve's temptation (note the parallel between the serpent and Satan, both of whom speak their appealing lies) and Israel's wilderness temptations (Jesus's quotations in vv. 4, 8, and 12 are all from Deut 6–8). Whereas Adam, Eve, and Israel failed to do God's will under temptation, Jesus succeeded.[2] This points to the fulfillment of God's purposes for not only Israel, but for all of humankind.

Matthew's genealogy also notes Jesus's descent from not only David (an essential qualification of the Messiah), but also Abraham (1:1). The significance of this at the beginning becomes clearer at the end: "Then Jesus came to them and said, 'All authority in heaven and on earth has been given to me. Therefore go and make disciples of all nations, baptizing them in the name of the Father and of the Son and of the Holy Spirit, and teaching them to obey everything I have commanded you. And surely I am with you always, to the very end of the age'" (Matt 28:18–20).

"All nations" translates *panta ta ethnē*, the same phrase the Septuagint used in Genesis 18:18 when God said of Abraham, "all nations on earth will be blessed through him" (see also 22:18), which in turn alludes to Genesis 12:3, "all peoples on earth (*pasai hai phulai*, a conceptual parallel for *panta ta ethnē*) will be blessed through you." God was now going to bless all nations through Abraham's people, understood as the church made up of Jews and gentiles.[3] The Great Commission may further reflect Genesis 18 when it calls for teaching disciples to obey Jesus's teaching, for teaching was pivotal for the Abrahamic covenant. Genesis 18:19 says, "For I have chosen him, so that he will direct his children and his household after him to keep the way of the Lord by doing what is right and just, so that the Lord will bring about for Abraham what he has

1. Beale, *New Testament Biblical Theology*, 388–89.

2. Among those who see an Adam-Israel-Christ typology here, see Beale, *New Testament Biblical Theology*, 391; Wright, *Luke for Everyone*, 43; Pao and Schnabel, "Luke," 287.

3. Carson, "Matthew," 596; Beale, *New Testament Biblical Theology*, 391.

promised him." The only way Abraham's nation would be blessed and be a means by which God blesses the world (through justification by faith; see Gal 3:8–9) would be if Abraham properly trained his progeny to obey God, and they in turn trained their progeny (see Deut 6:20–25; Ps 78). In a similar way, the only way the people of God (Jew and gentile) will enjoy the new covenant blessings is if Jesus's followers properly train their spiritual progeny to obey God.

Peter made the same connections in his sermon to the (probably mostly Jewish) onlookers at the temple in Acts 3:25–26. "He said to Abraham, 'Through your offspring all peoples on earth will be blessed.' When God raised up his servant, he sent him first to you to bless you by turning each of you from your wicked ways." The blessings of God would come from the risen Lord to those who turned to God from their sins. Paul made the same application to gentiles in Galatians 3:7–8 when he says, "Understand, then, that those who have faith are children of Abraham. Scripture foresaw that God would justify the Gentiles by faith, and announced the gospel in advance to Abraham: 'All nations will be blessed through you.' So those who rely on faith are blessed along with Abraham, the man of faith."

Returning to Matthew's teaching, the blessings and curses of Leviticus 26 and Deuteronomy 28 are fulfilled (5:17–18) through the Beatitudes. Those who are poor in spirit, mourning, meek, hungry and thirsty for righteousness, merciful, pure in heart, peacemakers, and persecuted stand to receive the blessings of the kingdom, comfort, the earth, righteousness/justice, mercy, to see God and to be God's children (5:3–10). Such blessings include profoundly spiritual ones like mercy and to "see" God. But they also include physical ones. "Blessed are the meek, for they will inherit the earth" (5:5) quotes Psalm 37:11, which adds that the heirs will "enjoy peace and prosperity." The righteous are promised they will inherit the land forever (Ps 37:29). Verse 11 may be an allusion or conceptual parallel to Leviticus 26:6, "I will grant peace in the land, and you will lie down and no one will make you afraid." Jesus further made clear the purpose God was working towards when he taught his followers to pray "your kingdom come, your will be done, on earth as it is in heaven" (Matt 6:10). Because these blessings for the church are built on the blessings promised to Adam, Abraham, and Israel, they are bound up with the ultimate accomplishment of the cultural commission and thus God's purposes in creation.

Matthew 22:20-21

There is some debate over whether Jesus's logion in Matthew 22:20-21//
Mark 12:16-17//Luke 20:24-25 alludes to the image of God.[4] The Phari-
sees and Herodians asked Jesus the question, "Is it right to pay the impe-
rial tax to Caesar or not?" (v. 17). They were trying to trap him on the
horns of a dilemma. He could either say "no" and open himself up to the
charge of siding with the revolutionaries seeking to overthrow Rome, a
charge that could get him crucified, or "yes" and alienate many fellow
Jews who saw paying the tax as an idolatrous act of loyalty to Caesar over
God. After all, the silver denarius used to pay this poll tax bore a bust of
Tiberius Caesar with an inscription that read, "Tiberius Caesar Augustus,
Son of the Divine Augustus." On the other side was Tiberius's mother
Livia with the words, "High Priest."[5] Religiously, it constituted idolatrous
blasphemy. Politically, it added insult to injury. As Justin Ukpong points
out, adult males of colonized peoples paying such a tax symbolized their
subjugation to the Romans.[6] Judas the Galilean, who largely had a Pharisaic outlook, said that Israel was to consider God their only ruler. He
and his compatriots revolted against the Romans in AD 6 over this very
tax and were brutally defeated and he himself executed the next year.
When Pontius Pilate introduced these particular coins in Jerusalem in
AD 26, many rioted.[7] Josephus saw Judas the Galilean as the author of the
"fourth sect," the Zealots, and blamed them for the Jewish revolt of AD
66-70 that resulted in the destruction of Jerusalem and the temple, but
Wright makes a strong case from Josephus's own writings that revolution
was in the air among many Jews outside the ranks of the Zealots in the
first century.[8] Thus, either horn of the dilemma Jesus chose would, presumably, enable Jesus's enemies to get him out of the way. The dialogue
proceeded, "But Jesus, knowing their evil intent, said, 'You hypocrites,
why are you trying to trap me? Show me the coin used for paying the tax.'

4. Mark was probably written in the late fifties to early sixties of the first century,
followed by Matthew and Luke in the sixties. The unanimous witness of second century church fathers that the traditionally identified authors wrote the gospels that bear
their names is impressive. See the arguments for this traditional view of the authorship
and date of the Synoptic Gospels in Carson et al., *Introduction*, 66-79, 92-99, 113-17.

5. Edwards, *Mark*, 363.

6. Ukpong, "Tribute to Caesar," 436.

7. Lints, *Identity and Idolatry*, 106n11.

8. See Josephus, *Ant.* 18.23. On the run up to the two revolts (AD 70 and 135), see
Wright, *New Testament*, 173.

They brought him a denarius, and he asked them, 'Whose image is this? And whose inscription?' 'Caesar's,' they replied" (Matt 22:18–21).

"Image" is *eikōn*, the Greek word the Septuagint uses to translate *ṣelem* in Genesis 1:26–27. Here it means "an object shaped to resemble the form or appearance of something, *likeness, portrait*."[9] Jesus responded, "So give back to Caesar what is Caesar's, and to God what is God's." Some interpreters believe "what is Caesar's" includes the coins that bear his image and inscription while "what is God's" includes the person made in God's image and bearing God's inscription (see Isa 44:5: "others will write on their hand, 'the Lord's'") so that one's obligations to God go above and beyond those to Caesar, though one should pay the tax to such authorities because God has appointed them to restrain evil and encourage good (in line with Rom 13:1–7 and 1 Pet 2:13–17). This is sometimes called the anti-Zealot interpretation.[10] If true, then the point of the image of God reference would be that people belong to God and thus owe him moral service and, indeed, their very selves.[11]

There are objections to this view. Robert Stein points out that "Jesus was not saying that all money bearing Caesar's image belonged to him. Taxes belonged to him, but not all money."[12] Technically, perhaps. But one may wonder what the image and inscription would then have to do with Jesus's logion, which he introduced with the inferential particle *toinyn* in Luke and *oun* in Matthew. John Nolland suggests that the genitives "of Caesar" and "of God" are best understood in the sense, "to which he has a right."[13] In this case, Caesar has a right to at least the tax money stamped with his image and inscription and, by implication, God has a right to human beings stamped with his image and inscription. This is probably the best way to do justice to the connection between image/inscription and logion indicated by the inferential particles.[14]

9. BDAG 281.

10. Giblin, "Things of God," 520–25; Nolland, *Matthew*, 898–99; Edwards, *Mark*, 364; Garland, *Mark*, 463. Augustine (*Serm.* 308A.7) and Origen (*Hom. Luc.* 39.4–6) also saw a reference to the image of God in humans here. See Just, *Luke*, 309–11.

11. Giblin, "Things of God," 524–25.

12. Stein, *Luke*, 498.

13. Nolland, *Matthew*, 898.

14. The other possibility is that Jesus is making an ironic remark to the effect that "the only thing to do with something like this is to give it straight back to its pagan owners!" The difference would be that Jesus is not acknowledging Caesar's place among the civil authorities God had put into place or worse, endorsing Caesar's empire. Jesus would be relegating the question of whom is to have power to a secondary

Another potential problem is that Jesus's accusers at his trial said that Jesus opposed payment of taxes to Caesar (Luke 23:2). To Ukpong, this supports the notion that Jesus was actually opposing paying the tax, the proper (in line with the Zealots) yet peaceful (in contrast to the Zealots) response to the colonial oppressor. Unlike Mark (14:56) and Matthew (26:59–60), Luke did not say that such accusations were false, though Pontius Pilate did not find a basis for a charge (23:4).[15] His reading takes seriously the typically non-explicit manner in which Jesus addressed questions with Messianic implications, which left listeners to deduce the proper answers from his questions and statements and introduced the possibility that not everyone would agree on what he meant—hence all the debate then and now. But his way of playing Luke off against Mark and Matthew is not convincing, especially in light of Pilate's declaration that he saw no valid charge against Jesus in Luke 23:4. And had some of his listeners taken Jesus's logion this way (as opposed to trying to manufacture the charge that he opposed payment of the tax apart from the logion), they likely would have immediately gone to the Roman authorities with their charge rather than continuing to ply Jesus with hot-button questions to trap him, as they in fact did (see Luke 20:27–44).

Ukpong brings up an important question: how would Jesus's answer leave anyone astonished (Luke 20:26)? If he was saying to go ahead and pay the tax, would he not have been giving one of the anticipated possible answers?[16] The trap would have worked and he would have lost

---

issue that need not be resolved right away. See Wright, *Jesus and the Victory*, 506; Ukpong, "Tribute to Caesar," 434–35. While it is true that the first part of the logion must take its place under the second part in importance and that the empire issue, in retrospect, was sorted out over a much longer period of time and without the help of Jewish revolutionaries, it is difficult not to think that Rom 13:1–7 and 1 Pet 2:13–17 build on this notion that God delegates power to civil authorities and that we have a duty to God to submit to the authorities unless they command disobedience to God, in which case one must obey God rather than men, as Peter pointed out in Acts 4:19 and 5:29. However, the general exhortation to submit to governing authorities need not make revolution inherently immoral any more than it makes civil disobedience inherently immoral. Rather, revolution may be the most moral option in view of how a government treats its people. The Maccabean Revolt (see 1–2 Maccabees) seems to have been necessary to save many Jewish lives and to preserve the Law and temple until the Messiah came to establish the kingdom of God in a new way, as Jesus did nearly two centuries later. On the ethics of civil disobedience and revolution, see Davis, *Evangelical Ethics*, 189–205.

15. Ukpong, "Tribute to Caesar," 442.

16. Ukpong, "Tribute to Caesar," 435.

credibility with many anti-Roman Jews. Of course, the same can be asked of Ukpong's partially pro-Zealot reading, which would have resulted in the charge of revolution rather than astonishment, but the need to explain the astonishment remains on the interpretation here defended. Ultimately, the profundity of Jesus's answer in the context of his visit to the temple caused the amazement. He had ridden into Jerusalem receiving praise as the Son of David sent by God to save Israel (Matt 21:9), which prompted the whole city to wonder who he was (v. 10). He then pre-enacted the temple's destruction as an act of judgment against the people of Israel who had failed to make it a "house of prayer for all nations" (Mark 11:17, quoting Isa 56:7), making it instead a "den of robbers" (Mark 11:17, quoting Jer 7:11). The quotation from Jeremiah is particularly significant in that God sent the empire of the day, Babylon, to destroy the temple and the city in short order, just as he was about to do a generation after Jesus using, of all people, the Romans so many Israelites expected the Messiah to crush (see Luke 19:41–44, which Jesus said just before going to the temple, and 21:20–24, which followed the temple visit), who were not only idolatrous themselves, but were led by one claiming to be the Son of God and High Priest! As discussed above, the Christological claim was that Jesus, as the true Son of God, was replacing the temple (of which he was also the true High Priest, according to Heb 7:11–28) as his forthcoming resurrection would show, after which he would ascend to the right hand of the Father and send the Holy Spirit into his church, thereby designating the church the temple as well (see John 2:18–21; Acts 2:1–13; Eph 2:19–22). He was, in the last week before his crucifixion, presenting himself as Israel's Messiah, temple, and Son of God in the Divine sense. His identity and authority were questioned (Luke 20:2), showing that this was the issue for the people to resolve, along with whether or not they would accept him and therefore acquiesce to his way of setting up the kingdom, sans Rome's immediate overthrow, yet under God's mighty hand. In the parable of the tenants, Jesus alluded to his Sonship and how he would not be received as such, but rather be killed by the tenants (Luke 20:13–15) who would themselves be overthrown (v. 16). Of course, God's point in planting the vineyard to begin with had been to produce the fruit of righteousness and justice (Isa 5:7). This is what the tenants refused to give the owner and is probably the most precise identification of "the things of God" in the larger context,[17] though the temple context

17. Though he disagrees with the image of God interpretation of the logion, Witherington rightly draws attention to the need to understand it as building on the point

and confrontation of idolatry suggest that worship is in view,[18] a matter closely related to living justly (see Isa 58; Amos 5:21–27). God's people, made in his image, are called to worship God and produce justice and righteousness for God. It is true that everyone is made in God's image, but this does not negate this interpretation, for it has always been God's desire that all people be included among his people (1 Tim 2:4–6).

Colossians 1:15

Paul's writings significantly develop the image of God concept. Because Paul's analysis is multifaceted, it will be helpful to order the material in accordance with redemptive history. First, Paul identifies Jesus as the image of God in two passages (Col 1:15 and 2 Cor 4:4)—the only biblical writer to do so explicitly. Second, Paul views all human beings as made in the image of God (1 Cor 11:7, in line with Gen 1:26–27 and 9:6). Third, Paul has a vision for the gradual transformation of Christians into the image of God that is best understood in terms of the "already" side of the "already and not yet" eschatological tension (Col 3:9–10; Eph 4:22–24; 2 Cor 3:18). Finally, on the "not yet" side of this tension, Paul looks forward to the completion of believers' transformation into the image of Christ at the resurrection (1 Cor 15:49 and Rom 8:29).[19]

---

of the parable of the tenants. See Witherington, *Mark*, 326.

18. Wright sees the last half of the logion as an echo of Ps 96:7, which calls Israel to worship Yahweh our King (Wright, *Jesus and the Victory*, 505–6).

19. Very few scholars deny that Paul wrote Romans and 1–2 Corinthians. But some critical scholars deny that Paul wrote Colossians and Ephesians. Colossians opens with the author claiming to be Paul (1:1), continues with "I, Paul" in 1:23, and ends with "I, Paul, write this greeting in my own hand" (4:18). The authenticity of this is supported by some links with Philemon, whose author was clearly Paul. As Carson, Moo, and Morris explain, "in both epistles, greetings are sent from Aristarchus, Mark, Epaphras, Luke, and Demas who were clearly with Paul when he wrote (Col 4:10–14; Philm 23–24). Onesimus, the slave at the center of the letter to Philemon, is sent with Tychicus and referred to as 'one of you' (Col 4:9). Archippus, our fellow soldier (Philm 2), is given a message to 'complete the work' he has received in the Lord (Col 4:17)." Carson et al., *Introduction*, 334. See also their responses to the typical arguments against Pauline authorship regarding language and style, theological themes, and relation to Ephesians on pp. 331–34. As to Ephesians, the author identifies himself as Paul (1:1 and 3:1), an identification that appears to have gone undisputed in the ancient church. Such claims put the burden of proof on those who claim inauthenticity. The theology of the letter is consistent with themes in the other Pauline letters, including Colossians. On these matters, see Carson et al., *Introduction*, 305–9.

The foundation for everything else Paul says about the subject is his statement that Jesus *is* the image of God. Colossians 1:15–20 says,

> The Son is the image of the invisible God, the firstborn over all creation. For in him all things were created: things in heaven and on earth, visible and invisible, whether thrones or powers or rulers or authorities; all things have been created through him and for him. He is before all things, and in him all things hold together. And he is the head of the body, the church; he is the beginning and the firstborn from among the dead, so that in everything he might have the supremacy. For God was pleased to have all his fullness dwell in him, and through him to reconcile to himself all things, whether things on earth or things in heaven, by making peace through his blood, shed on the cross.

Some detail will be needed to show the connections between Colossians 1 and the biblical storyline as a means of discerning the meaning and role of the image in the unfolding purposes of God. The verbal correspondence between Genesis 1:27 LXX (*eikona theou*) and Colossians 1:15 (*eikōn tou theou*) leads many commentators to see this passage as an echo of the Genesis passage.[20] Genesis 1:26 uses the plural pronouns "us" and "our" in the phrase, "Let us make mankind in our image, in our likeness," pointing to plurality in the one God. Genesis 1:2 points to the Holy Spirit's inclusion in this plurality and Colossians 1:15 points to Jesus's inclusion, specifically as the pattern in which people were made by the Triune God. He is the image; humans are made according to the image.[21] Christ is the "Creator, ruler and goal of it all."[22] *Eikōn* ("image") here means "that which has the same form as something else . . . *living*

---

20. Moo, *Colossians and Philemon*, 117; Melick, *Philippians, Colossians, Philemon*, 215; Witherington, *Philemon, Colossians, and Ephesians*, 133; Beale, "Colossians," 852; Simpson and Bruce, *Ephesians and Colossians*, 193. One dissenting voice is Dunn, *Colossians and Philemon*, 87–88. Dunn does not think Genesis 1:26–27 is in mind here, but rather the Hellenistic Jewish identification of the image of God with divine Wisdom (e.g., Wis. 7:26; Philo, *Leg.* 1.43; *Fug.* 101; *Somn.* 1.239). But, as Moo points out, Paul was probably alluding to both traditions, as the wisdom tradition itself has Genesis 1 as its starting point. But "in place of the Jewish tradition, which finds the image to be expressed in wisdom or the word, the hymn claims that the original image is to be found in the person of Jesus Christ, God's Son." Moo, *Colossians and Philemon*, 118–19. In comparing Wisdom of Solomon with Colossians 1, Witherington is probably right in saying that "What is said there about the personified Wisdom of God Paul now says about Christ. See Witherington, *Philemon, Colossians, and Ephesians*, 130–31.

21. Moo, *Colossians and Philemon*, 118.

22. Simpson and Bruce, *Ephesians*, 198.

image," as in 1 Corinthians 15:49.[23] Murray Harris points out that "the degree of resemblance between the archetype and the copy must be determined by the word's context. Given 1:19 and 2:9, εἰκών here signifies that Jesus is an exact, as well as a visible representation of God."[24] Jesus is the revealer of God to the world. As John 1:18 says, "No one has ever seen God, but the one and only Son, who is himself God and is in closest relationship with the Father, has made him known." Gerhard Kittle believes the emphasis lies on "the equality of the εἰκών with the original,"[25] which would naturally enable the Son to reveal and represent the Father. The thought is much like Hebrews 1:3, "The Son is the radiance of God's glory and the exact representation of his being." Thus, the Son is equal with God and reveals him visibly to humanity.

In relation to humans, Ben Witherington points out that there is a paradox here: the one who is compared to Adam (as in Rom 5:12–19 and 1 Cor 15:45–49) and was "made in human likeness" (Phil 2:7) existed as the image before Adam and was the pattern in which Adam was made.[26] The preincarnate identification of Jesus Christ as the image of God is like saying, "the Prime Minister studied economics at Oxford."[27] It views Christ before creation and his incarnation in terms of the role he would play in creation after his incarnation. The essential point is that as one who is fully human and fully divine, he is in a unique position to do both what humans were intended to do, rule over creation under God (Gen 1:26–28; Psalm 8), and what only God can do, save the world (Isa 45).[28] That is, he is uniquely qualified to restore God's rule and human rule in creation. In fact, in Colossians 1:6 the gospel of Jesus is pictured as "bearing fruit and growing throughout the whole world." Jesus and his people are fulfilling at least part of the mandate of Genesis 1:28 through making disciples. The church's transformation of character into servants of God is described in similar terms: "bearing fruit in every good work, growing in the knowledge of God" (v. 10).[29] Rather than viewing this as a spiritualization of the mandate, it is better to see training the younger generations

---

23. BDAG 281–82.

24. Harris, *Colossians & Philemon*, 43.

25. Kittel, "εἰκών," 395.

26. Witherington, *Philemon, Colossians, and Ephesians*, 133.

27. Wright, *Climax of the Covenant*, 95.

28. Wright, *Climax of the Covenant*, 95.

29. On this allusion, see Beale, "Colossians," 851.

in righteousness as implicit in the mandate, as Genesis 18:18–19 suggests.[30] Here again, the cultural commission and the Great Commission overlap, and that based on an Adam-Christ typology that Paul develops elsewhere (see on 1 Cor 15 below). Jesus has come to accomplish what Adam and Eve were supposed to accomplish, what Israel as a whole (as a corporate Adam) was supposed to accomplish, but failed to do. Jesus succeeds where they failed. It will become clear below that those united with Jesus follow his lead in accomplishing these purposes.

In Genesis 5:1–3 the image of God was passed on from father to son, connecting the idea of sonship with that of the image. Here in Colossians, the image is the Son the Father loves (the relative pronoun *hos*, "who," in v. 15, refers back to "the Son he loves" in v. 13). In the Old Testament, the "son" of God appellation was at times applied to Israel as a whole (e.g., Exod 4:22; Jer 31:9; Hos 11:1) and at other times to the Messiah in particular (e.g., 2 Sam 7:14; 1 Chr 17:13; Ps 2:7; Ps 89:26), and without overtones of deity in either case. Paul's notion of Jesus's sonship builds on these. He introduces Christ this way in Romans 1:2–4: "the gospel . . . regarding his Son, who as to his earthly life was a descendant of David, and who through the Spirit of holiness was appointed the Son of God in power by his resurrection from the dead: Jesus Christ our Lord." This concept parallels "firstborn from among the dead, so that in everything he might have the supremacy" in Colossians 1:18. His sonship, demonstrated by the resurrection that launched the new creation, meant a few things, as N. T. Wright explains. "The resurrection, in other words, declares that Jesus really is God's Son: not only in the sense that he is the Messiah, though Paul certainly intends that here, not only in the sense that he is the world's true lord, though Paul intends that too, but also in the sense that he is the one in whom the living God, Israel's God, has become personally present in the world, has become one of the human creatures that were made from the beginning in the image of the same God."[31]

The story traced through Scripture thus far has as a central motif God's intention to reign as king over all creation. The image motif developed thus far shows that God intended humans to be a part of this plan as rulers of the land and animals, following God's lead as beneficent stewards of creation. But Satan successfully tempted humanity to

---

30. Similarly, see Beale, *Temple*, 264–65.
31. Wright, *Resurrection*, 722.

rebel against God, thus establishing his own influence in creation, a sort of rival kingdom. Adam and Eve and eventually Israel and the nations would experience distance from God, that is, exile, as a punishment (see Gen 3:23–24; 2 Chr 36:15–22; Eph 2:11–12). But God had promised restoration that would bless Jew and gentile alike, a return from exile in conjunction with the full establishment of his kingdom and the resurrection of the dead (e.g., throughout Isa 40–55; Ezek 36–37). Colossians continues this story in 1:12–14: "and giving joyful thanks to the Father, who has qualified you to share in the inheritance of his holy people in the kingdom of light. For he has rescued us from the dominion of darkness and brought us into the kingdom of the Son he loves, in whom we have redemption, the forgiveness of sins." Through the work of Christ, believers are redeemed out of bondage to the devil's kingdom, their sins having been forgiven. This redemption is built on the model of the Exodus. God freed Israel from slavery in Egypt and led them in power to possess the promised land, their inheritance. But because of idolatry and unfaithfulness to the covenant, God eventually sent Israel into exile in Assyria and Babylon. In beginning to bring Israel back from exile, God was signaling that the time of forgiveness and restoration was beginning. In fact, N. T. Wright makes a persuasive case that "forgiveness of sins is another way of saying 'return from exile.'"[32] At the very least, the latter is a/the primary consequence of the former. That verse 14 puts redemption in apposition to forgiveness of sins shows this connection. When God forgives sins, a person (or people's) exile is over since sin was the reason for exilic punishment. The return from exile is modeled on the Exodus, the original redemption. In the same way that Israel was once enslaved to Egypt, all people, Jew and gentile alike, are enslaved to sin under the influence/ dominion of Satan. But through the sacrifice of Christ, the ransom, believers are set free from this bondage (see John 8:31–47). That freedom, like many aspects of salvation in the New Testament, must be understood as already under way, but not yet fully consummated.

Colossians 1:13–14 parallels Paul's summary of what God commissioned him to do in Acts 26:17b–18.[33] "I am sending you to them to open their eyes and turn them from darkness to light, and from the power of Satan to God, so that they may receive forgiveness of sins and

32. Wright, *Jesus and the Victory*, 268–74. Especially illustrative of this connection are Jer 31:31–34; 33:4–11; 36:24–26, 33; Isa 40:1–2; 43:25—44:3.

33. Witherington, *Philemon, Colossians, and Ephesians*, 126–27; Melick, *Philippians, Colossians, Philemon*, 206.

a place among those who are sanctified by faith in me." The switch from Satan's power/dominion to God's, the light versus dark contrast, the reference to forgiveness/redemption, and the notion of receiving a share/ inheritance among God's people tie the two passages together. Further, the Acts passage itself reflects Isaiah 42:7, where the Servant of the Lord is charged with the responsibility "to open eyes that are blind, to free captives from prison and to release from the dungeon those who sit in darkness."[34] In Isaiah, opening blind eyes surely reverses the judgment of God in 'blinding' idolaters to the truth, which was referred to when Isaiah was commissioned in 6:9–10 (discussed above). Sitting in darkness in 42:7 is also the judgment of God, this time referring to the upcoming Babylonian exile. Yet those being freed include gentiles (v. 6) as a part of a worldwide kingdom of justice (vv. 1 and 4), suggesting the wider application of the exile idea mentioned earlier: all people are in exile before they come to know God. Duguid defines the theological meaning of exile this way: "the experience of pain and suffering that results from the knowledge that there is a home where one belongs, yet for the present one is unable to return there."[35] In Eden and Israel, the home was where God dwelt with his people. Temple theology built on this. The end of exile thus involves a peace with God that draws one near to him (Eph 2:13–22). In an interesting twist, the New Testament portrays believers as those who, though forgiven of sin and indwelt by God as his temple (Matt 28:20; Eph 2:13–22) and present citizens of the heavenly Jerusalem (Gal 4:25–26; Phil 3:20; Heb 12:22), are aliens, strangers, and exiles in the world (1 Pet 1:1, 2:11; Jas 1:1) on a journey to the new promised land, the New Jerusalem, which will come down to earth out of heaven when God renews creation (Heb 4:9–11; 13:14; Rev 21–22).[36] Exile from God before conversion, then, is a reality for Jew and gentile alike and the end of that exile upon conversion is an already and not yet reality for the New Testament people of God.

Like the Acts and Colossians texts, the kingdom of the Servant/ Christ supplants another kingdom, freeing those under its sway, both Jew and gentile, thus releasing them from punishment. This Servant Song of Isaiah 42 is about Jesus Christ (Luke 2:32; Matt 3:17; 12:18–21), yet aspects of Jesus's work as the Servant are passed on to Paul and Barnabas (see Acts

---

34. Marshall, "Acts," 599.

35. Duguid, "Exile," 475.

36. On all of this, see Duguid, "Exile," 475–78.

13:46–47, where they quote a portion of the Servant Song in Isa 49:6 as God's command to them to "bring salvation to the ends of the earth").[37]

Jewish and gentile believers now stand in a position to share in the inheritance (*klēros*) in the kingdom of the Son (Col 1:12). This is one of the few passages in Scripture that implies or states a distinction between the kingdom of God and the kingdom of Christ (see Matt 13:41; 25:31). In 1 Corinthians 15:24–28, the kingdom of Christ is transitional to the ultimate kingdom of God. Having a share in the inheritance implies that believers have become children of God (Paul makes this clear elsewhere, as in Rom 8:14–17), a prerequisite to inheriting what God promises his children. Throughout the Old Testament, "inheritance" (LXX *klēros*) often referred to the land of Israel, which God possessed and then allotted to Israelite families after the conquest (e.g., 1 Sam 26:19; Jer 2:7; Ezek 38:16; Joel 1:6; Ps 68:9). Here in Colossians 1, the inheritance is in the kingdom of Christ and, as verses 15–20 make clear, Christ reconciles and reigns over all things in heaven and on earth. It is difficult not to see the inheritance in line with Jesus's promise that the meek will inherit the earth (Matt 5:5, quoting Ps 37:11) and his prayer that God's kingdom come "on earth as it is in heaven" (Matt 6:10). This is so especially in light of Paul's own picture of the inheritance of God's children: the new creation in Romans 8:17–25.[38] But the hope/inheritance is presently kept for us in heaven (Col 1:5, as in 1 Pet 1:4).

Colossians 1:18–20 puts Christ at the head of the new creation by virtue of his resurrection after having reconciled to himself "all things [*ta panta*], whether things on earth or things in heaven, by making peace through his blood, shed on the cross." Calvin says this only includes humans and angels,[39] which seems reasonable in light of the personal connotations of *apokatallassō* reflected in the translation "reconcile" in verse

---

37. This makes sense on the notion of corporate representation discussed above. In Isaiah 49:3, the Servant is called Israel, but two verses later, the Servant's task is to gather Israel to himself, suggesting a distinction between the Servant and Israel. Since the NT is clear that Jesus is the Servant, he must also represent Israel. If Jesus can represent Israel, he can also represent the NT people of God. Thus, Jesus's Servant tasks can be given to Paul, Barnabas, and others in a way that brings them into the category of the Servant. We are united with Jesus Christ (see Rom 6:1–11).

38. Helpful for the biblical use of *klēros* is Eichler, "Inheritance, Lot, Portion," 295–303. On the NT expansion of the OT land promises along the lines sketched here, with a reference to Col 1:12–14, see Wright, *Faithfulness of God*, 366–67.

39. Calvin, *Philippians, Colossians, and 1–2 Thessalonians*, 155.

22 and Ephesians 2:16.[40] People are clearly included in the term (this is the point of v. 22), but in verse 20 it surely includes all things in earth and heaven as well. As Moo points out, neuter forms of *pas* occur five other times in the context (twice each in vv. 16 and 17 and once in v. 18), all referring to everything in creation.[41] This presupposes that something has happened since creation to disrupt the original harmony between God and humans, God and spiritual beings, and God and nature. The fall in Genesis 3 and the spread of the rebellion throughout the entire human race is the obvious explanation of human enmity with God (Rom 3:23, 5:12). As part of humans' punishment for rebellion, God cursed the ground he had entrusted to their care, causing pain in work (Gen 3:16–19). Nature itself "groans as in the pains of childbirth," waiting to be "liberated from its bondage to decay and brought into the freedom and glory of the children of God" (Rom 8:21–22). Some of the spiritual powers also rebelled against God (Jude 6). Reconciliation or pacification, as it is sometimes called, for each category happens in a way appropriate to the object. Nature did not rebel and is not morally free and thus is being brought into harmony by being renewed, a unilateral act of God. Angels, who are morally free, had their opportunity to either obey God or rebel against him and do not appear to have any further opportunity to get back on God's side. Thus, rebellious angels are set to endure eternal separation from God and punishment (Jude 6; Matt 25:41). In what sense are they pacified then? Paul answers that in Colossians 2:15: "And having disarmed the powers and authorities, he made a public spectacle of them, triumphing over them by the cross." As the conquering king, Christ defeats the powers who oppose him and his just and peaceful rule by lovingly enduring the punishment for human sin, thus freeing his people from both the bondage to and penalty for the sins they had been led into by demonic forces. Humans are in an interesting position in that their pacification may take one of two forms. They may "receive Christ Jesus as Lord" (Col 2:6) and thus receive forgiveness and life (vv. 6–14), as well as peace and participation in the new creation (Rom 5:1–2; 2 Cor 5:17–19) in a new relationship with God as sons and daughters (Rom 8:14–17). Or they may continue in rebellion and be defeated and judged along with the rebellious spiritual powers (see Matt 25:41; Rev 20:11–15). Pacification thus does not entail universalism, yet it does bring justice and order to

40. See Büchsel, "Ἀλλάσσω," 259.

41. Moo, *Colossians and Philemon*, 134–35. See also BDAG 112; Vorländer and Brown, "Reconciliation," 172.

all creation—already, but not yet fully. Melick, whose analysis is reflected here, sums up the meaning of reconciliation nicely.

> Thus reconciliation may be effected by voluntary submission to Jesus, which brings the blessings of salvation, or by involuntary submission, being conquered by the power of his might. Reconciliation must be defined in this context, therefore, as all things being put into proper relation to Christ. Those who respond to his voice will be brought into a relationship of grace and blessing. Those who oppose and reject him will receive eternal punishment involving removal from God's blessings and the active outpouring of his judgment. In the end, everyone and everything will be reconciled in this sense. Everyone and everything will be subordinated to Christ.[42]

This whole analysis has shown the centrality of kingdom authority and order in creation, which was once firmly in place but must now be restored. This theme was evident in Genesis 1, 2, 9, Psalm 8, and throughout Daniel and is repeatedly emphasized by Paul in Colossians 1. It enhances this point that Paul calls Jesus the "firstborn" (*prōtotokos*) in creation and new creation (vv. 15 and 18). God had called Israel his firstborn son in Exodus 4:22. It is possible there is a thought of Jesus as representative of Israel here, too (as in Isa 49:3–5, discussed above). More likely, Paul is alluding to Psalm 89:27, quoted here with verses 28 and 29 to show the Messianic significance that went well beyond David. "And I will appoint him to be my firstborn [LXX *prōtotokon*], the most exalted of the kings of the earth. I will maintain my love to him forever, and my covenant with him will never fail. I will establish his line forever, his throne as long as the heavens endure." As Moo says of this psalm, "this latter text is probably especially important for Colossians 1:15, since Psalm 89 rings with messianic allusions, and Paul has just been describing Christ in messianic/kingly terms (vv. 12–14).[43] Thus, Paul uses *prōtotokos* to refer to "the superior rank and dignity of Christ."[44] He holds this rank in creation by virtue of his deity (the thought of preexistence may be here)

---

42. Melick, *Philippians, Colossians, Philemon*, 227. In agreement with this line of interpretation are Moo, *Colossians and Philemon*, 134–37 and Dunn, *Colossians and Philemon*, 103–4.

43. Moo, *Colossians and Philemon*, 119.

44. Michaelis, "Πρῶτος," 879. Against the Arian interpretation that the term portrays Christ as a created being lesser than God, see Melick, *Philippians, Colossians, Philemon*, 215–17. And note the use of the same term in Heb 1:6 of Christ, who is then called "God," applying Ps 45:6–7, which is about *Elohim*, to Christ.

and in new creation by virtue of being the pioneer, "the firstborn among many brothers and sisters" to be resurrected (Rom 8:29). He is therefore the rightful king of creation and new creation.

His authority to restore all things and rule is grounded in the fact that "God was pleased (*eudokēsen*) to have all his fullness dwell (*katoikēsai*) in him (*en autō*)" (v. 19). This is likely an allusion to Psalm 68:16 (67:17 LXX): "the mountain where (*en autō*) God chooses (*eudokeō*) to reign (*katoikein*), where the Lord himself will dwell forever."[45] In the psalm, the dwelling of God was his sanctuary, the temple in Jerusalem (v. 17). The prayer was for God to arise and save his people by defeating and subjugating his enemies (see vv. 1–3, 14, 18, 29–32), closely related to themes seen throughout the context of Colossians 1 and 2. Whereas it was the temple in Jerusalem that symbolized God's presence and reign over the earth (Ps 68:24, 32), now it is Jesus who is God present with humanity reigning as king. In Beale's words, "Thus, one reason why Christ should 'come to have first place in everything' (Col 1:18b) is that he is God and is the inauguration of the eschatological temple, in which God's fullness and wisdom have begun to dwell."[46]

To summarize, when Paul calls Jesus the image of God in Colossians 1, he is teaching that Jesus reveals the invisible God, since he is both visible (embodied) and fully divine. He is setting up Jesus as the paradigm human, the pattern in which humans were created and are being recreated through resurrection (3:1 and 10 develop this thought), and the one through whom God's purposes for humans are being accomplished. And he is emphasizing that Jesus is the king of creation who not only holds it all together, but who is bringing peace to it all by fully establishing his beneficent kingdom through his death on the cross in spite of all opposition to his rule.

---

45. Moo, *Colossians and Philemon*, 133; Beale, "Colossians," 856–57.

46. Beale, "Colossians," 857. Paul's use of *pleroma* (fullness) seems to be motivated by a desire to counter the false teachers' apparent claim that the Colossians needed to follow their philosophy with its rules to experience fullness (Col 2:1–8, 20–23). On the contrary, Paul tells them, "in Christ all the fullness of the Deity lives in bodily form, and in Christ you have been brought to fullness" (Col 2:9–10a). See Moo, *Colossians and Philemon*, 132.

2 Corinthians 4:4

The other passage in which Paul identifies Jesus as the image of God is 2 Corinthians 4:4–6.

> The god of this age has blinded the minds of unbelievers, so that they cannot see the light of the gospel that displays the glory of Christ, who is the image of God. For what we preach is not ourselves, but Jesus Christ as Lord, and ourselves as your servants for Jesus' sake. For God, who said, "Let light shine out of darkness," made his light shine in our hearts to give us the light of the knowledge of God's glory displayed in the face of Christ.

This text has in common with Colossians 1 an emphasis on the authority of Christ. There are a few indications of this. First, there is the confrontation between God and Satan, who is "the god of this age" (v. 4), who rules the dominion (*exousia*) of darkness (Col 1:13).[47] Elsewhere Paul calls him "the ruler of the kingdom (*exousia*) of the air" (Eph 2:2) and says he has taken people "captive to do his will" (2 Tim 2:26). This is similar to Jesus's own characterization of the devil as "the prince of this world" in John 12:31, 14:30, and 16:11 (see also Luke 4:6). He opposes Jesus as darkness opposes light (as in Col 1:13), here by 'blinding' unbelievers in the sense of preventing them from knowing the truth (v. 4). It is possible that this is another side of the reality that people become like what they revere, trust, or follow. Those who trust in Christ become more like him. Likewise, those who follow the ways of the god of this age become more like him. The result is blindness and spiritual collapse leading to destruction (see "perishing" in v. 3).[48] God defeats this work of the devil by an act of "all-surpassing power" (v. 7): just as God originally made light shine when he created the world (Paul alludes to Gen 1:3), He also enlightens the hearts of budding believers (v. 6) in an act of new creation upon their hearing the preaching of the gospel. Paul anticipates his reference to the new creation, of which every person who comes to Christ becomes a part (5:17).[49]

---

47. Harris, *Second Corinthians*, 327; Witherington, *1 and 2 Corinthians*, 386. Tertullian argued that "the god of this age" is God because he is the only true God (*Marc.* 5.11), but this was apparently motivated by the desire to refute Marcion's teaching that there is an inferior creator in contrast to the superior savior God. See Garland, *2 Corinthians*, 210.

48. Garland, *2 Corinthians*, 210.

49. Harris, *Second Corinthians*, 335; Garland, *2 Corinthians*, 216; Balla, "2 Corinthians," 763.

Another indication that authority is emphasized here is the way Paul refers to the content of the gospel as "Jesus Christ as Lord, and us as your servants for Jesus' sake" (v. 5). "Christ," of course, is Greek for *māsiaḥ*, the Hebrew term for the anointed king in David's line who is to reign over the earth. Victor Hamilton remarks that "while it may designate an office such as the high priest (Lev 4:3), *māsiaḥ* is almost exclusively reserved as a synonym for 'king' (*melek*)."[50] And the royal overtones of *kyrios* ("Lord") are clear, as it frequently means "one who is in a position of authority, *lord, master*."[51]

Finally, the gospel displays the "glory of Christ" (v. 4), or more precisely, "God's glory displayed in the face of Christ" (v. 6). Paul's use of *doxa* follows the meaning of *kābôd*, which it often translates. Glory in the Old Testament referred especially to the dignity and honor enjoyed by authority figures, whether God as the "king of glory" (Psa 24:7–10) or humans as those God crowned with glory and honor to rule over the animals (Ps 8:5). When used of God, it sometimes includes visible manifestations of light marking his special presence (Exod 16:7, 10; 24:17). Paul had just been talking about that very subject in 3:7–8 (reflecting on Exod 34:29–35). And the Lord showed his glory at the tent of meeting or temple in particular, since the purpose of these structures was to symbolize the presence and reign of God (Lev 9:6, 23; Num 14:10; 16:19; 20:6; Exod 40:34–37; 2 Chr 7:1–3).[52] The Exodus 32–40 background is particularly in view in 2 Corinthians 3 and 4. After the sin of the golden calf, Israel was becoming as spiritually dull as the idol they worshiped and God was indicating that he might destroy them (32:10) or not go with them to the promised land (33:3). This, of course, would threaten the covenant promise to give Abraham and his descendants the land (Gen 12:1–3) as well as God's promise to dwell there with Israel as their king on his mountain, a new Eden (Exod 15:17–18). But God ended up going with them and being their king, as was demonstrated when he filled the tabernacle. "Then the cloud covered the tent of meeting, and the glory of the Lord filled the tabernacle. Moses could not enter the tent of meeting because the cloud had settled on it, and the glory of the Lord filled the tabernacle" (Exod 40:34–35). In this light, N. T. Wright picks up the

---

50. Hamilton, "מָשַׁח," 531. See 1 Sam 2:10; 2 Sam 22:51; and Ps 18:50. On the same royal dignity overtones in *Christos* in Pauline usage, see Grundmann et al., "Χρίω, Χριστός," 542.

51. BDAG 577.

52. See Spicq, "δόξα," 365–66.

allusions as Paul brings them to bear on Jesus in 2 Corinthians 3 and 4:
"The God who abandoned Israel at the exile, because of idolatry and sin,
but who promised to return one day, as he had done in Exodus after the
threat of withdrawing his 'presence,' has returned at last in and as Jesus
the Messiah."[53] Jesus is the meaning to which the temple had pointed.

As the temple, Jesus displays the glory of God, yet not in a spec-
tacular visual, at least not presently, but rather believers perceive Jesus's
divine authority and greatness by faith when God enlightens them to do
so as they hear the gospel.[54] As Wright points out, "That is why Paul had
to *argue* in chapter 3 that the revelation of the new covenant in Christ is
in fact glorious—because the Corinthians were disposed to doubt it."[55]
Hence the talk of "jars of clay," "wasting away on the outside," and bearing
the death of Christ in verses 4:7–18. In spite of all appearances, God was
coming to reign in and through Christ and has included his people in this
glorious plan.

If Jesus shares the glory of the Father, he also visibly reveals him, even
if not in the spectacularly visual way portrayed in, e.g., Revelation 1:12–16.
This is surely central to the meaning of the image here, as in Colossians
1:15. Murray Harris is especially clear and compelling on this point.

> As God's εἰκών, Christ both shares and expresses God's nature.
> He is the precise and visible representation of the invisible God
> (Col. 1:15, where τοῦ ἀοράτου is added to εἰκὼν τοῦ θεοῦ). An
> εἰκών is a "likeness" (German *Bild*) or a "visible expression" *(Ab-
> bild)*. The degree of resemblance between the original and the
> copy must be assessed by the word's context, but it could vary
> from a partial or superficial resemblance to a complete or es-
> sential likeness. Given passages such as Phil. 2:6; Col. 1:19; 2:9,
> we may safely assume that for Paul εἰκών here, as in Col. 1:15,
> signifies that Christ is an exact representation *(Ebenbild)* as well
> as a visible expression of God.[56]

As in Colossians, this thought that Christ visibly represents the invisible God seems intimately connected with the ruling function of God
as king of his creation. Certainly, the concepts are alongside one another.
But if the analysis thus far is on target that "image" carries a connotation

53. Wright, *Faithfulness of God*, 679.

54. Harris, *Second Corinthians*, 330–31; Garland, *2 Corinthians*, 212.

55. Wright, *Resurrection*, 385.

56. Harris, *Second Corinthians*, 331. See also Garland, *2 Corinthians*, 212; Witherington, *Conflict and Community in Corinth*, 386.

of authority, then the authority of Christ is within the overlapping meanings of "glory," "Lord," "Christ," and "image" here.

Both 1 Corinthians 4:4 and Colossians 1:15 mean that Jesus is the image of God in a unique way, a primary way that other humans are not. Kilner presses this point: "People are created 'in' or 'according to' God's image. Christ, in the words of the New Testament (e.g., 2 Cor. 4:4; Col. 1:15) simply *is* the image of God (no preposition) ... With Christ not overtly in view as a reference point in the Old Testament, the recognition there would simply have been that people are not yet God's image but are intended to be so."[57]

Kilner also makes a methodological point of this. Rather than beginning in Genesis, which does not explicitly say what the image consists of, he says, "The New Testament affirms explicitly that Christ is God's image, so unpacking the meaning of that affirmation is the surest place to begin. Then we will be in a better position to consider the meaning of the Genesis and other biblical texts. *We cannot interpret Old Testament texts as if the authors had New Testament ideas in view* [emphasis mine]. However, we can interpret them with the expectation that they do not contradict what the New Testament reveals were God's purposes from 'before the beginning.'"[58]

It is wise to keep this clear statement of the New Testament in view when reading the Old Testament image texts. Using the assumptions of Vosian biblical theology, one can improve on the italicized statement: one cannot interpret Old Testament texts as if the *human* authors had New Testament ideas in view, but one can interpret them as though the *divine* author did.[59] It is more than a matter of not contradicting subsequent revelation; it is a matter of building an edifice of truth bit by bit through authors who did not understand the finished product as it would be known a thousand years in the future. But God knew the full truth and planned its gradual unfolding in special revelation to authors who understood in part. Hearers and readers can understand the Old Testament more clearly in the light of Christ, the fulfillment of its message; indeed, Christ both expects and enables them to do so. After his resurrection, he said to his followers, "'This is what I told you while I was still with

57. Kilner, *Dignity and Destiny*, 89.

58. Kilner, *Dignity and Destiny*, 53.

59. The reasoning here is from Vos's guiding principles of biblical theology, namely "the infallible character of revelation," "the objectivity of the groundwork of revelation," and "plenary inspiration." See Vos, *Biblical Theology*, 11–14.

you: Everything must be fulfilled that is written about me in the Law
of Moses, the Prophets and the Psalms.' Then he opened their minds so
they could understand the Scriptures. He told them, 'This is what is written: The Messiah will suffer and rise from the dead on the third day, and
repentance for the forgiveness of sins will be preached in his name to all
nations, beginning at Jerusalem'" (Luke 24:44–47). It is one thing to say
that the prophecies were clear enough to recognize the fulfillment when
it happens. Jesus said that to these disciples and to the two on the road
to Emmaus (vv. 25–26). It is another thing to use his death, resurrection,
and mission as interpretive keys to help them understand the Scriptures
more clearly, as he did here. The Old Testament quotes and allusions in
Luke's account had been making the point all along and continue in Acts.
Pao and Schnabel provide a helpful guide to those quotes and allusions.

> The statement in 24:46, that Jesus's death fulfills Scripture, is
> supported by references to OT passages in other parts of the
> Gospel of Luke; see the references to Ps 118:22 (Luke 20:17), Isa
> 53:12 (Luke 22:37), Ps 31:5 (Luke 23:46), and Ps 22:7, 18; 69:21
> (Luke 23:34–36). See also the references in the book of Acts,
> where Jesus's death is interpreted with reference to Ps 118:22
> (Acts 4:11), Ps 2:1–2 (Acts 4:25–26), and Isa 53:7–8 (Acts 8:32–
> 33); note also the reference to Ps 16:8–11 (Acts 2:25–28; 13:35)
> and Isa 55:3 (Acts 13:34) to explain Jesus's resurrection . . . Note
> that Isa 49:6 is alluded to in Luke 2:32, quoted in Acts 13:47, and
> echoed in Acts 1:8 . . . Granted that the connection between the
> programmatic statements in 24:47 and in Acts 1:8 is deliberate,
> 24:47 may be regarded as an allusion to Isa 49:6 and thus as
> a reference to the Isaianic new-exodus program as announced
> in Luke 4:16–30, pushed forward with the introduction of the
> Gentiles . . . The allusion to Isa 49:6 "provides continuity with
> the past history of the people of God while at the same time
> justifying the move to the Gentiles and the eventual redefinition
> of the people of God" (Pao 2000: 91).[60]

As Oss puts it, "Earlier portions of the canon were understood more
clearly in the light of Jesus Christ and the expanding canon . . . Progressive revelation and the formation of the canon contribute to the perspective that the Bible is a single literary work produced ultimately by a single
divine author."[61] This is not to minimize the importance of the biblical

60. Pao and Schnabel, "Luke," 401. They cite Pao, *Acts and the Isaianic New Exodus*,
91.

61. Oss, "Canon as Context," 112.

authors' humanity, but it does emphasize God as the source of the truths revealed. As Peter says, "For prophecy never had its origin in the human will, but prophets, though human, spoke from God as they were carried along by the Holy Spirit" (2 Pet 1:21).

1 Corinthians 11:7

Paul also makes it clear that humans are still made in God's image and likeness after the fall. In 1 Corinthians 11:7, Paul says man "is the image and glory of God." "Is" translates *hyparchōn*, a present participle that signifies the current, ongoing reality that man is the image of God. Thus, the fall did not change this fact.[62] Again, this statement is the only biblical text that says anyone other than Jesus *is* the image of God, in contrast to the typical phrasing that humans are made *in* the image of God. It is the exception to the rule and one probably should not make much of it. Piper seems to be correct that there is some flexibility in how the concept is stated in Scripture.[63] Jesus is clearly said to be the image, and that in a unique, revelatory way. One learns what God is like because God the Son images him perfectly. At the very least, one can affirm that even if an ordinary person is the image of God, Jesus is the image of God *par excellence* and is therefore the pattern of what a human being should be.

The problem for modern interpreters is that Paul only says that the man (*anēr*) is the image and glory of God, "but woman (*gynē*) is the glory of man. For man did not come from woman, but woman from man" (1 Cor 11:7b–8). It is important to keep in mind that there is a big difference between saying women *are not* made in God's image and not specifically mentioning that women *are* made in God's image. Jouette M. Bassler writes that "Paul does not deny that women are created in God's image, but Paul also does not affirm it, and this silence is significant."[64]

In order to discover how significant Paul's statement may or may not be, the procedure here will be to attend to the main point he makes, posit the most likely background situation, and use other Pauline passages on the image of God to shed light on his meaning here. One should note that the reconstruction of the situation in Corinth and thus how Paul is addressing it are notoriously difficult to determine, resulting in a

---

62. This is especially emphasized in Kilner, *Dignity and Destiny*, 139–40.

63. Piper, "Image of God."

64. Bassler, "1 Corinthians," 562.

dizzying array of interpretations by various scholars over the centuries. Fee, for example, repeatedly makes this point to emphasize the need for interpreters' humility.[65]

Nevertheless, Paul's main point seems pretty clear: Corinthian women should wear veils on their heads when they pray or prophesy in church gatherings (v. 5).[66] Reconstructions of the situation in Corinth should begin with the fact that Paul seems to be arguing for retaining an obvious distinction between the two genders in worship settings. Some of the Corinthians must have been blurring that distinction for one reason or another.[67] When Paul says in Galatians 3:28 that "there is no longer male and female" (NRSV), he was not obliterating gender distinctiveness. Rather, according to James D. G. Dunn, "what Paul attacks in this version of a common theological affirmation in Hellenistic Christianity is the assumption that the slave or the woman is disadvantaged before God or, still more, is an inferior species in the eyes of God (cf. 1:10)."[68] Paul encouraged women as well as men to prophesy and pray (see chapters 12 and 14); he just wanted the gender distinction in place for some reason.

The reason seems to have centered on the issue of who may have been honored or shamed by one's behavior or dress. In worship as in all of life, "whatever you do, do it all for the glory of God" (1 Cor 10:31). It is probably no coincidence that these words appear just before the discussion of women's veils. This brings up the possibility that things may be done to glorify someone else and/or result in shaming/dishonoring someone and/or distracting the gathered worshipers from God, robbing him of the glory due him. One may use his/her liberty to negative effect, as Paul had just made clear a few verses before: "'I have the right to do anything,' you say—but not everything is beneficial. 'I have the right to do anything'—but not everything is constructive. No one should seek their own good, but the good of others" (vv. 23–24; see also 6:12).[69] Thus, one must seek the good of others and, ultimately, the glorification of God. As

---

65. E.g., Fee, *First Corinthians*, 512.

66. Bassler, "1 Corinthians," 562–63; Witherington, *Conflict and Community in Corinth*, 235; Thiselton, *First Corinthians*, 801–2; Ciampa and Rosner, "1 Corinthians," 522; Fee, *First Corinthians*, 495.

67. Thiselton, *First Corinthians*, 803–4; Bassler, "1 Corinthians," 562; Fee, *First Corinthians*, 502; Witherington, *Conflict and Community in Corinth*, 238.

68. Dunn, *Galatians*, 207.

69. On the freedom vs. order tension and the need to freely choose what is most beneficial for others and God-honoring, see Thiselton, *First Corinthians*, 829.

Ray Ciampa and Brain Rosner put it, "Paul's ultimate concern seems to be related to the manifestation of glory and shame in worship, particularly that all be done to the glory of God (cf. 10:31), and not to glorify or shame anyone else. Humanly directed glory is to be avoided, as well as humanly or divinely directed shame."[70]

But who would it shame and how if a woman prophesied or prayed in church without a veil? Craig Keener fills in some vital background here. "Women's hair was a common object of lust in antiquity, and in much of the eastern Mediterranean women were expected to cover their hair. To fail to cover their hair was thought to provoke male lust as a bathing suit is thought to provoke it in some cultures today. Head covering prevailed in Jewish Palestine (where it extended even to a face veil) and elsewhere."[71]

Similarly, Anthony Thiselton, citing the work of Aline Rousselle and Dale Martin, says that a veil meant that a woman was unavailable for sexual interest. If a woman was going to pray or prophesy, this could draw attention to her, whether intentionally or unintentionally. One dare not attract the wrong sort of attention if one can do something to prevent it and the resulting shame (or loss of respectability) of one's family. As Thiselton puts it, "self-advertisement, especially if it relates to perceptions of the worship leader as an object of sexual attraction, diverts attention from God who should be the center of undivided attention. *To employ a dress code which hints at sexual availability while leading worship is unthinkable*" (emphasis his).[72] Paul is apparently dealing with a specific problem that calls for a specific remedy.[73] Were Paul dealing with a lot of

---

70. Ciampa and Rosner, "1 Corinthians," 504.

71. Keener, *Bible Background*, 1 Cor 11:2–16.

72. Thiselton, *First Corinthians*, 829. On women's hair as the focus of sexual attraction in Roman culture, see Ciampa and Rosner, "1 Corinthians," 516–18 and the works there cited. That Corinth was infamously promiscuous hardly needs to be pointed out. It is plausible that Jews in Corinth would have viewed a relaxation of standards of dress such as this as a move towards licentiousness. Keener is probably correct that the Greek practice of baring their heads for worship and the Roman practice of covering their heads is probably not the relevant issue since such customs did not "divide along gender lines." Keener, *Bible Background*, 1 Cor 11:2–16, vs. Witherington, *Conflict and Community in Corinth*, 233–35.

73. Sometimes in our culture, any talk of the importance of women dressing modestly so as not to incite lust is thought to blame her for his lust. This is then conflated with blaming victims of rape rather than rapists. The counterpoint is then made that modesty is not important, as if that follows. The nuanced view is that if a woman is dressed in a way that would likely and predictably pique male lust in a church setting, the male is totally responsible for lust, for he could look away or focus on God, and the

male worshipers who wore low-cut tops in an apparent attempt to show off their chest hair to women who found that alluring, he presumably would have targeted such men with a similar exhortation, and for the same reason.

In this light, it is easier to understand what Paul means that a woman who prays or prophesies without a veil dishonors her head (v. 5), probably meaning her husband or possibly her father if she is single (see *anēr* in v. 3, which can mean "man" or "husband" depending on the context[74]). Paul associates glory closely with image in verse 7, not because they are exactly the same, but possibly because they are closely related in Psalm 8:5. God made people "a little lower than God," (NRSV; this is a conceptual parallel of being made in the image of God), crowning them with glory and honor. Being made in God's image means people have a certain rank and status as those charged with and equipped to rule creation under God, filling it with his glory. Paul calling the woman the glory of man does not deny that she is also crowned with glory and honor, it just means one can be the glory of more than one being just as one can bear the image of more than one being. Ciampa and Rosner say that Paul transitions from image to glory because glory counterbalances shame in verses 4–6.[75] Paul also thinks in terms of glory as a visible manifestation in a passage with parallels to this one, 2 Corinthians 3–4.[76] God's glory was reflected in Moses's face, who then "put a veil over his face to keep the people of Israel from gazing at the end of the glory that was being set aside" (3:13). This sets up verse 18, which speaks of humans reflecting God's glory more and more. The analogy to 1 Corinthians 11 has to do with the visibility of God's and man's glory (though in 2 Cor 3:18, the visibility is metaphorical for apparent inner, spiritual transformation). Ciampa and Rosner say, "Paul has a similar glory in mind for the woman and that it is appropriate for her to wear a veil to keep people from gawking at man's glory in the church."[77] When Paul says, "a woman ought to have authority

---

woman is responsible for not taking reasonable measures to keep the focus off of her beauty. Similarly, in cases of rape, the rapist is totally responsible. The need for modesty does not change that fact. To remove the issue of dress and the motives behind how people dress from moral scrutiny is unnecessary and unwise, even while we insist on the absolute responsibility lookers and aggressors bear for their lust and actions.

74. BDAG 79.

75. Ciampa and Rosner, "1 Corinthians," 523.

76. BDAG 257.

77. Ciampa and Rosner, "1 Corinthians," 526.

over her own head" (v. 10), he probably means to "keep control of (how people perceive) their heads" because the issue here remains autonomy versus restraint.[78] She should freely choose the route of glorifying God and not shamefully drawing attention to herself.

Paul does not deny here or anywhere else that women are made in God's image. The reason he did not affirm women's creation in God's image here must be because that is not the issue he is dealing with in the Corinthian church. Had the Corinthians denied such status to women, Paul no doubt would have set them straight. His other teachings on the image of God suggest this. Most relevant is Genesis 1:27: "So God created mankind in his own image, in the image of God he created them; male *and female* he created them" (emphasis mine). Females are just as much made in God's image and likeness as males, according to the clear teaching of Genesis. The burden of proof must be on anyone who would deny this.

Yet it has been denied, in whole or in part, and that by very influential Christians. In the third century, Tertullian told each woman, "You destroyed so easily God's image, man."[79] Two centuries later, Augustine formed a more complicated view that declared women to be made in God's image in a way, yet not fully as men were, taking 1 Corinthians 11:7 to be a denial of women's full participation in the image. "The woman together with her own husband is the image of God, so that that whole substance may be one image; but when she is referred separately to her quality of *help-meet*, which regards the woman herself alone, then she is not the image of God; but as regards the man alone, he is the image of God as fully and completely as when the woman too is joined with him in one."[80] Thomas Aquinas followed the Augustinian view, more or less, saying,

> The image of God, in its principal signification, namely the intellectual nature, is found both in man and in women. Hence after the words, To the image of God He created him, it is added, Male and female He created them (Gen. 1:27). Moreover it is said "them," in the plural, as Augustine (*Gen. lit.* 3.22) remarks, lest it should be thought that both sexes were united in one individual. But in a secondary sense the image of God is found in man, and not in woman, for man is the beginning and end of woman, just as God is the beginning and end of every creature.

78. Thiselton, *First Corinthians*, 839.

79. Tertullian, *Cult. fem.* 1.1.

80. Augustine, *Trin.* 12.7.10.

So when the Apostle had said that man is the image and glory
of God, but woman is the glory of man, he adds his reason for
saying this: For man is not of woman, but woman of man; and
man was not created for woman, but woman for man.[81]

John Calvin similarly said that the woman, "though in the second
degree, was created in the image of God."[82]

Paul was not qualifying Genesis 1:27 and assigning the woman to
secondary status as made in God's image to a lesser extent than the man.
He said the woman was the glory of man to exhort the Corinthians to
neither glorify anyone but God nor shame a husband or father while
praying or prophesying. It seems that these theologians did not do justice
to the *ad hoc* nature of Paul's words, nor the clear implication of equality
in Genesis 1:27.[83]

Acts 17:28–29

When Paul preached in Athens, he went out of his way to find common
ground with his audience and use it to begin his presentation before
the Areopagus. Beginning with an altar for an unknown god, he pro-
claimed to them the one true God they did not know (Acts 17:23). God
had given them much out of his common grace so that people might
seek him and find him (vv. 26–27). Paul encourages them to seek after
God anew since their efforts to find him have only led them to a coun-
terintuitive idolatry. Yet God is not far from them; rather, people all
depend on him for life. Paul quotes the Cretan philosopher Epimenides
(c. 600 BC), who spoke of Zeus, yet who said something that Paul could
truly say of Yahweh: "'For in him we live and move and have our being'" (Acts 17:28).[84] Not only does this suggest the nearness of God to

81. Aquinas, *Summa Theologica*, pts. 1, Q. 93, art. 4 (p. 495). For analysis of Augustine and Aquinas on this point, see Borresen, "Imago Dei," 360–63.

82. Calvin, *Genesis*, 129. For analysis of Calvin and some who followed a similar
view after the Reformation, see Kilner, *Dignity and Destiny*, 34–35.

83. It is not necessary here to delve into the hotly contested issue of the meaning of
"head" (*kephalē*) in verse 3. Whether it is a metaphor for rank, source, or prominence
(without connotations of authority) is not relevant to whether or not women are made
in the image of God. The word could carry any of the three meanings and still every
woman is made in God's image and just as valuable as every man. Those interested in
the debate should consult the even-handed discussion in Thiselton, *First Corinthians*,
812–22 and the works cited there.

84. Nunnally, *Acts*, 310.

people, it also supports his point that God does not depend on them, they depend on him (vv. 24–25).

It is at this point that Paul quotes a second poet, this time the fourth-century BC Stoic Aratus of Cilicia (where Paul himself hailed from): "'We are his offspring'" (v. 28).[85] As David Peterson points out,

> The poet will have understood these words in a pantheistic sense, but Paul appears to have viewed them in the light of the image of God theology in Genesis 1:26–27 ... He recognized that a search for God had been taking place in the Greco-Roman world, but condemned the result—the idolatry which was everywhere present and the ignorance of the true God which it betrayed (vv. 22–25). In short, he indicated that the search had been ineffective because of human blindness and stubbornness (cf. Rom 1:18–32). Paul goes on to encourage a new seeking after God on the basis of his gospel about Jesus and the resurrection (vv. 30–31). The words of Aratus are used to affirm that, in a sense, all human beings are God's 'family' *(genos, offspring)*.[86]

There is widespread agreement among commentators that "offspring" is an allusion to humanity being made in God's image in Genesis 1:26–27.[87] It seems that this allusion to the image serves two functions here. First, it supports Paul's call for his hearers to seek God and find him in verse 27. Since every person is related to God, God wants every person to pursue a relationship with him who is never far away. Friedrich Büchsel's definition of *genos* ("offspring") demonstrates this relational connection: "'Posterity,' 'family': common in the NT. In Ac. 17:28 the quotation from Arat. Phaen., 5 follows Stoic belief in ascribing relationship with God to all men on the basis of their existence."[88] Here, relationship with God does not imply that everyone is willingly carrying on a relationship with God, but that human beings by their very nature stand in relationship to God, a fact that makes possible, desirable, and enjoyable any actual relationship with God that may follow from it. Similarly, Ned Stonehouse says that from the fact that humans are made in God's image can be

---

85. Aratus, *Phaen.* 5.

86. Peterson, *Acts*, 499–500.

87. Bruce, *Acts*, 340; Marshall, "Acts," 595; Stonehouse, "Areopagus Address," 18; Horton, *Acts*, 300–301; Nunnally, *Acts*, 310; Wright, *Acts for Everyone*, 91; Witherington, *Acts*, 530; Polhill, *Acts*, 376.

88. Büchsel, "Γίνομαι," 1:684–85.

inferred that they are "made to respond religiously to the Creator."[89] F. F. Bruce also interprets this relationally but is quick to distinguish the sort of relationship nonbelievers have with God from the sort of relationship believers have with God. The latter are God's children in a unique sense (Gal 3:26). Of Acts 17, Bruce explains, "But Paul is dealing here with the responsibility of all human beings as creatures of God to give him the honor which is his due."[90] This is an important distinction. Whereas all people stand in a sort of filial relationship to God as his children, not all children want to know, trust, or obey their Father. The Christian doctrine of adoption may be stated in a way that sounds too much like there is no prior, given relationship to God before one is adopted into his family upon conversion. But the idea need not be expressed in such a way that it ignores that prior relationship. The distinction is between those who have saving faith (with all that faith implies) and those who do not. In any case, Paul's words make it clear that the image of God has to do with humans being children of God. People stand in relation to him, whether they like it or not. This is the necessary foundation of anyone enjoying fellowship with God as a son or daughter.

The second way the quotation functions is to aid Paul's critique of idolatry. This is clear from the conclusion Paul draws from the idea in verse 29: "Therefore since we are God's offspring, we should not think that the divine being is like gold or silver or stone—an image made by human design and skill." As Wave Nunnally points out, the logic of the argument is twofold: "(1) If we are related to God but do not have the characteristics of idols, then we know he also does not have the characteristics of idols. (2) If God made humankind, it is illogical to think that humankind can go back and make God. Children do not create parents."[91] The idea that God is the Creator, Father, Sustainer, and Judge is clear enough to call all people to worship, relationship, and accountability to him even on the basis of natural revelation. Here is an implication of the revelatory nature of the image of God. If Jesus is the image of God, he clearly reveals what God is like. If people are made according to the image of God, then they reveal some things about God. Human nature teaches humanity some things about God, such as that he is not like the handcrafted idols people make. But the decisive revelation of God has come in Jesus Christ, whom

89. Stonehouse, "Areopagus," 18.

90. Bruce, *Acts*, 340.

91. Nunnally, *Acts*, 310.

the Father raised from the dead, thus proving that he is the rightful King and Judge of the world (vv. 30–31).

Colossians 3:9–10

People are still made in God's image. But does that necessarily mean that sin has not had any effect on the image and likeness of God? Is there any change needed that somehow relates to the image of God? There are three Pauline texts that have a bearing on those questions in the "already" period of the "already and not yet" eschatological timetable. That is, these texts state and imply things about regenerated people and a process in which they are engaged as a core aspect of their salvation: sanctification.

Colossians 3:9–10 says, "Do not lie to each other, since you have taken off your old self with its practices and have put on the new self, which is being renewed in knowledge in the image of its Creator." This last phrase clearly echoes Genesis 1:26–27 so that Paul is again engaging in intertextual interpretation.[92] Recall that Paul had echoed Genesis 1:28 in 1:6 and 10 to say that both the gospel and the church in Colossae were bearing fruit. And 1:15 had referred to the Son of God as the image of God. As Beale remarks, "Thus, Gen. 1:26–28 is in Paul's mind at points throughout this epistle."[93]

"New self" translates *neon*, with "self" supplied from "old self" (*palaion anthrōpon*) in verse 9. But "self" is an inadequate rendering. Humanity is viewed corporately rather than individually here, as the parallel in Ephesians makes clear. Ephesians 2:15 says, "His purpose was to create in himself one new humanity [*kainon anthrōpon*] out of the two, thus making peace." When *kainon anthrōpon* is then used in 4:23 (the Ephesian parallel to Col 3:9–10), it should also be understood in this corporate sense rather than in the individual sense of "new self" found in NIV, HCSB, NRSV, ESV, and NASB. "New man" is the translation in KJV, NKJV, and LEB, which could possibly be understood in a corporate sense, though without the benefit of gender neutrality. "New humanity" is the term that best captures the corporate sense inclusively and will be the terminology used here for both Colossians 3:10 and Ephesians 4:24. Also in support of the corporate view is the fact that verse 11 expands on

---

92. Beale, "Colossians," 865; Simpson and Bruce, *Ephesians*, 272; Dunn, *Colossians and Philemon*, 221–22; Kilner, *Dignity and Destiny*, 253–54.

93. Beale, "Colossians," 865.

the new humanity in saying, "Here [*hopou*] there is no Gentile or Jew, circumcised or uncircumcised, barbarian, Scythian, slave or free, but Christ is all, and is in all." In the new humanity, there are no such distinctions, but rather their most important identifying feature is Christ in them all.[94] This is similar to the collective humanity in Genesis 1:27 and sets up the moral exhortations in the following verses, which focus heavily on relational virtues and practices.

"Putting off" the old humanity and "putting on" the new humanity happened at conversion, when believers died with Christ (v. 3; see Rom 6:6) and were raised with him (v. 4).[95] As Moo explains, what we took off was "our 'Adamic identification, with its servitude to sin . . . and it is our 'Christic' identification, with its power over sin, that we have 'put on.'"[96] Paul refers to the same event as clothing oneself with Christ in Galatians 3:27 and Romans 13:14.[97] It provides no difficulty to say that the new humanity is both the whole people of God and Jesus Christ since he identifies Christ as the head of his body, the church (Col 1:18; Eph 1:22–23). Paul everywhere assumes and applies his core belief that the people of God are in union with Jesus Christ. Before conversion, people were dominated by sin; afterwards, they have the power and freedom to change. The theme of old creation versus new creation, the former headed by Adam and the latter by Christ, is clearly in view. This is why a psychological reading wherein believers simultaneously have both an old and new nature within them that fight with one another is not correct. Rather, Paul's anthropology is eschatological, where old humanity belongs to the old age of sin and death, but new humanity belongs to the age to come already, but not yet fully.[98]

94. The arguments for a corporate sense come from Moo, *Colossians and Philemon*, 267–68; Wright, *Resurrection*, 240; Kilner, *Dignity and Destiny*, 252–53.

95. *Apekdysamenoi* and *endysamenoi* in vv. 9–10 are causal adverbial participles. See Harris, *Colossians & Philemon*, 150–52.

96. Moo, *Colossians and Philemon*, 268. This is evident in that Paul's earlier discussion of this subject in Romans 6 followed right on the heels of the Adam-Christ typology in Romans 5:12–21. Verse 19 illustrates this corporate identity wherein Adam is conceived as our head: "For just as through the disobedience of the one man the many were made sinners, so also through the obedience of the one man the many will be made righteous."

97. Moo, *Colossians and Philemon*, 268; Dunn, *Colossians and Philemon*, 221.

98. Moo, *Colossians and Philemon*, 268; Melick, *Philippians, Colossians, Philemon*, 295–96.

The new humanity is to be renewed. *Anakainoumenon* ("being renewed") is a present passive participle that makes clear that God is engaged in a continuous process of changing believers. God does this by granting knowledge (*epignosis*, "full knowledge"[99]). Paul appears to be saying that God is providing the knowledge of good and evil to the new humanity and that this knowledge is a key to renewal in the image of God. Above it was argued that the tree of the knowledge of good and evil was a probation tree. The knowledge could be gained disobediently by eating from the tree or obediently by trusting God and not eating the fruit, in which case God would have provided that knowledge, and that without the wreckage humanity has experienced because Adam and Eve (and everyone) chose to be disobedient. Paul seems to focus on lying and knowledge in verses 9–10 because Adam and Eve were duped by a lie in their desire to gain knowledge in the forbidden manner.[100] Eve's summary of God's command regarding the tree was not entirely accurate, which left the door open to deception. Later on, the Colossians were also tempted to deem God's provision of knowledge and wisdom inadequate and instead listen to the false teachers. Thus, he warns them, "See to it that no one takes you captive through hollow and deceptive philosophy, which de-pends on human tradition and the elemental spiritual forces of this world rather than on Christ" (2:8). No, Christ is the sufficient source of all they need; he is the "mystery of God . . . in whom are hidden all the treasures of wisdom and knowledge" (2:2b–3). In Christ is "all the fullness of the Deity . . . in bodily form" and in him the Colossians "have been brought to fullness" (2:9–10a). Paul illuminates the nature and content of this knowl-edge. "We continually ask God to fill you with the knowledge [*epignōsis*, as in 3:10] of his will through all the wisdom and understanding that the Spirit gives, so that you may live a life worthy of the Lord and please him in every way: bearing fruit in every good work, growing in the knowledge [again, *epignōsis*] of God, being strengthened with all power according to his glorious might so that you may have great endurance and patience, and giving joyful thanks to the Father" (Col 1:9–12).

The knowledge here is the knowledge of God and of his will and does not stop at mere intellectual knowledge about God. J. I. Packer cap-tures the thought of similar passages like 2 Corinthians 8:1–3 and Psalm 119 well when he says, "Our aim in studying the Godhead must be to

99. L&N 1:335–36.

100. Beale, "Colossians," 866; Dunn, *Colossians and Philemon*, 221–22; Moo, *Co-lossians and Philemon*, 269; Kilner, *Dignity and Destiny*, 253.

know God himself the better . . . As he is the subject of our study, and our helper in it, so he must himself be the end of it."[101] One cannot know God personally without knowing something about him, yet knowing about him without personally knowing him would be pointless. How much more pointless would it be to have the raw intellectual capacity to reason while failing to employ it towards this ultimate end? Verse 9 also includes knowledge of God's will, and that for the purpose of pleasing God and "bearing fruit in every good work" accompanied by growing knowledge of God (v. 10).[102] Again, this alludes to Genesis 1:28, "Be fruitful and multiply," broadening the concept beyond sexual reproduction to being productive "in every good work." In contrast to being God's enemies in their minds/attitudes because of their evil behavior (Col 1:23), the picture is of people increasingly knowing God personally, discovering his will, doing it with the powerful help of the Holy Spirit, and accomplishing the cultural commission. Here, knowing God's will and doing God's will go together so that the mind, heart, and will are going the same direction. Knowing God is the chief goal. Harris helpfully surveys the various ways one may take "in knowledge" (*eis epignōsin*) in 3:10. Other than a vague locative equivalent of *en* that seems unlikely, the other four options all express variations of the same basic idea: whether it is directional (NASB), telic (GNB), consecutive (NEB), or temporal (Barclay), the preposition indicates the (intended) result of renewal in the image of God. Harris translates it in the temporal sense: "until it reaches full knowledge of him."[103] Colossians 1:9–10 then clarifies what accompanies such knowledge: worship, work, purpose, and power.

The restoration goes right to the root of the problem as it has expressed itself since the garden of Eden. Elsewhere, in Romans 1, knowing about God but failing to worship and thank him results in ignorance (another way to look at the blinding action of the god of this world Paul spoke of in 2 Cor 4:4), idolatry, and every kind of depravity (vv. 18–32). This must be reversed. Thus, Paul writes in Romans 12:1–2, "Therefore, I urge you, brothers and sisters, in view of God's mercy, to offer your bodies as a living sacrifice, holy and pleasing to God—this is your true and proper worship. Do not conform to the pattern of this world, but be

---

101. Packer, *Knowing God*, 18.

102. Moo, *Colossians and Philemon*, 269. Calvin said that "it is not the reason merely that is rectified, but also the will." Calvin, *Philippians, Colossians, 1–2 Thessalonians*, 211.

103. Harris, *Colossians & Philemon*, 152–55.

transformed by the renewing of your mind. Then you will be able to test and approve what God's will is—his good, pleasing, and perfect will."

Believers offering themselves to God is worship and is fitting in view of all God has done for them in Christ (developed throughout Romans). Rather than conforming to the world's pattern (recall that chasing idols results in becoming like them), believers are being conformed to the pattern of God's Son (8:29, on which see below), which happens by the renewing of their minds, and this results in knowing and approving of God's will, which involves willingly doing it. Thus, humans can become more like the all-knowing God by knowing him, and this is closely tied to worship and obedience. Going one step further, all of redeemed humanity knowing the Lord is a necessary condition of the restoration of the proper order of creation brought about by the just reign of the Spirit-empowered, Davidic branch in Isaiah 11. As verse 9 says, "They will neither harm nor destroy on all my holy mountain, for the earth will be filled with the knowledge of the LORD as the waters cover the sea." Again, the link is made between knowing God personally and a well-ordered creation project led by the Messiah and his people.

The renewal has knowledge of God and his will as its goal and doing his will is the assumed corollary. Colossians 3 expands on this moral transformation in a communal way. The old humanity believers are to take off includes many vices of an antisocial nature, from various sexual sins to greed to rage to slander (vv. 5–8). Notably, greed is called idolatry. In a context where the solution is knowing and becoming like the Creator, the problem includes worship of a created thing.

On the other hand, the virtues believers are to put on are enumerated in verses 12–14 and are conspicuously social in nature. "Therefore, as God's chosen people, holy and dearly loved, clothe yourselves with compassion, kindness, humility, gentleness and patience. Bear with each other and forgive one another if any of you has a grievance against someone. Forgive as the Lord forgave you. And over all these virtues put on love, which binds them all together in perfect unity."

The first social connection to note here is between God and his people who are dearly loved. Along with the reference to God as our Father in verse 17, this seems to apply the Father and Son relationship between the Father and Jesus in 1:15 to the relationship between God and his people. The filial relationship will show up in other image texts below.

It was noted earlier that humanity's creation in God's image was foundational to designating Israel a "kingdom of priests" (Exod 19:5–6), language 1 Peter 2:9 uses of the church so that believers' identity and mission are in continuity with Israel's in some ways. Likewise, here in verse 12, Paul applies Israel terms to the church: "God's chosen people, holy and dearly loved."[104] Adam and Eve, made in God's image, were given the cultural commission, which was passed on to Noah and then Abraham and Israel, and ultimately to the church. In any case, it is clear that verses 12–14 develop what it means to be renewed in knowledge in the image of our Creator in verse 10. Dunn captures the link between vv. 10–11 and verse 12.

> The negative "put off" sequence was completed in 3:9, and the "put on" sequence began in 3:10. But 3:10–11 were more a statement of principle, the transformation of conversion-initiation being seen in the wholeness of its effect, the putting on of a completely fresh personality. Now we come to the particulars, the clothes, as it were, which the new person should wear. The verb (ἐνδύσασθε) is the same as in 3:10, though now clearly in the imperative. It is as a result of that decisive step and engagement with Christ (οὖν) that a whole set of particular consequences must follow.[105]

Basically, if believers put on the new humanity at conversion, they must put on the virtues of the new humanity, the virtues of Jesus, and these must show up in their behavior, especially in how each member of the new humanity treats the others. Believers must become in character and practice what they are in principle.[106] Verses 15–17 continue this moral and relational emphasis by calling for peace, thanksgiving, soaking in Scripture, teaching it to one another through song (a corrective to the kind of inaccurate knowledge of God's word that led Eve and countless others into sin, perhaps including the Colossians), and doing everything in the name of the Lord Jesus.

Calvin speaks of the image as "the rectitude and integrity of the whole soul, so that man reflects, like a mirror, the wisdom, righteousness, and goodness of God."[107] Many scholars see here a moral component in the meaning of God's image.[108] This passage is an important reason that

104. See Moo, *Colossians and Philemon*, 275.

105. Dunn, *Colossians and Philemon*, 227.

106. See the similar statements in Moo, *Colossians and Philemon*, 268; Melick, *Philippians, Colossians, Philemon*, 296.

107. Calvin, *Philippians, Colossians, 1–2 Thessalonians*, 211–12.

108. Dunn, *Colossians and Philemon*, 221–22; Moo, *Colossians and Philemon*,

one's concept of being made according to the image of God must include moral and social aspects along with knowledge (rightly construed relationally and intellectually).

An important question this passage raises is about how sin impacts the image of God in humanity, if at all. It is often said that the image of God in humans was marred or damaged or perhaps even lost after the fall. Melick, for example, says "the goal of renewal is the image of the Creator. What was lost in the fall into sin is gained through the application of grace . . . That image was marred when they sinned."[109] Dunn writes,

> The idea that in the "fall" the divine image was lost or damaged may be implied here . . . though its explicit expression is the product of subsequent Christian theology (contrast Gen. 5:1–3; 9:6; 1 Cor. 11:7; Jas. 3:9) . . . Perhaps more to the point here, "image" is a dynamic concept, as its use in reference to divine Wisdom and Christ (1:15) confirms. Consequently it does not imply a static status but a relationship, one in which the "image," to remain "fresh" (νέος, "new"), must continue in contact with the one whose image it is.[110]

Hoekema sees a similar implication here. "If something needs to be renewed it is not yet perfect."[111] How would he describe the image as it is now in fallen people? "The fact that the image of God must be restored in us implies that there is a sense in which that image has been distorted. Though, as we have seen, some Bible passages teach that there is a sense in which even fallen man is still an image-bearer of God, these texts clearly imply that there is a sense in which we no longer image God properly because of our sin, and that therefore we need to be restored to that image. The image of God in this sense is not static but dynamic."[112]

But whether or not one thinks that the image of God is damaged, lost, or defaced by sin depends on where one sees the locus of the image of God. If the locus is in believers, then this implication might make sense. If the locus is outside the believer, then this implication does not make sense. Jesus is himself the image of God. In fact, Melick, who said the image is marred or lost (in whole or in part?), correctly sees

---

268–69; Melick, *Philippians, Colossians, Philemon*, 296–97; Kilner, *Dignity and Destiny*, 255–58; Hoekema, *Created in God's Image*, 25–28; Kittel, "Εἰκών," 394.

109. Melick, *Philippians, Colossians, Philemon*, 296–97.

110. Dunn, *Colossians and Philemon*, 222.

111. Hoekema, *Created in God's Image*, 25.

112. Hoekema, *Created in God's Image*, 28.

kata eikona (according to the image) as referring to the Creator as the standard, which parallels Paul's statement that Jesus is the image of God in 1:15.[113] Hoekema, just before his statement that the image of God in humans needs to be renewed, also acknowledges that Jesus is the image of God, yet does not seem to follow that defining thought through in his discussion of the possible effects of sin on the image. Rather, it seems that when he says Jesus is the image, he means "Jesus is a visual example of what the image of God is. There is no better way of seeing the image of God than to look at Jesus Christ."[114] Rather than locating the image in Jesus alone, he locates it in each person, with Jesus being the exemplary human. Yet defining Jesus as the unique image, the paradigm according to which humans were made and are remade, and humans as those made in his image, makes good sense in Colossians, the only book that contains both the teaching that Jesus is the image and that humans are in the process of being renewed in his image.

Thus, Jesus is the image, the paradigm, the pattern according to which human beings were made and are being remade. The locus of the image is Jesus himself as the exemplary human being, the one we should all be like in character, values, and behavior.

Kilner then draws out the implications of this notion.

> Paul's characterizing the image of God in Christ mentioned in 3:10 as a fixed standard that is guiding the renewal taking place is significant. There is no image changing here—people as the new humanity are changing according to what the image is and requires. As noted above, this is consistent with the rest of the Bible's teaching that when humanity fell in early Genesis, God's image did not change, people did. God's image, including God's intentions and standards, remains constant as God is over time. Humanity, though, changes, first for the worse and later, in Christ, for the better.[115]

Kilner emphasizes that which is static and constant: the image itself, Jesus, along with the Divine intentions and standards for humanity that Jesus represents. People still have a connection with God, whether any given individual responds to God's overtures to become an adopted child of God (see below on Romans 8) or not. God's purposes for people are

---

113. Melick, *Philippians, Colossians, Philemon*, 297.

114. Hoekema, *Created in God's Image*, 22.

115. Kilner, *Dignity and Destiny*, 257.

what they are regardless of the extent to which any given individual fulfills them. These factors that do not vary from person to person ground human dignity. But what admits of degrees, the dynamic aspect of being in God's image, Kilner speaks of this way: "in Christ they increasingly reflect God's own attributes [i.e., the moral virtues throughout Col 3], to God's glory. Being a Christian, then, involves having a commitment to the person and pattern of Christ. It requires being the person and living the life that echoes Christ's own."[116] Kilner agrees with something discussed earlier, that one may reflect Adam and false idols. But rather than eliminating or damaging God's image, which is Jesus, it simply obscures one's true identity as made in the image of God.[117] And obscuring who one truly is does not make one something other than one is and therefore does not make one less valuable. It is becoming clearer that what it means to be made in the image of God cannot be reduced to only static aspects or dynamic ones but must include both.

Ephesians 4:22–24

Like Colossians 3, Ephesians 4:22–24 contains the language of "putting off" and "putting on" along with a possible reference to the image of God. The passage begins, "You were taught, with regard to your former way of life, to put off your old self, which is being corrupted by its deceitful desires" (v. 22). As in the parallel in Colossians, a number of disharmonious vices and behaviors are proscribed. It is significant that here Paul echoes his teaching in Romans 1 about the mess pre-Christian gentiles had gotten themselves into. He speaks of the "futility of their thinking" and how they are "darkened in their understanding" (vv. 17–18), echoing Romans 1:21 ("their thinking became futile and their foolish hearts were darkened"). Both passages echo Deuteronomy 29:4, which tells those Israelites who saw the wonders God did in Egypt, "but to this day the Lord has not given you a mind that understands or eyes that see or ears that hear." This may have alluded to the golden calf episode in particular. Similarly, the cause of futile thinking in Romans 1 is that though they knew about God's eternal power and divinity through nature (v. 20), they "suppressed the truth by their wickedness" (18) and refused to glorify and thank God (v. 21). Paul alludes to this in Ephesians 4:18 with the phrase "separated

116. Kilner, *Dignity and Destiny*, 258.
117. Kilner, *Dignity and Destiny*, 259.

from the life of God because of the ignorance that is in them due to the hardening of their hearts." But it is not as though they worshiped no one or nothing. They "exchanged the glory of the immortal God for images made to look like a mortal human being and birds and animals and reptiles" (Rom 1:23, echoing Ps 106:19–20). Ephesians also contrasts serving God with idolatry in 5:5. "For of this you can be sure: No immoral, impure or greedy person—such a person is an idolater—has any inheritance in the kingdom of Christ and of God." One cannot simultaneously serve God and an idol. It may be that both passages assume that these Gentiles became as ignorant as the idols they worshiped, the theme in a number of Old Testament passages mentioned earlier. Ephesians is emphatic that the gentiles were responsible for their sad condition.[118] And that makes God's punishment just. "They became callous and gave themselves over to promiscuity for the practice of every kind of impurity with a desire for more and more" (4:19 HCSB). In Romans 1, "God gave them over in the sinful desires of their hearts to sexual impurity for the degrading of their bodies with one another" (v. 24). Depravity was both their crime and their punishment for idolatry.

On the other side of this is the transformation that results from worshiping and following Christ. Ephesians 4:24 continues the clothing metaphor, "to be made new in the attitude of your minds; and to put on the new self, created to be like God (*ton kata theon*) in true righteousness and holiness." "New self" translates *kainon anthrōpon*, a phrase pregnant with meaning in Ephesians. The mystery of God's will that has now been revealed is "to bring unity to all things in heaven and on earth under Christ" (Eph 1:9–10). Of the things on earth that are not in unity under Christ, Jews and gentiles come into focus in chapter 2. The gentiles, once alienated from God, the people of God, and the covenant (2:12), are now brought near by Christ (2:13). Thus, the two groups are made one new humanity (*kainon anthrōpon* in v. 15), one body (v. 16, which has particular application to the local church in 4:12), and one temple in which God dwells by his Spirit (vv. 19–22). Richard Hays observes that this unity becomes the foundation of all of the ecclesiological and ethical exhortations in the second half of Ephesians, which focus on manifesting unity and love (e.g., 4:1–3, 25; 5:31).[119] Thus, "new humanity" in 4:24

---

118. O'Brien, *Ephesians*, 321.

119. Hays, *Moral Vision*, 62–63.

means the people of God as a whole in whom God dwells. Similar to Genesis 1:26, humanity is viewed as a whole.[120]

As Kilner explains, Adam and Eve had initiated a whole new way to be human that was very different from God's pattern in that it was a counterfeit humanity (a costume). The real way to be human, the real way to image God, was restored by Christ, the true image of God. Now God's people must "put on" this new way.[121] The new humanity is being created (in the sense of an inaugurated but not yet consummated new creation) *ton kata theon* ("according to God"), an allusion to or conceptual parallel of *kat' eikona theou* ("according to the image of God") in Genesis 1:27 (LXX).[122] Being newly created according to God's image here means a change in the spirit (*pneumati*) of one's mind (*noos*), terms that overlap and refer to the source of a person's inner life (mind, will, and emotions).[123] A renewed mind would be more able and willing to accept the truth and put it into practice. Being renewed also means having true righteousness (*dikaiosynē*) and holiness (*hosiotēs*). God is both righteous (Ps 116:5) and holy (Lev 19:2). God is both the One who renews believers and the Prototype and Paragon for their renewal.[124] The moral similarity as part of what it means to be made in the image of God is clear. "True" likely describes this righteousness and holiness because there were false forms of righteousness and holiness on offer, and that in connection with human philosophies and false wisdom. Colossians is clearer about this (see 2:1–20), though Ephesians 4:14 alludes to this as well. The truth of the gospel is necessary for salvation, sanctification, mutual edification in the church, and spiritual protection (1:13; 4:15, 21; 6:14) and forms disciples who speak the truth (4:25; 5:9).

Such righteousness and holiness should be increasingly true of God's people in light of this lofty purpose of God, which is yet to be completed. The moral exhortations are designed to aid that process and include encouragements to work hard, tell the truth, and speak only beneficial words to others (Eph 4:25–31). Then Paul adds these words that illuminate our subject: "Be kind and compassionate to one another, forgiving each other, just as in Christ God forgave you. Follow God's example, therefore, as

---

120. Kilner, *Dignity and Destiny*, 261–62.

121. Kilner, *Dignity and Destiny*, 262.

122. Witherington, *Philemon, Colossians, and Ephesians*, 298–99; O'Brien, *Ephesians*, 332.

123. BDAG 680 and 833, respectively.

124. Simpson and Bruce, *Ephesians*, 106.

dearly loved children and walk in the way of love, just as Christ loved us and gave himself up for us as a fragrant offering and sacrifice to God" (Eph 4:32—5:2). Because believers are made in God's image, children of God, God intends for them to resemble him in character and behavior towards others. The imitation of God as children imitate their father is based on the image of God in which they were created once before and in which they are now being recreated. This was done so believers would engage in the good works God has in mind (Eph 2:10). What good works? As in Colossians, Ephesians alludes to Genesis 1:26–28 to suggest that Christ is leading the new humanity in "filling everything in every way" (1:23). God has placed all things under Jesus's feet (1:22, echoing Ps 8:6 along with 110:1). God was restoring the original unity of creation and dominion of humanity under the Creator.[125] Of course, there are more good works encouraged in Ephesians, but not less.

2 Corinthians 3:18

The same gradual moral progression is in view in 2 Corinthians 3:18. "And we all, who with unveiled faces contemplate the Lord's glory, are being transformed into his image with ever-increasing glory, which comes from the Lord, who is the Spirit." What makes the passage particularly understandable is attention to the background Paul alludes to. God had written the Ten Commandments with his own "finger" on stone tablets. Exodus's emphatic repetition of this fact (Exod 24:12; 31:18; 32:15–16) is surely a refutation of any suggestion that God did not really say those things (cf. Gen 3:1 and contemporary objections to the inspiration of Scripture). Yet the rebellion of Israel in subsequent generations that brought upon them the exile, the ultimate Divine curse, pointed to the need for a supernatural work of moral transformation. Jeremiah 31:31–34 prophesied this work.

> "The days are coming," declares the Lord,
> "when I will make a new covenant
> with the people of Israel
> and with the people of Judah.
> It will not be like the covenant
> I made with their ancestors
> when I took them by the hand

125. Thielman, "Ephesians," 814.

to lead them out of Egypt,
because they broke my covenant,
though I was a husband to them,"
declares the Lord.
"This is the covenant I will make with the people of Israel
after that time," declares the Lord.
"I will put my law in their minds
and write it on their hearts.
I will be their God,
and they will be my people.
No longer will they teach their neighbor,
or say to one another, 'Know the Lord,'
because they will all know me,
from the least of them to the greatest,"
declares the Lord.
"For I will forgive their wickedness
and will remember their sins no more."

Jeremiah's prophecy speaks of many of the main aspects of salvation: forgiveness of sins, a personal relationship with God, corporate unity as the bride of God, the universal knowledge of God (redeemed society), and moral transformation. Second Corinthians 3:3 echoes the phrase "write it [the law] on their hearts" in verse 33 (in turn echoing the Exodus references to God writing the law on stone). The implication of verse 32 is that this will work, i.e., because God will put the law in their minds and hearts, they will not break the covenant, unlike their predecessors.

Similarly, Ezekiel prophesied, "I will give them an undivided heart and put a new spirit in them; I will remove from them their heart of stone and give them a heart of flesh. Then they will follow my decrees and be careful to keep my laws. They will be my people, and I will be their God" (Ezek 11:19–20). Paul alludes to this when he says the Corinthians are "a letter from Christ . . . written not with ink but with the Spirit of the living God . . . on tablets of human hearts" (2 Cor 3:3). Like Jeremiah, Ezekiel emphasizes that this work of God will be effective at transforming the moral behavior and character of the people of God. In other words, God's people will now obey the Torah wholeheartedly because of the Spirit within. And both prophets connected this moral transformation with the promise that God will be their God and they will be his people. In Leviticus 26:11–12, which expands upon the earlier intimations in Genesis 17:7 and Exodus 6:7, this promise is connected with the promise that God will establish his dwelling (tabernacle/temple) among them and walk among them.

Ezekiel 36:26–28 picks up these same themes. "I will give you a new heart and put a new spirit in you; I will remove from you your heart of stone and give you a heart of flesh. And I will put my Spirit in you and move you to follow my decrees and be careful to keep my laws. Then you will live in the land I gave your ancestors; you will be my people, and I will be your God."

Here again, Paul is echoing the prophecy that God would put the Spirit into believers and write the law on their hearts. This is probably why verses 17–18 refer to the Spirit as "the Lord."[126] *Kyriou* here probably has Yahweh in view (see Exod 34:34, which Paul has been talking about in the context). The overall purpose for his line of argument is to show that, in spite of some Corinthians' doubts, his apostolic ministry has a letter of recommendation from God that is written on their own hearts, in fulfillment of God's promises. N. T. Wright explains, "Paul develops this picture in an implicit dialogue with the description of the original giving of the law on Mount Sinai, telescoping together the 'tables of stone' in Exodus with the 'stony hearts' of Ezekiel. The ministry he has exercised in Corinth, he suggests, has fulfilled the prophetic promises by producing this new kind of 'letter', written with the spirit of the living God on the 'tablets' of fleshly, beating hearts. And they, the Corinthians, are the living proof of this fulfillment: You are a letter from the Messiah, with us as the messengers."[127]

The theological lens through which to view this moral transformation is the image of God. Jesus, the image of God, is what believers contemplate or "see" (perceive) by the enlightening work of God (4:4–6).[128] The result of perceiving Christ supernaturally is "that those who look are changed into the likeness of what they see (→ μεταμορφόομαι), i.e., they

126. *Pneumatos* appears to be in epexegetical apposition to *kyriou* here. See Harris, *Second Corinthians*, 318.

127. Wright, *Faithfulness of God*, 981.

128. "Contemplate" translates *katoptrizomenoi*, "look at something as in a mirror, contemplate something," though some scholars prefer "reflect" (BDAG 535). Some find both ideas in the word. Harris notes that "reflection is rather contained by implication in the subsequent word εἰκών, which is visible representation (or reflection) of some reality" (Harris, *Second Corinthians*, 314). True, but glory also connotes visible representation (even if metaphorical, as in "glory" here) and the context compares Moses seeing the Lord and reflecting his glory with us seeing/contemplating the Lord as through a mirror and reflecting his glory. Thus, both connotations are present, if not in the word, certainly in the context.

themselves acquire a share in the δόξα."[129] Here again, people become like what they worship, whether the god of this age (4:4) or Jesus.[130] Believers see better than the saints of the Mosaic covenant (1 Cor 3:7–11), yet not as well as all the people of God will when they see Jesus face to face (1 Cor 13:12), which will complete their transformation (1 John 3:2). This transformation, as in Romans 8:4–11, takes place by the power of the Holy Spirit continuously (*metamorphoō* is a present passive verb) in an act of new creation (2 Cor 5:17). The Holy Spirit frees believers (v. 17), probably from the law of sin and death, as in Romans 8:2. Sin has the effect of veiling/blinding people (2 Cor 3:15; this is the aim of the god of this world in 2 Cor 4:3–4) until this freeing and enlightening work comes. This transformation comes "from" (*apo*) the Spirit. The Spirit is the source or cause, supplying the life, power, and freedom to do right and grow in the fruit of the Spirit, but believers must willingly "keep in step with the Spirit" (Gal 5:25).[131] As in a dance, one can lead but the other must follow or the dance may end on the floor.

A key issue for our study is the relationship between "image" and "glory." Are they the same thing, different, or overlapping? Beale cites this passage as an example in which the two are used synonymously.[132] But, Kilner counters, one could not speak of a transformation to greater degrees of the image of God because Jesus is the image, the unchanging standard, according to which we have been made and are being remade.[133] Degrees pertain to glory in believers, not to Jesus the image. True enough. But two distinctions are needed here. First, there is the distinction between Jesus the image and all humans, who are made according to the image, which Kilner emphasizes. But Colossians 3:18 is clearly about believers, not Jesus, whereas 4:4 is about Jesus, the image. Second, a distinction should be made between aspects of believers being made in the image/likeness that are static, admitting of no degrees, and are shared equally by all humans and aspects that do admit of degrees and are not necessarily shared equally by all believers at this point in time (though they may in the future). Genesis 9:6 and James 3:9 ground the value of people in their being made in God's image and likeness with

129. Kittel, "Ἔσοπτρον, Κατοπτρίζομαι," 696–97.

130. Garland, *2 Corinthians*, 209–10.

131. See BDAG 105–6; Harris, *Second Corinthians*, 317.

132. Beale, *We Become What We Worship*, 214.

133. Kilner, *Dignity and Destiny*, 244–45.

the consequence that they are not to be murdered or even cursed. The implication of equality is clear in that these texts use the general terms *ādām* and *anthrōpos*, making no distinction among human beings as to value. It seems that either being made in the image of God admits of no degrees in any aspect or it admits of no degrees in some aspect(s), the aspect(s) that grounds human value.

On the other hand, Colossians 3 and Ephesians 4 speak of being renewed in the image or likeness of God. And in Hoekema's words, "if something needs to be renewed it is not yet perfect."[134] And what may be renewed admits of degrees of renewal, as the phrase "with ever-increasing glory" (*apo doxēs eis doxan*) in 3:18 indicates. Harris points out that Paul is returning to the contrast between the old covenant and the new in comparing the fading glory of Moses with the increasing glory of the new covenant people of God. *Apo* indicates source and *eis* result so that Paul has in mind a measure of glory God grants people upon regeneration and the increasing glory he grants believers throughout sanctification that culminates in their perfect sanctification/glorification upon resurrection (see Rom 8:29).[135] Thus, there is a moral aspect of people's likeness to God that admits of degrees and thus cannot be the basis of human value since each human's value is equal, though our moral similarity to God is clearly not. Jesus is the unchanging image and standard whereas the aspect of one's being in the image that pertains to one's moral character, which admits of degrees and change, seems to overlap with glory. This may better explain 1 Corinthians 11:7, which uses the two terms in parallel. This interpretation rejects the old distinction between image and likeness and the notion that glory is synonymous with likeness (as opposed to image). Rather, image and likeness are synonyms and glory significantly overlaps with both of them.

It is possible that the referent of the terms is the same (moral and spiritual likeness to God), but some of the connotations are somewhat distinct. Image connotes visible royal representation and similarity, here in moral character, and glory implies visible/apparent increasing honorableness in moral character as a reflection of Jesus's great moral character and is connected with the rule of Jesus and his people (Ps 8:5; Heb

---

134. Hoekema, *Created in God's Image*, 25. Of course, Hoekema is not thinking here of Kilner's distinction between Jesus as the image and humans made according to the image, but the idea that the need for renewal implies imperfection (and degrees of moral similarity).

135. Harris, *Second Corinthians*, 316.

2:6–11). Specifically, Paul mentions endurance, honesty, and renouncing secret and shameful ways as examples of moral transformation in this context (4:1–2, 7–12).

The intent of bringing glory into the discussion here relates to the Exodus context discussed above wherein Moses's face shone with the glory of God literally as he met with God in the tent of meeting. God revealed that he would go with Israel into Canaan after all, which he made spectacularly obvious when "the glory of the LORD filled the tabernacle" (Exod 40:35). Jesus replaced the temple as the one to which the temple symbol pointed: God is with his people and reigning among them. But, having ascended to heaven and taken his seat on the throne at the right hand of God, he sent the Holy Spirit into his people, who are therefore the temple, as Paul says a few chapters later (2 Cor 6:16).[136] Whereas the glory of the tabernacle was shown in visible, external light, the increasing glory in God's people is not outward but inward, yet nevertheless apparent.[137] Paul says, "Though outwardly we are wasting away, yet inwardly we are being renewed day by day. For our light and momentary troubles are achieving for us an eternal glory that far outweighs them all. So we fix our eyes not on what is seen, but on what is unseen, since what is seen is temporary, but what is unseen is eternal" (2 Cor 4:16b–18).

Because glory in Psalm 8 has royal overtones, it would be well to note Spicq's connection of sharing in Jesus's glory with both spiritual transformation and the dignity of ruling with Christ.

> Beginning in the present, these contemplate Christ's glory and are metamorphosed in his image "from glory to glory," the objects of increasing illumination. The life-giving glory of Christ becomes ours and emphasizes our spiritual likeness to the Lord; through this refraction we resemble his image more and more "with unveiled faces." Furthermore, "when Christ, our life, is manifested, then you will be manifested with him *en doxē*" [Col.

---

136. Wright, *Faithfulness of God*, 983–84.

137. Some commentators see glory as inner spiritual transformation, though they do not pick up the temple allusion. See Harris, *Second Corinthians*, 315–16; Witherington, *Conflict and Community in Corinth*, 381–82; Garland, *2 Corinthians*, 200. Kilner's analysis of glory as moral transformation, which varies from person to person and in the same person at different times, is similar, though he insists that the image does not change (nor any aspect of it, by implication); rather, people change. And though he does not emphasize the royal aspect of the image overall, he does admit that human rulership over creation will be possible once the resurrection completes believers' transformation/glorification. See Kilner, *Dignity and Destiny*, 241–52.

3:4], that is, in splendor and in the greatest dignity (2 Cor. 4:17), symbolized as an incorruptible crown [1 Pet. 5:4].[138]

Thus, image and glory overlap, yet there are unique connotations of glory that help Paul make particular points in the context, namely, that it increases (metaphorically getting brighter and brighter) and that God has filled believers as his temple in the new covenant era. In this way, our moral likeness to God increases.[139] Kilner, though arguing that the two terms are not synonyms, nevertheless acknowledges that the two terms are connected; that both image (as it pertains to believers rather than Christ) and glory have to do with reflecting God's attributes more and more; and that glory implies the ability of other people to recognize the transformation of believers' character.[140]

1 Corinthians 15:49

Now Paul's teaching about the "not yet" side of the already and not yet eschatological tension, the completion of believers' transformation into the image of Christ at the resurrection, must be examined. It will become clear that Paul is interpreting Genesis 1 and 2 in the light of the risen Christ. A person can bear more than one image. Seth bore God's image (with the dignity and purpose that implies) and Adam's image (with the sin and weakness that implies) and was a precursor to the rest of humanity doing so. Thus, sin causes one to not purely image God. 1 Corinthians 15:49 refers to this in saying believers "have borne the image of the earthly (*choiky*) man," an adjective Paul may well have coined from *chous* (soil, dust) to characterize humanity, not as souls trapped in earthly tombs or prisons, but as frail and corruptible here in this fallen state.[141] Death came to all through this earthly man, Paul says in 15:21–22, establishing his Adam-Christ typology. In referring to humanity as earthly in verse 49, Paul is continuing his discussion of Genesis 2:7 (see vv. 45–48), which says, "Then the Lord God formed a man (*ādām*) from the dust (*āpār*) of

---

138. Spicq, "δόξα," 371–72.

139. This parallels Paul's teaching in Romans 2:7 that seeking glory, honor, and immortality by doing good is a proper goal of people, which we fall short of (3:23, which also implies our glory is a reflection of God's glory), and that God intends to glorify us when he raises us, conforming us to the image of his Son (8:29).

140. Kilner, *Dignity and Destiny*, 64–65.

141. Schweizer, "Χοϊκός," 472–73, 477.

the ground (*ādāmah*) and breathed into his nostrils the breath of life, and the man became a living being."

Philo also provided an interpretation of Genesis 2:7 in the first century and connected it with the image of God using similar terminology. He reflected, "'And God created man, taking a lump of clay from the earth, and breathed into his face the breath of life: and man became a living soul.' The races of men are twofold; for one is the heavenly man, and the other the earthly man. Now the heavenly man, as being born in the image of God, has no participation in any corruptible or earthlike essence."[142]

He refers to the heavenly man as "the first man"[143] and "eldest son,"[144] but the earthly man as "the second kind of man."[145] This ontological distinction takes on ethical significance, as is seen in his parallel exposition of the same Genesis passage.

> After this, Moses says that "God made man, having taken clay from the earth, and he breathed into his face the breath of life." And by this expression he shows most clearly that there is a vast difference between man as generated now, and the first man who was made according to the image of God. For man as formed now is perceptible to the external senses, partaking of qualities, consisting of body and soul, man or woman, by nature mortal. But man, made according to the image of God, was an idea, or a genus, or a seal, perceptible only by the intellect, incorporeal, neither male nor female, imperishable by nature. But he asserts that the formation of the individual man, perceptible by the external senses is a composition of earthy substance, and divine spirit. For that the body was created by the Creator taking a lump of clay, and fashioning the human form out of it; but that the soul proceeds from no created thing at all, but from the Father and Ruler of all things. For when he uses the expression, "he breathed into," etc., he means nothing else than the divine spirit proceeding from that happy and blessed nature, sent to take up its habitation here on earth, for the advantage of our race, in order that, even if man is mortal according to that portion of him which is visible, he may at all events be immortal according to that portion which is invisible; and for this reason,

142. Philo, *Leg.* 1.31.

143. Philo, *Opif.* 134.

144. Philo, *Conf.* 63.

145. Philo, *Leg.* 2.5.

one may properly say that man is on the boundaries of a better and an immortal nature, partaking of each as far as it is necessary for him; and that he was born at the same time, both mortal and the immortal. Mortal as to his body, but immortal as to his intellect.[146]

People can either follow the better part of themselves, the soul or mind, or else the "dead corpse connected with us, that is . . . the body."[147] Salvation for Philo was to follow the better part and eventually leave the dead corpse behind, being freed from bodily life and conformed completely to the image of God.[148] Death, on this view, is more of a friend than an enemy. Eduard Schweizer calls this the mythology of two men and rightly says it stems from Platonism and the *Sophia* tradition.[149] Because Philo and Paul both interpret Genesis 2:7 using language about the image of God and a first man and second/last man, scholars have wondered what the relationship is between the two. Had Paul read Philo? If so, was this passage influenced by Philo or a reaction to Philo? Thiselton is probably right that one need not resolve the question of whether Paul had read Philo or not. What matters is that both writers were probably familiar with the kind of thinking reflected in Philo's work. Paul is probably offering a polemic against the mythology of two men that appears to have influenced some Corinthians to deny the general resurrection (see 1 Cor. 15:12).[150]

Paul explains the nature of resurrection hope this way in 1 Corinthians 15:42–49.

> So will it be with the resurrection of the dead. The body that is sown is perishable, it is raised imperishable; it is sown in dishonor, it is raised in glory; it is sown in weakness, it is raised in power; it is sown a natural body, it is raised a spiritual body. If there is a natural body, there is also a spiritual body. So it is written: "The first man Adam became a living being"; the last Adam, a life-giving spirit. The spiritual did not come first, but the natural, and after that the spiritual. The first man was of the dust of the earth; the second man is of heaven. As was the

---

146. Philo, *Opif.* 134–35.

147. Philo, *Gig.* 14–15.

148. Philo, *Gig.* 14; *Opif.* 134–35.

149. Schweizer, "Χοϊκός," 9:477.

150. Thiselton, *First Corinthians*, 1284. Similarly, see Barrett, *First Corinthians*, 374–75.

earthly man, so are those who are of the earth; and as is the heavenly man, so also are those who are of heaven. And just as we have borne the image of the earthly man, so shall we bear the image of the heavenly man.

In denying the general resurrection, some of the Corinthians seemed to be embracing Philo's hope of bodily death leading to incorporeal immortality.[151] Paul responds to the Corinthians' hope, arguing that Christian hope includes the resurrection of the body, which transforms the body rather than destroys it (*sōma* occurs repeatedly in Paul's argument). What, then, do the descriptions of the post-resurrection body say about human beings the image of God?

The seed and plant analogy of verses 36–38 demonstrates continuity of identity so that the person's new body grows out of the old one, just as Jesus's corpse became his post-resurrection body.[152] Luke 24:36–43 particularly emphasizes the continuity of Jesus's identity ("It is I myself" in v. 39), the physicality of Jesus's body (the disciples saw, heard, and felt him; Jesus also said he was not a ghost and then ate bread in front of them), and the connection between continuity of identity and physicality ("It is I myself" is sandwiched between the encouragements, "Look at my hands and my feet" and "Touch me and see" in v. 39).[153]

But there is also considerable discontinuity, as the contrasts in verses 42–45 make clear. "Sown" (*speiretai*) refers to the pre-resurrection (of those who die) or pre-transformation (of those who survive until Jesus comes; v. 51 covers that possibility) state of a *living* person,[154] for it would make no sense to speak of a soul-animated dead body in verse 44. The first contrast is that the body "is sown perishable (*phthora*), it is raised

---

151. Wright, *Resurrection*, 353. Fee thinks some of the Corinthians may have had an over-realized eschatology, thinking they had already attained the ultimate spiritual existence in spite of still being embodied (Fee, *First Corinthians*, 790–91). Though pride was an enormous issue in Corinth (e.g., 1 Cor 11:18–19), it is more plausible to see the pervasive influence of Platonic anthropological dualism as the basis for some Corinthians' denial of the resurrection (see 15:12) and thus the target of Paul's polemic. Nor would this be the first time he dealt with that sort of thinking in Greece (see Acts 17:31–32).

152. Thiselton, *First Corinthians*, 1271; Fee, *First Corinthians*, 782.

153. The intermediate state between death and resurrection in paradise, which Jesus had spoken of in 23:43, seems to be a necessary but unnatural state for beings God designed to be whole beings with both physical and non-physical aspects. The implication is that Jesus's identity was preserved in this soul-only, disembodied state, awaiting the reunification of his whole being on the third day.

154. Ciampa and Rosner, "1 Corinthians," 811.

imperishable" (*aphtharsia*; v. 42). Usually this is understood in terms of duration: temporary versus permanent life (as in NIV above, NRSV, ESV, RSV, NASB).[155] Indeed, the word can mean "abortion" or "total destruction of an entity."[156] But Thiselton argues for a qualitative sense. *Phthora*, he says, "denotes decreasing capacities and increasing weaknesses, issuing in exhaustion and stagnation, i.e., in a state of decay."[157] Paul uses the term in Romans 8:21 of creation's "bondage to decay" (*phthoras*).[158] He also uses the verbal cognate in 1 Corinthians 15:33, 2 Corinthians 11:3, 1 Timothy 6:5, 2 Timothy 3:8, and Ephesians 4:22 of moral corruption, a sense the word has at times in the Septuagint (e.g., Gen 6:11; Exod 32:7; Hos 9:9).[159] If the qualitative sense is on target, and it seems to be, that means its opposite (*aphtharsia*) would "*not* be *permanence* or *everlasting duration*, but *ethical, aesthetic, and psychosocial flourishing and abundance*, even perhaps *perfection*, and certainly *fullness of life*" (emphasis his).[160] BDAG defines this positive word only negatively as "the state of not being subject to decay/dissolution/interruption, incorruptibility, immortality,"[161] yet "not subject to decay" points beyond duration to qualitative considerations, or at least the idea that it is not just about not dying, but avoiding the slow process that leads to dying as well.[162] Anyone over sixty years old can testify that there is a difference between slowly losing abilities and actually dying, though the former moves in the direction of the latter. If the qualitative sense is correct, then verse 53, which says, "For the perishable must clothe itself with the imperishable, and the mortal with immortality," is not using parallelism, but is complementing the qualitative sense (*phtharton* vs. *aphtharsian*) with the durative (*thnētos* vs. *athanasian*). In any case, the qualitative implies the durative, though not necessarily vice versa. It certainly is attractive and its resultant satisfaction and joy comports well with the vision of human

---

155. See Ellingworth and Hatton, *1 Corinthians*, 360; Fee, *First Corinthians*, 784; Ciampa and Rosner, "1 Corinthians," 811.

156. BDAG 1055.

157. Thiselton, *First Corinthians*, 1272.

158. See meaning 1, "breakdown of organic matter, dissolution, deterioration, corruption" in BDAG 1055. Our passage is listed under this meaning.

159. Meaning 4, "inward depravity" in BDAG 1055.

160. Thiselton, *First Corinthians*, 1272.

161. BDAG 155.

162. Wright, *Resurrection*, 347 combines the notions of decaying, dying, and disintegrating and their negations here.

flourishing, productivity, and joy in many "blessing" passages (e.g., Lev 26:3–13; Matt 5:3–12; Isa 65:17–25). In the flow of the argument, being dust and returning to dust will be undone in believers' final state of permanent flourishing.

Secondly, the body "is sown in dishonor, it is raised in glory" (v. 43). "Dishonor" (*atimia*) is the negation of the honor (*timē*) with which humans were crowned by God at creation, parallel to glory (*doxa*) in Psalm 8:5 (LXX). It can also be understood in light of Paul's contrast, addressing the same subject, in Philippians 3:21, where he says Jesus "will transform our lowly bodies so that they will be like his glorious body." *Tapeinōsis* ("lowly") means "an unpretentious state or condition, *lowliness, humility, humble station*."[163] This lowly condition does not stem from being physical, but from being sinful and therefore corruptible.[164] The fear and shame of Genesis 3:7–10 may lie in the background. Israel experienced a similar shame as result of the exile, the punishment for their sins—a shame God would remove and replace with honor (Zeph 3:18–20). Wright says that in both Philippians 3:21 and here, the thought is that "the new body will have both a status . . . and a capability of which the present body knows nothing. The sense, arising from the previous paragraph, is of human beings becoming what they were made to be, attaining at last their proper *doxa* instead of the shameful, dishonoring status and character they presently know."[165] The honor and glory of humans made in God's image and put in charge of creation will be restored to fullness (Wright overstated the loss of *doxa* as though it were a complete loss, perhaps because Paul so emphasizes the discontinuity here), but through the kingdom-establishing work of Christ, which Paul looks forward to as finished work in 1 Corinthians 15:27: "for he has put everything under his feet" (quoting Ps 8:6). Christ shares his status and authority with his people (see Heb 2:10 and discussion below). Nor is it only human beings who have glory. All sorts of things in creation have some sort of glory, including the sun, moon, stars, and earthly bodies of various animals, as verses 40–41 assert. In the case of the stars, glory may come in the form

---

163. BDAG 990.

164. Wright, *Resurrection*, 231.

165. Wright, *Resurrection*, 347. Thiselton says radiance may be the meaning here on the analogy of the joy in one's facial expression upon seeing a loved one after an absence (Thiselton, *First Corinthians*, 1274). This is possible, as are other ways glory might be visibly obvious, but the renewed status and responsibility of humans (Ps 8:5; note that v. 27 echoes Ps 8:6) seems to be the primary point.

of light, but the same cannot be said for animals. As Wright remarks, "it is no shame to a dog that it does not shine, or to a star that it does not bark."[166] Thus, the point of saying believers' bodies will be raised in glory is not that they will literally emanate light, but that they, like the rest of creation, will come to be exactly what God designed them to be from the beginning, before the fall, with all the capabilities, roles, responsibilities, and status that implies for each thing and being in creation.

Third, the body "is sown in weakness, it is raised in power" (v. 43). Thiselton explains, "just as power in this epistle repeatedly denotes the capacity to carry through purposes or actions with operative effectiveness, so weakness denotes an incapacity to achieve such competency and the spiral of consequent frustration and deenergization through maximal unsuccessful effort and distraction."[167] This dovetails with the problem of decaying in verse 42 and its reversal in human flourishing. A new operative effectiveness is supplied by the Holy Spirit, as the fourth and last contrast will make clear. But it is worth asking, what would be the purpose for which God makes us effective if not to reign with Christ in the new creation, thus fulfilling the cultural commission? First Corinthians 6:2–3 says God's people will judge both the world and angels, pointing to some eschatological responsibilities. God only gives power for a purpose.

The fourth contrast is "it is sown a natural (*psychikos*) body, it is raised a spiritual (*pneumatikos*) body" (v. 44). There is some confusion surrounding this wording. The RSV, NRSV, and REB render *psychikos* "physical" and *pneumatikos* "spiritual" so that the contrast is understood to be about what these bodies are composed of. Many translations justifiably render the terms "natural" and "spiritual" (NIV, HCSB, KJV, LEB, NLT, ESV, NASB, NKJV), but the connotation is exactly the same to those with Platonic dualistic assumptions about mere soul-salvation—a set of assumptions Paul does not share. Indeed, the words connote something quite different when read from a different set of assumptions. BDAG gives "the physical" as a possible meaning of *psychikos* just after a very different definition, one that makes better sense of its use throughout 1 Corinthian and in James: "an unspiritual person, one who merely functions bodily, without being touched by the Spirit of God 1 Cor 2:14 . . .

---

166. Wright, *Resurrection*, 346.
167. Thiselton, *First Corinthians*, 1274.

a physical body 15:44ab. The wisdom that does not come from above is called ἐπίγειος, ψυχική (unspiritual), δαιμονιώδης Js 3:15."[168]

John Shelby Spong defends the non-physical understanding of Jesus's resurrection and believers' this way: "It was not a 'flesh and blood' body fit to inhabit this earth. It was rather a 'spiritual body' designed for life in the kingdom of God. That is a vast difference. 'Flesh and blood cannot inherit the kingdom of God,' Paul asserted, 'nor does the perishable inherit the imperishable' (1 Cor. 15:50). I do not know how Paul could have been any more specific."[169]

But this non-physical concept of the resurrection and kingdom should be rejected for the following reasons. First, as both Thiselton and Wright point out, adjectives ending in -*inos* regularly refer to composition (what something is made of), whereas those ending in -*ikos* regularly refer to functions, characteristics, or modes of being.[170] This is not a hard rule, though it strongly suggests Paul would have found a different way to denote physical versus non-physical composition. Marcus Borg alludes to this when he says "the Greek phrase behind 'physical body' means literally 'a body animated by soul,' and the second phrase means 'a body animated by spirit,'" yet he nevertheless argues from the context (especially v. 50, as Spong did) that Paul must mean physical versus non-physical.[171] That will be examined shortly.

Second, as Wright points out, had Paul wanted to contrast physical and nonphysical bodies (and was willing to go against convention by using adjectives ending in *ikos*), he actually could have used *psychikos* for the *non*-physical one. For many in the ancient Hellenized world, *psychē* meant "soul" so that *psychikos* might have been rendered "soulish."[172] We will see below that this word was not understood according to Greek dualistic thought here, but rather stood for the Hebrew *nepeš* in Genesis 2:7, which Paul interprets in the following verses.

Third, the physical versus non-physical meanings would make no sense in other passages in 1 Corinthians that use the same terms. For example, take 1 Corinthian 2:14–15. "But the natural (*psychikos*) man does not accept the things of the Spirit of God, for they are foolishness to him,

---

168. BDAG 1100. See also L&N 1:693.

169. Spong, *Resurrection: Myth or Reality?*, 50.

170. Thiselton, *First Corinthians*, 1276; Wright, *Resurrection*, 351–52.

171. In Borg and Wright, *Meaning of Jesus*, 133.

172. Wright, *Resurrection*, 351.

and he is not able to understand *them*, because they are spiritually discerned. Now the spiritual (*pneumatikos*) *person* discerns all *things*, but he himself is judged by no one" (LEB). Paul obviously does not mean that the spiritual person is not physical. Similarly, in 3:1, Paul says, "And I, brothers, was not able to speak to you as to spiritual *people*, but as to fleshly (*sarkinos*) *people*, as to infants in Christ" (LEB). Both spiritual and fleshly people are physical. The issue, as Wright explains, is "whether they are indwelt, guided and made wise by the creator's Spirit, or whether they are living at the level of life common to all humankind (*psychikos*), or whether indeed they are living at the level of life common to all corruptible creation (*sarkinos*)."[173] The spiritual gifts in 1 Corinthians 12 and 14 enable one to do things by the power of the Holy Spirit that would otherwise be impossible, often using the body in some way, as in speaking in tongues, interpreting tongues, healing the sick, and working other miracles.[174]

Fourth, these other references to spirituality in 1 Corinthians have a great deal to do with the Holy Spirit. He enables people who have received him to understand things he has revealed (2:10–15) and he gives gifts to the church for mutual edification (12:4–7). Second Corinthians 3:18 (with Ezek 36:27 in the background) and Romans 8:9–11 particularly emphasize the role of the Holy Spirit in the sanctification and glorification process of being conformed to the image of Christ. Here, as Wright points out, Paul is going beyond merely describing the resurrection body and specifying how this will be achieved: by the life-giving power of the Holy Spirit.[175] Thus, C. K. Barrett explains, "*spiritual* does not describe a higher aspect of man's life; the noun spirit (πνεῦμα) on which it is based refers to the Spirit of God, and the *spiritual body* is the new body, animated by the Spirit of God, with which the same man will be clothed and equipped in the age to come."[176] Verse 45 will call the last Adam (Jesus) "a life-giving Spirit" (HCSB). The Father and Son give life (John 5:21), as does the Spirit (John 6:63). The roles of the Son and Spirit are intertwined at this point.

Fifth, verse 50 does not support the notion that the spiritual body will be nonphysical. It says, "flesh and blood cannot inherit the kingdom of God, nor does the perishable inherit the imperishable." The two

---

173. Wright, *Resurrection*, 349–50.

174. Wright, *Resurrection*, 350.

175. Wright, *Resurrection*, 354. Likewise Barrett, *First Corinthians*, 372; Witherington, *Conflict and Community in Corinth*, 308.

176. Barrett, *First Corinthians*, 372–73.

phrases are parallel to each other so that "flesh and blood" corresponds to "the perishable" whereas "the kingdom of God" corresponds to "the imperishable." The point would be that transformation is needed to inherit God's kingdom. Wright explains,

> "Flesh and blood" is a way of referring to ordinary, corruptible, decaying human existence. It does not simply mean, as it has so often been taken to mean, "physical humanity" in the normal modern sense, but "the present physical humanity (as opposed to the future one), which is subject to decay and death." The referent of the phrase is not the presently dead but the presently living, who need not to be raised but to be changed; and this brings us back to the dual focus of verses 53 and 54. Both categories of humans need to acquire the new, transformed type of body.[177]

Thiselton also argues that verse 50 is not about the composition of the body, pointing out that in the course of the argument, "the negatives decay (v. 42), humiliation, and weakness (v. 43) do not denote 'substances' but modes of existence or life."[178] Verse 50 addresses the change in mode from that of decay, humiliation, and weakness characterized in terms of believers' current flesh and blood to one of incorruptibility.[179] This view of verse 50 has the distinct advantage of being consistent with Luke 24:39–43, where the risen Jesus, who is the pattern for believers' resurrected selves, goes to some lengths to prove to the disciples that he is physically alive. "'Look at my hands and my feet. It is I myself! Touch me and see; a ghost does not have flesh and bones, as you see I have.' When he had said this, he showed them his hands and feet. And while they still did not believe it because of joy and amazement, he asked them, 'Do you have anything here to eat?' They gave him a piece of broiled fish, and he took it and ate it in their presence."[180]

---

177. Wright, *Resurrection*, 359.

178. Thiselton, *First Corinthians*, 1276.

179. Thiselton, *First Corinthians*, 1292. Similarly, see Fee, *First Corinthians*, 798–99.

180. Millard Erickson argues that though Jesus was physical and tangible here, that was before a second stage of his transformation made him non-physical, adapting him to heavenly, nonphysical existence (*Christian Theology*, 1199, 1226–34). Positing such a second stage has serious problems. First, an adaptation to nonphysical existence is not stated anywhere in Scripture. Second, Erickson's treatment of the final state ignores texts about the transformation of the present creation. As Charles Hodge points out, "the destruction spoken of [in 2 Pet 3:10–12] is elsewhere called a παλιγγενεσία, regeneration (Matt 19:28); an ἀποκάταστασις, a restoration (Acts 3:21); a deliverance

Thus, the contrast is not between physical and non-physical. *Psychikos* translates *nepeš* in Genesis 2:7 LXX, which Paul quotes in verse 45. As discussed earlier, *nepeš ḥayyāh* means "living being" and refers to the whole person. It is this Hebrew category that influences Paul's thought rather than the Greek dualistic concept of an immaterial soul as a part of human beings, according to Eduard Schweizer. *Psychikos* is a neutral or even positive concept in and of itself, for God created human beings. But in the context of the contrast with the spiritual body post-Eden, this speaks of an earthly orientation that is corruptible. Such a person is not inclined towards the spiritual and does not understand or accept things that are spiritually discerned (1 Cor 2:14) but is rather fixed on all things earthly. Because the earth is under demonic influence, its wisdom can be described as earthly (*epigeios*), unspiritual (*psychikos*), demonic (Jas 3:15). Jude 19 shows a similarly pessimistic assessment of how humans live when left to their own devices: "These are the people who divide you, who follow mere natural (*psychikos*) instincts and do not have the Spirit."[181] Such people seek things rather than the kingdom (Matt 6:25–34), love self and pleasure rather than God (2 Tim 3:2–5), and behave like animals (2 Pet 2:12).

Fee also rejects the notion that composition is at issue in the contrast between the two terms. "Rather, they describe the one body in terms of its essential characteristics as earthly, on the one hand, and therefore belonging to the life of the present age, and as heavenly, on the other, and therefore belonging to the life of the Spirit in the age to come."[182] Yes, though it seems like something more is being said. Wright, in keeping with the tendency of adjectives ending in *-ikos* to describe functions, characteristics, or modes of being, says *psychikos* captures "the sense of aliveness, operating through breath and blood, energy and purpose, which is common to humankind . . . Ordinary human life."[183] In contrast,

---

from the bondage of corruption (Rom. 8:21)." Hodge, *Systematic Theology*, 3:852. Third, as my father-in-law Kerry McRoberts once queried in a phone conversation with me, how would Erickson explain Jesus's abilities to disappear and go through locked doors (Luke 24:31; John 20:19) if he had not yet been adapted to his heavenly, nonphysical existence? It seems that Jesus was simultaneously physical and endowed with such abilities. The doctrine of believers' resurrection must be able to accommodate both physicality and new abilities, continuity and non-continuity with present existence, even if that requires a strong element of mystery.

181. Schweizer et al., "Ψυχή," 662–63.

182. Fee, *First Corinthians*, 786.

183. Wright, *Resurrection*, 350.

pneumatikos "describes, not what something is composed of, but what it is animated by. It is the difference between speaking of a ship made of steel or wood on the one hand and a ship driven by steam or wind on the other."[184] Thiselton's view is similar, seeing the contrast as between "people moved by entirely human drives . . . unspiritual" and people involved in "a mode and pattern of intersubjective life directed by the Holy Spirit."[185] He then summarizes the thrust of verses 42–44:

> The point is, rather, that a resurrection mode of existence characterized by the reversal of decay, splendor, power, and being constituted by (the direction, control, and character of) the (Holy) Spirit would be expected not to be reduced in potential from the physical capacities which biblical traditions value, but enhanced above and beyond them in ways that both assimilate and transcend them.[186]

That the biblical perspective values physicality should be clear from the very passage Paul has been talking about in 1 Corinthians 15, namely Genesis 1, which says seven times that God deemed his creation good, even very good (vv. 4, 10, 12, 18, 21, 25, and 31). This positive valuation of creation, coupled with the more holistic Hebrew concept of human beings, leads to the very different understanding of "natural" and "spiritual" defended here, one that would be difficult to capture in a translation. This view holds promise to put into some sort of perspective both the physicality and the more mysterious aspects of Jesus's post-resurrection body, since believers' will be like his. Some of his followers had trouble recognizing him at first (John 20:14–15; 21:12; Luke 24:13–20). Jesus could inexplicably enter locked rooms (John 20:19). Theology must retain both the continuity and discontinuity of the pre- and post-resurrection body to do justice to the counsel of Scripture.

The argument of 1 Corinthians 15 would have been jarring to those who had always thought of body and immortality as mutually exclusive. Yet Paul sees the transforming power of the man from heaven, Jesus, as the means by which believers will be transformed, hence the phrase, "the last Adam, a life-giving Spirit" in verse 45. Here Paul reverses Philo's order and rejects the two man myth along with the system of (merely) soul-salvation that went along with it. Wright explains, "And

184. Wright, *Resurrection*, 352.

185. Thiselton, *First Corinthians*, 1277–78.

186. Thiselton, *First Corinthians*, 1279.

the 'heavenly man' is not one who, unsullied by the world of creation, remains in a purely non-physical state; he is the lord who will come from heaven (verses 47–49, corresponding closely to Philippians 3:20–21). He will enable other humans, not to escape from the physical world back to an original 'image of God', but to go on to bear, in the newly resurrected body, the 'image of the man from heaven.'"[187]

Though many modern translations and commentators think the future tense *phoresomen* ("we will bear") is original in verse 49, the hortatory subjunctive *phoresōmen* is to be preferred.[188] The exhortation would be, as in Colossians 3:9–10 and Ephesians 4:23, to put on the new self, the moral pattern of Christ. Christians need not wait for the Holy Spirit to do so at the resurrection, for they are already endowed with the Spirit and are already in the process of being raised with Christ (Col 3:1). The Spirit will lead them (Gal 5:18) and they must follow (Gal 5:25), with the result that the virtues love, joy, peace, forbearance, kindness, goodness, faithfulness, gentleness and self-control (Gal 5:22–23) will blossom in their character just as they do in the character of their Lord.

Though this passage does not give an exhaustive description of post-resurrection existence, it is clear that the body is part of the whole person made in God's image, an assumption we saw in Genesis 1:26–28. Believers' bodies will be imperishable, glorious, powerful to serve God, and Spirit-animated. There is no thought of becoming divine, only of

187. Wright, *Resurrection*, 353. Similarly, see Keener, *Bible Background*, 488.

188. There are a few reasons to prefer *phoresōmen*, "let us bear," as original over *phoresomen*, "we shall bear." The external evidence is far more impressive, as Bruce Metzger, who defends the future, admits. See Metzger, *Textual Commentary*, 502. It is also much more widespread geographically. The very thing that inclines Metzger and others to prefer the future, namely that it reads so well in this didactic (as opposed to hortatory) context, is the very thing that makes this the easier reading. One would not likely change to the harder reading intentionally. See Fee, *First Corinthians*, 787n5. Barrett, Thiselton, and others explain it as an accidental mishearing (omicron vs. omega) and thus rely on context to decide the issue. Barrett, *First Corinthians*, 369n2; Thiselton, *First Corinthians*, 1289. But Fee's reasoning is more convincing when he says, "B et al. would thus inadvertently have the original, not as 'copies' of it but as independent attempts to correct the 'error' . . . Far better to make sense of what best explains how the other came about than to assume that the context cannot here be hortatory." It is nevertheless justifiable to include 1 Cor 15 among the texts about the "not yet" transformation into the image of God because of the forward-looking stance throughout verses 20–55 (esp. vv. 42–44 and 51–55). The exhortation to bear Christ's image would be as an ethical anticipation of the completion of sanctification at the resurrection and thus akin to Colossians 3 and Ephesians 4, but set in an emphatically eschatological context.

resembling the excellencies of Jesus and imaging him in a way befit-
ting created humans. Jesus remains distinctly divine, eternally existent,
infinite in power and wisdom, and thus transcendent in those respects.
But as to humanity and virtue, he is the paradigm and believers will be
conformed to that paradigm.

It was noted that Paul alluded to Psalm 8:6 in verse 27. It is time to
glean something more from this.

> Then the end will come, when he hands over the kingdom to
> God the Father after he has destroyed all dominion, authority
> and power. For he must reign until he has put all his enemies
> under his feet. The last enemy to be destroyed is death. For he
> "has put everything under his feet." Now when it says that "ev-
> erything" has been put under him, it is clear that this does not
> include God himself, who put everything under Christ. When
> he has done this, then the Son himself will be made subject to
> him who put everything under him, so that God may be all in
> all. (1 Cor 15:24–28)

This is one of five allusions to Psalm 8 in the New Testament (Phil
3:21; Eph 1:22; Heb 2:6–8; 1 Pet 3:22). Paul here combines it with Psalm
110:1 in verse 25 to say that everything, including the enemies of Christ,
will be put under the authority of Jesus in the kingdom of God. The significance of echoing Psalm 8 seems to lie in the fact that it will be through
the kingdom of God that Jesus will regain the dominion over creation
that Adam lost (to some degree) by rebelling against God.[189] This is why
the last Adam must also be the Davidic Messiah. Now the rebellion is
over and the death that resulted is defeated by the resurrection, for sin
has been forgiven. Humans are no longer dust destined to return to dust.
God rules over his creation (as in Ps 8:1–2, 9), with humanity under him
led by Christ, the representative and paradigm of the new humanity (v.
49).[190] In this resurrection chapter, the new creation is presented as the
realm in which God's original purpose for humanity to exercise godly
dominion over creation is finally realized in full. This seems to be the
purpose behind giving us the direction and power of the Holy Spirit in
full at the resurrection.

---

189. Ciampa and Rosner, "1 Corinthians," 745–46.

190. Barrett, *First Corinthians*, 376.

Romans 8:29

Romans 8 speaks of the glorious future in a similar way. Paul says, "For those God foreknew he also predestined to be conformed to the image of his Son, that he might be the firstborn among many brothers and sisters. And those he predestined, he also called; those he called, he also justified; those he justified, he also glorified" (Rom 8:29–30). Though much discussion and debate surrounds the meaning of predestination, the main point Paul makes is about the goal toward which believers are predestined: to be conformed to the image of God's Son and glorified. Jesus came in humans' likeness (8:3; see also Phil 2:7) so that humans might be conformed to his image. "Conformed" (*symmorphous*) is an adjective meaning "pertaining to having a similar form, nature, or style, *similar in form*."[191] Paul uses the same term in Philippians 3:21 of resurrection bodies when he says that Jesus Christ "will transform our lowly bodies so that they will be like (*symmorphon*) his glorious body." The latter passage looks forward to glorification when Jesus returns and 2 Corinthians 3:18 envisages glorification as something that happens gradually until that time. Is Romans 8:29 about the already or the not yet aspect of glorification? Witherington and Hyatt see the aorist *edoxasen* as looking back upon our future glorification as if it had been completed.[192] If so, this would highlight the certainty of that future event, grounded as it is in God's predestined plan. But God calls and justifies his people before that day, the latter in anticipation of the final verdict on judgment day. Believers "have been justified" (Rom 5:1), yet they will be justified (Rom 2:13–16). In this same "already and not yet" timetable, believers are in the process of being glorified, a process that is under way and will be completed. Joseph Fitzmyer sees the term as not only "a gracious anticipation, but as a present experience. Cf. 2 Cor 3:18, 4:4b–6."[193] In the present context, this makes more sense. The agency of the Holy Spirit throughout the Christians' lives brings life and righteousness in a process that culminates with the resurrection. In the words of verses 10c–11, "the Spirit gives life because of righteousness. And if the Spirit of him who raised Jesus from the dead is living in you, he who raised Christ from the dead will also give life to your mortal bodies because of his Spirit who lives in you." The Spirit leads believers, helps them put to death bodily sins (vv. 13–14),

191. BDAG 958.
192. Witherington and Hyatt, *Romans*, 230.
193. Fitzmyer, *Romans*, 526. See also Mounce, *Romans*, 183.

and gives them assurance that they are God's children (vv. 14–17). Thus, Paul views glorification as a process that begins at conversion, continues throughout believers' lives, and culminates at the resurrection. And it is clearly viewed as a moral transformation, along with the other nuances of glorification seen in 1 Corinthians 15, namely a reversal of shame and restoration of purpose, responsibility, and status. God assures believers that all of this will happen by giving them the Spirit as the "firstfruits" (*aparchēn*). Fitzmyer explains, "'Firstfruits' was often used in the sense of 'earnest money,' a guarantee of what was to come, like *arrabōn*, 2 Cor 1:22; 5:5 (cf. G. Delling, *TDNT* 1.486; A. Sand, *EDNT* 1.116–17). In this sense Paul understands the Spirit as the 'firstfruits' of the glory that is the Christian destiny. The Spirit, which has been received, is thus the guarantee or pledge of the glory assured for Christians."[194]

Believers eagerly await their destiny, when they will be conformed to the image (*eikōn*) of his Son. Here again is the two Adam concept. Drawing on Romans 5:12–20, Moo correctly correlates the Adamic concepts there and 1 Corinthians 15. "Adam, created in God's 'image' (LXX εἰκών) has tragically 'transformed' that image into one that is 'earthly,' sin-marred; and this image is what is now imprinted on all who were descended from him."[195] One can adjust this idea to fit the teaching that Jesus is the image and that it is our reflection of him that is marred by sin. Genesis 1:26 said Adam was made in the image of God; now Jesus is the pattern, the image, into which believing humanity is destined to be transformed.

Both 1 Corinthians 15 and Romans 8 say that this conforming to the image of Jesus will take place in the eschatological future, at the resurrection. Romans 8 makes this clear in verse 23, which says adoption to sonship/daughtership is completed when believers' bodies are redeemed. Verse 29 says that the purpose for which Christians are being conformed to Jesus's image is so that they will become the brothers and sisters who follow in the wake of the firstborn, preeminent (*prōtotokos*) Son, a reference to Jesus's status shown by his being the first to rise from the dead (like "firstborn from among the dead" in Col 1:18). Thus, believers attain sonship/daughtership by means of adoption into God's family, a process already under way (Rom 8:14–17), but not yet consummated until the resurrection (v. 23). This has powerful

---

194. Fitzmyer, *Romans*, 510; Witherington and Hyatt, *Romans*, 224; Mounce, *Romans*, 185.

195. Moo, *Romans*, 534n151.

overtones of an intimate family relationship with God, a central benefit and purpose of salvation (Rom 5:1).

Emil Brunner says this sonship meaning of the image of God is "entirely new" in terms of the development of the biblical doctrine. It moves the idea from the periphery to the center of the New Testament gospel. It gives rise to the "imitation of God" as an ethical imperative and makes the prospect of becoming completely like Jesus the "sum-total of the hope of salvation."[196] Certainly the image in general and sonship/daughtership does move to the heart of the gospel in the New Testament (particularly in Paul and John), though it would be well to remember the seed of the connection between image and offspring in Genesis 5:1–3. The family resemblance of Adam and Seth was put alongside the passing on of the likeness of God to Seth. The notion of being able to image more than one being (if they differ from one another in some pertinent way) was intimated and apparently became part of Paul's basis for Adam-Christ typology. Humanity desperately needed to leave behind moral likeness to Adam for likeness to the last Adam. Paul also has a Father and son relationship between God and Israel in mind as background for the filial concept. This relationship began with the Exodus (Exod 4:22; Hos 11:1) and included discipline and moral training in the desert (Deut 8:2–5). This relationship was the basis for some moral exhortation in Deuteronomy 14:1–2. The tender Fatherly love of God for Israel is vividly portrayed in Hosea 11:3–4. "It was I who taught Ephraim to walk, taking them by the arms; but they did not realize it was I who healed them. I led them with cords of human kindness, with ties of love. To them I was like one who lifts a little child to the cheek, and I bent down to feed them." Because of his Fatherly love, he cannot give up on them (Hos 11:8–9). God will call Israel's king his son (2 Sam 7:14), a prophecy fulfilled by Solomon (1 Chr 17:13), yet this should be seen as a partial fulfillment. When Gabriel announced Jesus's coming birth to Mary, he applied the prophecy to Jesus, underlining Jesus's role as the anointed king of Israel who would reign forever (cf. Luke 1:31–33 with 2 Sam 7:11–16[197]), not only over Israel, but over all the nations on earth (see Ps 2:7–8, which is applied to Jesus in Acts 13:33; Heb 1:5; 5:5). Of course, Jesus was also to be God's Son in the unique Divine sense as well, which is the subject of Gabriel's explanation of the miraculous conception in Luke 1:35–37. But

196. Brunner, *Man in Revolt*, 501.

197. Stein, *Luke*, 84; Marshall, *Luke*, 67.

the royal sense as a royal representative of Israel, the corporate son of God, is important for our adoption to sonship/daughtership. "Through the Spirit of holiness" Jesus was "appointed the Son of God in power by his resurrection from the dead" (Rom 1:4).

Paul plots an analogous trajectory for God's people. As God had called Israel to be his adopted children (Rom 9:4), he predestines the new people of God (Jew and gentile) to be his adopted children (Eph 1:5). This comes about through union with Jesus (Gal 3:26–27) and the indwelling Holy Spirit (Rom 8:15; Gal 4:5–6). Because of the context of moral transformation in Romans 8:1–17 and Galatians 4 and 5, and with the prophecy of the coming Holy Spirit's transforming power in mind (Ezek 36:26), Roy Ciampa concludes, "Thus when Paul speaks of the 'Spirit of adoption' in 8:15 he may have fused together promises linking the Spirit with divine adoption and with the spiritual and moral transformation of the restored people of God."[198] Just as Jesus's appointment to sonship (in the kingly sense) happened at the resurrection, so believers' adoption is completed at the resurrection (Rom 8:23).[199] The writer to the Hebrews will likewise connect Jesus's sonship with our own. When the sons and daughters of God become like the only begotten Son of God, who is the exact representation of the Father, believers become like their heavenly Father.

One result of being God's children is in verse 17: "Now if we are children, then we are heirs—heirs of God and co-heirs with Christ, if indeed we share in his sufferings in order that we may also share in his glory." Here "glory" refers to what believers stand to inherit as heirs, as the following verse makes clear: "For I consider that the sufferings of this present time are not worth comparing with the glory that is to be revealed to us" (ESV). Moo defends the NEB translation of the last phrase, "which is in store for us."[200] This includes the revelation of the children of God (v. 19), such status not being obvious to observers in the midst of the trouble, hardship, persecution, famine, nakedness, danger, and sword believers

198. Ciampa, "Adoption," 377–78. Much of this discussion of adoption was informed by his analysis.

199. For a similar connection of these themes, see Beale, *New Testament Biblical Theology*, 442.

200. The preposition is not *en* ("in," which would restrict the glory to what is in us and exclude nature, which is the subject of vv. 19–22), it is *eis*, which is translated "to" in HCSB, NRSV, LEB, NLT, ESV, NASB, and RSV (cf. "in" in NIV, KJV, and NKJV). But, as Moo points out, "to" sounds like believers are merely receiving revelation about the glory. Rather, "Paul's choice of *eis* . . . suggests that the glory reaches out and includes us in its scope." This is best captured by the NEB. Moo, *Romans*, 512n21.

often face this side of the resurrection (v. 35). This glory also includes the liberation of creation (*ktisis*) from "its bondage to decay" (v. 21), for which it "groans" with longing (vv. 19 and 22). Though sometimes *ktisis* refers to human beings (Mark 16:15) or all created things including humans (2 Pet 3:4), Witherington explains why it must refer to nature apart from humans. "Verse 23 clearly enough contrasts believers with creation, and this seems to rule out inclusion of believers here. Verse 20 seems to rule out non-believers as well, or even humanity in general, since at least Adam was not subject to such futility or suffering without a choice. So *ktisis* here probably refers to subhuman creatures and nature."[201] God will liberate the ground from the curse he put on it to punish humanity for sin (Gen 3:17–19).[202] The decay (*phthora*), as in 1 Corinthians 15:42, refers to diminishing vitality. Fitzmyer describes this condition as "not only perishability and putrefaction, but also powerlessness, lack of beauty, vitality, and strength."[203] Related to this is the futility (*mataiotēs*) of creation's condition, which Witherington and Hyatt describe as "'ineffectiveness,' inability to reach its goal and *raison d'être*."[204] What creation "groans" for, what would get creation back to effectively fulfilling the role for which God made it, is to share in the freedom and glory of God's children (v. 21).

Human beings similarly groan, awaiting adoption to sonship/daughtership (v. 23) and the resurrection, which is here in apposition to "the redemption of our bodies," probably to bring out that parallel between the bondage and freedom of both creation and people (v. 23). As in 1 Corinthians 15, the renewal of people is set alongside something God will do to nature (see 1 Cor 15:27 and Ps 8:6, which refers back to Gen 1).

The overall impression is one of putting things right that have gone terribly wrong after God had created them good in the first place. Calling the children of God heirs of all this seems to be a conceptual parallel, if not allusion, to Psalm 37:11, which Jesus quotes in Matthew 5:5: "Blessed are the meek, for they will inherit the earth." This claim is strengthened by what Paul had said in Romans 4:13: "Abraham and his offspring received the promise that he would be heir of the world." Combining the senses

---

201. Witherington and Hyatt, *Romans*, 222–23. See also Foerster, "Κτίζω, Κτίσις," 1028–29.

202. Barrett, *Romans*, 156; Kruse, *Romans*, 347; Mounce, *Romans*, 184; Witherington and Hyatt, *Romans*, 223. Vs. Fitzmyer, *Romans*, 507.

203. Fitzmyer, *Romans*, 509.

204. Witherington and Hyatt, *Romans*, 223. This is consistent with "state of being without use or value, *emptiness, futility, purposelessness*" in BDAG 621.

of 1 Corinthians 15:47–49 with Romans 8:18–30 concerning humanity's relationship to the ground (in light of Genesis 2), people were created from dust, yet originally destined for glory. However, they rebelled and the punishment was that the ground would resist their efforts to subdue it and cause them pain until they return to it in death. But as of Jesus's saving work on the cross and in the resurrection, God's people are once again destined for glory.

James 3:9

James appeals to the image of God in his moral teaching about speech.[205] "With the tongue we praise our Lord and Father, and with it we curse human beings, who have been made in God's likeness. Out of the same mouth come praise and cursing. My brothers and sisters, this should not be. Can both fresh water and salt water flow from the same spring? My brothers and sisters, can a fig tree bear olives, or a grapevine bear figs? Neither can a salt spring produce fresh water" (Jas 3:9–12).

There are a few things to notice about James's concept of the likeness of God. First, verse 9 is a clear allusion to Genesis 1:26. James says humans are made in the "likeness" (*homoiōsin*) of God, the same term used by the Septuagint to translate *dəmut* in Genesis 1:26.[206] This means that the cursed one (the receiver/object of the action) is to be respected by the curser (the giver/subject of the action). But verses 10–12 turn to the curser and challenge him/her to be a source of "fresh water" and

---

205. The author identifies himself as James in 1:1. Though the New Testament mentions four men of that name, the early church fathers generally thought the Lord's brother wrote the epistle, though by no means all of them did (Eusebius, *Hist. eccl.* 3.25.3; 2.23.25). Scholars who deny that this James was the author find it hard to imagine the brother of Jesus not mentioning his unique relationship with him or the post-resurrection appearance of Jesus to him. These arguments carry some weight, though brevity and the nature of the problems James addresses in the epistle surely have much to do with what is and is not said. For example, he is not addressing those who deny the resurrection, which would surely prompt him to mention Jesus's appearance to him (just as some Corinthians' denial of the general resurrection prompted Paul to bring up Jesus's post-resurrection appearances to over 500 people, including James in 1 Cor 15:5–8). At any rate, the way he quotes and alludes to a number of Jesus's teachings in his short letter strongly suggests he heard these teachings in person, as Jesus's family members probably would have. James the Lord's brother probably wrote in the 40s before the Jerusalem Council. See Carson et al., *Introduction*, 410–14.

206. Loh and Hatton, *James*, 116; Richardson, *James*, 157; Davids, *James*, 146; Moo, *James*, 163.

produce according to its kind. These verses do not explicitly appeal to the Christian's renewal in the likeness of God as other passages do, but one certainly could do so. One must both live up to the image of God and treat others as those made in God's image. The image is relevant to both the subject and object, the giver and receiver, of human actions.

Second, he says people "have been made" in God's likeness using a perfect participle, *gegonotas*, showing that humanity was and still is made in God's likeness. Whatever else sin has done to people, it has not erased the likeness of God.[207] These people made in God's image are not just believers. He likely would have used some term to designate believers specifically if he thought that only believers are made in God's likeness. Rather, he uses *tous anthrōpous*, the plural of the generic term for human beings of either gender.[208] This means that all nonbelievers as well as believers are made in God's likeness.[209] Kilner is probably right in saying "it is precisely those who apparently warrant cursing most—whom James is identifying as being in God's likeness. The passage appears to be stressing that the reason for respecting people is rooted in something other than their attractive attributes."[210] Peter Davids points out that James's use of "we" in the cursing scenario, though probably short of a confession of his personal sin, suggests that he thinks of himself and the teachers of verse 1 as sharing in the temptation to curse others.[211] If so, then the implication that believers are not to judge others as meriting a curse may be present here. Punishment is God's responsibility, not the Christian's (as in Rom 12:19–21).

Though James does not say so explicitly, a probable inference is that there are some actions/words towards one made in God's likeness that would be consistent with the blessing believers speak to God. This does not mean people should worship one another, obviously. It may be more like "bless and do not curse" in Romans 12:14 and saying "only what is helpful for building others up according to their needs, that it may benefit those who listen" (Eph 4:29). Such words are probably included in the fresh water that flows from the spring believers should be (v. 11), the tree producing fruit according to its kind (v. 12), the good and humble deeds

207. Richardson, *James*, 157–58; Hoekema, *Created in God's Image*, 20.

208. BDAG 81–82.

209. Hoekema, *Created in God's Image*, 20.

210. Kilner, *Dignity and Destiny*, 128.

211. Davids, *James*, 147. So too Loh and Hatton, *James*, 115.

(v. 13), and the enacting of peace-loving, considerate, merciful, good, and sincere wisdom (vv. 17–18).

Third, rather than *image* (*eikōn*) of God, James uses the term *likeness* (*homoiōsin*), which means "state of being similar, likeness, resemblance."[212] Contrary to teaching that humans still have the structural image of God but not the likeness, morally construed, after the fall (as in, e.g., Irenaeus), James says all people, believing and unbelieving, have the likeness of God and makes no distinction with regard to degrees or extent. Logically, this could mean all people are equally like God or that all are equally like God in a certain respect, the one that grounds human value. Or it could mean that humans simply do not have the prerogative to judge how much like God other people are before deciding how to treat them. These possibilities will be discussed below. In any case, the two times Scripture appeals to the creation of an object of action as one made in the image or likeness of God (here and Gen 9:6), it puts all human beings into the category without distinction. All human beings are equally made in the image of God. Any attempt to distinguish one human being from another on the basis of whether or not they fit a set of criteria for inclusion among bearers of God's image and likeness is foreign to biblical thinking and smacks of justifying the oppression of the non-included human being. The same is true of any attempt to determine the present degree to which a person presently resembles God so as to determine the extent to which one must treat them with respect. Believers are not to be in the business of judging who is in and who is out of the group bearing God's likeness nor grading the extent to which they do or do not resemble God. They must treat everyone in accordance with how much God values them, and God values human beings equally.

Fourth, the only other explicit appeal to the object of an action's being made in the image or likeness of God forbade murder (Gen 9:6). James goes further and forbids even speaking against someone. This is consistent with Jesus's teaching that believers should not only refrain from murder but (on the same principle) refrain from calling them names (Matt 5:21–22). Jesus's exhortation is in the context of an overall concern for peace that requires reconciliation when someone has something against another (Matt 5:23–26), a teaching James either alludes to or parallels in 3:17–18.

212. BDAG 708.

Fifth, James assumes that it is inconsistent to praise God but speak against a person because the person is made in God's likeness. Here he implies that a person represents God in a way that makes an attack on the person tantamount to an attack on God. James is consistent with (though not demonstrably dependent on) Jesus's teaching that the way people treat "the least of these" is the way they have treated him (Matt 25:31–46). In turn, this stands in continuity with the Old Testament wisdom tradition. Middleton explains, "This NT text echoes the OT wisdom tradition that people somehow represent their maker, so that oppression or kindness shown to the poor and needy are equivalent to insult or honor shown to God (Prov 14:31; 17:5; cf. 22:2)."[213]

Sixth, this notion of humans made in the likeness of God follows right on the heels of a reference to human dominion over animals. "All kinds of animals, birds, reptiles and sea creatures are being tamed and have been tamed by mankind, but no human being can tame the tongue. It is a restless evil, full of deadly poison" (vv. 7–8). Kilner views this as irrelevant to the appeal in verses 9–12, saying "but James does not appeal to people to control their tongues as part of their rulership responsibilities in God's image. Rather, in verse 9 James invokes only the creation, in God's image, of those being cursed—with no apparent reference to any rulership on their part."[214] Again, Kilner is arguing that the image does not mean rulership, and in making that case, he sometimes downplays contextual clues about human dominion. Here, it is true that James does not directly connect dominion with the exhortation about words. But when James alludes to Genesis 1:26 and/or 28 in both verses 7 and 9, it is hard to believe that it is a coincidence. Granted that the arguments are different in verses 7–8 and 9–12. Possibly dominion and image went together so thoroughly in James's mind (as a reader of Scripture) that the one point naturally reminded him of another argument he could use, for likeness to God is a multifaceted concept. In any case, this text will neither help one distance the image/likeness from dominion nor establish dominion as the essence of the image.

213. Middleton, "Image of God," 396.

214. Kilner, *Dignity and Destiny*, 199.

Hebrews 2:5–11

Hebrews develops the image of God concept in a way similar to Paul.[215]

> It is not to angels that he has subjected the world to come, about which we are speaking. But there is a place where someone has testified:
>
> "What is mankind that you are mindful of them,
> a son of man that you care for him?
> You made them a little lower than the angels;
> you crowned them with glory and honor
> and put everything under their feet."
>
> In putting everything under them, God left nothing that is not subject to them. Yet at present we do not see everything

---

215. That Paul did not write Hebrews is especially clear from 2:3: "This salvation, which was first announced by the Lord, was confirmed to us by those who heard him." Paul insisted he had learned the gospel directly from Jesus Christ (Gal 1:11–12). And the author does not identify himself, as Paul almost always does. Also, the emphasis on Jesus as High Priest throughout Hebrews finds little treatment in Paul. The letter's teaching certainly complements Paul's in a number of areas (see below), though it is mostly lacking typical Pauline emphases like justification by faith and the resurrection. Carson, Moo, and Morris summarize what we can know about the matter: "In all likelihood the author was a Hellenistic Jew who had become a Christian, a second-generation believer (Heb 2:3). He was steeped in the LXX (none of his numerous quotations from the Old Testament depends on the Hebrew) and, judging by his excellent vocabulary and Greek style, had enjoyed a good education." Carson et al., *Introduction*, 397 (see 394–97 for a good summary and evaluation of the evidence). Barnabas may satisfy most of these criteria and adds the qualification of being a Levite (Acts 4:36), making him a decent candidate (see Tertullian, *Pud.* 20), but the case for him or anyone else does not rise above the level of circumstantial evidence. In the end we must admit with Origen that only God knows who wrote Hebrews (according to Eusebius, *Hist. eccl.* 6.25.14). We do, however, have good evidence it was written in the first century, as 1 Clement 36:1–6 uses Hebrews 1 and was probably written by AD 96. Another consideration puts the book before the destruction of the temple in AD 70. The author referred to the Mosaic covenant as "obsolete" and said it "will soon disappear" (8:13). But sacrifices were still being offered in the temple, as 10:1–2 makes clear: "The law is only a shadow of the good things that are coming—not the realities themselves. For this reason it can never, by the same sacrifices repeated endlessly year after year, make perfect those who draw near to worship. Otherwise, would they not have stopped being offered?" (Heb 10:1–2). Carson et al. write, "It is difficult not to conclude that the sacrifices were still being offered when the author wrote such lines as these . . . True, this is an argument from silence; but it is a powerful argument from silence because, given the nature of his polemic, we expect noise: it is hard to imagine how the author could maintain such silence if he were writing after the destruction of the temple." Carson et al., *Introduction*, 399–400.

subject to them. But we do see Jesus, who was made lower than the angels for a little while, now crowned with glory and honor because he suffered death, so that by the grace of God he might taste death for everyone.

In bringing many sons and daughters to glory, it was fitting that God, for whom and through whom everything exists, should make the pioneer of their salvation perfect through what he suffered. Both the one who makes people holy and those who are made holy are of the same family. So Jesus is not ashamed to call them brothers and sisters.

Several things should be noted as relevant to the image and likeness of God. First, the argument of chapters 1 and 2, buttressed by Old Testament quotations, establishes both an Adamic and Davidic/Messianic framework for understanding the work of Christ in reference to Psalm 8. Hebrews 1:2–4 says, "in these last days [God] has spoken to us by his Son, whom he appointed heir of all things, and through whom also he made the universe. The Son is the radiance of God's glory and the exact representation of his being, sustaining all things by his powerful word. After he had provided purification for sins, he sat down at the right hand of the Majesty in heaven. So he became as much superior to the angels as the name he has inherited is superior to theirs."

"Exact representation" translates *charaktēr*, a synonym of *eikōn* that emphasizes the exact resemblance of the Son to the Father. This is then a conceptual equivalent to calling the Son the image of God.[216] The passage shares several similarities with Colossians 1:15–23. The idea of Jesus as image/exact resemblance is connected with sonship: the Son is like his Father (Col 1:15, 19; Heb 1:3). Jesus reveals what God is like (Col 1:15; see the phrase that parallels "exact representation of his being," "the radiance of God's glory" in v. 3). God created the universe through Jesus, who has a governing and sustaining role in it (Col 1:17; Heb 1:3). Jesus is enthroned as king (Col 1:16, 18; Heb 1:3–4). Jesus brought about reconciliation between God and creation (Col 1:20) by providing purification for human sin (Heb 1:3). The rest of Hebrews 1 then establishes the superiority of Jesus to angels, quoting such Messianic passages as Psalm 2:7 in verse 5, 2 Samuel 7:14 (from the Davidic covenant) in verse 5, Psalm 45:6–7 in verses 8–9, and Psalm 110:1 in verse 13. The basic point here is that God has appointed the Son, not angels, to rule God's eternal

---

216. Wilckens, "Χαρακτήρ," 422; Gess, "Χαρακτήρ," 289; Ellingworth, *Hebrews*, 99; Beale, *New Testament Biblical Theology*, 462; Kilner, *Dignity and Destiny*, 59, 67.

kingdom (see v. 8). After a warning not to neglect the salvation the Lord announced to us in verses 1–4, Hebrews 2 picks up this very point about the Son's authority in contrast to angels. As Paul Ellingworth points out, the author probably thinks of angels as having authority in the present age, in line with the Septuagint reading of Deuteronomy 32:8, "he set up boundaries for the nations according to the number of the angels of God." This reading went along with similar notions in Daniel 10:13–14 and 12:1 (see also Sir 17:17; 1 En. 60:15–21; 89:70–76; Jub 35:17). But they will not rule the world to come.[217]

No, that is the role of the Son. This is where 2:5 picks up where chapter 1 had left off. "It is not to angels that he has subjected the world to come, about which we are speaking," but rather to the Son, as the quotation from Psalm 8 will show. What is the world to come and where in 1:1—2:4 had it been mentioned? "The world to come" (*oikoumenēn tēn mellousan*) equals "the coming age" (*mellontos aiōnos*) of Hebrews 6:5[218] equals the new creation of Revelation 21–22. This is the New Testament concept of the present world/age (place and time) dominated by sin and death giving way to a promised future world/age dominated by righteousness and life (shared with apocalyptic writings such as Eth. En. 48:7; 2 En. 65:1—66:6; 71:15; 2 Esd 7:113) that God's people will be resurrected to enjoy (1 Cor 15:20–28).[219] In Hebrews, believers are on a journey towards that place/age just as Old Testament Israel journeyed from Egypt to the promised land (see the typology of 4:1, 9–11; 11:10–16; 13:14), yet they are in some sense currently there participating in that place/age (4:3; 6:5; 12:22, 28). It is heavenly in character (12:22), yet the reign of Christ there fulfills promises of ruling the earth in Hebrews 2:5–10.[220]

Where had the world to come been mentioned before Hebrews 2:5? Hebrews 1:2 called Jesus "heir of all things," probably an allusion to Psalm 2:8, "Ask me, and I will make the nations your inheritance, the ends of the earth your possession."[221] The verse before that, Psalm 2:7, was then quoted in Hebrews 1:5 to say that the Son has been appointed to rule (where

217. Ellingworth, *Hebrews*, 147. The translation of Deut 32:8 is from Brannan et al., *Lexham English Septuagint*.

218. BDAG 700.

219. Sasse, "Αἰών, Αἰώνιος," 206–7.

220. For a view of the age to come that emphasizes discontinuity between the present world and the future one, see Ellingworth, *Hebrews*, 146. For a view that emphasizes continuity and the renewal of creation, see Wright, *Resurrection*, 457–61.

221. Beale, *New Testament Biblical Theology*, 464.

being God's son recalls the promise to David of a line of sons/descendants who will rule forever in 2 Sam 7:14). Hebrews picks up this very thought: the Son's kingdom will be eternal (1:8–9, quoting Ps 45:6–7), in contrast to the universe in its present condition. God will destroy the earth and heavens in judgment as part of setting things right for all the evil done on the earth (1:10–12, quoting Ps 102:25–27). Verse 13 quotes Psalm 110:1, which goes on to speak of the king extending his rule from Zion, ruling in the midst of his enemies (vv. 2–6), very much like Psalm 2:5–12. As in 1 Corinthians 15:25–27, Psalm 110:1 is combined with Psalm 8:6 to bring the Adamic and Davidic functions of Jesus's work together. The general point to be made is that ruling the earth is the responsibility of humans made in God's image and the subject of Genesis 1:26–28, which is exposited in Psalm 8, which is, in turn, exposited in Hebrews 2. Jesus fulfills not only that original cultural commission, but also the promises of an eternal kingdom in David's line. In other words, Christ is both the end-time Adam and the end-time Davidic king. The point about a Davidic king is obvious from the citations from Psalms 2 and 110 and 2 Samuel 7, but the Adamic background and its link to the Davidic concept should be traced. Beale explains that an Adamic background

> is apparent in that the commission of Gen 1:26, 28, which included "ruling over . . . all the earth," was applied to the patriarchs with the language of "possess the gate of their enemies" and imparting a blessing to "all the nations of the earth" (Gen 22:17–18), the latter of which is directly connected with being "given all these lands" (Gen 26:3–4). This is obvious "inheritance" language. Psalm 2:8 is likely a partial development of the reiteration of Gen 1:26, 28 in the patriarchal promises, perhaps especially Gen 22:17–18 and Ps 72:17, where an individual king is promised to have sovereignty over all the nations of the earth. Like Heb 1:2, Rom 4:13 explicitly applies these promises to the whole earth (Abraham "would be heir of the cosmos"), and Heb 11:13–16 applies these promises to the entire new cosmos, where Gen 22:17 is not coincidentally cited as partial support (perhaps together with Gen 32:12).[222]

Granted this, it is easy to see how the Davidic, Messianic background of Hebrews 1 leads to the Adamic background of Hebrews 2. Through the Davidic, Messianic kingdom, Adam's commission is accomplished.

---

222. Beale, *New Testament Biblical Theology*, 463. Beale apparently means that Hebrews 11:12 cites Genesis 22:17.

Because of the enemies of God's kingdom, a strong king was needed to reestablish that kingdom on earth. Christ has done that through the cross and resurrection. The Messiah as the last Adam is going to accomplish what Adam did not: just dominion throughout all creation.[223] But this awaits the world to come for consummated fulfillment. Hebrews 2:14–18 emphasizes the fact that Jesus is fully human since this is a necessary qualification for him to be of the same family and die for humanity, thus breaking the devil's power over them (wielded through the fear of death). He is utterly qualified to be their high priest and thus help them in temptation. In a similar vein as this last thought, the Hebrews author says that Jesus was tempted in all the ways people are yet did not sin (4:15). It is hard not to see a contrast with Adam there. Jesus helps people overcome sin because, unlike Adam, he overcame.

Does Hebrews 2 relate the image of God conceptual equivalent "a little lower than God/angels" to Christ alone, to God's people, to humanity in general, or to some combination of them? The third option, humanity in general, can be ruled out because whereas Genesis 1 did so refer, the author had no reason to distinguish God's people from those who continued the rebellion against him since the fall had not yet happened at that point. Psalm 8 was reflecting on Genesis and humanity in general without reference to that distinction. But Hebrews 2 clearly assumes a distinction between redeemed and unredeemed humanity in verses 10–18. "A little lower than" Elohim in Psalm 8:5 originally referred to human status or place above the rest of creation but below God,[224] that is, to humanity made in the image of God. Though Hebrews follows the Septuagint in translating *Elohim* "angels," one can argue that since angels were thought of as having authority over humans in the present world, the human position is still the same either way: to be below angels is also to be below God in the order of authority. This position of being in God's image is surely part of *ēlattōsas* in Hebrews 2:7: Jesus became like humans and thus was in the same position (see v. 17). But, as Ellingworth and Nida point out, Hebrews uses *brachy* of time to specifically apply the words to Christ: "(a) for a little while in the past, Jesus was made lower than the angels; (b) now ... we see Jesus crowned with glory and honor; (c) in the future, we shall see Jesus ... as ruler over all things."[225] Like Paul, the Hebrews author says

223. Allen, *Hebrews*, 212.

224. Bratcher and Reyburn, *Psalms*, 82.

225. Ellingworth and Nida, *Hebrews*, 34.

Jesus became like humanity (2:17) to make humanity like him (glorified, holy sons/daughters in vv. 10–11; see also Phil 2:5–11 and Rom 8:29). In any case, applying Psalm 8:6 to Jesus does not replace humans with Jesus but sets Jesus forth as humanity's representative leader and the originator/pioneer of salvation (see *archēgos* in v. 10). As Allen puts it, "the author typologically connected Psalm 8 with Christ, understood (as in Paul) as the last Adam, the representative man, who achieves for humanity the dominion that had been lost due to Adam's sin."[226]

Jesus (individually) was crowned with glory and honor, not just in the original sense in which Adam and Eve were (and humans still are, to some extent), but in the sense of being exalted to the throne at the right hand of the Father now (1:3),[227] a precursor to the world to come being completely subjected to him. Though Adam and Eve presumably conformed to the moral image in the pre-fall probationary period, they did not conform so well as "the radiance of God's glory and the exact representation of [God's] being" (Heb 1:3). They were not creators like Jesus was. He was the pattern in which they were formed, so his glory goes beyond theirs (see Matt 17:1–13; 2 Pet 1:16–18; Rev 1:9–18). Jesus merited this exaltation by willingly suffering for (*hyper*, on behalf of) people (v. 9). This is one of many references in Hebrews to Jesus being the atoning, substitutionary sacrifice (see, e.g., 1:3; 2:17; 7:27; 9:11–14). This is as in Revelation 5:9, where Jesus is said to be worthy to judge the world as its king (that is, open the seven seals) because he was slain to purchase people from all people groups for God. The world should only be ruled by him who is willing to obey the Father's will and suffer for others. Again, this is like Philippians 2:8–9. Jesus was made perfect (*teleiōsai*) through his suffering. Gerhard Delling says the author of Hebrews uses the term in a cultic and ethical sense, though one can readily discern a telic note as well: "If the τελειοῦσθαι which Jesus experienced does not mean liberation from guilt, the categories used even with reference to him are ethical. God has qualified Jesus, the → υἱός (5:8–9; 7:28), "to come before him" in priestly action. He has done so by the suffering (2:10) in which Jesus confirmed his obedience, 5:8f."[228] O'Brien calls this a "vocational"

226. Allen, *Hebrews*, 227.
227. O'Brien, *Hebrews*, 92.
228. Delling, "Τελειόω," 83.

understanding of the term in which Jesus is equipped for his high priestly responsibilities (see 2:14–18).[229]

As Jesus was made fit for his high priestly office, so he makes holy his brothers and sisters. The link between what the Father did to Jesus and what Jesus does to people is brought out by Ellingworth. "Ἁγιάζω means 'to make ἅγιος,' that is, primarily, to dedicate or consecrate to God as belonging exclusively to him (cf. Num 16:5; John 17:17–19); and secondarily, to purify from sin (1:3; 9:14). Ἁγιάζω thus reflects the cultic and ethical aspects of τελειόω in v. 10."[230] Jesus ("the one who makes people holy") and believers ("those who are made holy") are "from one" (*ex henos*), probably referring to common descent from Abraham. Jesus and Jewish believers, of course, hail from Abraham biologically, but gentiles hail from Abraham spiritually by virtue of having the faith of Abraham, as Romans 4:10–17 argues. Here is another point at which the author seems to show familiarity with Pauline thought.[231]

The author follows this with "so Jesus is not ashamed to call them brothers and sisters" (v. 11). O'Brien says the reason he is not ashamed is because believers are of the same family. That is true as far as it goes, but this is a *holy* family, and that seems relevant here, as he mentions in a footnote.[232] The author has been talking about how fitting it was for God to perfect the one who makes believers holy and brings them to glory. And there is nothing automatic about feeling proud of one's family members. Being Abraham's children, set apart for God, cleansed from sin, and glorified means Jesus is not ashamed of believers, but rather proud of them. This is reminiscent of being sown in dishonor and raised in glory (1 Cor 15:43) as the culmination of a sanctification process in which

229. O'Brien, *Hebrews*, 107. Similar is Ellingworth, *Hebrews*, 163.

230. Ellingworth, *Hebrews*, 163–64.

231. Ellingworth, *Hebrews*, 164–65 defends this understanding in part from the reference to Abrahamic descent in v. 16, but with some hesitation. The more common understanding is to see in this a reference to having God as a common Father (this is explicit in NLT, NRSV, HCSB, NASB, and seems to be implied in NIV). Ellingworth rightly argues that this "would be too general to support the argument, since this would not differentiate the Son and the sons on the one hand from the angels on the other (as v. 16 will require)" (p. 165).

232. O'Brien, *Hebrews*, 100. Footnote 142 approvingly cites F. F. Bruce, who believes the atonement of sins and our sanctification is part of the reason Jesus is not ashamed of believers. Notice that 11:16 says God is not ashamed to be called the God of those who walk in faith, and this comes in the middle of the discussion of Abraham's faith in 11:8–19.

believers are "transformed into his image with ever-increasing glory" (2 Cor 3:18). It seems likely that glory retains its connotations, not only of moral transformation (as its connection with holiness here suggests), but the status and responsibilities of humanity made in God's image that are the subject of Psalm 8:5–6 (quoted in Heb 2:7–8). Jesus, the representative man (or last Adam, to use Pauline language), is glorified because of his suffering and comes into his kingdom authority, reigning over the earth. He brings his brothers and sisters into glory, under himself and ultimately the Father, and by this means the cultural commission is accomplished not only *for* them, but *through* them because Jesus has now qualified them for this responsibility. Hebrews 12:10–11 speaks of God training and disciplining believers "in order that we may share in his holiness." The result is righteousness and peace. This seems like a partial parallel to the way that Jesus learned obedience through suffering. Jesus, of course, was not disciplined for sin (see 12:4 on the believers' struggle against sin) because he did not sin (4:15). But he was trained by suffering and hardship, and God's people are as well. If Hebrews 2 makes it clear that this trained Jesus for his high priestly role and perhaps his kingly role as well (as Psalm 8 seems to suggest in Hebrews 2), does this not suggest that similar hardship trains believers for a role in the kingdom of priests? Genesis 1–2 and Daniel 7 in particular show that it is not just the fact of human dominion, but the manner in which they exercise it, that matters to God. Hebrews 2 tells us something about the moral and functional aspects of the image of God: God made people a little lower than God and angels so that they may rule the animals and the earth; now he is remaking them in the image for the same purpose, but now in the world to come. The Father, the Son, and the children of God together, now in proper order, exercise dominion.

1 John 3:2–3

Another passage that specifically refers to the image or likeness of God is 1 John 3:2–3.[233] "Dear friends, now we are children of God, and what

---

233. There is evidence to support the contention that the apostle John wrote 1 John, perhaps in the early 90s. The author claims to be an eyewitness of Jesus bearing testimony of what he has seen to non-eyewitness readers (1:1, 3; 4:14; 5:6–7). Which eyewitness he was is suggested by the many similarities between 1 John and the Gospel of John such as the prologues of both (cf. 1 John 1:1–4 with John 1:1–18) and the many polarities (light vs. darkness, love vs. hate, life vs. death, etc.) in both. Church fathers

we will be has not yet been made known. But we know that when Christ appears, we shall be like (*homoioi*) him, for we shall see him as he is. All who have this hope in him purify themselves, just as he is pure." Several things should be noted about our subject.

First, this is about being remade in the likeness of God and thus alludes to and builds on the work of Genesis 1:26.[234] This is clear from the use of *homioi*, a cognate of *homoiōsis* in Genesis 1:26 (LXX). John says the appropriate response to this hope is for believers to purify (*hagnizei*) themselves just as he is pure. In a non-cultic context such as this, *hagnizei* certainly takes on its moral sense, "to cause to be morally pure."[235] This is about becoming more like Jesus morally.[236] "Just as (*kathos*) he is pure" sets Jesus forth as the moral "pattern . . . the standard or goal toward which we are to move."[237]

Secondly, John states the cause of this completed transformation: "for we shall see him as he is." "For" is *hoti*, whose causal sense is emphasized in the translation "because" in the HCSB, LEB, ESV, and NASB. Colin Kruse brings out the significance of the present tense "is" (*estin*) at the end of verse 2: "not seeing him as he was in the days of his earthly ministry, nor seeing him with the eyes of faith, but seeing him as he now is in heavenly glory."[238] Contemplating the Lord's glory is what God uses to transform believers more into his image in this age (2 Cor 3:18) and that process culminates in a climactic seeing that results in a completed transformation (see 1 Cor 13:12). That believers do not fully know him as he is in his glory now corresponds with the fact that they do not yet fully know what they will be like when they are like him.

Third, this brings up the question of when this will take place. John has two times in view here: the second coming in the future and the present of any given believer's life. He had just referred to Jesus's second

began quoting and alluding to 1 John by AD 96 (1 Clem 49:5; 50:3; see 1 John 2:5; 4:12, 17–18). By the mid-second century John was named as the epistle's author by Papias of Hierapolis (according to Eusebius, *Hist. eccl.* 3.39.17). Attempts to historically reconstruct a Johannine school responsible for these writings, the main alternative theory to the traditional view, seem speculative and ill-founded. On all this, see Carson et al., *Introduction*, 446–51, 151–57.

234. Derickson, *First, Second, and Third John*, 286.

235. BDAG 12.

236. Derickson, *First, Second, and Third John*, 286; Kruse, *Letters of John*, 116; Akin, *1, 2, 3 John*, 137–38.

237. Akin, *1, 2, 3 John*, 138; Haas et al., *First John*, 85.

238. Kruse, *Letters of John*, 116.

coming in 2:28, which will make the king physically present with his people (the nuance of *parousia* at the end of the verse) with the result that he will be visible to them (the nuance of *phanerōthē* earlier in the verse).[239] The referent of *phanerōthē* in verse 2 is not Christ but "what we will be" (*ti esometha*), which is also the referent of the cognate *ephanerōthē* earlier in the verse.[240] Nevertheless, the time referent is the second coming since that is when "what we will be" will be revealed to the world, the result of seeing him.

Now John works from the future to the present by describing how the Christians' hope for the future is to influence them in the present. "All who have this hope in him purify themselves, just as he is pure" (v. 3). Marinus de Jonge brings out the nuances of the New Testament concept of hope. "There are to be distinguished four main semantic components which combine in various ways to represent the concept of 'hope.' These are, (1) time, for hope always looks to the future; (2) anticipation, for there is always some goal to the time span; (3) confidence, namely, that the goal hoped for will occur; and (4) desire, since the goal of hoping is represented as a valued object or experience."[241]

John is saying that in the future, when Jesus returns (component 1), two major goals of the Christian life, namely seeing Jesus and becoming like him (component 2), which John is confident will happen (component 3), will take place. Those who desire this wonderful experience (component 4) will respond in a certain way now. This is the way in which the "not yet" inspires us in the "already" timeframe. That which believers do not yet have in fullness drives them on towards it in the present. Just as a person who wants to play in the National Football League practices football in the present to prepare, the person who wants to be like Jesus tries to imitate him in the present.

The final observation is that becoming like Jesus is again connected with being children of God (see above on Romans 8). In the teaching leading right up into 3:2–3 John said, "If you know that he is righteous, you know that everyone who does what is right has been born of him. See what great love the Father has lavished on us, that we should be called children of God! And that is what we are! The reason the world does not know us is that it did not know him. Dear friends, now we are

---

239. Akin, *1, 2, 3 John*, 130.

240. Derickson, *First, Second, and Third John*, 285; Akin, *1, 2, 3 John*, 137–38.

241. Haas et al., *First John*, 84.

children of God, and what we will be has not yet been made known" (1 John 2:29—3:2).

That believers are children of God speaks of their intimate relationship with God as adopted members of his family.[242] They have been grafted into the family God began to create when he called Israel his son, as Akin points out (citing Deut 1:31; 8:5; 14:1; 32:6; Ps 103:13; Prov 3:12; Isa 63:16; 64:8; Jer 31:9, 20; Hos 11; Mal 1:6; 2:10). But what is the connection between the fact that believers are God's children and their moral similarity to Jesus? First John 2:29 contains a clue: the telltale sign of a child of God is imitating God's righteousness. Jesus made a similar point when he pointed to his disciples and said, "Here are my mother and my brothers. For whoever does the will of my Father in heaven is my brother and sister and mother" (Matt 12:49–50). The family moral resemblance is not only vertical in comparison with God but horizontal in comparison with one another. The other side of that truth is in 3:1: those who do not know God do not know his children either. As Akin puts it, "the child of God is unknown by the world because they have different fathers (i.e., God and Satan)."[243] There is a family resemblance, and that resemblance is moral in nature. Of course, this assumes a link between likeness to God and likeness to Christ implicit in 1 John. Paul made that connection explicit when he told the Colossians "the Son is the image of the invisible God" (Col 1:15). John may have had such an understanding. It certainly would make sense of 2:28—3:3. At least one can say that John elsewhere emphasizes the oneness of the Father and the Son (John 10:30–38). At a more basic level, sin separates people from God, so if they are to have a close familial relationship with God, they will need to be purified of sins. In this way, the relational and moral goals of the Christian life work together to bring people closer to God, and the image of God overlaps with both concepts by pointing to their relationship with and moral similarity to their adoptive Father.

---

242. Haas et al., *First John*, 81.

243. Akin, *1, 2, 3 John*, 134. See John 8:42–47 on the imitation of one's "father," whether God or the devil.

Revelation 13:14–15

The final image passage comes in the last book of the Bible, Revelation.[244] Just as Daniel 7 presented a parody of the creation order and human dominion, so John presents a parody of the order of creation using a rich combination of Old Testament passages, including Daniel 7. The vision commences with a presentation of the unholy trinity, a clear parody of the Holy Trinity. Christians worship God the Father, Son, and Holy Spirit (Rev 1:4–6). The idolatrous inhabitants of the earth worship the devil, the antichrist, and the false prophet, particularly the first two (Rev 13:4, 8; see 16:13 for "false prophet").[245] The false father figure is the devil,

---

244. The author calls himself John with no additional identifiers in 1:1, 4, 9; 22:8. The testimony of the early church that John the apostle wrote Revelation is stronger than the testimony supporting the authorship of any other NT book. Second-century writings that so attribute the book include Justin, *Dial.* 81; the lost commentary on Rev by Melito, bishop of Sardis, according to Eusebius, *Hist. eccl.* 4.26.2; Irenaeus, *Haer.* 3.11.1, 4.20.11, and 4.35.2; Muratorian Canon; and possibly Papias. This attribution was not unanimous. Dionysius disagreed with it in the third century (so Eusebius, *Hist. eccl.* 7.25.7–27). Critics today usually deny the apostle's authorship as well, and for often similar reasons, such as differences in Greek style and themes with John's Gospel and epistles and the fact that John identified himself as a prophet rather than an apostle (see 1:3; 10:8–11; 22:7). The latter point is not convincing because 1:3 and 22:7 characterize the book as a prophecy, which it is. Can apostles not write prophecies? And 10:8–11 is about John as a prophet, but that role does not preclude the role of apostle. See Boxall, *Revelation*, 7. The theory that someone wrote pseudonymously in John's name is not convincing, as such authors tended to specifically identify the notable biblical person they were claiming to be. One would not just write "John," but would specify "John the apostle" or something similar (Boxall, *Revelation*, 6). The popular critical theory today posits a Johannine school, people connected in some way with the apostle, who sought to preserve his teachings by writing John's Gospel, epistles, and the Apocalypse. But such source-critical analyses are speculative, complicated, and unnecessary. The different genres and occasions of the various Johannine writings explain differences among them while common authorship explains similarities such as the polarities of light vs. dark, true vs. false, and the identification of Jesus as the Word and the lamb. On all of this, see Carson et al., *Introduction*, 151–57, 470–72. As to when it was written, the preponderance of evidence tells against the late 60s and for the 90s. Revelation reflects a persecution of the church as it was being written. There is no evidence the Neronian persecution extended beyond Rome or stemmed from anything other than Nero's desire to pin the fire on Christians. But the evidence of persecution in Asia Minor during Domitian's time is substantial. See Eusebius, *Hist. eccl.* 3.17, 20 (citing Hegesippus and Tertullian); 4.26 (citing Melito of Sardis), and Tertullian, *Apol.* 5. And see Beale, *Revelation*, 14–15 on the cult of Domitian in Asia Minor, the probable background of Rev 13.

245. Fee, *Revelation*, 177–78, 187; Mounce, *Revelation*, 265; Beale, *We Become What We Worship*, 262; Patterson, *Revelation*, 272.

portrayed as a dragon, who tries unsuccessfully to destroy God's people and the Messiah in Revelation 12. But he is not done. In the next verse, he calls forth his false Christ, a beast out of the chaotic sea (like Dan 7:2–3) that combines the terrifying attributes of the four distinct beasts of the four Daniel 7 empires, a lion, bear, leopard, and indescribable monster with ten horns (Rev 13:1–2). Human empires and their rulers here behave more like brutal beasts than like God. Because each beast in Daniel 7 was a distinct kingdom (see v. 23), some interpreters say this beast also appears to be a kingdom rather than merely one king and is generally identified as either the Roman Empire or some revived approximation of it.[246] One probably does not need to set this up as an "either/or." Daniel 7:17 also identifies the four beasts as four kings. The king represents the kingdom in each case. This opens up the possibility of the beast as a kingdom and its prime representative. As the Father gave Christ the throne of the world (Rom 1:3–4), so the devil gives the antichrist the throne of the same world (Rev 13:2), setting up the conflict that ensues.

The identification of this beast as the antichrist is seen in that 1 John portrays the antichrist as denying that Jesus is the Christ (the anointed king of the world; 2:18) while the beast usurps this kingly role and blasphemes God (Rev 13:2, 6).[247] *Anti* in the New Testament generally means "in place of"[248] so that antichrist means "one who is opposed to Christ, in the sense of usurping the role of Christ—'antichrist.'"[249] Jesus warned his followers to look out for people who would deceive others into following them and thus usurp his role. He called them false Christs (Matt 24:4–5). He also warned against false prophets who would perform signs to aid in the deception (Matt 24:24). Similarly, Paul describes "the man of lawlessness," who will "oppose and will exalt himself over everything that is called God or is worshiped, so that he sets himself up in God's temple, proclaiming himself to be God" (2 Thess 2:3–4). He will also use signs and wonders to deceive people into serving him (2 Thess 2:9). The most obvious indication in Revelation 13 that the beast is mimicking Christ is its fatal wound that is healed (v. 3). Here is resurrection on the cheap, packaged to deceive people, perhaps including those in the church who lack discernment and loyalty to

---

246. Boxall, *Revelation*, 187–88; Mounce, *Revelation*, 253; Beale, *Revelation*, 684; Fee, *Revelation*, 180.

247. Beale, *Revelation*, 686.

248. Büchsel, "Ἀντί," 372.

249. L&N 542.

Christ. This person and/or empire seeks exaltation to the world's throne
and to conquer God's people (vv. 7–10; see Dan 7:21).[250]

The third person of the counterfeit trinity is the second beast or
false prophet. Its close relationship with the dragon/devil is seen in that it
spoke like a dragon and its close relationship with the beast/antichrist is
reflected in its lamb-like horns (v. 11; cf. the portrayal of Jesus as a lamb
in 5:6). What could be more harmless than a Jesus-like little lamb? But
its function is to deceive people into worshiping the beast (vv. 12–14), a
distortion of the Holy Spirit's role as "the Spirit of prophecy who bears
witness to Jesus" (Rev 19:10; see also John 16:12–15).[251] This it does by
means of false prophecies (16:13; 19:20; 20:10) and miraculous signs. Not
only does it point to the "resurrection" of the beast as a sign that seems
to accredit it to the world as its legitimate ruler/empire (v. 12), but it performs other signs, including calling down fire from heaven in imitation
of the prophet Elijah (1 Kgs 18:38; 2 Kgs 1:10).

One of the signs the second beast performs involves an image. "Because of the signs it was given power to perform on behalf of the first
beast, it deceived the inhabitants of the earth. It ordered them to set up
an image in honor of the beast who was wounded by the sword and yet
lived. The second beast was given power to give breath to the image of
the first beast, so that the image could speak and cause all who refused to
worship the image to be killed" (13:14–15). There is early primary-source
evidence of significant persecution in the time of Domitian, which was
at the end of the first century, when John probably wrote Revelation.[252]

---

250. It will not be necessary for the purposes of this section to resolve the question of whether the beast is an individual person (Patterson, *Revelation*, 282; though
acknowledging the beast's corporate representation of a kingdom as well, LaHaye, *Revelation*, 176–80 focuses on the beast as an individual), a kingdom (Mounce, *Revelation*,
251–53; Boxall, *Revelation*, 187; Fee, *Revelation*, 180), or both (Walvoord, *Revelation*,
197–99; Beale, *Revelation*, 683–91). This decision impacts the interpretation of the
healing or resurrection. Since Satan cannot raise the dead (vs. LaHaye, *Revelation*,
180), some interpreters see the resurrection as a metaphor for a declining empire being revived (e.g., Walvoord, *Revelation*, 199–200; Mounce, *Revelation*, 253 seems to
lean in this direction) or as an allusion to the Nero *redivivus* myth, perhaps combined
with the declining empire being revived (Boxall, *Revelation*, 188; Fee, *Revelation*, 181).
Such varied approaches are compatible with the interpretation of the image of God to
be offered below.

251. Mounce, *Revelation*, 258.

252. 1 Clement 1:1 refers to repeated calamities that were happening to the church.
In 7:1, Clement compares the present circumstance of the church to the persecutions
suffered by Peter, Paul, and other believers. Chapter 39 describes people jeering and

And there is impressive evidence that something like this was occurring in the very cities in Asia Minor to which John addressed the book of Revelation. Ian Boxall points out that

> By the first century CE, all but Thyatira among Revelation's seven cities had temples of the imperial cult, while there is evidence in five for imperial altars and priests (Laodicea and Philadelphia excepted . . .). Given its influence on public buildings, statuary, coinage and city festivals, the worship of the emperor, alongside that of the gods, would have pervaded virtually every aspect of life. Non-participation would have been severely frowned upon by the local authorities and probably the local populace.[253]

Except for a disagreement over Thyatira, Beale concurs, adding that such pressure towards emperor worship had been building throughout the century.

> The command to perform idolatry alludes partly to the pressure placed on the populace and the churches in Asia Minor to give homage to the image of Caesar as a divine being. By the end of the first century AD all the cities addressed in the Apocalypse's letters had temples dedicated to the deity of Caesar, the first established in Pergamum in 29 BC (see on 2:9–10, 12–13). Earlier, Emperor Caligula established temples dedicated to his own deity and even tried to place an image of himself in the holy of holies in the Jerusalem temple (Josephus, *Ant.* 18.261–62; *War* 2.184–87; Philo, *Legat.* 184–96, 346–48).[254]

The similarities would not have been lost on John's original audience. Both Boxall and Beale point out that there is evidence from that period of trickery, ventriloquism, and false lightning being used in temples to evoke awe for the emperor among worshipers. Such phenomena may lie behind the image speaking. Yet one cannot rule out real Satan-empowered miracles. Also, Beale is probably right in saying, "Because of the transtemporal nature of ch. 13 seen so far, the 'image' transcends narrow reference only to an idol of Caesar and includes any substitute for the truth of God in any age."[255] That is, the church throughout the ages can expect similar attempts by grandiose statist tyrants and their

mocking Christians. See also Pliny, *Ep.* 10.96–97; Dio Cassius, *Hist. rom.* 67.14.

253. Boxall, *Revelation*, 189.

254. Beale, *Revelation*, 710.

255. Beale, *Revelation*, 711.

sycophants to coerce worship of the tyrants and absolute loyalty to the state. In fact, this does not sound unfamiliar in modern times, when socialist states have sought control of their citizens' speech, religious beliefs, religious practices, education, health care, environment, weapons, business practices, artistic expression, and money for the ruling class's purposes. If the state is viewed as the provider of everything needed to live in return for citizens' votes (demonstrating loyalty) and if the state demands obedience to its dictates rather than obedience to God (which has happened many times through the centuries right to the present day, including in the United States), has it not put itself in God's place? Overt worship may be simply a further step in an implied attempt to usurp God's role as provider, king, teacher, healer, etc. And this may come to a head once again and in a climactic way prior to Christ's return. Before moving on from this point, it is important to notice that false worship is a parody of true worship. False worship here is both evoked by deception and coerced by force, whereas true worship is offered freely, reverently, and gratefully to the one who is the rightful source of blessings and who evokes awe in anyone who can perceive the basic truth about God.

That this passage has something to do with the image of God can be shown by the cumulative weight of a few observations. First, it uses the same term for "image," *eikōn*, as the Septuagint of Genesis 1:26–27 as well as the New Testament passages on the image. Second, the vision rather obviously echoes Daniel 3, where Nebuchadnezzar sets up an image that the "nations and people of every language" must worship or die. And nearly everyone does (Dan 3:4–7), except for Shadrach, Meshach, and Abednego (v. 12). Likewise, second beast orders the inhabitants of the earth to set up an image of the first beast and worship it or else be killed (Rev 13:15). Shadrach, Meshach, and Abednego defy the order, saying that God can save them if he wants, but even if he does not, they will serve him alone (Dan 3:16–18). They are then saved by one who looks like a son of the gods (v. 25).[256] Likewise, God's people must not worship the beast or exchange God's mark upon them for the beast's mark (cf. Rev 14:1 with 13:16) even though such refusal could result in being killed (Rev 13:15) or going into captivity. Patient endurance and faithfulness is needed (v. 10), at least until the son of God comes to vindicate and save

---

256. Interestingly, 1 Clement 45 also draws inspiration from the righteous defiance and ultimate vindication of Shadrach, Meshach, and Abednego in that period of persecution.

his people (19:11–21).[257] Third, as in Daniel 3, the issue of worship, far from being a mere private spiritual issue, is a public and political one as well. Dominion over the earth and nations is at issue in both texts. It was noted in the discussion of Daniel above that Nebuchadnezzar seems to have been using the worship of the image he had set up as an aid to political unity in his diverse kingdom. Likewise, worship of the beast (Rev 13:15) clearly strengthens its claim to rule over "every tribe, people, language and nation" (Rev 13:7). These people must receive a mark designating their loyalty to the beast to participate in the economic life of his empire (vv. 16–17). The image of God has repeatedly been linked with dominion on earth. Now the image of the beast is linked with dominion as well. So not only is the Holy Trinity parodied here, but the creation of humans in God's image is parodied as well. Strengthening this point is a fourth consideration. The second beast gives breath to the image so that it can speak (Rev 13:15) in apparent imitation of God breathing into the man Adam, made in God's image (Genesis 2:7.)[258] "Breath" is *pneuma*, another indication that the second beast parodies the Holy Spirit.

Therefore, this text does say something about the image of God. But what? First, this text is about worship, in this case misdirected towards the image of the antichrist, who is a human being. Worshiping images of humans is foolish and leads to moral degradation and judgment (Rom 1:23–32). Ultimately, the devil who sent and authorized the antichrist is being worshiped by this act. John did not express the thought this way, but one could set up a contrast between worshiping the image of the antichrist, who is not the image of God, and worshiping the image of God who is Christ. In any case, Revelation repeatedly insists that worship is to be directed towards God the Father, Son, and Holy Spirit (see Rev 1:4–6, 17; 4:8–11; 5:6–14; 7:9–12; 11:15–18; 15:1–4; 19:1–10; 22:9).

Second, the link with human dominion has already been mentioned, but there is a difference in humanity's position in the antichrist's kingdom

257. For the parallels between Rev 13 and Dan 3, see Beale, *Revelation*, 711–12.

258. Kilner, *Dignity and Destiny*, 258. It is also true that this act imitates what happened to the two witnesses in Rev 11:11–12. "But after the three and a half days the breath of life from God entered them, and they stood on their feet, and terror struck those who saw them. Then they heard a loud voice from heaven saying to them, 'Come up here.' And they went up to heaven in a cloud, while their enemies looked on." See Boxall, *Revelation*, 195. Breathing life into people has been a divine act since that first instance in Gen 2:7. The resurrection of the two witnesses and the parody of this creative power by the second beast are both signs used to persuade people to follow either Christ or the antichrist.

and in Christ's kingdom. In the antichrist's kingdom, humanity bows to the image of the antichrist and has no apparent royal role themselves. The state, assisted by false prophecy and false religion, will become the boot on everyone's neck and, at the same time, the thing without which no one can function in the world. This is much as it was in Daniel, where people were to worship King Nebuchadnezzar's god, thus consolidating his power, and where the beasts were not inclined to share power. The fourth beast, for example, "had large iron teeth; it crushed and devoured its victims and trampled underfoot whatever was left" (Dan 7:7), probably including the previous empire. Contrast the son of man in Daniel, who was given authority over all nations and peoples by the Ancient of Days (Dan 7:9–13) and shared this kingdom with his people (vv. 18 and 22). "Then the sovereignty, power and greatness of all the kingdoms under heaven will be handed over to the holy people of the Most High. His kingdom will be an everlasting kingdom, and all rulers will worship and obey him" (v. 27). Likewise, in Revelation, those who do not worship the image are granted authority to reign with Christ. "I saw thrones on which were seated those who had been given authority to judge. And I saw the souls of those who had been beheaded because of their testimony about Jesus and because of the word of God. They had not worshiped the beast or its image and had not received its mark on their foreheads or their hands. They came to life and reigned with Christ a thousand years" (Rev 20:4). This stands in sharp contrast to the beast and those who worship his image.

> Then I saw the beast and the kings of the earth and their armies gathered together to wage war against the rider on the horse and his army. But the beast was captured, and with it the false prophet who had performed the signs on its behalf. With these signs he had deluded those who had received the mark of the beast and worshiped its image. The two of them were thrown alive into the fiery lake of burning sulfur. The rest were killed with the sword coming out of the mouth of the rider on the horse, and all the birds gorged themselves on their flesh. (Rev 19:11–21)

This is the final answer to the blasphemous rhetorical question by which worshipers justified their allegiance to the antichrist (Rev 13:4): "Who is like the beast? Who can wage war against it?" As Beale points out, "The expression of Satanic incomparability is an ironic use of OT phraseology applied to Yahweh (cf. esp. Exod 8:10; 15:11; Deut 3:24; Isa 40:18, 25;

44:7; 46:5; Ps 35:10; 71:19; 86:8; 89:8; 113:5; Mic 7:18). This is a further attempt at Satanic imitation of God."[259] It ends in utter destruction for Satan and his followers alike (Rev 20:10).

Third, in light of what has just been said, the original order of creation is very much in view in Revelation 13, just as it was in Daniel 2, 3, 4, and 7. God is over people, made in his image, who are over animals and land. But when people both usurp God and imitate beasts instead of God in how they treat one another, the creation order is in disarray. God will set things in order again, putting humanity (not just one nation) under God, and all else under humanity. It is the fully divine and fully human Jesus Christ that is uniquely qualified to bring about this order.

Fourth, as was just touched upon, people become what they worship. One who worships the beast becomes beastly. One who worships God becomes godly. As Beale states, "Thus the conclusion about the name connoting identification with either Christ (or God) or the beast entails specifically identification with the presence of and likeness to the character of the one worshiped."[260] What justifies this conclusion? Verse 9 had inserted into the middle of this introduction to the unholy trinity, "Whoever has ears, let them hear." This sensory organ malfunction language, as discussed above, tends to occur in contexts about idolatry and originated in the account of the golden calf in Exodus 32, which described "stiff-necked people" and so on. They were coming to resemble the stubbornness of the animal they worshiped. Similarly, it would seem that some will have been rendered incapable of hearing (v. 9) and wisdom (v. 18) by being so bound up with all things earth (the nuance of "inhabitants of the earth" in v. 8) and vulnerable to deception into thinking the beast is incomparably great (vv. 4 and 14).[261] Idolatry blinds people to all else but the idol they cherish. But anyone not so bound and deceived is urged to hear and understand.

Additional background may come from the phylacteries ancient Israel was encouraged to wear. Beale makes the connection this way.

> God told Israel that the Torah was to "be for a sign on your hand, and as a reminder on your forehead" in order to remind them continually of their commitment and loyalty to God (Exod 13:9; so also Exod 13:16; Deut 6:8; 11:18). These were phylacteries

---

259. Beale, *Revelation*, 694.

260. Beale, *We Become What We Worship*, 259.

261. Beale, *We Become What We Worship*, 254–55.

(leather pouches) containing portions of Scripture worn on the forehead and arm. The New Testament equivalent is the invisible seal or name of God (see on Rev 7:2–8). The forehead represents their ideological commitment and the hand the practical out-working of that commitment. Likewise, as a travesty of the signs of membership in the Old Testament community of faith, the beast's marks on the foreheads and the hands of the worshipers refers to their loyal, consistent and wholehearted commitment to him and hence identification with him.[262]

Likewise, Kilner notes, "Those who choose to worship the beast become like the beast—a sort of image of the beast. They literally bear an image of the beast on their right hands or foreheads. (The word for image in vv. 16–17 here, *charagma*, is the same word Paul uses for an idol/image in Acts 17:29)."[263] It should be noted that God the Father's name written on his people's foreheads is mentioned right after the mark of the beast (14:1). That the presence of God is closely associated with his name being written on people's foreheads is clear in 22:4. Whichever name people have written on their forehead or hand indicates their ideological, practical, and personal commitment to and imitation of the one named.

Fifth, it is deeply ironic that the image of the beast becomes an occasion of a government violating people's right to life here. Being made in the image of God is the very thing that Genesis 9:6 uses to explain why human governments must take extreme care to protect humans from murder. But here humans are being murdered because of an image.[264] Once again the parody of God's order of things is shown. The counterfeit is a brutal reversal of the original.

Concluding Reflections on the Image of God in the New Testament

The main developments of the image of God concept can be summarized briefly in story form. The cultural commission had been going forward to some extent throughout the Old Testament period. People were somewhat blessed at times, they multiplied and increasingly filled the earth, they trained their children in varying degrees of righteousness, they

---

262. Beale, *We Become What We Worship*, 256.

263. Kilner, *Dignity and Destiny*, 158.

264. Kilner, *Dignity and Destiny*, 158.

farmed land, built civilizations, gained scientific knowledge, developed ways of putting their knowledge to use for some noble purposes, and engaged in a variety of positive cultural practices—all of which meant that God's purposes were not at a standstill. His plans for humanity and creation were moving forward, yet humanity continued to rebel against God and engage in every form of idolatry and depravity, becoming more and more like the things they worshiped and less and less like God in moral character. Israel had a remnant of God's sons and daughters, but the nation had also fallen into idolatry and depravity, for which he exiled them, casting them out of his presence. He then began to restore them to a certain degree, yet the prophets spoke of such a grand restoration that much more was expected.

When Jesus came on the scene, he said he was bringing about that restoration, that he was bringing in the kingdom of God (Mark 1:15; Luke 4:18–19, quoting Isa 61:1–2). This kingdom was a matter of restoring God's presence and dominion in creation as well as human dominion under him, as the combination of Psalms 8:4–6 and 110:1 in Hebrews 2:6–8 and 1 Corinthians 15:25–27 make clear. Creation is disputed territory. The devil and his agents want to control kingdoms and nations and be worshiped by all humanity (e.g., Rev 13). If people were created in God's image so that they may exercise dominion, Jesus the image of God has to be the ultimate king and has to win an ultimate victory over these enemies to reestablish order in a fallen world.

All humans are equally made in the image and likeness of God, so they must treat each other with proper respect, not murdering each other or even cursing each other. Morally, they reflect God's virtues of love, righteousness, and holiness much less in their sinfulness. God remedies this through the priestly work of Jesus on the cross in that Jesus died in their place. God forgives and purifies those who have faith in Christ. Jesus becomes the pattern of their new creation, their renewal to reflect the image of God fully. God adopts them as his sons and daughters, brothers and sisters of Christ and one another. They conform to their elder brother, who is perfectly like God because he is God the Son. This equips them for their royal and priestly responsibilities. As N. T. Wright puts it, "The goal is the new heaven and new earth, with human beings raised from the dead to be the renewed world's rulers and priests."[265] As God's priestly servants they will serve him (Rev 22:3) and as his image-reflecting royal

---

265. Wright, *After You Believe*, 67.

children they will reign under him (Rev 22:5).[266] The earth will be full of his glorious presence (Rev 21:11, 22–25). Yet in the present age, they are in the process of moving in this direction by the presence and empowerment of the Holy Spirit (2 Cor 3:18). And as priests, they are ministers of reconciliation, urging the people of the world to be reconciled to God (2 Cor 5:19–20). This is another way to state the Great Commission (Matt 28:18–20), which is a means by which the cultural commission is to be accomplished by the image of God and those who reflect his image.

---

266. The late first-century or early second-century Barn. 6:11–19 overlaps this telling of the story at several points.

Chapter 3

A Systematic Theology of the Image of God

IT REMAINS TO TAKE the ideas from the biblical theology of the image of God and present it in the logical form of a systematic theology in conversation with influential past and present theologians. The intent here is to show how the biblical theology has steered the conclusions and suggested categories for the systematic theology. The defense of each exegetical move was provided above and need not be repeated. Here are the questions to be answered, in order:

- In what does the image of God consist?

- What was God's purpose for making humanity in his image and likeness?

- How does sin impact the image and likeness of God?

- How will God fully conform believers to the image of his Son?

In What Does the Image of God Consist?

Here the major options in the history of theology must be considered, namely the structural/substantive view, the relational view, and the royal/functional view. Some theologians combine elements of two or more of these views. Each view will be described and evaluated. Then, picking up certain emphases of a couple of them, a combinational perspective called the royal family view will be set forth and defended.

The Structural View

The dominant position throughout church history has been the structural or substantive approach that says that one or more human attributes or capacities constitute(s) the image of God. Most often, reason has been identified as the image, though Irenaeus included free will as well.[1] The likeness was something else, namely the moral similarity to God. Humans retained the former after the fall, but not the latter. Though Irenaeus spoke of Jesus as the image, the emphasis appears to be on the rational capacities within humanity as constituting the image.[2]

The same can be said of Augustine,[3] who also held to the image versus likeness distinction and added that humans are made in the image of the Trinity.[4] Humans are not, of course, equal in value to the Trinity, but there is a certain similarity in that memory, understanding, and will in the human soul are distinguishable and yet of one substance, analogous to the way the Father, Son, and Holy Spirit are one substance, yet three persons.[5] The image serves its proper end only as the three aspects are directed towards God. "Let it then remember its God, after whose image it is made, and let it understand and love him. Or to say the same thing more briefly, let it worship God."[6] Short of doing so, the human has the capacity for this, and that is the relic of God's likeness. Stanley Grenz also notes that in contrast to the Greek Fathers, Augustine's concept of the image and likeness gives little attention to dominion on earth.[7]

Aquinas carried on the patristic and Augustinian distinction between image and likeness,[8] seeing the latter as a gift of grace (*supernaturalis donum gratiae*) that enabled human minds to rule their lower passions.[9] This gift was lost when humanity fell but is restored through

1. Irenaeus, *Haer.* 4.4.3.

2. Irenaeus, *Haer.* 5.6.1–2.

3. So Grenz, *Social God*, 153.

4. Augustine, *Trin.* 7.6.12

5. Augustine, *Trin.* 10.11–12

6. Augustine, *Trin.* 14.12.15.

7. Grenz, *Social God*, 156.

8. Aquinas, *Summa Theologica*, 1.93.9.

9. Aquinas, *Summa Theologica*, 1.95.1. Hoekema, *Created in God's Image*, 36 downplays Aquinas's distinction between image (as reason) and likeness (as righteousness) based on 1.93.9, *ad.* 3: "Nor is it unfitting to use the term image from one point of view, and from another the term likeness." But he did make a distinction just before that, in his explanation of his own view: "But likeness may be considered in another

sanctification and eventual resurrection. But even without this grace, humans have a natural capacity to know of God and love him in some sense. That is the first stage in which the image exists in humans.

> I answer that, Since man is said to be the image of God by reason of his intellectual nature, he is the most perfectly like God according to that in which he can best imitate God in his intellectual nature. Now the intellectual nature imitates God chiefly in this, that God understands and loves Himself. And so we see that the image of God is in man in three ways. First, because man possesses a natural aptitude for understanding and loving God; and this aptitude consists in the very nature of the mind, which is common to all men. Secondly, because man actually or habitually knows and loves God, though imperfectly; and this image consists in the conformity of grace. Thirdly, because man knows and loves God perfectly; and this image consists in the likeness of glory.[10]

Also, similar to Augustine, he held a concept of how humans image the Trinity. In his words, "Now the Divine Persons are distinct from each other by reason of the procession of the Word from the Speaker, and the procession of Love joining Both. But in our soul word 'cannot exist without actual thought,' as Augustine says (*Trin.* 14.7). Therefore, first and chiefly, the image of the Trinity is to be found in the acts of the mind, that is, namely, as from the knowledge which we possess, by thinking we form an internal word, and thence break forth into love."[11]

"In our soul" reflects Aquinas's linking of the image with the immaterial soul more than with the whole self, though he did agree that humans are composites of body and soul, the latter being the form of the former.[12] He also said that Jesus is the divine image, but as Grenz notes, the centrality of this fact acknowledged by many church fathers fell by the wayside. It was humans who were the image of God.[13]

---

way, as signifying the expression and perfection of the image. In this sense Damascene says (*De Fid. Orth.* 2.12) that 'the image implies an intelligent being, endowed with free choice and self-movement, whereas likeness implies a likeness of power, as far as this may be possible in man.' In the same sense likeness is said to belong to the love of virtue, for there is no virtue without love of virtue." He qualifies the distinction, but he makes it nonetheless.

10. Aquinas, *Summa Theologica*, 1.93.4.

11. Aquinas, *Summa Theologica*, 1.93.7.

12. Aquinas, *Summa Theologica* 1.75.5; 1.76.1.

13. Grenz, *Social God*, 158.

In the Reformation period, John Calvin did away with the old distinction between image and likeness, seeing the two terms as Hebrew repetition,[14] a view Reformed theologians generally follow to this day.[15] He also rejected Augustine's notion of the three things in humanity that image the Trinity.[16] A number of endowments in the structure of human nature mirror God.

> I have, indeed, no doubt but he intends, by the first, the distinguished endowments which clearly manifest that men were formed after the image of God, and created to the hope of a blessed and immortal life. The reason with which they are endued, and by which they can distinguish between good and evil; the principle of religion which is planted in them; their intercourse with each other, which is preserved from being broken up by certain sacred bonds; the regard to what is becoming, and the sense of shame which guilt awakens in them, as well as their continuing to be governed by laws; all these things are clear indications of pre-eminent and celestial wisdom.[17]

These endowments are primarily in the soul, though the body also reflects God's image.

> Therefore, although the soul is not man, yet it is not absurd for man, in respect to his soul, to be called God's image; even though I retain the principle I just now set forward, that the likeness of God extends to the whole excellence by which man's nature towers over all the kinds of living creatures. Accordingly, the integrity with which Adam was endowed is expressed by this word, when he had full possession of right understanding, when he had his affections kept within the bounds of reason, all his senses tempered in right order, and he truly referred his excellence to exceptional gifts bestowed upon him by his Maker. And although the primary seat of the divine image was in the mind and heart, or in the soul and its powers, yet there was no part of man, not even the body itself, in which some sparks did not glow.[18]

---

14. Calvin, *Inst.* 1.15.3.

15. E.g., Hodge, *Systematic Theology*, 2:96; Hoekema, *Created in God's Image*, 13.

16. Calvin, *Inst.* 1.15.4.

17. Calvin, *Psalms*, 102 (on 8:5–6). For the language of mirroring God, see *Inst.* 1.15.4.

18. Calvin, *Inst.* 1.15.3.

Grenz argues that Calvin's is a basically relational view of the image. He explains, "the faculties of intellect and will, which, Calvin agrees, the soul possesses, do not in and of themselves constitute the *imago Dei*. Rather, in his estimation, the divine image entails the proper working of these powers, enabling the human person to 'mount up even to God and eternal bliss.'"[19] It is true that Calvin includes humanity's relational capacity ("their intercourse with each other" in the above quote from his commentary on Psalm 8) in the image, but he does so as one example of an endowment that manifests the image of God. Though Calvin surely did emphasize what God intended for people to do with those endowments relationally as well as morally, Erickson is right to classify Calvin's as a structural/substantive view.[20]

Calvin's influence can be seen in the view of Niebuhr, who holds a substantive view that does not focus on just one endowment of human beings but incorporates a broader range of considerations. He distinguishes between humanity's essential nature and virtue/perfection. He first delineates the essential nature. "To the essential nature of man belong, on the one hand, all his natural endowments, and determinations, his physical and social impulses, his sexual and racial differentiations, in short, his character as a creature imbedded in the natural order. On the other hand, his essential nature also includes the freedom of his spirit, his transcendence over natural process and finally his self-transcendence."[21]

The virtue/perfection aspect of the image includes faith, hope, and love. Here a person's freedom must be used to reflect these virtues. This doctrine is stated in contrast to the Roman Catholic notion of an original knowledge of God and original righteousness that were withdrawn from humans at the fall.[22]

My seminary professor, Wayne Grudem, teaches something even broader. He defines the image of God this way: "The fact that man is in the image of God means that man is like God and represents God."[23] Rather than narrowing down the ways humans are like God, he says the likeness to God "refers to every way in which man is like God."[24] He then

19. Grenz, *Social God*, 167. Grenz cites Calvin, *Inst.* 1.15.7–8.

20. Erickson, *Christian Theology*, 501.

21. Niebuhr, *Nature and Destiny*, 1:270.

22. Niebuhr, *Nature and Destiny*, 1:270–71.

23. Grudem, *Systematic Theology*, 442.

24. Grudem, *Systematic Theology*, 443.

discusses numerous similarities between God and humans that animals do not share, grouped under the categories "moral aspects," "spiritual aspects," "mental aspects," "relational aspect," and "physical aspects."[25] This is similar to Erickson's statement that the communicable attributes of God constitute the image of God. Human nature or personality includes mind, will, and emotions, and these are what make up the image and enable relationships with God, people, and nature.[26] Philip Edgcumbe Hughes also includes personality, spirituality, rationality, morality, and authority as aspects or manifestations of God's image in humans, though his view lays a particularly strong emphasis on the fact that Jesus is the image whereas people are made in his image.[27] Hoekema points out that the Reformed tradition often makes the distinction between the broader and narrower senses of the image, the former including the structural aspects like reason and will and the latter including functions like worshiping, relating, and ruling creation.[28] Variations of the structural approach have continued to influence many theologians down to the present day.[29]

Is some version of the substantive view correct? It seems clear that image and likeness do not refer to separate aspects of a person. Rather, the two concepts overlap and refer to the idea that humans, as whole beings, represent God in creation and bear similarities to him.

A frequent criticism of this view is that it reads Platonic and Aristotelian concepts into the biblical teaching.[30] Perhaps this is most seen in the frequent exaltation of reason to preeminence among the human capacities identified with the image, as in Calvin, citing Ephesians 4:23–24.[31] It is true that Ephesians 4 speaks of the renewal of the mind, construed

25. Grudem, *Systematic Theology*, 445–49.

26. Erickson, *Christian Theology*, 514.

27. Hughes, *True Image*, 51–61. His point about Jesus being the image is discussed on p. 34. Not all theologians build their anthropology directly on a Christological foundation. On the Christ-centered anthropologies of Gregory of Nyssa, Julian of Norwich, Martin Luther, Friedrich Schleiermacher, Karl Barth, John Zizioulas, and James Cone, see Cortez, *Christological Anthropology*.

28. Hoekema, *Created in God's Image*, 69–70.

29. Pope, *Compendium of Christian Theology*, 1:423–26; Miley, *Systematic Theology*, 1:407; Hoekema, *Created in God's Image*, ix; Packer, *Knowing Man*, 20–23; Berkhof, *Systematic Theology*, 203–5; Hodge, *Systematic Theology*, 2:99; Thiessen, *Lectures in Systematic Theology*, 219–22.

30. Erickson, *Christian Theology*, 512; Niebuhr, *Nature and Destiny*, 1:152–54; Brunner, *Man in Revolt*, 43–44; Kilner, *Dignity and Destiny*, 178–83.

31. Calvin, *Inst.* 1.15.4.

as the whole inner life of thinking, will, and emotion. Colossians 3:10 takes us back to Genesis 3, when humanity tried to gain knowledge the wrong way. God now gives this to his people in Christ, a knowledge that is both intellectual and personal. As Packer says, one must know about God in order to know God personally, and knowing God personally is the proper purpose of studying God.[32] Eternal life is, first and foremost, knowing God (John 17:3). This knowledge is also a knowledge of God's will that includes a willingness to do it. In this way, reason is needed to love God and the will is needed to follow his ways and gain his virtues so as to put them into practice, especially in how believers treat others and accomplish the cultural commission. In both contexts, the key virtue is love (Eph 5:1; Col 3:14). In view of this, Hoekema is surely correct that rationality "is by no means the heart of the image of God."[33] Yet knowledge, in concert with these other virtues, appears to be part of what it means for humans to properly image God. It is worth pointing out that these texts put the accent on the end result (knowledge) rather than the natural capacity (reason).[34]

The freedom of human beings is everywhere presupposed, for every command of Scripture assumes people can and must obey God. The punishment of people for rebellion assumes they should have freely obeyed. But nowhere in Scripture is freedom specifically included in the image of God. Obedience as a part of holiness assumes that the person has freely decided to obey God (though "it is God who works in you to will and to act in order to fulfill his good purpose" [Phil 2:13]). The obedience rather than the presupposed freedom is a part of humans becoming more like God. Knowledge rather than its prerequisite rationality is a key to being renewed in God's image. Similarly, the righteousness and holiness of character rather than the freedom by which people make decisions that lead to righteous and holy character is part of what it means to reflect God's righteousness and holiness. Perhaps, then, the human reflection of the image of God does not refer to human nature or personhood in general, as the broadest structural concepts of the image hold (Grudem, Erickson, Hughes, Niebuhr, etc.), but rather emphasize things that presuppose such capacities. Increasing knowledge, righteousness, and holiness are set

32. Packer, *Knowing God*, 18.

33. Hoekema, *Created in God's Image*, 35.

34. Hodge, writing from a structural point of view, nevertheless gets at this point in saying, "By knowledge is not meant merely the faculty of cognition, the ability to acquire knowledge, but the contents of that faculty." Hodge, *Systematic Theology*, 2:101.

forth in Colossians 3 and Ephesians 4–5 as what it means to be renewed in God's image. Shall the church base the doctrine of the image of God on what these passages presuppose or on what they actually say?

Rationality and freedom are not ends in themselves, but rather means to ends. Brunner may overstate it slightly, but his point is nevertheless well-taken that reason, creativity, and freedom "do not contain their own meaning, but their meaning is love, true community."[35] Thus, proponents of the structural view are right to see the moral aspects, and love in particular as the highest virtue, as part of what it means for humans to be in the image and likeness of God, in view of Colossians 3:1–17 and Ephesians 4:17—5:20. And a practical benefit of this view is that Christians are challenged to imitate God in every way possible.[36] Ephesians 4:24 and 5:1–2 certainly emphasize believers imitating Jesus in the context of transformation into his image.

Related to the overemphasis on mental capacities, as Kilner points out, is the body-soul dualism presupposed in setting forth purely mental or spiritual capacities as the essence of the human likeness to God. This demeans the body as a lesser part of human beings.[37] Clearly the Hebraic view sees humans as whole beings. Their most important command/purpose is to "love the Lord your God with all your heart and with all your soul and with all your mind and with all your strength" (Mark 12:30). It requires the whole self with its material and non-material aspects to love God. And one cannot exercise godly dominion in creation as a mind detached from a body. The passages about God's image are not as concerned to satisfy ontological curiosity about the nature of humanity and their various aspects as to point to God's purposes for people as whole beings.

Another problem in the structural view is that it tends to draw the circle too large. Grudem, for example, provides many comparisons of abilities humans possess that animals do not (or at least not as much).[38] For instance, he says that whereas his young son is capable of understanding his father's instruction to go get a screwdriver from his workbench, a chimpanzee never could.[39] While that may be true, that does not

---

35. Brunner, *Man in Revolt*, 74.

36. E.g., Grudem, *Systematic Theology*, 449.

37. Kilner, *Dignity and Destiny*, 186.

38. Grudem, *Systematic Theology*, 448–49.

39. Grudem, *Systematic Theology*, 446.

mean the use of language is part of the image of God.[40] This is no minor point. Broaden the list of things included in the image of God too far and theology may lose sight of what Scripture sets forth as central in favor of what is peripheral or what is not included in any image text. Grudem has committed the former error by neglecting the stated purpose of the image of God in Genesis 1:26–28: dominion. He only mentions it in a footnote.[41] Yet its importance is evident in several passages in both testaments. The latter error may crop up when capacities like reason, freedom, and creativity are put at the heart of the image of God concept. Surely knowledge, righteousness, and holiness deserve more emphasis than reason, freedom, or creativity, which are not set forth as such in image texts. This is not to diminish the importance of these human capacities, but to say that they are not the essence of what it means to be made in God's image and may not even be included in the concept. They appear to be presupposed. The way such capacities are used, however, figures prominently in some of the passages examined above. The use of freedom to obey or disobey God is central to the creation and fall narratives. Genesis 4 highlights human inventions that stem from creativity as a way of tracking human progress in accomplishing the cultural commission. These capacities are vitally important to knowing God and exercising godly dominion in creation, but the image texts focus on the uses of such capacities rather than the capacities themselves.

The Relational View

A relational view of the image of God has been proposed by Emil Brunner. He distinguishes between formal and material aspects of the image. The formal image consists in humanity's relationship to God as a matter of objective fact. Humans are responsible to God and called into loving relationship to him, whether they respond positively or negatively to him. The material image refers to the actual response of faith, love, and obedience or the lack thereof.[42] Brunner's distinction is not between different parts of a person's being. He said "man is to be understood as a unity, from the point of view of man's relation to God, without the

40. For arguments against assuming that differences between people and animals tell us what the image of God is about, see Kilner, *Dignity and Destiny*, 109–12.

41. Grudem, *Systematic Theology*, 443n8.

42. Summarized in Kilner, *Dignity and Destiny*, 212.

distinction between nature and super-nature; this unified 'theological' nature is perverted by sin, but in this perversion it still always reveals the traces of the image of God in the human structure."[43] As noted above, Brunner sees sonship as a New Testament innovation on the concept of the image. He then pulls together some related concepts in a summary statement of his overall position.

> Sonship to God is spoken of as likeness to God, of the "imita-tion" of God, of "being holy as he is holy." Thus, with the idea of "sonship," or of being "children of God," the *Imago* doctrine, especially in connection with the doctrine of the original "son-ship" of Jesus Christ, comes into the very center of the New Testament message. "To be like him" (1 John 3:2) becomes ab-solutely the sum-total of the hope of salvation, and thus of the message of the New Testament as a whole. From this point of view alone, therefore, can we understand why the concept of the *Imago* has gained such an outstanding position in Christian doctrine, and especially in the theologians of the Reformation. In the New Testament, as has already been shown above, in the text—through the relation of the *Imago* to the Primal *Imago*, Je-sus Christ, to the Word of God, and thus to faith, the concept of the *Imago* is torn out of its Old Testament structural or morpho-logical rigidity, and the dynamic understanding of the *Imago*, as being-in-the-Word through faith, is established, which is the basic idea of my whole work.[44]

Brunner sees dominion as proceeding from being made in God's image. "The fact that man has been made in the Image of God, is primar-ily expressed—even if it does not consist in this—in man's position of pre-eminence which he now holds in the created world . . . as is expressed in Psalm viii."[45] Such an acknowledgement is fairly typical of those who hold relational as well as substantive views.

Karl Barth emphasizes that the proper starting point for anthropol-ogy is Christology.[46] Jesus is the image of God, the prototype for human beings, who are made *in* the image of God.[47] A human being is a visible counterpart to God, uniquely capable of being addressed by him in an

---

43. Brunner, *Man in Revolt*, 514.

44. Brunner, *Man in Revolt*, 501.

45. Brunner, *Man in Revolt*, 500.

46. Barth, *CD* 3/2 132.

47. Barth, *CD* 3/1 197–201.

I-Thou relationship. Barth believes that the differentiation of Adam and Eve as male and female in Genesis 1:27, following immediately after God's stated intent to create humans in his image and likeness, shows that the image is a fundamentally relational concept.[48] In the Divine deliberation of verse 26, the plurality of the Godhead (if not specifically the Trinity) was indicated, giving the human unity and diversity a divine reference point. Human dominion is a consequence of being made in the image, enabled by humanity's higher dignity and might.[49]

Dietrich Bonhoeffer also holds a relational view, but he relates it more closely to human dominion. He states it in terms of freedom for (rather than from) relationship to God first and foremost, then to one another, then to creation as stewards. Yet people are not exercising proper dominion. He calls technology "the power with which the earth seizes hold of humankind and masters it."[50] In an age in which people stare spellbound at cell phone screens for hours a day, Bonhoeffer's claim appears to be on solid ground—to say nothing of nuclear weapons and the many other dangers to life and limb posed by technology. Why do people fail to exercise dominion?

> The reason why we fail to rule, however, is because we do not know the world as God's creation and do not accept the dominion we have as God-given but seize hold of it for ourselves. There is no "being-free-from" without a "being-free-for." There is no dominion without serving God; in losing the one humankind necessarily loses the other. Without God, without their brothers and sisters, human beings lose the earth. Already in sentimentally shying away from exercising dominion over the earth, however, human beings have forever lost God and their brothers and sisters. God, the brother and sister, and the earth belong together. For those who have once lost the earth, however, for us human beings in the middle, there is no way back to the earth except via God and our brothers and sisters. From the inception humankind's way to the earth has been possible only as God's way to humankind. Only where God and the brother, the sister, come to them can human beings find their way back to the earth. Human freedom for God and the other person and

---

48. Barth, *CD* 3/1:183–85.

49. Barth, *CD* 3/1:187.

50. Bonhoeffer, *Creation and Fall*, 67.

human freedom from the creature in dominion over it constitute the first human beings' likeness to God.[51]

Jürgen Moltmann also views the image of God relationally, using
the language of freedom reminiscent of Bonhoeffer.[52] He then relates it to
dominion through the notion that the image represents God in creation
and acts in his name.[53] But people must do this according to the servant
pattern of Christ (rather than the violent usurping pattern of the beasts
of Daniel 7).[54] Karl Rahner and Herbert Vorgrimler have also advanced
this relational understanding that includes dominion in the context of
Roman Catholic theology.[55]

Stanley Grenz argues for a communal understanding, a variation of
the relational view. As with every other area of his theology, Grenz bases
this on his emphatically Trinitarian theology,[56] seeing human beings as
fundamentally relational because we reflect the fundamentally relational
Trinity of Father, Son, and Holy Spirit. Unlike Augustine, however, Grenz
does not look for three aspects of a human being to correspond to the
three persons of the Trinity in an analogy of being. Rather, the analogy is
one of relationship. He summarizes,

> In the final analysis, then, the *imago Dei* is not merely relational;
> it is not simply the I-Thou relationship of two persons standing
> face-to-face. Instead, it is ultimately communal. It is the escha-
> tological destiny of the new humanity as the representation of
> God within creation. The character of the triune God comes to
> expression through humans in community. Wherever commu-
> nity emerges, human sexuality understood in its foundational
> sense—the incompleteness endemic to embodied existence,
> together with the quest for completeness that draws humans out
> of isolation into bonded relationship—is at work. This sexuality
> gives rise to the primal male-female relationship—marriage. Yet
> more important is the role of sexuality in bringing humans into
> community with Christ and with his disciples in the fellowship
> of his church. This community forms the context for all humans,

51. Bonhoeffer, *Creation and Fall*, 67.

52. Moltmann, *Man*, 67.

53. Moltmann, *Man*, 108.

54. Moltmann, *Man*, 110–13.

55. Rahner and Vorgrimler, *Dictionary of Theology*, 228.

56. Note how Grenz narrates the outline of his systematic theology around the
motif of the Trinity. Grenz, *Theology for the Community of God*, 640–47.

male and female, to come together in harmonious creative relationships of various types. But more important, it is this connection that will eternally draw humankind into participation in the very life of the triune God, as the Spirit molds humans into one great chorus of praise to the Father through the Son, which in turn will mark the Father's eternal glorification of the new humanity in the Son.[57]

It is not the individual *per se* that is made in the image of God, it is persons in community, the social/ecclesial self. Christ lives in believers by his Spirit so that they are an extension of him. But Grenz denies that this undermines the importance of the individual, dissolving him/her into "an undifferentiated collective." Individuals remain objects of Jesus's love and are responsible to him.[58] There are a couple of ways people participate in the life of the triune God. One is by being adopted sons and daughters of God, thus sharing the sort of filial relationship with the Father that Jesus the Son of God has (Matt 6:9). Another way is the moral imitation of Christ by the power of the indwelling Holy Spirit.[59]

Elsewhere, Grenz poses the question of how the image of God is present in all people, not just the Christian community. He says there is a sense in which all humans are made in God's image, namely in that each person has the potential to participate in God's eschatological purposes. God assigns worth to each person, loves each one, and holds each one responsible.[60] One might characterize this as a static rather than dynamic reality that is about God's love for all people and his purpose that all people enjoy and return his love. It is a way to account for the statements in Scripture that all human beings are made in God's image even after the fall, but without recourse to human capacities like reason, will, memory, and so forth as in the structural view. Jesus, however, is the image of God, and those in union with him are thereby uniquely related to the image. Believers are in the process of transformation that will culminate in the resurrection, fully conforming them to the image of God.[61] Rather than viewing this as a return to Adam and Eve's state before the fall, Grenz sees this as the culmination of God's creation purposes for humans that will only be realized in the *eschaton*. In this eschatological orientation, as in

57. Grenz, *Social God*, 303.

58. Grenz, *Social God*, 333.

59. Grenz, *Social God*, 325.

60. Grenz, *Theology*, 2780–85.

61. Grenz, *Social God*, 278.

other ways, Grenz follows his mentor, Wolfhart Pannenberg, who said, "In the story of the human race, then, the image of God was not achieved fully at the outset. It was still in process . . . This full actualization is our destiny, one that was historically achieved with Jesus Christ and in which others may participate by transformation into the image of Christ."[62]

A final variation of a relational view must be considered because its proponent, John Kilner, is an important conversation partner in this work. He emphasizes that the only time Scripture defines the image of God, the image is said to be Jesus Christ (Col 1:15; 2 Cor 4:4). Humans are made in the image and likeness of God, that is, according to the pattern of Jesus the image.[63] This is usually acknowledged by interpreters, as we have seen, yet is sometimes left behind when it comes to the question of how sin impacts the image of God. Kilner seeks to base his doctrine firmly and consistently on the fact that Jesus is the image of God. That is, he wants to build anthropology on Christology.

People being made in the image and likeness of God is a single concept, since these two terms overlap and do not refer to separate aspects of human beings.[64] Kilner believes the image and likeness concept can best be summarized by the terms "connection" and "reflection." Regarding Jesus, Kilner explains, "Christ is intimately connected with God as God's exact imprint; as Christ, as the radiance of God's glory, magnificently reflects who God is and what God does."[65] As applied to human beings other than Christ, the image is a likeness image rather than an imprint image.[66] He says,

> Humanity is profoundly connected with God by virtue of God's eternal purposes for humanity. God intends for people to reflect who God is and what God does, though they may fall short of actually doing so now. While they do not warrant the title of "God's image" yet, they have dignity grounded in their destiny to become God's image—and so warrant that title once they are fully conformed to Christ. Until then, people are just "in" or "according to" God's image—always accountable to the standard of

---

62. Pannenberg, *Systematic Theology*, 2:217.

63. Kilner, *Dignity and Destiny*, 88–89.

64. Kilner, *Dignity and Destiny*, 124–26.

65. Kilner, *Dignity and Destiny*, 66.

66. Kilner, *Dignity and Destiny*, 59.

God's image, and developing toward that image as God enables and people endeavor.[67]

The eschatological orientation here is important. Humanity was not a full reflection of God the Son even before the fall. Development was needed and was God's goal for humanity, to be experienced once their whole selves became imperishable. The effect of the fall was that humans "lost most of our ability to reflect God," though this does not mean the image of God was damaged because Jesus is the image and was not and is not damaged in any way by human sin. Humans, however, are damaged and in need of renewal in the image of Christ.[68] But because human dignity is not based on the degree to which they currently reflect God but rather on their connectedness to God and his intention that they ultimately reflect him, their full dignity is intact. In his words, being in God's image is "more about God than about people."[69] Each person's current reflection of God may differ, but this has no bearing on each one's value. Dignity is an objective, static fact in that God bestows such dignity on everyone and intends for everyone to participate in the glorious destiny he offers. This grounds human dignity and full equality regardless of anyone's abilities, health, age, moral condition, relationship with God, or any other factor.[70]

It may be wondered why Kilner's view is classified under the relational category since his view sounds distinct from the other relational views we have considered. It stems from the term "connection." When discussing the relational view, Kilner remarks, "If all that someone means by associating relationship with image is that people have some connection with God that cannot be damaged and that serves as a basis for human dignity and human destiny, then such a view is in line with the biblically grounded understanding that the present book affirms."[71] Of course, he knows that is not all the relational views tend to affirm about the image. But it does show a general affinity with relational views. Kilner does see dominion as a purpose of the image, though he emphasizes that it is not what the image means. He has an unfortunate tendency to call rulership an attribute rather than a function. It is fair to say that

---

67. Kilner, *Dignity and Destiny*, 123.

68. Kilner, *Dignity and Destiny*, 132.

69. Kilner, *Dignity and Destiny*, 325.

70. Kilner, *Dignity and Destiny*, 313–16.

71. Kilner, *Dignity and Destiny*, 214.

his view does not fit well with royal/functional views overall.[72] As for the structural view, Kilner repeatedly emphasizes that the ways humans presently reflect God's attributes (including reason, relationship, and rulership) does not constitute the human likeness to God.[73] This might lead one to think such attributes have no share in his image doctrine, but not so. The accent is on the word *presently*. He says, "All people remain in God's image, not because they have wonderful God-like attributes such as reason, but because God's intention that they reflect them to God's glory has not changed ... This distinction between intended versus actual attributes is crucial."[74] Intended attributes, not attributes such as they are this side of the resurrection, count in reflecting God. Yet his view should not be included under the structural view because the latter generally sees the current state of these attributes as how humans, even fallen ones, image God, and therefore have great value. But Kilner bases human value squarely on humanity's connection with and future reflection of God.[75]

Is some version of the relational view the proper view of the image of God? The emphasis on the centrality of human relatedness to God is a vital presupposition of the gospel and of the image of God. God does offer each person love and relationship with himself and all of humanity. That love for God is an important aspect of the image of God is clear from the connection Genesis 5, Romans 8, Colossians 1, Hebrews 2, and 1 John 3 make between the image of God and sonship/daughtership.

Kilner makes a good point that the formal aspect of the relationship with God would be better conveyed by the term "connection" since "relationship" can easily be (mis)understood to imply participation on the part of people.[76] There are many people who refuse to participate in a relationship with God because they love their sin more than they love God. But this does not change the fact that they are connected to God, made in his likeness.

Some authors point out that Brunner's view, like Barth's, bears the marks of the existentialism that was so common in the first half of the twentieth century.[77] For Erickson, this means a "de-emphasis on essences

---

72. Kilner, *Dignity and Destiny*, 206–7.

73. E.g., Kilner, *Dignity and Destiny*, 177 and 227.

74. Kilner, *Dignity and Destiny*, 184.

75. Kilner, *Dignity and Destiny*, 311.

76. Kilner, *Dignity and Destiny*, 214n172.

77. Kilner, *Dignity and Destiny*, 220; Piper, "Image of God."

or substances" in favor of will and action.[78] On the other hand, the structural view is vulnerable to the opposite error because it overemphasizes substances, under Greek philosophical influence, perhaps at the expense of will and action. The Bible addresses issues of human substance in passages other than the image ones.[79] One need not adopt a structural view of the image to paint a biblically accurate picture of the things in human nature that enable a relationship with God. It should also be emphasized that not all relational views demonstrate the marks of existentialism like Barth's and Brunner's do. For example, Grenz's view sounds more like it is influenced by postmodern communitarianism.[80] Of course, the identification of existentialism does not automatically disqualify Barth's and Brunner's views. But Barth's notion that the creation of male and female explains the relational meaning of God's image seems to read into Genesis 1:26–27. Phyllis Bird says of Barth's view of Genesis 1 that he "has advanced only a novel and arresting variation of the classical Trinitarian interpretation, an interpretation characterized by the distinctly modern concept of an 'I-Thou' relationship, which is foreign to the ancient writer's thought and intention."[81] On the other hand, Grenz's communitarian view, if not pressed too far, coheres with the biblical teaching on "humankind" (Gen 1:27 NRSV) and on the new, corporate humanity in Colossians 3 and Ephesians 4. So the question is not so much about whether the *zeitgeist* influences one's view of the image, but whether the *zeitgeist* brings to one's attention what God reveals in Scripture or blocks one from seeing it in any given instance.

An additional point relates to sticking with the emphasis of the image texts. Bonhoeffer says, "Human freedom for God and the other person and human freedom from the creature in dominion over it constitute the first human beings' likeness to God."[82] In light of what was said about freedom above, it would be better to emphasize love and righteousness rather than the freedom presupposed by love and righteousness. Existentialism favors the concept of freedom presupposed by loving relationship, but Scripture sets forth the love itself between God and us and us and

78. Erickson, *Christian Theology*, 508.

79. E.g., Num 5:2; 6:6; Matt 10:28; 1 Thess 5:23; Heb 4:12; 12:23; Jas 2:26; Rev 6:9. For a helpful discussion of this, see Grenz, *Theology*, 2458–637.

80. For the general assessment that Grenz has uncritically accepted postmodernism, see Carson, "Domesticating the Gospel," 45.

81. Bird, "Male and Female He Created Them," 132.

82. Bonhoeffer, *Creation and Fall*, 67.

each other as central. This is so even though freedom is a part of the fall narrative, specifically implied when God gives Adam and Eve a choice of whether or not to eat from the tree of the knowledge of good and evil. The emphasis in image texts is not upstream with freedom, but downstream with obedience. Love, though only implied in the Genesis narrative (by God's blessing Adam and Eve, providing for them, placing them in his own garden, and walking among them), is strongly emphasized in Colossians 3, Ephesians 4–5, and implicitly in the filial emphasis in Romans 8 and Hebrews 2. Sticking to the main emphases of the image texts narrows the image concept, in this case illuminating the filial relationship and the centrality of righteousness.

The Royal/Functional View

The royal/functional view emphasizes human dominion over creation in its understanding of the image of God. The precise way in which image and dominion are related may vary. Clines says that human dominion "cannot be definitive of the image" for such would be too narrow. But because dominion is such an immediate consequence of the image, "it loses the character of a mere derivative of the image and virtually becomes a constitutive part of the image itself." He appeals to the phrase "so that they may rule" in Genesis 1:26 for support.[83] Numerous Old Testament scholars see dominion as a/the stated purpose for God's creating humans in his image and likeness in Genesis 1. For some, humans occupy the role of representatives of God in creation, carrying out his dominion-related purposes (procreation, filling the earth, subduing the earth, ruling over the animals, building godly cultures, etc.).

That is the view of Middleton, who says that the image of God refers to "human rule, that is, the exercise of power on God's behalf in creation," implying both a representational sense (similarity to God) and a representative sense (the function of ruling as God's representatives).[84] The latter sense may have been in Middleton's mind when he spoke of human beings carrying out the cultural commission by building cities, making music, crafting tools for efficient and effective work, farming, and so on (as is evident in Genesis 4). There is an analogy with God when it comes to such activities and the qualities it takes to carry them out: "Just as God

83. Clines, "Image of God," 96.
84. Middleton, *Liberating Image*, 88.

constructed the cosmos (heaven and earth) by wisdom, understanding, and knowledge (Prov 3:19–20), so humans require this very same triad of qualities when they build a house (Prov 24:3–4)."[85] Against the background of the temple as a microcosm of creation, Middleton sees the human vocation as mediating God's presence in creation. In humanity's role as representatives of God, they are to imitate his love, generosity, peacefulness, and care, being a blessing to the creation he has entrusted to their care and towards one another. This is in sharp contrast to violent, oppressive, and selfish ways humans sometimes have used and continue to use power on one another, animals, and the created order. To bring *shalom* to everyone and everything they touch is a priestly responsibility. Jesus is the paradigm of this, the image of God, the model for the new humanity to follow as the Holy Spirit leads and empowers them, progressively conforming them to his image until the resurrection completes the process. The purposes for which God made people in his image will be fulfilled in the new creation, when all the earth is filled with God's glory, the cultural mandate is fulfilled (in the New Jerusalem), and community is properly formed.[86]

To say that dominion is God's purpose for making people in his image implies to some a distinction between dominion and image. Beale, for example, after explaining that images represent the sovereign presence of the one imaged in the ancient Near East, says, "Nevertheless, there is likely an additional ontological aspect of the 'image' by which humanity was enabled to reflect the functional image. For example, Adam was made in the volitional, rational, and moral image of God, so that, with regard to the latter, he was to reflect moral attributes such as righteousness, knowledge, holiness, love, faithfulness, and integrity (for the first three attributes as part of the divine image, see Eph 4:24; Col 3:10), and above all he was to reflect God's glory."[87]

Thus, proponents of the royal view may combine an emphasis on human dominion under God with ontological/structural characteristics and/or relational considerations. J. Rodman Williams, for example, reflects an eclectic approach that includes all three major views on the image of God. Man is to reflect God in his dominion, being, and character.[88] The

---

85. Middleton, "Image of God," 395.

86. Middleton, "Image of God," 396–97.

87. Beale, *New Testament Biblical Theology*, 32.

88. Williams, *Renewal Theology*, 201–8.

reverse is true as well: structural views of the image sometimes include human dominion and relationships (with God, others, and creation) and relational models of the image sometimes include dominion and/or structural characteristics. In such eclectic views, the differences are sometimes a matter of which consideration receives the most emphasis or the precise way the various elements relate to each other. These are, of course, not the only differences, but seeing the issue this way helps people to understand that the lines between the various schools of thought are sometimes fluid. The tendency to combine the insights of these views is strong.

Is some version of the royal/functional view correct? Erickson answers in the negative, saying that Genesis 1:26 distinguishes the image of God and its consequence, dominion, with the two hortatory expressions, "Let us make man in our image, after our likeness," and "let them have dominion."[89] But Kilner, who also answers in the negative, says that the relationship between image and dominion is closer than is implied by the term "consequence." God created humans in his image and likeness "so that they may rule."[90] Purpose rather than consequence more accurately describes the relationship. Yet even that may not be close enough. Once again, rule is implied in *ṣelem* and is the purpose for which God made people in his image. He made them rulers so that they might rule. But now believers must make sure to filter this truth through the lens of Jesus Christ. Since Jesus is himself the image of God, the divine Son, people are made according to his pattern, as royal sons and daughters of God, in order that they might represent God and carry out his beneficent rule by caring for creation and fulfilling the cultural commission.

This brings up another objection by Kilner: human rule is marred and even lost. "At present we do not see everything subject to them. But we do see Jesus" (Heb 2:8–9). Human participation in God's reign is a future reality, not a present one.[91] But there are many different activities involved in rulership, including procreating, raising godly offspring, farming, taming and caring for animals, making scientific discoveries, developing new technologies to aid them in all such tasks, resisting evil, enforcing justice, etc. Surely progress has been made in many of these areas. Even by the time Genesis 4 was written, there had apparently been some progress. By the time James 3:7 was written, even more progress

---

89. Erickson, *Christian Theology*, 512.

90. Kilner, *Dignity and Destiny*, 207.

91. Kilner, *Dignity and Destiny*, 204.

had been made: "All kinds of animals, birds, reptiles and sea creatures are being tamed and have been tamed by mankind." God supplies people with the ability to make some progress on these fronts just by common grace, to say nothing of saving grace. Hebrews 2:8–9 probably does not mean that no progress at all has been made towards human dominion, but rather that human dominion has not yet been fully accomplished. Dominion comes in degrees. It is already under way, but not yet fully accomplished. Bonhoeffer also pointed to human failure to rule: "We do not rule; instead we are ruled. The thing, the world, rules humankind; humankind is a prisoner, a slave, of the world, and its dominion is an illusion. Technology is the power with which the earth seizes hold of humankind and masters it."[92] Yet he does not eliminate the royal function from his image of God doctrine, even in its current phase. He rather paints the picture of human failure to exercise dominion apart from Christ.[93] But again, the restoration of humanity begins before the *eschaton*, so does not their ability to exercise proper dominion grow before the *eschaton*? Recall that Ephesians spoke of "the church, which is his body, the fullness of him who fills everything in every way" (Eph 1:22–23). This suggests that Christ is accomplishing the cultural commission through his people even now. And Revelation 21:26 says "the glory and honor of the nations will be brought into" the New Jerusalem, suggesting that there were cultural artifacts God accepts as worship. Such artifacts seem to be things made before the new creation. Human dominion should be viewed within the already and not yet timetable that makes sense of so many other biblical teachings like resurrection, adoption, and the kingdom of God. Humans exercise dominion already, but in a sinful and incomplete way. Whatever dominion that is good and proper is a foretaste of the dominion of the world to come.

One of Kilner's objections to the notion that rulership is what it means to be made in God's image is that, if it were, we would expect to see the notion in all the image texts. Yet we do not.[94] But the redemptive-historical analysis above has shown that dominion is a major theme throughout many of the image texts. This Kilner does not acknowledge because he narrows the context down too much in some image passages. For example, he says that in Genesis 9, dominion over animals in verses

92. Bonhoeffer, *Creation and Fall*, 67.
93. Bonhoeffer, *Creation and Fall*, 66.
94. Kilner, *Dignity and Destiny*, 202.

2–5b is left behind by the time God's image comes up in verse 6. Yet the image gives the reason people will be held accountable for the shedding of human blood, as also animals will be held accountable for killing humans (not vice versa). Similarly, James 3:7 mentions humans taming animals before going on in verse 9 to forbid cursing humans. But Kilner does not see how the latter relates to the former. In this way, he discounts rulership in some image passages. He says that Colossians 3:10 is not about rulership. It is true that rule is not the emphasis in Colossians 3. Rather, moral transformation is the focus. But Colossians 1:15–18 is about Jesus's rulership as the image of God. Surely when Paul comes back to the subject of the image of God in chapter 3, one should understand ruling with Christ as relevant to the believer's transformation in some way. The point may be implicit, but it may well parallel the thought in Hebrews 2 that Jesus makes his brothers and sisters holy and thus qualified to rule the earth under him. Paul is connecting believers with Christ in terms of a filial relationship with God and human dominion, implying what Revelation 2:26–27 comes out and says, that believers will reign with Christ (applying the Psalm 2 Messianic rule over the nations to Christians who overcome deception and temptation). Kilner similarly says Ephesians 4:24 lacks any reference to ruling, but the parallel with Colossians suggests the same implicit connection between the reign of Christ and the reign of his people, with an emphasis on the righteous character God's people will need. Kilner says Romans 8:29 is not about rulership yet verses 19–23 parallel creation's and our own groaning for liberation and renewal. The creation groans because God had cursed it to punish people for sinning. Humanity's adoption and resurrection mean its days of being cursed are over. This presumes human dominion: their actions profoundly affect the world with which they have been entrusted as stewards. One passage he correctly sees no apparent reference to rulership in is 2 Corinthians 3:18.[95] But this is no real difficulty since it, like Colossians 3 and Ephesians 4–5, is making a point about increasing moral transformation. Hebrews 2 makes a similar point about Christ making his brothers and sisters holy, which is necessary for them to exercise the dominion that Christ is going to bring about. Rulership is a predominant theme in the image texts and should not be marginalized in the overall image doctrine, even this side of the resurrection.

---

95. See Kilner, *Dignity and Destiny*, 202–3.

Again, Kilner objects that not everyone has the same capacity to rule, so this concept of the image would mean some are more in God's image than others and thus more valuable.[96] Recall that Kilner sees human dominion in the new creation as a purpose for which people were made in God's image and as an intended reflection of God. That is surely the case. Whereas people cannot reliably speculate on how exactly God views people, it seems safe to suggest that God is not limited by time. He probably views people in terms of his purposes for them, purposes that are logically prior to creation and that run on into the new creation. His view is probably not restricted to the current moment in anyone's life. Further, the effects of the fall are on all people, no matter what their abilities. People have a tendency to think others are less valuable than themselves for various reasons like disabilities or a lack of empowerment in a given society, as Kilner suggests. Yet rather than this being a reasonable inference from the dominion concept of the image, it seems to be a sinful and opportunistic distortion of the idea, especially in view of the wide variety of ways humans exercise dominion—a fact some may easily lose sight of if focusing on their own particular niche in the world. Rather than focusing on the object of such a negative evaluation, perhaps people should focus on the subject of the evaluation. The person who looks down upon another as if she is not as much like God is himself failing to reflect God by that very condescending attitude.

A Royal Family View

This is the view defended in this dissertation. It is not a new view, but one that first and foremost attempts to do justice to the redemptive-historical analysis of the image of God provided above and, secondly, learns from the major views and sets them forth in a way that attempts to maximize the strengths and avoid certain weaknesses of those views. It can be called a royal family view because it seems that being God's children, reflecting God's righteous character, and exercising dominion are deeply interrelated.

It seems best to express the idea in the form of a story, since even the moral and doctrinal passages, and more obviously the narrative passages, are a story. God made human beings to be his children, and the children of a king are royalty, with the responsibilities and privileges that come with being in a royal family. The responsibilities stem from the king's

96. Kilner, *Dignity and Destiny*, 205.

creation project, a world he wants to fill with living beings of all sorts, including his own "progeny." Thus, he created and appointed his children to farm, garden, build civilizations, watch over everything, steward the earth's resources, and look after the animals. They were the only ones who really could do such a thing, provided they multiplied themselves and filled the earth. They would act on his behalf and in his interests and for the good of all they oversaw. And he would walk among them in close fellowship because he loves them and wants them to love him and each another. The more they love him, the more they will love one another and take care of the earth and its animals, as well as keep evil, the privation of good, from spoiling the entire project. Imitating his benevolent character, they will work for the flourishing of all their Father had made and this, in turn, will lead to their intended flourishing. As God's children, all human beings would imitate his pattern of work punctuated by rest and his self-giving love, holiness, and righteousness. All would grow in wisdom as they made discoveries, explored and filled the world, and most of all, got to know their Father over the whole course of their lives. These children have the mark of their Father's glory in them and as they fill the earth, they fill it with God's glory and extend his dominion worldwide.

But Adam and Eve rebelled against God. As one consequence, God the Father was not the only one being imitated. Adam and Eve were too, and so was the devil himself. There came to be a division in humanity between those who know God and those who know about him but refuse to love and obey him. No one in either group is perfect, but generally those in the former group repent and trust in God and try to imitate and obey him as their Father, whereas those in the latter group do not. Are people in both groups still children of God or only the penitent faithful? Both are children of God in some sense. "We are his offspring," Paul told the Athenians in Acts 17:28. God created each and every human being to be his child.[97] This purpose predates any individual's life, choices, sins, or death. It even predates the fall in that God purposed to create all people before he actually did. When God views people, it seems that he does not merely see their present acts or condition, but also their place in his affections and purposes that both predate creation and carry on into the eternal future in the new creation. He is not bound by time, so his view of human beings is not bound by time. Thus, when his intended children imitate someone other than him for their ruin, he still views them in

---

97. Berkhof, *Systematic Theology*, 202. Similarly, see Brunner, *Man in Revolt*, 500–501.

terms of his eternal love and beneficent purposes for them, even if he deals with them in space and time according to their actions and character and even if there are conditions that must be met to participate in his beneficent purposes. Fallen and unrepentant people are God's children by his design, purpose, and love, but not by their will. Nothing they can ever do will change the fact that they are related to their Creator. All people have such a connection with God whether they want it or not. Like the prodigal son of Luke 15:11–32, rebellious children of God have chosen to run from their father so they may live as they wish, with disastrous results. Their straying has led to humiliation, the result of the Father's exilic discipline (Jer 31:18–19; Hos 11:5–7). The highway to hell is far less fun than the party AC/DC imagines.

But something changes when prodigals return to the Father. It is not God's love for them, nor his purposes for them. It is, among other things, their willingness to return and live as his children, under his authority and blessing. There is a willingness to be associated with him, to come clean for wrongdoings (note the penitent prodigal son in Luke 15:17 and 21, perhaps echoing penitent Israel in Jer 31:19 and Hos 11:10), to seek help in leaving vices behind and gaining virtues of character in kind with the Father and his preeminent Son, Jesus, the very pattern of how the rest of humanity should be. Only through the work of Jesus to take the punishment for sins and break the power of sin over people would any of them ever return—or rather be drawn back in—by the compassionate Father, who is overjoyed to receive them (Luke 15:20–24; Jer 31:20; Hos 11:8). As N. T. Wright remarks, the parable of the prodigal son could also be called "the parable of the Running Father."[98]

Through the Son, who is in a sense humanity's elder brother but in another sense ontologically one with the Father, previously exiled offspring approach the Father and resume a personal relationship and their place in the creation project (Jer 31:18 and Hos 11:10–11). They are said to be adopted as God's children and enjoy the benefits of a personal relationship with the Father and stand to inherit all that the Father has promised those who return to him. Again, it is not that people were not God's children, but their willful absence from and mutiny against the Father's authority changed the dynamics of the relationship as experienced in a fallen world. The term "adoption" (*huiothesia*; see Rom 8:15, 9:4; Eph

---

98. Wright, *Luke For Everyone*, 187. Elders did not stoop to something as undignified as running in that society, which underscores the great compassion and love of the father for his returning son in the parable and of God for his returning children in reality.

1:5; Gal 4:5) highlights the new filial and legal circumstance of being a willing part of God's family as compared with the flight from and rebellion against him that drove a wedge between people and their Father and rendered them disqualified to inherit what he promised his redeemed children. The Holy Spirit assures them of their filial relationship with the Father as they are drawn into the love of the Trinity. The Spirit also empowers and enlivens them to become Christlike and godly in imitation of their elder brother and Father, as well as empowering them to be courageous witnesses so that others will be drawn into this filial relationship and eternal creation plan.

It is not as though humanity in rebellion against God totally fail to accomplish the cultural commission. The Father has ways of seeing to it that his purposes in the creation project get accomplished even by rebellious people, whose basic desires are nevertheless God-given. The world is now full of people, the earth is being farmed, discoveries are being made, natural resources are being used in ever more creative ways to improve lives, animals are being watched over and tamed, etc. And much of this is done by people who have not returned to the Father. But those who have returned to the Father have the opportunity to intentionally and effectively accomplish the Father's purposes in creation, empowered by the Holy Spirit, inspired by humanity's paradigm Jesus, and accompanied by the Father until Jesus returns. Then he will fully establish justice, unity, and peace on earth in the final, consummated eternal kingdom of God in a renewed creation wherein the dominion of God and his resurrected children is fully accomplished and their relationship with the Father is fully enjoyed with no hint of the rebellion or wickedness that had previously marred life in the world.

Jesus is the image of God who both reveals what God is like and provides the pattern, the paradigm of character, knowledge, righteousness, holiness, and love that the rest of God's children are to imitate by Divine power. He is the royal Son who rules over creation at the Father's side. Believers are the children of the King, royal by nature in principle, but only experientially if they fully accept the Father's terms by which to participate again in the filial and legal relationship with the Father. Because Jesus is the image and people are made in the image, it is not accurate to say that the image is damaged by sin. Jesus remains sinless. But the human reflection of God's knowledge, love, righteousness, and holiness in their character and actions is deeply affected by sin, a fact seen in all aspects of human nature, relationships, and life on earth.

Humanity's being made in God's image, then, means God made them and intends to renew them according to the pattern of Jesus Christ, who is the image of God. He is the Son of God (albeit in a unique, divine way); they are sons and daughters of God. He is set to reign supreme over God's kingdom in creation; they are set to reign with him over creation. He is perfectly loving, righteous, holy, and wise; they grow in love, righteousness, holiness, and wisdom until God perfects them according to the paradigm of Jesus's character. All people are connected to the Father whether they want to be or not. All people are invited to share in this destiny whether they choose to take part or not. *Thus, a human being made in God's image is a royal son/daughter by nature who is meant to enjoy relationships with God and his family and reflect his virtuous character while sharing dominion in creation with the family.* They are that by design whether they are believers or not, but nonbelievers forfeit the filial and legal benefits when they refuse to associate with God and his children. People may resume that relationship with the Father by repentance and faith. Only if they do so will they be empowered and guided by the Holy Spirit to the point of fully reflecting the knowledge, righteousness, holiness, and love of God progressively this side of the resurrection and fully at the resurrection. What nonbelievers do not forfeit is dignity, that is, objective value. God values all people equally whether believer or nonbeliever, male or female, heterosexual or LGBTQ+, slave or free, of whatever ethnicity or nationality. Because God loves people as a good father loves his children, even the rebellious ones, they all have objective value, an idea to be considered further in the next chapter.

God also values his children instrumentally and functionally like a farmer values his children's contributions to the work of the farm. But obviously, no loving father merely values his children instrumentally. They are ends and not merely means. But like all beings created for purposes that include non-relational ones along with the relational ones, they are means as well. If all God cared about with regard to his children was a good relationship, he might well have created them as souls floating around a non-physical dimension, enjoying him and one another, but not as embodied beings put in charge of a physical creation project with a commission. The creation is not only the backdrop for their relationship with God, though it is that, it is also something God values in itself, and the creation project is something God intended to engage in with his children. What God called good they should regard as good as well. They were made for creation like muscle cars were made for the street. It is their natural habitat. The Father designed it for them and them for it. He made it clear how much he values this creation project by walking among humanity in it (in Eden), sending his Son into it as a human, raising his Son physically from the dead, and promising he will return and renew creation and dwell among them forever.

These contributions to the creation project are beautifully paralleled in C. S. Lewis's creation story in *The Chronicles of Narnia*. After Aslan (who represents Jesus) created the world in which Narnia was set, he appointed a cab driver and his wife Nellie to be the first king and queen of Narnia. They were astonished at such a daunting task and so Aslan blessed them and, calling them "my children," described what he expected of them, saying,

> You shall rule and name all these creatures, and do justice among them, and protect them from their enemies when enemies arise. And enemies will arise, for there is an evil Witch in this world . . . Can you use a spade and a plow and raise food out of the earth? . . . Can you rule these creatures kindly and fairly, remembering that they are not slaves like the dumb beasts of the world you were born in, but Talking Beasts and free subjects? . . . And would you bring up your children and grandchildren to do the same? . . . And you wouldn't have favorites either among your own children or among the other creatures or let any hold another under or use it hardly? . . . And if enemies came against the land (for enemies will arise) and there was war, would you be the first in the charge and the last in the retreat?[99]

Though the parallels are not perfect, they are clear. The Creator relates to the couple as a father relates to his children. He blesses them and appoints them for important responsibilities. He enumerates their responsibilities: farming, naming the animals, ensuring impartial justice, treating those under their care as free creatures rather than slaves, opposing evil, and teaching their descendants to carry on these same responsibilities. As they multiply, they and their progeny establish new nations, build civilizations, and carry out all such responsibilities until the climactic battle culminates in the victory of good over evil and the new creation ensues.[100]

The above summary is not meant to be a comprehensive statement of Christian doctrine in story form, but to outline the story of God's

99. Lewis, *Magician's Nephew*, 149–52.

100. The battle and new creation are the subject of Lewis, *Last Battle*, 143–211.

family and creation project as it relates specifically to the image of God. The analyses of various theologians have brought certain things to light and should be acknowledged. The influence of relational views is evident in the idea of a connection that gives humans dignity as those loved and valued by God (Kilner). This connection exists whether individual people accept or reject God, an idea common in all relational views, particularly emphasized in Barth, Brunner, and Kilner. The emphasis on sonship/daughtership, particularly the relational emphasis, is inspired by Brunner's insight that the theme moved to the center of the New Testament concept of the image, though the beginnings of the idea can be seen in Genesis 5:1–3. The emphasis on not only relationship with God, but relationship with everyone else in a large family picks up Grenz's communitarian emphasis, though without buying into the whole thought about the socially constructed self so prevalent in postmodern thought. Perhaps most inspiring of all was Bonhoeffer's view that relationship with God, one another, and all creation are deeply intertwined. This makes sense of the royal connotation of *ṣelem* and means that the many interpreters who argue against the royal/functional view because, they say, dominion as a consequence or purpose should be distinguished from the image that enables or grounds dominion, have missed something. When a king has children, they are royal automatically. Their part in the kingdom is part of their purpose simply by their being a part of that family. The family and what they are doing together are deeply interconnected and should not be separated in a way that makes relationship less important than dominion nor dominion superfluous. This is so even though eternal life is knowing God (John 17:3), giving relationship with God precedence over functional dominion. But those functional considerations are exactly what are needed to explain why the Old Testament spends so much time telling the story of God reestablishing dominion in the Old Testament through his kingdom of priests, his holy nation, particularly through the Davidic dynasty, as well as why the central theme of Jesus's teaching was the kingdom of God. As important as individual salvation is, the biblical hope Jesus taught believers to pray for was for God's kingdom to come on earth (Matt 6:10). The Bible begins with creation and ends with new creation, so the creational context matters to God.

The influence of the royal/functional views has also been evident throughout this work. The focus on the cultural commission and how it connects with the Great Commission aligns with Beale's, Dempster's, and Christopher Wright's writings. Middleton's emphasis on imitating the beneficent dominion of God is retained here as well. N. T. Wright's notion of the creation and new creation project with God as its King and humans serving as his kingdom of priests is found in this overall story as well. And the royal connotations of *ṣelem* in the ancient Near East so commonly noted among those who emphasize the dominion aspect of the image is a building block of this view.

A few remarks about synthesizing the biblical material are needed. First, it seems justifiable to omit capacities like reason, free will, and relational abilities from the image of God because they were not, in and of themselves, set forth in the image texts as being what it means to be made in God's image and likeness. It is certainly true that only beings with such personal capacities (inherent, natural capacities rather than currently exercisable ones, but that point must be developed below) could be in God's image. After all, to have a personal relationship with God, one must be a person. And personal relationship is the primary purpose for which he created people as his children. Likewise, in order to exercise godly dominion, representing the personal God, they must be personal beings. Yet that does not make such personal capacities part of God's image. They seem to be presupposed since the image texts that speak of renewal in God's image speak, not in terms of the capacities themselves, but outcomes that presuppose such capacities like knowledge, holiness, righteousness, and love. It may be that when God speaks of human likeness to himself, he has these capacities in mind too. But if that were the case, why would he not name these capacities in the image texts?

On a related note, when one sees possible warrant in a number of different views, it is very tempting to simply combine all of those views into a larger perspective. Perhaps it is better to include too much than too little in one's doctrine of the image so as not to miss something. But examples examined earlier cast such a wide net that a key biblical emphasis, in Grudem's case, dominion, was lost in the shuffle. The doctrine of the image of God confronts people with the human purpose, and it seems that a clear and sharp understanding of that purpose is important enough to commend the value of deciding from among the various views. One must narrow down the concept as much as Scripture does, but no further.

The relational, Father-child context of the image concept is clear from the many times it was assumed or included in image texts: Genesis 5:1–3; Acts 17:28–29; Colossians 1:15 and 3:17; Ephesians 5:1–2; Romans 8:14–30 (repeatedly); James 3:9; Hebrews 2:10–14; and 1 John 3:1–3. Brunner is surely correct that believer's filial relationship with God is at the heart of the concept. Any doctrine of the image of God that lacks this would be incomplete.

The theme of dominion is central in a number of texts, some of which also include the filial relationship, which will be noted in parentheses here: Genesis 1:26–27 and 9:6; Psalm 8; Daniel 2:35; Colossians 1:15–20 (includes the filial relationship); 2 Corinthians 4:4–6; Romans 8:18–29 (includes the filial relationship); 1 Corinthians 15:20–58; James 3:9 (see vv. 7–8; includes the filial relationship); and Hebrews 2:5–13 (includes the filial relationship); Revelation 13:14–15. By comparing these two lists, it seems clear that the image of God doctrine must include both filial and royal components and attempt to relate them to each other in keeping with the teaching of those texts. The view here defended is an attempt to do so.

The theme of moral virtue was clear in several texts. We will note in parentheses when there is also a filial and/or dominion-oriented theme included as well: Colossians 3:1–17 (includes the filial relationship); Ephesians 4:17—5:20 (includes the filial relationship); 2 Corinthians 3:18; 1 Corinthians 15:49 (includes dominion); Hebrews 2:5–13 (includes both the filial relationship and dominion); and 1 John 3:1–3 (includes the filial relationship). Two of these texts (Col 3:13 and Eph 4:32—5:2) teach believers to imitate their Father and/or Jesus. Hebrews 2:10–13 says Jesus makes us holy so that he will not be ashamed to call believers his brothers and sisters, which suggests family likeness in terms of holiness. This comports with Matthew 5:48 and Luke 6:36, which teach believers to imitate the Father's perfection and mercy. Figure 1 visually represents the findings of the last three paragraphs for the sake of clarity and easy reference.

In spite of the filial relationship evident in multiple image texts, Kilner takes issue with equating the parent-child relationship with what it means to be made in God's image, though he does agree that they should be associated somewhat on the basis of Romans 8:29; Hebrews 2:11; 1 John 3:2; Genesis 5:1–3; Luke 3:38; and Acts 17:28–29.[101] But, he says, saying that all people are God's children is not entirely accurate. Only those who believe and receive Christ are God's children (John 1:12). Paul argues that "it is not the children by physical descent who are God's children, but rather the children of the promise who are regarded as Abraham's offspring" (Rom 9:8). In verse 26, he quotes Hosea 1:10, "In

---

101. Kilner, *Dignity and Destiny*, 295–97.

the very place where it was said to them, 'You are not my people,' there
they will be called 'children of the living God.'" In Hosea's day, Israel had
abandoned God and consequently God disowned them, only to later
bring them back. In Paul's day, it was the gentiles who had not been his
people but were now being welcomed as children of God. Jesus made a
distinction between children of the devil and God's children (John 8:42–
47; see also 1 John 3:10).[102]

IMAGE TEXT	FILIAL?	DOMINION?	VIRTUE?
GEN 1:26–27	Implicit?	Yes	
GEN 5:1–3	Yes		
GEN 9:6		Yes	
EXOD 20:4–6			
PS 8:5		Yes	
DAN 2:35, 3:1		Yes	
MATT 22:20–21			Implicit?
COL 1:15	Yes	Yes	
2 COR 4:4		Yes	
1 COR 11:7		Yes	
ACTS 17:28–29	Yes		
COL 3:9–10	Yes		Yes
EPH 4:22–24	Yes		Yes
2 COR 3:18			Yes
1 COR 15:49		Yes	Yes
ROM 8:29	Yes	Yes	Yes
JAS 3:9	Yes	Yes	
HEB 2:5–11	Yes	Yes	Yes
1 JN 3:2–3	Yes		Yes
REV 13:14–15		Yes	

But even in saying that the equation of image and being children of
God is problematic, Kilner qualifies his statement by saying "only Christians are God's children *in the fullest sense* [emphasis mine]."[103] Again,
only the penitent and faithful are God's children in the sense of adopted
or received back into the filial and legal relationship. As Kilner says, Paul
does use a generic term for offspring, *genos*, in Acts 17:28–29, as opposed
to the more intimate *teknon* in passages like Romans 8:17 and Ephesians
5:1. But that makes good sense on the royal family view. Rebellious children who forfeit the close relationship as well as their inheritance rights
are related to their Father but are not close enough to warrant the more
intimate term. As for the children of the devil, the issue in Jesus's dialogue with his opponents in John 8 was who they were following. His

102. Kilner, *Dignity and Destiny*, 296–97.
103. Kilner, *Dignity and Destiny*, 297.

opponents were children of Abraham, ethnically speaking. But if they were Abraham's children in the sense of having Abraham's faith, they would not be trying to kill Jesus, as they were, for Abraham would not have done so (vv. 39–40). In trying to kill Jesus, they were imitating the devil (vv. 41 and 44). Had they been God's children in the salvific sense, they would have loved Jesus (v. 44). It seems that there is a sort of reverse adoption, wherein you can be an adopted child of the devil just by virtue of imitating his evil behavior. But even this does not change the fundamental fact that people are connected with God, as Kilner agrees. To call humans God's "offspring" names that connection. And adoption takes people from being mere offspring to being sons and daughters at peace with their Father.

What Was God's Purpose for Making Humanity in His Image and Likeness?

Genesis 1:26–28 makes clear that at least one of God's purposes, the very first stated purpose, for creating humans in his image and likeness was that human beings will exercise dominion on earth. This dominion over land and creatures is to be carried out in accordance with the benevolence and generosity God displayed towards all of his creation and creatures, including people. Genesis 2 pictures God placing Adam and Eve in the garden of Eden to "work it and take care of it" (Gen 2:15), the beginning of the accomplishment of the cultural commission to exercise dominion. They also bore children, another key aspect of dominion (Gen 4:1–2; 5:1–3). If trained properly, children would do "what is right and just" and so receive the Abrahamic promises of land, descendants, blessings, and in turn be a blessing to others (Gen 18:19; 12:1–3), a covenant God established to get the creation project back on track after the fall. The resulting godly culture contrasts with the ungodly cultures seen throughout biblical history, notably Babel (Gen 11) and its seed, Babylon (Isa 13; Rev 17–18). The kingdom of God produces people who yield the good fruit of righteousness and justice (Isa 5:1–7 and Matt 21:33–46). Dominion involves all sorts of human endeavors like agriculture, animal husbandry, procreation, family life, the cultivation of the arts (Gen 4:19–21), and the building of cities and cultures (Rev 21–22). Charlie Self offers a partial list of ways Christians have engaged in such endeavors in obedience to Scripture and to the benefit of the world:

abolition movements to end all forms of slavery;

establishing fair legal systems;

charitable efforts, especially in caring for the broken, poor, and vulnerable;

affirming the sanctity of every human life, from conception to coronation;

creating environments for entrepreneurs to flourish and to lift the community's economy and welfare;

education expansions and reforms;

intellectual inquiry and the organization and preservation of knowledge;

framing the role of government as subsidiary to church, family, and conscience, yet a partner with other agencies for good;

fostering the arts, including music and visual expressions.[104]

Humanity, crowned with glory and honor (Ps 8:5), is responsible to glorify and worship God and to bear his glorious presence throughout the earth. Solomon prays that he may rule with justice (Ps 72:1–2) over all the earth (v. 8) so that "all nations will be blessed through him" (v. 17). Then he prays for the end result of all of this: "Praise be to his glorious name forever; may the whole earth be filled with his glory" (v. 19). The kingdom of God through David's lineage thus becomes crucial for the accomplishment of God's dominion purpose.

In the New Testament, the image of God was associated with sonship and daughtership (e.g., Rom 8:29), perhaps picking up on the connection in Genesis 5:1–3. This suggests that relational intimacy with God is a purpose of creating us in God's image. God wants a large family of children who bear a family resemblance to him, reflecting his righteousness, holiness, knowledge, and especially love (Col 3:10; Eph 4:22–24). Thus, one could speak of a moral purpose for being created in God's image. The relational purpose is not entirely distinct from the moral one, nor are either of these purposes cut off from the royal/functional purpose. They are intertwined. Humanity's Father planned the creation project as a family project and has a niche within it for each son and daughter with our various talents and interests. The character and behavior of each son and daughter matters with respect to their relationship with God in that sin is mutiny that alienates them from him. "Without holiness no one will see the Lord" (Heb 12:14). And vices like selfishness, rage, envy, and hatred damage people's relational harmony with each other as brothers and sisters. Believers' moral character also makes an enormous difference in how they go about dominion: like beasts or like the Father? For selfish gain or for the flourishing of all God made?

104. Self, *Flourishing Churches and Communities*, 510–20.

But what is the primary purpose for the image and likeness? Perhaps it would be best to set this question in the context of the larger question, "What is the chief and highest end of [humanity]?" The Westminster Larger Catechism has it right in saying "[Humanity's] chief end is to glorify God, and fully to enjoy him forever."[105] Worship and relationship with God are primary. This is both responsibility and human fulfillment, for nothing and no one else satisfies people like God does (Ps 43:4). The three purposes and responsibilities of the image of God all involve people in worship, bringing God glory, and relational intimacy with him. For example, the blessings of Leviticus 26 and Deuteronomy 28 were life-giving and joy-producing, but also things that enabled the accomplishment of the cultural commission. In order to be blessed, the conditions of love for God and obedience to God (Deut 6:5–6) had to be met. Yet the greatest blessing Israel could receive for meeting these conditions was enjoying the personal presence of God with Israel. Leviticus 26:12 says, "I will walk [*hālak*, as in Gen 3:8 when God walked in the Garden of Eden to interact with Adam and Eve] among you and be your God, and you will be my people." Obeying God in the cultural commission and Mosaic Covenant (which were intertwined though distinguishable) required relationship with God and resulted in an even greater enjoyment of God, along with secondary considerations like land, peace, prosperity, and so on. Thus, the highest purpose of humans is to glorify and enjoy God.

How Does Sin Impact the Image and Likeness of God?

Sin has deeply impacted human dominion, which was a central purpose of the image and likeness of God in Genesis 1 and Psalm 8. Human dominion under God is not as effective apart from a proper relationship with God (Lev 26). The blessing of God has always been vital to dominion and all flourishing (Gen 1:28). After Adam and Eve sinned, God punished humanity in a number of ways. The ground was cursed rather than blessed (though not absolutely or always; see Leviticus 26) in order to make the execution of human dominion over nature painful (Gen 3:17–19). In the same way, childbirth, also central to dominion in that more people made in God's image were needed to carry it out, was made painful (Gen 3:16). Animals kill each other and humans and vice-versa (Gen 9:1–6). Clearly human willingness to carry out God's

105. Grudem, *Systematic Theology*, 441n4.

purposes is not as it should be. People thus do not represent God as much as they should. Even so God's purposes are being accomplished, even by those who are not intentionally obedient. The doctrine of common grace ought to be taken seriously. Agriculture, animal husbandry, procreation, child-rearing, cultural development, artistic endeavors, education, government, work of all sorts, scientific and technological advancement all point to some progress towards the accomplishment of the cultural commission, though far short of the fulfillment in the new creation (Heb 2:5–11). The repercussions of sin on nature and animal life are nowhere more plainly observed than in the story of the flood that brought widespread destruction to earth and animals (Gen 6–9). All of these things, in turn, would affect human beings in various ways.

Genesis 5:1–3 teaches that humans after the fall are still made in God's image, yet also reflect the image of Adam, who fell into rebellion. This seems to be a seed of the later idea that people would need to be conformed to the image anew (Rom 8:29). But consider for a moment the biblical teaching about sin between the fall in Genesis 3 and the image of Adam in Genesis 5. When Cain failed to worship God fully in Genesis 4, God said to Cain, "Why are you angry? Why is your face downcast? If you do what is right, will you not be accepted? But if you do not do what is right, sin is crouching at your door; it desires to have you, but you must rule over it" (Gen 4:6–7). God personifies sin as a would-be dominator of human actions. If Cain did what was right, sin would not be able to master him. This assumes Cain could master sin, though the text does not satisfy theological curiosity about how. But if he did not do what was right, sin would gain a foothold and dominate his actions. He did the latter and the consequences became more than he could bear (4:10–16). The sins of Cain became the sins of his family, though God's grace was shown to them as they began to create a culture with mixed elements of good and evil (Gen 4:19–24).

Cain's lack of righteousness did not reflect God's righteousness. Genesis says the likeness of Adam was passed down to another of his sons in the context of a human race now bound to die, sometimes calling on the Lord (Gen 4:26), sometimes even walking with the Lord (Gen 5:22), but overall descending to the sad pre-flood reality. "The Lord saw how great the wickedness of the human race had become on the earth, and that every inclination of the thoughts of the human heart was only evil all the time" (Gen 6:5). Though Genesis had narrated the introduction of murder into the human story in Genesis 4 as something sudden and jarring, it portrayed the descent into this pre-flood evil as something that happened gradually over time (as the intervening genealogies in chapters 4 and 5 make clear). There was a sort of collective or corporate spread of sin reflected in the human failure and sometimes refusal to carry out the cultural commission. God was not worshiped or depended upon as he should have been, but rather disobeyed. This no doubt caused many problems for individuals (Cain being the prime example), but the emphasis of Genesis 3–11 is clearly on the whole of humanity. By Genesis 11, the cultural commission to, among other things, fill the earth is openly rejected in favor of a new plan: "Come, let us build ourselves a city, with a tower that reaches to the heavens, so that we may make a name for ourselves; otherwise we will be scattered over the face of the whole earth" (v. 4). God nevertheless got his way when He "scattered them from there over all the earth, and they stopped building the city" (v. 8). This is why one must remember that God sees to it his purposes for creation, including human dominion, are being accomplished in spite of human neglect or outright refusal to carry them out. In any case, such a corporate emphasis in hamartiology requires an equally corporate emphasis in soteriology, hence the importance of the kingdom of God and the body of Christ in the New Testament. This corporate emphasis should not come at the expense of the individual, but rather both aspects should be held together.

The Old Testament never says the image or likeness of God was damaged, but it says a great deal about the sinful actions and character of people. The New Testament teaches that Jesus is the image of God. As Kilner insists, "the image of God is the standard of who people are created to be—embodied in the person of Christ—and that standard is not diminished in any way because of sin."[106] This is the very truth that seems to be forgotten when theologians (who generally acknowledge that Jesus is the image of God) portray the image and likeness of God as being lost (in whole or in part), damaged, or destroyed. Hoekema can be considered a moderate representative of this viewpoint. He acknowledges that Jesus is "the image of God par excellence."[107] Soon after, he explains that after human beings fell into sin, the image was not annihilated but it was perverted. Humans still possessed structural endowments, which Hoekema considers part of the image of God, but people now use them for corrupt purposes. This had a powerful effect on humanity's relationships to God,

---

106. Kilner, *Dignity and Destiny*, 134.

107. Hoekema, *Created in God's Image*, 73.

other people, and nature by introducing into them alienation, rebellion, hatred, indifference, manipulation, and so forth.[108]

Calvin was somewhat less restrained in his description of sin's effect on the image of God. On the one hand, he says God's image in us was not totally annihilated but was deformed.[109] On the other hand, "Although some obscure lineaments of that image are found remaining in us; yet are they so vitiated and maimed, that they may truly be said to be destroyed. For besides the deformity which everywhere appears unsightly, this evil also is added, that no part is free from the infection of sin."[110] Hoekema rightly criticizes Calvin for these inconsistent claims.[111]

Kilner has meticulously documented similar descriptions, noting particular theologians' use of a number of terms for what they say has happened to the image of God because of sin. These include

> "lost," "obliterated," "destroyed," "forfeited," "shattered," "effaced," "ceased," "mortally wounded," "erased," "extinguished," "annihilated," "sinned away," "smashed," "wiped out," "negated," "taken away"—or else "virtually lost," "mutilated," "almost blotted out," "all but obliterated," "almost entirely extinguished," "maimed," "vitiated," "worn out," "almost effaced," "ruined," "radically limited," "spoiled," "wasted away,"—or in any case "partly lost," "eroded," "impaired," "degenerated," "reduced," "diminished," "disrupted," "malfunctioning," "harmed," "impoverished," "damaged," "bent," "weakened," "broken," "cracked," "fragmented," "perverted," "corrupted," "defiled," "warped," "disease-ridden," "twisted," "infected," "tainted," "stained," "blotted," "marred," "defaced," "deformed," "disfigured"—or at the very least "sullied," "blemished," "desecrated," "tarnished," "confused," "blurred," or "distorted."[112]

Because the Bible nowhere describes the image of God this way, such descriptions of what has happened to the image must be inferences from the fact that God renews people in his image (Eph 4:23–24; Col 3:9–10) and will eventually conform them completely to the image of his Son (Rom 8:29). But if it is true that Jesus is the image, not just in the sense of the most excellent example of the image to set before the less

108. Hoekema, *Created in God's Image*, 83–85.

109. Calvin, *Inst.* 1.15.4.

110. Calvin, *Genesis*, 95.

111. Hoekema, *Created in God's Image*, 48.

112. Kilner, *Dignity and Destiny*, 175. See pp. 160–74 for the many sources cited there.

excellent images, but in the sense that Jesus actually is the pattern, the paradigm, the model used to create and renew believers, the only image of God there is, then none of the adjectives in the paragraph above can be accurate because none of them properly apply to Jesus. Kilner argues that "what the Bible says about God's image does not consistently make sense unless it is true that God's image remains undamaged."[113] He is thinking of texts like Genesis 9:6 and James 3:9 that affirm that humans are made in God's image/likeness even after the fall.

The image of God is not damaged, but rather human beings are damaged by sin. As Calvin says, every part of a human being is infected by sin. The doctrine of total depravity in that sense is on target. All aspects of human beings are infected by sin, including the heart, soul, mind, strength, and thus body. People as a whole and in all their parts are dead in transgressions and sins, disobedient children of wrath who follow the ways of the world rather than God's ways and who also follow the devil's ways (Eph 2:1–3).[114] They are steeped in idolatry (Rom 1:21–23) and become like that which they serve (Ps 135:15–18). They become selfish (Gal 5:20). As Brunner says, being made in the image of God becomes the occasion of temptation. "The copy wants to be the model itself, the one who ought to answer wishes to be the 'word itself,' the planet wants to be the sun, a star in its own light. Man 'can' do this, thanks to the gift of the Creator."[115] People also have a tendency to stoop down to become more like animals than like God in behavior and character, an enormous irony considering God put them under himself and over the animals when he gave them dominion in creation.[116] The same thing is seen in Daniel 4 and 7. But this does not mean they actually become less human. Being human is a category that one is either in or out of on a substance view of persons and is biologically determined. Brunner is an example of a theologian who goes too far when he says, "If any human being were ever to respond to God in harmony with his Word, and upon the basis of his Word, in believing love, he would be truly human."[117] In context, he clearly means the person would be living out the knowledge of his creatureliness and Divine purpose, living a life of love and responsibility

---

113. Kilner, *Dignity and Destiny*, 147. In agreement that the image is not lost or damaged is Barth, *CD* 3/1:200.

114. See Augustine, *Conf.* 7:21.

115. Brunner, *Man in Revolt*, 133.

116. See Augustine, *Conf.* 7.16

117. Brunner, *Man in Revolt*, 53.

to God. This is a Christian adaptation of the existentialist concept that existence precedes essence; biological humanness precedes real and experiential humanness. But speaking this way can lead one to think there are degrees of humanness and therefore value. Worse, it seems to imply nonbelievers are not fully human and therefore not fully valuable. What would become of human rights in a nation with such a notion? It is best not to speak of human purpose that way.

Apart from Christ, people are not righteous and do not seek God. They lie, slander, curse others, are prone to divisiveness and violence, and do not fear God (Rom 3:10–18). Such Scriptures do not mean that it is impossible for nonbelievers to do anything good. For example, God has entrusted people in government with authority to administer justice for the good of everyone (Rom 13:1–7). Nonbelievers sometimes do that, and this is a means by which God restrains evil, an act of his common grace. King Cyrus of Persia did something good in setting the people of Judah free from captivity to go home and rebuild the temple (Ezra 1:1–4). God appointed him for that purpose (Isa 44:24—45:7). Such acts are not meritorious for salvation (Rom 3:20), for our sins cannot be cancelled out by our good deeds and our good deeds are not necessarily done for the best of reasons. But there is little use denying that a nonbelieving mother does well when she engages in selfless and altruistic acts for her children, for example. As Grudem points out, inherited corruption does not mean people are as bad as they could possibly be. Just laws, family and societal expectations, and conscience restrain them from doing all the evil they would otherwise do and encourage them to do some good in areas like family life, education, science, technology, the legal system, and the arts.[118]

Sin does not only damage individuals, but also society. The corporate aspects of sin are evident in the dividing wall of hostility between Jew and gentile and any groups who hate one another (Eph 2:14). They are seen in "bitterness, rage and anger, brawling and slander, along with every form of malice" (Eph 4:31). They are seen in the pride, divisions, and condescending arrogance Paul corrected in the Corinthian church (1 Cor 11:17–34). The disputes and enmities between nations often reflect such sinfulness at the corporate level (see Isa 2:4) and show humanity as a whole failing to reflect the unity and diversity in loving relationship so evident in the Father, Son, and Holy Spirit.

---

118. Grudem, *Systematic Theology*, 496–97.

What then can be said about the effect of sin on human creation in God's image and likeness? If becoming more honest, for example, means being renewed in the image of the Creator (Col 3:9–10), then lying makes one less like God in that respect. The image is not damaged, but people may conform to the image's moral pattern more or less with respect to any given virtue or action. It should be noted that one may conform poorly on the matter of honesty but well on the matter of gentleness. There are many virtues in play in an evaluation of a person's moral character. From image passages that encourage renewal in God's image one should infer, not that the image is damaged or lost, but that believers' present degree of moral conformity to the image is not as much as God intends. Their character is not enough like that of Jesus, nor is their behavior. Kilner speaks of human attributes which God intended to reflect his own as being "badly stunted in sinful people."[119] Such people "may be exercising some reason, following some moral guidelines, managing their lives and environment to some degree, and maintaining relationships somewhat well. Nevertheless, 'the mind that is set on the flesh is hostile to God . . . and cannot please God'" (citing Rom 8:7–8).[120] The image is not damaged by sin, but believers' reflection of Jesus's righteousness, holiness, knowledge, and love is damaged. As a result, the total human reflection of God's goodness is less than God intended.

How Will God Fully Conform Believers to the Image of His Son?

Humanity's Father sent his Son in human likeness to perform his saving work in order to make people like him (Romans 8), reflecting his love, knowledge, holiness, and righteousness in character (Col 3:10). Hoekema says, "Sanctification, therefore, ought to be understood as the progressive renewal of man in the image of God."[121] This is true in the sense that it is not the image itself, but rather conformity to the image, that is lacking and in need of such renewal.

Sanctification is to happen in three phases. The first is regeneration, when the Holy Spirit makes believers alive with Christ morally and spiritually (Eph 2:5–6). This begins a transformation of character that

---

119. Kilner, *Dignity and Destiny*, 289.

120. Kilner, *Dignity and Destiny*, 290.

121. Hoekema, *Created in God's Image*, 86.

continues in phase two, sanctification.[122] This is to progress throughout
life as believers strive to put off the old humanity and put on the new one
and as God creates them to be like him (Eph 4:22–24). But this process
must culminate in phase three, the resurrection, their glorification, when
they will be totally transformed into the image of God's Son (Rom 8:29).[123]
Seeing Jesus will be a key means to this transformation (1 John 3:2; 2
Cor 3:18). The Holy Spirit gives them the vitality to begin, continue, and
complete this process of sanctification. Paul says, "But if Christ is in you,
then even though your body is subject to death because of sin, the Spirit
gives life because of righteousness. And if the Spirit of him who raised
Jesus from the dead is living in you, he who raised Christ from the dead
will also give life to your mortal bodies because of his Spirit who lives in
you" (Rom 8:10–11).

The Holy Spirit's role is to guide and empower believers. Their role
is to follow his lead and draw upon his power through prayer, the Word
of God, dependence on God, and obedience (see Gal 5:13–26; Eph 5:25).
1 John 3:2–3 makes clear that if they really hope to be perfected in the
image of Christ one day, they will purify themselves (shorthand for their
compliance in the process) in the present.

In terms of resemblance/likeness to God, which is a nuance of "image" and the clear idea of "likeness," Ephesians 4–5 is especially relevant,
particularly in pointing out the way for the church as a whole to form a
new humanity that reflects the image of God in a corporate sense. God's
people are to "be kind and compassionate to one another, forgiving each
other, just as in Christ God forgave you" (Eph 4:32). They are to imitate
Jesus by walking "in the way of love" (Eph 5:1). These virtues and actions
form a sharp contrast with the preceding verse: "Get rid of all bitterness,
rage and anger, brawling and slander, along with every form of malice" (v.
31). The implication is that bitterness and brawling are not the way of love
Christ walked in or the way God has treated us. The church is made up of
brothers and sisters who must learn to get along, help and strengthen one
another, and live out the loving unity in diversity so evident in the inter-
Trinitarian relationships. The church is, in a profound sense, the means
of the reunification of humanity. At the end of a fascinating discussion of
the corporate image of God, Robert Jenson says, "So what does all this

122. "Sanctification" can be used in a narrow sense, as in the second phase, or in a
broad sense that includes all three phases.

123. On the three phases of sanctification, see Erickson, *Christian Theology*, 1,000–
1001; Grudem, *Systematic Theology*, 747–50.

come to? That the church is the communal home of humanity, and that all other communities live by acknowledged or unacknowledged longing to be the church. Which brings us back to Luther on Genesis: had we not fallen, there would have been just the church and her members."[124] This is quite like what was said earlier, that God had always meant for all people to be his family, his sons and daughters, brothers and sisters of one another. The renewal of his image renews each member but also the family as a whole.

Concluding Reflections

The image of God is only defined as Jesus Christ himself. Systematic theologians should acknowledge this in the sense, not merely that he epitomizes what images of God should be, but that he is the only image, the paradigm for humanity. This explains why Scripture never says the image of God is damaged yet does say God's people are being conformed to the image. That Jesus is the Son of God is not incidental to his being the image of God but reveals something of the nature of the image concept: to bear God's image and likeness is what his well-trained children do. Humans stand in relation to God, of course, whether they accept or reject him, just as children of parents are their children whether they love or hate their parents. And God loves his children who reject him. They are still valuable to him, which seems to be why he patiently gives people more time to repent and have eternal life before the final consummation (2 Pet 3:9). The more one rebels against God, the less like him one is morally. Yet this does not decrease one's value, which is based on God's intentional creation and filial love. But once the time comes, he will perfect his willing children according to the pattern of his perfect Son Jesus in a renewal and reunification that will encompass the entire created order. Then he will be among his people forever. They will enjoy him, serve him, and reign with him in a utopian vision that will bring the entire creation project to its natural completion for all eternity.

---

124. Jenson, "*Anima Ecclesiastica*," 1025–27.

Chapter 4

The Image of God and Human Sacredness

THE DOCTRINE OF THE image of God in humans has enormous ethical implications. A convenient way to categorize two broad areas of ethical implications is to distinguish between people as the subjects of action and people as the objects of action. The former group could also be called the treater, actor, or giver of action. The latter group could also be called the treated, acted upon, or receiver of action. On the one hand, in learning the way of Christ, believers discover the sorts of virtues and actions that are appropriate for a person being renewed in God's image and likeness and what sorts of vices and actions are not appropriate. This is the guidance to the subject/treater/actor/giver of action. On the other hand, believers learn how to treat another person and how not to treat another person in view of the fact that s/he is made in God's image. This person is the treated/acted upon/receiver of action.[1] James 3 combines both kinds of guidance. On the one hand, the believer should be a source of praise, "fresh water," or "good fruit" (vv. 10–12). S/he is the subject of the action/ speech in view. On the other hand, it is inappropriate to curse people who are made in God's image (v. 9). That is, such a being should not be treated that way, for that is tantamount to cursing God. The treated/acted upon/receiver has great value and represents the Creator. Thus, the image of God both gives believers a paradigm to follow for moral development and a needed perspective about the value of those with whom they interact. A fitting way to say this is that there are appropriate ways for brothers and sisters to treat fellow brothers and sisters whether those brothers and sisters willingly associate with their Father or not.

---

1. Middleton, "Image of God," 396, also makes such a distinction.

The rest of this chapter will concern the objects/receivers of action. That is, how ought one treat those who are made in God's image? Of what value are people made in God's image and why?

The Claim That the Image of God Grounds Human Value

It is common for Christians to claim that the Christian worldview grounds, or provides a solid basis for, the belief that human beings are valuable and thus ought not to be treated in ways unbefitting beings of such value. In a very influential book, Francis Schaeffer and C. Everett Koop, former Surgeon General of the United States, constantly appeal to the fact that people are made in God's image to promote an ethic that respects the value of human life in a culture in which such a view is eroding. Holding to the Judeo-Christian view rather than a pre-Christian Roman view, people "viewed human life as unique—to be protected and loved— because each individual is created in the image of God."[2] Similarly, Nigel M. de S. Cameron, in seeking to urge the medical community to renew its commitment to the Hippocratic Oath and its ancient synthesis with the Judeo-Christian view of humanity and the world, says that it is the *imago Dei* "that constitutes human being from the divine perspective; and here lies the source of the inestimable dignity of the human creature. Men and women, in their very nature, reflect something of the dignity and worth of God himself."[3]

It will be necessary to define some important terms as they arise. As David Gushee notes, dignity in such a context refers to the "worth" or "value" that explains why every human is worthy of respect. Christians who would interact with secular bioethicists often use this common term even though they have available to them the language of sanctity and sacredness, terms that not only underline the value of people, but also allude to the divine source of value.[4] This understanding of dignity is important because some secularists who criticize conservative bioethicists' reasoning based on dignity have badly misunderstood the idea. For example, in a widely read piece called "The Stupidity of Dignity," Steven Pinker's arguments against the use of dignity as a guiding concept

---

2. Schaeffer and Koop, *Whatever Happened to the Human Race?*, 284.

3. Cameron, *New Medicine*, 172. Similarly, see Davis, *Evangelical Ethics*, 3; Klusendorf, *Case for Life*, 58, 137, 140–41.

4. Gushee, *Sacredness of Human Life*, 20.

in bioethics assume that dignity has to do with acting or being treated in a dignified way. As examples of undignified experiences, he mentions things like undergoing a pelvic examination or going through certain airport security procedures, saying that people willingly choose these things for something they think is worth the trade-off.[5] Though some writers might possibly be talking about dignity in that sense occasionally, the frequent and obvious meaning in bioethics literature is surely worth or value.[6] It seems that Pinker has knocked down a straw man rather than a real one. And, along with Ruth Macklin, he has not explained why two of his principles of bioethics, autonomy and respect for persons, are normative in the first place. If a person has no objective value, why does his/her autonomy matter? Why must one show respect for such a being?[7]

Many Christians have contrasted the way human value is grounded in the Christian worldview with how it is grounded in philosophical naturalism. C. Ben Mitchell and his many coauthors explain,

> A further point of tension in ethics arises in the grounding for the critical notion of human dignity. In an evolutionary view of the world holding that human beings are the products of matter, energy, and physical processes, with no such thing as a human nature—not to mention anything like the image of God—human dignity has nothing on which to ultimately ground it. If human beings are the product of blind, random evolutionary forces, then there is no fundamental reason to treat human beings with any respect or dignity at all. It is not an accident that the notion of human dignity arose in settings informed by a view of a human being as having an essence that grounds one's identity. More specifically, the modern notions of human dignity arose out of a commitment to human beings being the product of a Creator, made in His image, and today, as naturalism gains dominance, human dignity is clearly a holdover from a Judeo-Christian heritage that has long been abandoned. Contrast that with the record of the majority of the most heinous human rights abuses in the twentieth century occurring in avowedly atheistic regimes such as communist nations. One cannot have a human nature in a physicalist view of a human

---

5. Pinker, "Stupidity of Dignity."

6. In addition to Gushee (cited above), see Sulmasy, "Dignity and Bioethics," 472, Gelernter, "Irreducibly Religious Character of Human Dignity," 394.

7. See Macklin, "Dignity Is a Useless Concept," 1419–20.

being. All one has is biology, and biology cannot ground concepts such as human dignity.[8]

Similarly, Bonhoeffer asks, "And where if not in God should there lie the criterion for the ultimate value of a life? In the subjective will to live?"[9] The implication is that only if God values people can people have objective value. If people are only left with subjective value (whatever value people/governments may put on themselves or others), then this is well short of a foundation for inalienable rights. Objective value is needed to ground inalienable human rights.[10] Positive rights (rights posited by government) are insufficient, a fact that should be obvious after communist governments, failing to posit certain of their own citizens' rights, exterminated nearly one hundred million of them in the twentieth century.[11]

Nor is this simply a way Christians and other religious people criticize nonreligious perspectives. Jean-Paul Sartre cautioned atheists about jettisoning God and then happily going on as though a thorough revision of their worldview were not necessary. God's absence results in human forlornness, which has consequences that must be faced, which his existentialism was meant to help atheists do.

> The existentialist, on the contrary, thinks it very distressing that God does not exist, because all possibility of finding values in a heaven of ideas disappears along with him; there can no longer be an *a priori* Good, since there is no infinite and perfect consciousness to think it. Nowhere is it written that the Good exists, that we must be honest, that we must not lie; because the fact is we are on a plane where there are only men. Dostoevsky said, "If God didn't exist, everything would be possible." That is the very starting point of existentialism. Indeed, everything is permissible if God does not exist, and as a result man is forlorn, because neither within him nor without does he find anything to cling to.[12]

Thus, nowhere is it written that people have value and consequently a right to life that must be respected. Human governments may demand that their citizens respect others in a legal positivist system, but it would

---

8. Mitchell et al., *Biotechnology*, 612–20.

9. Bonhoeffer, *Ethics*, 163–64.

10. On this, see Montgomery, *Human Rights and Human Dignity*, 81–188.

11. See Panné et al., *Black Book of Communism*.

12. Sartre, "Existentialism," 451.

not be ethically wrong to disobey such a dictate, however unwise it may be practically. And governments do no wrong if they do not posit the right to life. Why must they? It is impossible to ground objective moral values in a naturalist worldview such as Secular Humanism. Nihilists and Existentialists such as Sartre acknowledge that and thus demonstrate greater consistency with their own presuppositions than naturalists who are nevertheless moral objectivists such as Pinker.[13]

For apologetic purposes, it is very important to be able to make this case. Christianity can provide a solid basis for human value and rights where naturalistic worldviews cannot. Naturalists may become more open to the Christian worldview when they see that their presuppositions imply a universe in which there are no objective values—if they hold more firmly to objective values than to naturalism. But in order for Christians to make this case, the image doctrine must be up to the task by providing that solid basis.

It should be pointed out before exploring that issue, however, that Christian ethicists like Robert George, Leon Kass, John Kilner, C. Ben Mitchell, and many others are right to find common ground from which to reason in bioethics discussions with people from secular perspectives. Christians can work with secular bioethicists on policies and standards that uphold human dignity even though their typically materialist worldview does not provide a solid ontological basis for that dignity. The distinction between epistemology and ontology is important here. Epistemologically, naturalists can know people have objective value while being unable to furnish ontological grounds for that value consistent with their naturalistic presuppositions. The Universal Declaration of Human Rights of the United Nations (1948) posits the "inherent dignity" and "equal and inalienable human rights" of people without a word about their basis.[14] H. Russel Botman is no doubt correct that the document implicitly reflects the biblical teaching that humans are made in the image of God.[15] Indeed, according to the eminent German philosopher Jürgen Habermas, the entire notion of human rights, including conscience

---

13. See Pinker, "The Moral Instinct." For a refutation of naturalistic attempts to found objective morality (including Pinker's), see Copan, "The Moral Argument," 174–90. See also the discussion surrounding a debate between William Lane Craig and Paul Kurtz in García and King, *Is Goodness Without God Good Enough?*

14. Montgomery, *Human Rights*, 219–37.

15. Botman, "Integrating Three Contemporary Discourses of Human Dignity," 1137.

rights, is the legacy of the Judeo-Christian principles of justice and love.[16] Yet cooperation with all people of goodwill to extend these protections to as many people as possible is surely a good thing, whatever perspective potential allies may espouse.

The point to be explored here is whether or not the royal family view of the image of God is up to the task of providing a solid foundation for the value/dignity/sacredness of human life. The apologetic function of an adequate biblical grounding for dignity has been mentioned. And the introduction pointed out many areas in which human beings are being mistreated in violation of the sacred value of human life. Perhaps biblical teaching on the image of God could make a difference as it has in many cultures. Of course, it is possible that improper teaching on the subject may contribute to the harm caused, particularly if it justifies treating people differently from one another. The assumption in Genesis 9:6 and James 3:9 is that humanity's creation in God's image establishes them as having great value, so great that it is tantamount to an attack on God to murder or even curse those made in his image. This means that it is a proper test of any theology of the image of God to ask whether it provides an adequate basis for human value. And the apologetic and ethical considerations mean that there is much at stake in the real world in finding out whether the royal family view passes the test. To put it to the test, first consider how the three common views of the image ground human value and whether any or all of those views actually do ground it firmly. Because the royal family view combines a particular variation of the relational view and royal/functional view, its grounding will be addressed under those views.

Image of God Theologies and Human Value

The concern here will be to survey how various theologies of the image actually ground human value/dignity/sacredness. It is not always clear which view of the image someone invoking the image holds. In Linda Woodhead's case, the reason she does not go into detail about the image is because she sees God's nature as beyond knowing. She explains, "If the divine essence (*ousia*) cannot be grasped, then surely the same is true of the human—if the human is indeed made in the image of God. If God and humanity are as closely related as Genesis suggests, then the impossibility

16. Habermas, *Time of Transitions*, 150–51.

of understanding or speaking of the divine nature also applies to human nature."[17] This insight should caution one against using or applying any doctrine of the image to justify harming people, as if one held the mysteries of God and his children in the palm of his/her hand. But the foregoing analysis suggests that more can be known about Jesus the image and about humans made in his image, even if it falls short of a full understanding. With that assumption in mind, what follows is an analysis of how each of the three major image views grounds human value.

The Structural/Substantive View

The structural view generally holds that what makes human beings valuable is the sort of beings we are, namely personal ones. The image of God has to do with human nature and human nature includes capacities like God's communicable attributes such as spiritual, rational, relational, and moral capacities.[18] Donal O'Mathuna holds that the whole human being, including the body, images God, in accord with the Hebrew holistic anthropology considered above. Though Jesus is the image of God, O'Mathuna in another passage describes the image in humans as "shattered."[19] As stated above, structuralists and others often describe the image this way, particularly as it pertains to how holy and righteous people are or are not.[20]

As David Gushee points out, the capacities associated with personhood, which are then considered to be included in or constitutive of being in God's image in structural views, bear similarities with the criteria of personhood pro-choice advocates offer to distinguish the merely human (particularly the unborn) from persons.[21] In their view, only persons deserve the right to life. Here are a few philosophers and their personhood criteria:

17. Woodhead, "Apophatic Anthropology," 3025–28.

18. Schaeffer, "Pollution and the Death of Man," 29; Schaeffer and Koop, *Whatever Happened to the Human Race?*, 408; Gelernter, "Irreducibly Religious Character," 396; Copan, "Moral Argument," 178.

19. O'Mathuna, "Bible and Abortion," 203–4.

20. "Structuralists" here is shorthand for adherents of a structural/substantive view of the image of God and does not refer to adherents of early twentieth century linguistic structuralism.

21. Gushee, *Sacredness of Human Life*, 45.

- Helga Kuhse and Peter Singer: "consciousness, the ability to be aware of one's surroundings, to be able to relate to others, perhaps even rationality and self-consciousness."[22]

- Michael Tooley: "a subject of past or current experiences involving at least some conscious thought, desires (necessary to have interests), and self-consciousness."[23]

- Mary Anne Warren: "Consciousness . . . reasoning . . . self-motivated activity . . . capacity to communicate . . . self-awareness."[24]

This is known as a functional view of personhood. Francis Beckwith accurately dubs it the "anti-equality case" since it does not hold that all humans have equal value, but rather that only some humans qualify as persons and thus have sufficient value upon which to base a right to life.[25] This is in contrast to the substance view of persons, which holds that all humans are necessarily persons and that all human persons have equal value from the time they begin to exist to the time they cease to exist, regardless of the extent to which they can exercise such personal capacities at any given time. Human rights are for all humans equally.[26]

But if the image of God includes or is constituted by such personal capacities, then does not the absence of the present ability to perform them (thinking, being self-aware, and so forth) mean that the human is not a person and does not bear the image of God, or at least not to the same extent as those who do so function? The present ability to exercise those capacities is critical to the functional view. Yet newborns, the temporarily comatose, and slumbering people do not have them either, and they are clearly persons. Only some of these beings create a problem for Kuhse, Singer, and Tooley, though, since they defend infanticide up to a certain stage.[27] The logic of their position leads inexorably to this inhumane conclusion. Jay Budziszewski focuses this line of criticism on Warren because, unlike Kuhse, Singer, and Tooley, she does not follow the logic of her own position to the approval of infanticide. He argues that functional definitions are fitting for automobiles and spacers, things with no inherent

---

22. Kuhse and Singer, "Moral Status of the Embryo," 184.

23. Tooley, "Abortion: Why a Liberal View Is Correct," 9–10.

24. Warren, "On the Moral and Legal Status of Abortion," 470.

25. Beckwith, *Defending Life*, 130, 134.

26. Beckwith, *Defending Life*, 132.

27. See Kuhse and Singer, *Should the Baby Live?*; Tooley, *Abortion and Infanticide*.

nature that can therefore be defined by humans' purposes for them. In contrast, human persons, made in God's image, have a nature and that nature does not depend on age or stage of development. People are not mere means, but also ends, subjects of rights.[28] Scott Klusendorf points out, "a substance functions in light of what it is and maintains its identity even if its ultimate capacities are never realized due to disability or injury. A dog that never develops his capacity to bark is still a dog by nature."[29] In short, people do not become persons by developing such mental capacities, they develop such mental capacities because they are persons.

But still, one wonders why mental capacities are assumed to be value-giving in the first place. The functionalist assumes such mental capacities must be presently exercisable, whereas the substance view defender assumes such mental capacities must be basic to the sort of being in question. But why assume that mental or spiritual capacities are specifically what makes humans valuable?

Also, if such capacities are assumed to be all there is to the image of God and all that makes people valuable, this tends towards a body-mind dualism foreign to holistic biblical anthropology. That is, the body is not included in what makes people valuable or worse, the body is not considered part of the self at all, but rather a mere instrument of the self, which is construed mentally and/or spiritually. The latter is clearly assumed by pro-choice functionalists, who say one can be a human without being a person. What is human in that statement is the body. What makes one a person is mental rather than physical. The same view seems to be assumed by various proponents and participants in the sexual revolution, such as people who have "friends with benefits," assuming one's body can engage in sex without any sort of emotional bonding with one's partner.[30] A wedge is driven between the body and emotions. Similar are gay people, whose bodies are designed for procreative union with the opposite sex, but whose desires (which are emotional/mental) are for the same sex.[31] Which is the true self, the body, the heart's desires, or both?

---

28. Budziszewski, *What We Can't Not Know*, 75–77.

29. Klusendorf, *Case for Life*, 50.

30. Denizet-Lewis, "Friends, Friends with Benefits and the Benefits of the Local Mall." Denizet-Lewis notes that those who engage in such hookups get into dating relationships as often as not, suggesting that the body and mind/heart are more integrated than mind-body dualism assumes. For further arguments in favor of such a unified view, see Budziszewski, *On the Meaning of Sex*, 292.

31. See Merritt, "Downfall of the Ex-Gay Movement," for the assumption that

Which should conform to which? The same holds for transgendered people. When a person born physically male thinks of himself as a woman
trapped in a man's body, often it is the mental construal of the self that
wins out over the clear design of the body.[32] Body-self dualism, then, has
become common both inside and outside the church.

Gushee and Kilner rightly point out that this notion that there are
humans who are not also persons is a denigration of the body at odds
with the anthropology of Scripture, which portrays the whole person as
made in God's image.[33] But good sense tells against it as well. Christopher
Kaczor points out several absurd conclusions that follow if the body is
not a part of the self.

> You are not a human being, you were not born . . . Your moth-
> er has never hugged you (since no one hugs the aims, desires,
> awareness that constitutes a person) . . . "You" pop in and out of
> existence along with your periodically present consciousness
> . . . Curing Dissociative Identity Disorder (DID), also known
> as multiple personality disorder, destroys "someone" since it
> destroys one or more sets of personalities with distinct aims,
> desires, and awareness, but this too is absurd. Finally, body-
> self dualism cannot adequately explain simple statements such
> as "you see."[34]

It is a plain scientific fact that human life begins as fertilization, as
numerous embryologists and biologists say. For example, Keith Moore
and his coauthors, in a widely-used embryology textbook, state, "Human
development begins at fertilization, when a sperm fuses with an oocyte
to form a single cell, the zygote. This highly specialized, totipotent cell
marks the beginning of each of us as a unique individual."[35] Similarly,
T. W. Sadler writes, "Development begins with fertilization, the process
by which the male gamete, the sperm, and the female gamete, the oocyte,

---

same-sex attraction is a permanent part of one's identity.

32. Michaelson, "What Does the Bible Teach About Transgender People?" Michaelson says, "Definitionally, sex is about chromosomes; gender is about cultural
practices. Sex is what is between our legs; gender is what is between our ears." For
examples of people saying they feel trapped in the wrong body and similar expressions
indicating body-self dualism, see Dallas, "Transsexual Dilemma."

33. Gushee, *Sacredness of Human Life*, 43; Kilner, *Dignity and Destiny*, 186.

34. Kaczor, *Ethics of Abortion*, 18–19. For an outstanding book-length treatment of
body-self dualism, its impact on our culture, arguments against it, and a holistic vision
of human flourishing, see Pearcey, *Love Thy Body*.

35. Moore et al., *Developing Human*, 11.

unite to give rise to a zygote."[36] Ronan O'Rahilly and Fabiola Müller agree. "Although life is a continuous process, fertilization . . . is a critical landmark because, under ordinary circumstances, a new genetically distinct human organism is formed when the chromosomes of the male and female pronuclei blend in the oocyte."[37] Maureen L. Condic, who teaches at the University of Utah School of Medicine, cites numerous medical texts and peer-reviewed journal articles that say the same thing.[38] It is beyond serious question and informed pro-choice advocates do not tend to challenge it. In fact, David Boonin stipulates the humanity of the embryo from the outset of his abortion defense. "Perhaps the most straightforward relation between you and me on the one hand and every human fetus from conception onward on the other is this: All are living members of the same species, *homo sapiens*. A human fetus, after all, is simply a human being at a very early stage in his or her development . . . A defense of abortion that seeks to engage critics of abortion on their own terms must therefore take this assumption as a given."[39] It is no doubt because this biological fact is so clear that the influential feminist and abortion supporter Naomi Wolf writes, "Clinging to a rhetoric about abortion in which there is no life and no death, we entangle our beliefs in a series of self-delusions, fibs and evasions. And we risk becoming precisely what our critics charge us with being: callous, selfish and casually destructive men and women who share a cheapened view of human life."[40]

If the above critique of body-self dualism is cogent and one must view humans holistically in ethical considerations, then one must view the human life that begins at fertilization as valuable. And the argument that there are humans that are not persons is not a biological and scientific one but a philosophical one, and not a well-supported one at that. Pro-choice advocates who argue this way make a distinction where there is no difference to justify abortion.

If one grants the premise that persons have value, there are strong philosophical arguments that all humans are persons and that personhood includes the body in its identity. But if secular bioethicists and others do not grant this, it might be helpful to provide some reason to believe

36. Sadler, *Langman's Medical Embryology*, 11.

37. O'Rahilly and Müller, *Human Embryology & Teratology*, 8.

38. Condic, "Origin of Human Life at Fertilization."

39. Boonin, "Defense of Abortion," 20–21.

40. Wolf, "Our Bodies, Our Souls," 26.

that the body and the personal capacities together are valuable or to widen the issue beyond personal capacities. At that point, it has become a battle of worldviews. It seems that something more than present capacities (vs. functionalism) or basic capacities (vs. a narrow structural view of the image of God with a substance view of persons, even construed holistically) is needed to ground human value. The latter surely helps us to see what sort of being is valued and to see that its size, level of development, environment, and degree of dependency are not relevant to its being a person (the SLED test).[41] But the notion that personal beings with rational and moral agency are valuable must ontologically rest on something more than a government or people's act of positing it. Positivism failed miserably in communist countries. Governments must be accountable to someone above their people for how they treat their people. Thus, a number of writers resist the tendency among Jewish and Christian ethicists to only speak in nonreligious terms like dignity, saying that this eliminates the basis for value from the discussion. Rather, the language of sanctity, sacredness, and the image of God carries an explanation of the grounds for human dignity/value.[42]

Kilner argues that there is great danger to human beings when the image of God is defined as ways people are presently like God because people inevitably vary in their capacities, which implies that people are not of equal value. Of course, if sin causes the image of God in people to be lost or damaged, then people may lack all value or at least equal value. The image of God may become a "high voltage" concept; "it can energize much or electrocute many."[43]

Kilner provides numerous examples of mistreatments justified by those who stated such a view of the image of God. He says, "This way of thinking has encouraged such abuses as mistreatment of impoverished and disabled people, the Nazi holocaust and exterminations of Native

41. Beckwith, *Defending Life*, 159–60. Concerning size, Shaquille O'Neal is not more valuable than Hillary Clinton, though he is a foot and a half taller. Concerning level of development, teenagers are not more valuable than toddlers. Concerning environment, where you are does not determine what you are, so living inside your mother does not make you something other than a person. Concerning degree of dependency, people who are dependent on medical technology are not less valuable than those who are not so dependent.

42. Gelernter, "Irreducibly Religious Character," 395; Budziszewski, *What We Can't Not Know*, 76; Browning, "Human Dignity, Human Complexity, and Human Goods," 4005–57.

43. Kilner, *Dignity and Destiny*, 37.

American groups, oppression of enslaved Africans (and their descendants) and women, and damaging of the natural environment."[44] Gushee registers the same concern: "It is not only mistaken but has proven problematic if not disastrous, time and again, to define the image of God in terms of any kind of quality that (some) human beings possess."[45]

It is shameful that people who called themselves Christians were sometimes among those who defended such practices. But it is important to keep three things in mind. One is that evil people like Adolf Hitler did not kill millions of people in concentration camps in obedience to Scripture, but in flagrant violation of the Golden Rule to "do to others what you would have them do to you" (Matt 7:12). A version of the image of God that loses sight of that is wrong on its face. Second, people can and sometimes will use anything, including Scripture and theology, to try to justify pursuing their desires. Paul says in Titus 3:3, "At one time we too were foolish, disobedient, deceived and enslaved by all kinds of passions and pleasures. We lived in malice and envy, being hated and hating one another." Hitler's hatred of Jews, extreme nationalism, outrage about the Treaty of Versailles, social Darwinism, and erroneous eugenics beliefs played decisive roles in what he did, and despite his efforts none of those things could be properly justified from Scripture.[46] Third, Kilner also carefully documents the many good things that believers have done to serve humanity based on the belief that all human beings are made in God's image. In fact, the list of such things includes the opposite of each of the acts some have justified with a faulty reading of the image. To wit, "Humanity's status in God's image, then, has served historically as a compelling impetus toward liberation. It has fostered respect and protection for those who have been wrongly oppressed, including impoverished, ill, and disabled people, as well as Native Americans, enslaved Africans and their descendants, and women. It has also inspired care for the natural environment."[47]

Recall that throughout much of the history of the church, the structural view of the image has been the dominant view. So how could such good and evil acts have both been justified using the structural view? Some non-theological contributing factors have been pointed out. As for the theological ones, it seems that a narrow focus on mental attributes

---

44. Kilner, *Dignity and Destiny*, 18. See his careful documentation in each case on pp. 17–37.

45. Gushee, *Sacredness of Human Life*, 44.

46. On all such factors and others, see Gushee, *Sacredness of Human Life*, 304–51.

47. Kilner, *Dignity and Destiny*, 17.

along with an emphasis on the devastating effects of sin on the image have created an opportunity for the misappropriation of the image. But thankfully, an emphasis on those passages that insist that human beings are still made in God's image after the fall (Gen 9:6; Jas 3:9), along with additional considerations in the image doctrine, have often prompted the church to treat human beings with the respect warranted. What are some of those additional considerations that may help ground human value for all humans on a structural view?

One consideration is the incarnation. Cameron says the timing and character of the incarnation establishes the full inclusion of the unborn in the human community. "For the human life of Jesus Christ began not at birth but at his miraculous conception; the Son of God took human flesh to himself in the person of a zygote."[48] Indeed, as Montgomery points out, only the heretical adoptionists held that Jesus became human later.[49]

Another consideration is the eschatological plan of God for humans to enjoy union with Jesus Christ. The connection with Jesus is the key here. John Behr brings an Eastern orthodox perspective to the issue.

> We acknowledge the point made by St. Gregory of Nyssa, that looking around us we do not directly see "images of God" everywhere, but men and women living broken lives, suffering, falling sick, and ultimately dying. However, rather than say that despite these empirical conditions, each of them is a person and so to be respected as such, it would be better to allow our interpretation of what we see to be conditioned by the light of Christ, so that we can say that what we see are images of God being fashioned, human beings in the making. All the toils and turmoils of the sea of life provide the framework and the means by which we grow into the stature of human nature manifest in Christ himself, the broken, suffering servant . . . It is therefore primarily in those who would previously not have been recognized—the autistic child, the mentally ill, the physically challenged, the derelict, homeless, imprisoned—that we see what it is to be human, and in so doing, and responding to them, that we become human ourselves. This is the dignity of the human being, a dignity which will never stand upon itself, but will always sacrifice itself.[50]

48. Cameron, *New Medicine*, 174.

49. Montgomery, "Christian View of the Fetus," 585.

50. Behr, "Promise of the Image," 37.

The emphasis here, in terms of the image of God doctrine, is on the moral similarity to Christ. Any lack of Christlike character in another is not cause to disrespect or mistreat him/her, but rather an opportunity to become more Christlike and thus more human oneself. N. T. Wright speaks of our purpose "to become genuine human beings, reflecting the God in whose image we're made, and doing so in worship on the one hand and in mission, in its full and large sense, on the other; and that we do this not least by following Jesus."[51]

The call to sacrificial love (Behr) and following Jesus in worship and mission (Wright) are welcome and biblical emphases. Behr's challenge to the subject not to look down at an object of treatment lest the subject debase himself/herself morally is vitally important. Applying that truth alone could have prevented many of the atrocities mentioned above. And an eschatological perspective on the image of God is evident in 2 Corinthians 3 and 1 John 3. Yet no Scripture passage uses the language of "more human," a term that implies that there is such a thing as "less human," even in the sense of a subject becoming less human for treating another as less than human. Either way, someone is becoming less human. It is not just that the idea can be (and has been) misused to treat people inhumanely, but that no biblical writer sets up the issue this way. It is also better philosophically to hold to the substance view of persons, which sees the category "human" as static and not admitting of degrees. One is either in or out; all or nothing. In Wright's concept, the degrees of humanness pertain to the individual's participation in God's purposes for his people. That surely does admit of degrees. But being human does not.

Fraser Watts also uses an eschatological framework in which human beings have dignity already in one sense, but not yet fully in another. The first sense is a static one: all people have equal dignity, which is the secular equivalent to the Christian teaching that humans are made in God's image and have sacred value. According to Watts, this is true and essential, but inadequate, a creational truth that is incomplete without the balance provided by eschatological redemption. A "relative or qualitative sense" of dignity is also needed.

> I suggest that we also need a qualitative concept of dignity that reflects the extent to which the potential that comes from being made in the image of God has been realized. The distinction between being made in the "image" of God, and growing into

---

51. Wright, *After You Believe*, 36.

his "likeness," has sometimes been used in this way. Though terminology has not been consistent, "image" has often been an absolute concept, while "likeness" has been a qualitative one. People differ in the extent to which they have realized the potential that comes from being created in the image of God. At the present time that fuller dignity to which all are called, and for which we can hope, is more completely realized in some people than in others. All, however, are called to a fuller realization of the dignity that is part of God's purposes. In this eschatological between-time, we need a qualitative or relative sense of dignity. When that dignity is completely realized in everyone, we will return to an absolute, universal concept of dignity that is manifest equally in all people.[52]

The main benefit of restoring the qualitative sense is the guidance and incentive to accomplish God's purposes that people may lack without it. On the other hand, the danger of reducing people to something less than they are is real. Watts discusses the perception among some that Darwinism presents a threat to human dignity, but he sees this as a confusion between the two senses of dignity. Human descent from primates means some behaviors might not be particularly dignified. But, he says, "qualitative forms of reductionism are acceptable, and need not lead on to the stronger, ontological forms of reductionism that are inconsistent with religious belief."[53] The key thing religious belief provides that has no analogate in secular thinking is the notion of dignity as gift from God. Though some secularists may regard the notion as patronizing or demeaning, Christians embrace God's gift of life and a human nature made in his image with gratitude.[54]

Watts is surely right to locate humanity eschatologically and to see character transformation as a process that must unfold until the resurrection perfects believers. He is also right to see human dignity in the first sense as static and something that humans share equally because God grants them such dignity. The problem is that these two senses of dignity are so different that it only adds to the confusion for Watts to continue to use the term of these two ideas. What is static is value, and that because God values all people equally. That is a gift, not something people become worthy of, nor is it some manner of behavior that can

---

52. Watts, "Human Dignity," 3234–40.

53. Watts, "Human Dignity," 3272–73.

54. Watts, "Human Dignity," 3305.

be described as dignified as opposed to shameful as in Watts' dynamic sense (he seems to use the term all three ways). The "dignified" sense is the one Pinker misunderstands Christian bioethicists to mean when they generally mean "value." Human beings do need to grow and develop more Christlike character. But this does not result in having greater value in God's eyes or warranting more of a right to life or liberty. It is true that some people are respected more than others for their sacrificial love, industriousness, leadership qualities, generosity, or other virtues and accomplishments. Paul says this is as it should be (in connection with a pastor, though the principle no doubt applies to other kinds of work): "The elders who direct the affairs of the church well are worthy of double honor, especially those whose work is preaching and teaching" (1 Tim 5:17). This may provide incentive to achieve more of one's potential. But this has nothing to do with being valued by God. Earned respect may have to do with subjective value, but human dignity is about objective value. There is a type of respect that every human being is due for simply being a human made in God's image. That does not change, regardless of what one accomplishes. It would be difficult not to continue to use the word "respect" in those two ways, but in view of the confusion surrounding "dignity," it would be best to regard it only as objective, equally shared, static value and not use dignity in any other sense in bioethical discussions so as to avoid confusion.

Though these last two views are not persuasive in exactly how they bring the eschatological dimension into the discussion of human value, there is a way to do so and it has already been mentioned. God does not seem to view human value only in terms of any one person's present condition. His connection to and purposes for people predate their creation and go on long after their lives in a fallen state have ended. From the beginning, God has had a destiny in mind that they would reflect his character perfectly. Their value to him pertains to their unique connection to him as his offspring. But he also seems to value them on a practical level for their contributions (by his grace) to his overall creation project, and that requires moral development. Any lack of such development this side of the resurrection does not decrease their present value. Dignity is static and objective in that it is a settled matter in the mind of God. That explains why he says repeatedly that humans are still made in God's image even after the fall and must therefore not be murdered or cursed (Gen 9:6; Jas 3:9; 1 Cor 11:7).

Can a substantive view of the image provide a solid foundation for the value/sacredness of every human being? No, if it focuses on the sort of beings humans are and measures worth by presently exercisable capacities. Advocates of substantive views may not personally measure worth that way, but if the logic of the position works out that way, that is a significant problem for the position. And no, if the image is said to be severely damaged, even by those who strongly affirm full and equal dignity. Again, it is the logic of the position that is at issue. If people were made in God's image in the beginning and that image is why they were valuable and that image was damaged by sin, then humanity is logically less valuable than at the beginning. A substantive view advocate may say that humanity's objective value stems from the fact that God their Creator values them. That is what it means to say that dignity/value is a gift. Such a connection with God is central to how the relational view grounds dignity. To the extent that particular substantive views draw upon that connection, they can indeed ground equal human value. Without this relational notion, it is difficult to see how substantive views of the image can provide grounds for the equal value of every human being at any age and in any condition.

Much of the danger Kilner and Gushee point to in substantive views that focus on capacities comes more from the sinful human attempt to take over the Divine prerogative of determining value. It is simply not up to human beings to assess each other's value and then decide how to treat one another accordingly. That would leave human value as a strictly subjective consideration. Rather, people must accept their creatureliness and God's authority over his creation. To usurp this Divine prerogative does not make one's behavior more godly but more beastly.

The Relational View

There are three passages in the gospels in which Jesus discusses the value of human life. In none of them does he explicitly mention the image of God, yet in each he mentions the fatherhood of God, which is central to the meaning of God creating us in his image. In his call to discipleship, Jesus says, "Whoever wants to be my disciple must deny themselves and take up their cross and follow me. For whoever wants to save their life will lose it, but whoever loses their life for me and for the gospel will save it. What good is it for someone to gain the whole world, yet forfeit their soul? Or what can anyone give in exchange for their soul? If anyone is ashamed of me and my words in this adulterous and sinful generation, the Son of Man will be ashamed of them when he comes in his Father's glory with the holy angels" (Mark 8:34–38).

Jesus is requiring absolute loyalty to himself, a loyalty that would prompt one to preach his message even if it results in martyrdom. Since the passage is about Jesus's expectation that disciples be loyal to himself as he was coming to rule by his Father's side in glory, the filial relationship in view is between the Father and Jesus. The fact that Jesus taught his followers to address God as "our Father" (Matt 6:9), however, makes it possible that their value has something to do with that relationship. This possibility will become more plausible if Jesus elsewhere grounds human value on the fact that the Father values his children.

The two uses of *psychē*, translated "life" in verse 35, are matched by two more in verses 36 and 37. Yet numerous translations have "soul" in verses 36 and 37 (NIV, KJV, NLT, ESV, NASB, NIV84, NKJV, AV). NRSV and LEB properly translate "life." The translation "soul" gives the impression that one particular part of the person is at issue here, but in fact it is the total person in view. *Psychē* was used for the Hebrew *nepeš* (e.g., Gen 2:7 LXX) which stands for the whole person. Jesus is not saying that one aspect of a person, the soul, is of so much worth that there is nothing one can exchange for it of equal value, but that the life of a person *as a whole* has such worth. This includes bodily life, which is why bodily healing and resurrection are included in biblical hope and not merely the survival of the soul or spirit in heaven. Something of humans survives the death of the body by God's enablement, and this preserves a person's identity and consciousness in the intermediate, disembodied state (Luke 23:43). But this is not the main hope of personal eschatology. Jesus is offering eternal life for the total person who is willing to surrender his/her life in this world.[55]

This eternal life clearly has some continuity with life on earth, or else why would Jesus use the same term "life"? God had once shortened life (Gen 6:3); now he is prolonging it indefinitely. Even if few find eternal life (Matt 7:13–14), the lives of people are no less valuable to God. This is the same assumption as in the flood narrative: when God punishes people with death for sin, it does not mean they have no value to him. It means they have freely chosen against him and his good purposes and

55. Cf. John 12:25, which has "hate their life," using "hate" in the comparative sense. One must prefer Christ to one's own earthly life in order to attain the incalculable good of eternal life.

thus forfeited their lives. But even as Noah preached righteousness to his generation before the flood (2 Pet 2:5), disciples of Jesus Christ have been preaching the gospel in order to make disciples of all nations (Matt 28:18–20), extending salvation all over the earth (Acts 13:46–47, quoting Isa 49:6). This fulfills the Abrahamic Covenant promise to bless all nations through Abraham's nation, including the spiritual descendants of Abraham and so encompassing Jewish and gentile Christians (Matt 8:11; Rom 4:9–17). This age is parallel to the age of Noah in that judgment has been forecast (though by fire rather than water per the Genesis 9 covenant), but God waits to bring it and the salvation that is its reverse side, for he is "not wanting anyone to perish, but everyone to come to repentance" (2 Pet 3:9). God would much rather the wicked turn from their wicked ways and live than to die in their sins because he loves the world of people (John 3:16).

If Mark 8 alludes to the inestimable worth of human life without using a word like "worth," Matthew 6:25–27 comes right out and says it. "Therefore I tell you, do not worry about your life, what you will eat or drink; or about your body, what you will wear. Is not life more than food, and the body more than clothes? Look at the birds of the air; they do not sow or reap or store away in barns, and yet your heavenly Father feeds them. Are you not much more valuable than they? Can any one of you by worrying add a single hour to your life?"

Jesus again uses *psychē* here of "life" and with a clear physical connotation, for a being without a body would not need food and water (v. 25). God feeds animals (which implies their worth to him, as in Genesis 1:30). Then Jesus uses an argument from lesser to greater: "Are you not much more valuable than they?" You (*hymeis*) is emphatic here, which probably explains the NIV's intensifying "much more."[56] BDAG defines the word translated "valuable," *diapherete*, as "differ to one's advantage from someone or something, *be worth more than, be superior to* τινός."[57] The only thing Jesus mentions that gives us a clue why God values people so much is his filial relationship to them (v. 26): the Father values his children. If the filial relationship is indeed central to what it means to be made in God's image, then it is hard not to see the assumption of Genesis 1 at work here: humans are more valuable than animals because humans

---

56. Carson, *Matthew*, 180.

57. BDAG 239 on *diapherō*.

are made in the image and likeness of God and are thus his children.[58] Disciples of Christ should trust in their loving Father to provide for them. Note that humans are more valuable than grass, as is obvious from the fact that they last longer (v. 30).[59]

Similarly, in Matthew 10:29–31 Jesus says, "Are not two sparrows sold for a penny? Yet not one of them will fall to the ground outside your Father's care. And even the very hairs of your head are all numbered. So don't be afraid; you are worth more than [again, *diapherete*] many sparrows." God values sparrows but does not stand in a Father-child relationship with them. Rather, Jesus says, "your Father" [not their Father] cares for them. Since you are worth more than many sparrows, how much more will Your Father take care of you?" In Matthew 12:11–12, the comparison is between a human and a sheep. "He said to them, 'If any of you has a sheep and it falls into a pit on the Sabbath, will you not take hold of it and lift it out? How much more valuable [*diapherei*] is a person than a sheep! Therefore it is lawful to do good on the Sabbath'" (cf. Luke 14:5). Unlike the previous two texts, this context lacks an immediate reference to God as Father. Yet the same anthropology is assumed to make the point that humans are more valuable than animals—sheep, in this case. For that reason, God authorizes (*exestin*) doing good to people on the Sabbath and therefore Jesus was right to heal the man with a withered hand (v. 10). Human beings have surpassing value to God because he made them to be his children.

And this seems to be the ultimate ground of human value. A personal note may provide clarity here. The moment our oldest daughter was born, the doctor who delivered her gasped as if something was wrong. She proceeded to show Kari and I that the umbilical cord was tied in a knot, which usually results in the death of the baby due to a lack of nourishment. But there Jamie was, alive and kicking like a frog. The doctor called her a miracle baby. As I held her for the first time I was filled with overwhelming love for her and gratitude to God for protecting her in the womb. Soon she was sleeping like a baby and I was crying like a baby. I felt the same way when Daphne was born with complications. If someone were to ask me why I love my daughters, I do not know of any answer I could give. I just do. A number of their capacities, virtues, and accomplishments over the years have been praiseworthy. They are intelligent, diligent, funny, mature,

---

58. Blomberg, *Matthew*, 125 sees an implied reference to God's image here, though not by way of the Fatherhood of God.

59. Nolland, *Matthew*, 313.

compassionate, and respectful. They get good grades and are effectively pursuing their chosen college majors and career paths. Jamie has been writing spellbinding novels on her way to her bachelor's degree. Daphne is showing scientific acumen, initially as a nursing student, but now as a biomedical sciences student on a pre-med track. I am very proud of them for such things, but none of them are *why* I love them. Is there anything that can ground value more than love can? Is there anything to which we must press beyond love to find grounds for value? Many people would regard love as the greatest of values.

Defenders of a structural view might reply that the nature of the one being loved matters. Generally, people are loved more than animals or inanimate objects, a fact that probably has something to do with the fact that they are personal beings capable of love and friendship, of freely choosing to have a relationship with the other. Some might say that such beings are worthy of greater love. If so, then freedom in human nature becomes an important presupposition for the love of God for human beings, a freedom that resembles his freedom. Without such freedom, love is not real because forced love is not love; programmed love is not love. Only freely chosen love is love. This point is well taken, but it does not mean freedom is what it means to be made in God's image or that freedom is part of the meaning of the image. Freedom is clearly presupposed in the human ability to relate, love, and choose good or evil. God does not love people because they are free, but because they are his children. It seems that he made them free personal beings so that they could be his children.

My love for my daughters only gives them subjective value in the sense of value to me. It does not make them objectively valuable, bearers of a right to life that no one, even their government, has the authority to take. It does not make it so that people other than my wife and I will value them. Only God's love can make someone valuable in such a way because he is the Creator and Governor of the universe. And the love he has for people needs no further grounding because there is nothing greater than the love of God. If he loves people and wants to protect them from anyone harming them, then that puts an obligation on everyone not to harm people. The fact that God is the moral Governor of the universe means that it would be in each person's best interest not to cross the Father or his other children in this matter. It is significant that God has designed the parents in a marriage relationship to procreate children in an act of free love that imitates God's act of freely and lovingly creating people—the very thing that gives them value. In essence, humans valuing each other (subjective value) imitates God's valuing of people (objective value). Humans not valuing each other, and especially their own offspring, fail to imitate God in this matter. This suggests that the subject's love is more important than the object's rationality, an important corrective to rationalistic functionalist criteria of personhood.

Contrast this notion of value based on God's love with Alison Jaggar's two ways a fetus may have value. "Fetuses may have moral value in two possible ways. If they are sentient . . . they have intrinsic value as beings whose interests should count in moral deliberation. In addition, when fetuses are perceived as approaching and welcome members of human families and communities, they may have moral value as objects of people's hopes, desires, and fears. Since both sorts of value admit of degrees, my view implies that all fetuses do not have the same moral worth."[60]

Why, from Jaggar's point of view, would anyone have intrinsic value? She does not go beyond asserting the value of sentient beings. But why think sentience is value-giving? As for her second way, it puts a great deal of power into the hands of human families and communities if their feelings and hopes bestow value and rights on a baby. Surely the hopes, desires, and fears of people is no foundation for inalienable rights or equal rights, as Jaggar herself admits. As Beckwith points out, "Every child a wanted child" reflects "the least virtuous and most repulsive aspect of 'machoism'—I can snuff you out because I'm bigger."[61] If people can grant rights, they can just as easily take them away, as communist governments have frequently done. Also, if fetuses are only valuable if they are the object of parents' (or a parent's) hopes, desires, and fears, does this make them mere means rather than ends? Are they only means to some purpose, like happiness? It sounds that way, though it is possible Jaggar assumes that parents hope for a relationship with the child and that this makes them personal beings. If so, then this again is subjective value. But something more than a subjective foundation for value will be needed for humans both inside and outside the womb. It could be that this is just Jaggar's way of referring to parental love for the child before birth. If so, then that is an imitation of the love of God for the child and is good, though subjective, in contrast to the objective value bestowed by God's love.

60. Jaggar, "Abortion Rights and Gender Justice Worldwide," 162.
61. Beckwith, *Politically Correct Death*, 65.

A number of theologians and ethicists ground the objective value of human life in the fact that humans are made in God's image, a reality that consists in or includes the fact that humans stand in relation to God and are loved by God and addressed by him in a call into a personal relationship.[62] This relation does not imply that each person loves God, as Brunner's teaching on the formal image makes clear. A positive response to God's call is not what gives people value; simply being loved by God does that. Because God does not owe anyone this love, but loves freely, this love is a gift. Human value is not inherent or intrinsic, it is derived from God. If there was no God who created us freely and lovingly for a purpose, then we just are. There is no value implied by simply existing, especially as a cosmic accident, even if you are smarter than Albert Einstein, more loving than Mother Teresa, and freer than a bird.

Gushee insists that human worth is not because of some human quality or characteristic. It is not an achievement, but an ascription by God, who created people for relationship with himself.[63] Gushee offers an excellent Christian definition of human sacredness with some implications.

> Human life is sacred: this means that God has consecrated each and every human being—without exception and in all circumstances—as a unique, incalculably precious being of elevated status and dignity. Through God's revelation in Scripture and incarnation in Jesus Christ, God has declared and demonstrated the sacred worth of human beings and will hold us accountable for responding appropriately. Such a response begins by adopting a posture of reverence and by accepting responsibility for the sacred gift that is human life. It includes offering due respect and care to each human being that we encounter. It extends to an obligation to protect human life from wanton destruction, desecration, or the violation of human rights. A full embrace of the sacredness of human life leads to a full-hearted commitment to foster human flourishing.[64]

It is clear that Gushee is concerned to provide grounds for negative rights such as the right to life and liberty—negative because they put an obligation on people to not kill or enslave anyone. But Gushee goes

---

62. Rae and Cox, *Bioethics*, 131–32; Montgomery, *Human Rights*, 207–8; Hittinger, "Toward an Adequate Anthropology," 74; Fowler, *Abortion*, 98; Kilner, *Dignity and Destiny*, 116–17; Mays, "Self in the Psalms and the Image of God," 625–29.

63. Gushee, *Sacredness of Human Life*, 44.

64. Gushee, *Sacredness of Human Life*, 33.

beyond that to say that those who believe in human sacredness are obligated to foster human flourishing. His book spells out numerous ways we can and should get involved.

Don S. Browning rightly specifies the filial nature of our connection with God in an interesting comparison with Kantian ethics.

> The metaphor of God the Creator assigns a special status to humans as made in God's image. The core of moral reason requires respect for both other and self as ends who must never be reduced to means and never commodified. The Jewish and Christian doctrine of the *imago Dei* gives ultimate seriousness to the status of humans as ends. Kant grounded respect for other and self on the basis of human rationality. This does not necessarily contradict also grounding respect on the basis of the *imago Dei*. Furthermore, basing respect on the primordial relation all humans have with the divine requires that we show respect to the neighbor with all the more seriousness. It is one thing to be a rational animal; it is something even more profound to be a child of God.[65]

Hans Reinders uses theological categories to consider the question of the value of a twelve year-old girl named Kelly, who was born micro-encephalic (part of her brain was missing), resulting in her living in what some would call a vegetative state. Some might even call hers a marginal case, as if full humanity or personhood was an attainment of those who could do particular things, with everyone else outside the circle. Or worse, they are in a sort of human minor league.[66] It is easy to see that the functional view of personhood leads to just this type of reductionism. To Reinders, the narrative in Scripture gives us a very different set of presuppositions with which to address the question of Kelly's humanity and worth. Reinders appeals primarily to the narrative elements of protology and eschatology to understand Kelly theologically. "What the Christian faith tells us about our final destiny, that we will be resurrected with Christ, is intended in the beginning. And what it tells us about our origin, that we are created in the image of God, is consummated in the end."[67] One must not start with a biological, psychological, or philosophical definition of a person, but rather a theological one. God created all humans in his image. Thus, "Christians claim that in the loving eyes of

65. Browning, "Human Dignity," 4031–36.

66. Reinders, "Human Dignity in the Absence of Agency," 1652.

67. Reinders, "Human Dignity in the Absence of Agency," 1668–69.

God the Father there are no marginal cases of being 'human.'"[68] Rather, he concludes this way:

> Having explained our dignity as originating from the act of communion by which God has first created us, and then has re-created us, we have shown that our humanity is a gift from the beginning to the end. We have received it, before we did anything, and we are promised the fullness of this gift in the end. This indicates why divine agency—not human agency—is the primary concept of theological anthropology. Because of what God does, we can see Kelly as a child of God who is lovable in his eyes just like any other of his children. When seen in that light, Kelly fits Jenson's description of personal being, according to which "a person is one whom other persons may address in hope of response." The hope of response in her case must be eschatological hope, the hope for what she and we will be in the final state of our existence, as Zizioulas did put it. Given that Christian hope, we may regard the acts of communion that include her in personal being as acts that prefigure the future of God.[69]

There is nothing like this in naturalism, for on its metaphysical assumptions death is personal extinction with no afterlife or resurrection. On functionalist assumptions, if a person is never self-aware or capable of rationality and so forth during her life, then she is on the margins or not a person and that will never change apart from relevant technological advancements. On the one hand, this means the Christian has no common ground to which to appeal in saying that Kelly is a person and therefore as valuable as anyone else. Having only theological ground to stand on ushers Christians to the margins of bioethics lest they be allowed to "impose their religion" on others. On the other hand, these theological resources ought to be highly valued for doing precisely what naturalistic humanism cannot: provide a foundation for both the intuitively grasped value of Kelly herself and the hope of Kelly actually flourishing in full health with the mental and relational capacities common to humanity. Are there not many parents with a special needs child who could be comforted by such a hope? To the Christian, this is no mere wish, but a certain hope based on the past fact of Jesus's resurrection from the dead. In that light, the very thought of killing humans not considered persons

---

68. Reinders, "Human Dignity in the Absence of Agency," 1685.

69. Reinders, "Human Dignity in the Absence of Agency," 1854–60. Similarly, see Polkinghorne, "Anthropology in an Evolutionary Context," 1321.

is an obvious affront to their worth, whether inside or outside the womb. Today, an estimated 67 percent of parents abort when they find out the child has Down syndrome. Pro-choice bioethicist Chris Kaposy laments this fact and makes a good case for choosing life for these children (as he and his wife did for their own) in the New York Times based on values such as unconditional love, acceptance, and empathy.[70] Nevertheless, there is nothing in a secular viewpoint like the Christian's foundation for Kelly's value and hope of total healing at the resurrection.

Others join Reinders in saying that Christian anthropology must draw resources from theology rather than appealing only to common ground in philosophical anthropology that lacks a narrative theological structure capable of making sense of our account of humanity and what actually makes humans valuable. Yet, rather than cutting Christians out of the great bioethical discussions of the day, there is a reason theological accounts of humanity should have a place at the table. Christoph Schwöbel insists that all accounts of human dignity rest on metaphysical assumptions that their advocates should make explicit for public debate. Christians should do the same, thereby making our claims publicly contestable.[71] There really is no metaphysical or worldview neutrality. Browning puts it this way: "The basic difference between theological anthropology and the anthropologies of other disciplines, thus, is not that theology is morally and metaphysically freighted and the others are not. It is rather that theological anthropology takes responsibility for its moral and metaphysical judgments while many other contemporary anthropologies do not. If this observation holds, then theology and the secular disciplines are on far more equal grounds than is generally recognized."[72] In this light, secular bioethicists bear just as much of the burden of proof for their naturalistic assumptions as Christians do for their theological ones.

It is valuable and vital for Christians to both appeal to common ground (e.g., dignity, patient consent, beneficence, justice, established facts, presuppositions of method like logic and the scientific method, etc.) in bioethical engagement and to use theological resources to ground what naturalistic perspectives cannot seem to: objective moral values, especially the value of human life. The latter is more of an apologetic endeavor and the former a social-political endeavor. Both are needed.

---

70. See Kaposy, "Ethical Case for Having a Baby with Down Syndrome."

71. Schwöbel, "Recovering Human Dignity," 644–54.

72. Browning, "Human Dignity," 3963–66.

It may be helpful to discuss a specific instance in which both of these sides of the debate come into play. Pro-choice philosopher David Boonin interacts with the sanctity of life argument against abortion. As he understands it, it states,

P1: The fetus is a human life from the moment of conception.

P2: Every human life is sacred.

P3: If the life of an individual is sacred, then the individual has a right to life.

C: The fetus has a right to life from the moment of conception.[73]

Boonin then points out that there are two different ways to understand the meaning of "sacred" here. One is religious: humans are made in God's image and exist in a special relation to God. If the pro-lifer is willing to acknowledge that the argument depends on this specifically religious concept, and if the concept is assumed to be true, then, Boonin says, "It is not difficult to see how an argument appealing to a claim about sanctity in the first sense might prove satisfactory."[74] He points out no problem with this argument at all. This supports the contention that the relational view of the image of God (which would include the royal family view) does indeed support the sanctity/sacredness/dignity/value of human life and the consequent political right to life.

Having said that, for those who do not accept its religious premises about God creating humans in his image and likeness and their therefore being related to God in a special way, the argument fails, Boonin says.[75] His point here is not to interact with apologetic arguments for these beliefs, for pro-life and pro-choice advocates alike should appeal to existing common ground in order to convince one another lest each side simply talk past the other from incommensurable positions.[76] For that very reason, few if any pro-lifers will concede that the pro-life argument depends exclusively on religious assumptions. Just as prohibitions of theft do not rely on exclusively religious reasons but have other types of reasons, so, too, prohibitions of abortion have both religious and non-religious reasons. Thus, Boonin interacts with the non-religious understanding of the sanctity of life argument. He says the non-theological sense of sacred

---

73. Boonin, *A Defense of Abortion*, 28. "P" stands for premise; "C" stands for conclusion.

74. Boonin, *A Defense of Abortion*, 28.

75. Boonin, *A Defense of Abortion*, 30.

76. Boonin, *A Defense of Abortion*, 9–14.

is "worthy of reverence or awe."[77] He concedes that a study of human embryonic development does indeed leave one with a sense of awe, but the same can be said of studying animal embryos. He concludes, "Why should it follow from the fact that the zygote is amazing, astonishing, or awesome, that we are only permitted to kill it under the sort of extreme circumstances that would also justify killing individuals like you and me?"[78] It is worth questioning why the latter individuals are worth so much if one does not assume God created humans in his image. Just before this, Boonin described humans and other species as "merely the tentative result of minor random variations guided by natural selection . . . So there is no reason for our evolutionary history to confer a moral status on us that it does not confer equally on all species that have survived this process."[79] So the question is, why is it impermissible to kill minor random variations? Humans might not want to be killed, but surely that does not make it objectively wrong (*prima facie*). Everyone knows it is in fact wrong, but naturalistic evolution cannot explain why nor provide objective moral values. Both sides should look for common ground yet consider one another's case for what is not currently common ground on such foundational issues.

The metaphysical problem aside, there is a problem with his conclusion. He assumes that there is a difference between the awesome zygote and "individuals like you and me." Or at least he assumes that pro-lifers mean something different when calling the zygote sacred than when we call "individuals like you and me" sacred. We do not; we mean the same thing: "highly valued and important."[80] Boonin clearly assumes the value of people old enough to read his book, a value so great that only extreme circumstances could justify killing them. And that is the common ground from which pro-life philosophers and ethicists argue for the substance view of persons over-against his own functional view of personhood. Indeed, the argument is that one should not arbitrarily choose one stage of development and attribute personhood and value according to the capacities typical at that stage of development. A personal being is a kind of substance, not a stage in a substance's development. A person goes through many stages of development and none of them ought to

---

77. Boonin, *Defense of Abortion*, 28.

78. Boonin, *Defense of Abortion*, 31–32.

79. Boonin, *Defense of Abortion*, 31.

80. See meaning 5b in Merriam-Webster's definition of the word "sacred."

define who is in and who is out of the fully human, rights-bearing community of persons. The argument is that none of the differences between
embryos and adults (size, level of development, environment, and degree
of dependency) justify killing the former and not the latter.

It should be noted that Boonin's entire work is an attempt to justify treating one group of humans very differently than another group
of humans. Even if he would likely not frame his work that way, that
is the effect of his argument. The Parable of the Good Samaritan (Luke
10:25–37) has something to say about such a procedure.

> On one occasion an expert in the law stood up to test Jesus.
> "Teacher," he asked, "what must I do to inherit eternal life?"
>
> "What is written in the Law?" he replied. "How do you
> read it?"
>
> He answered, "'Love the Lord your God with all your heart
> and with all your soul and with all your strength and with all
> your mind'; and, 'Love your neighbor as yourself.'"
>
> "You have answered correctly," Jesus replied. "Do this and
> you will live."
>
> But he wanted to justify himself, so he asked Jesus, "And
> who is my neighbor?"
>
> In reply Jesus said: "A man was going down from Jerusalem
> to Jericho, when he was attacked by robbers. They stripped him
> of his clothes, beat him and went away, leaving him half dead.
> A priest happened to be going down the same road, and when
> he saw the man, he passed by on the other side. So too, a Levite,
> when he came to the place and saw him, passed by on the other
> side. But a Samaritan, as he traveled, came where the man was;
> and when he saw him, he took pity on him. He went to him and
> bandaged his wounds, pouring on oil and wine. Then he put the
> man on his own donkey, brought him to an inn and took care
> of him. The next day he took out two denarii and gave them to
> the innkeeper. 'Look after him,' he said, 'and when I return, I will
> reimburse you for any extra expense you may have.'
>
> "Which of these three do you think was a neighbor to the
> man who fell into the hands of robbers?"
>
> The expert in the law replied, "The one who had mercy
> on him."
>
> Jesus told him, "Go and do likewise."

Richard Hays applies the parable to the issue of abortion this way.

> When we ask, "Is the fetus a person?" we are asking the same
> sort of limiting, self-justifying question that the lawyer asked

Jesus: "Who is my neighbor?" Jesus, by answering the lawyer's question with this parable, rejects casuistic attempts to circumscribe our moral concern by defining the other as belonging to a category outside the scope of our obligation. To define the unborn child as a nonperson is to narrow the scope of moral concern, whereas Jesus calls upon us to widen it by showing mercy and actively intervening on behalf of the helpless. The Samaritan is a paradigm of love that goes beyond ordinary obligation and thus creates a neighbor relation where none existed before. The concluding word of the parable addresses us all: "Go and do likewise."[81]

Again, people have tried to justify the enslavement, mistreatment, and murder of groups of people by defining them out of the human race, personhood, or image of God. This includes Native Americans, black people, people from South and Central America, Jews, and others. Yet, rather than learning from this inhumane pattern so as not to repeat it, some people are still justifying violence against those they do not deem persons. This not only fails to recognize a neighbor relation where there is one, but the justifying of the inaction or harm is itself very unneighborly. That is why Jesus's answer turns the question from "who is my neighbor?" to "who was a neighbor?" He wanted the legal expert to ponder whether he was being a good neighbor rather than evaluating the other's status. Ironically, pro-choice progressives, who often pride themselves on being more inclusive than their political rivals, refuse to include an entire category of humans/persons, namely the unborn. Their position is exclusivist and results in the same sort of inhumane acts as other exclusivists who have enslaved, mistreated, and murdered those deemed "less than" the rest of humanity.[82]

81. Hays, *Moral Vision*, 451. It is noteworthy that Hays says that the sacredness of human life has no basis in the NT and does not ground the prohibition of murder. Rather, human beings lack the authority to take what is not theirs, namely human life, which belongs to God (454–55). But this reason itself presupposes the sacred value of life. Why would a person need special authority to take something that has no value? Perhaps it is because God values life so much that he only delegates us authority to take it in limited circumstances. The NT basis for the notion of human sacredness includes Mark 8:34–38; Matt 6:25–30; 10:29–31 (discussed above).

82. In another irony, abortionist Dr. Willie Parker appeals to the Parable of the Good Samaritan to defend his abortion practice. A pregnant woman is in need, much as the man who was beaten and robbed was in need. Her need is for a safe ending of her pregnancy. As a physician, Dr. Parker is in a position to help and will not turn away as the priest and Levite did, but rather will help her as the Samaritan helped the man.

Full and equal human inclusivity should be applied not only to the unborn, but to those with Down Syndrome, mental illness, terminal diseases, rival nations, political enemies, and every other category of people. Lest Boonin or anyone else dismiss this as a theological argument, it surely appeals to secular values like love, inclusion, compassion for the helpless, neighbor relations, equality, and obligations to others. Surely these concepts are welcome in moral discourse, regardless of who spoke of them, for they can also be intuitively perceived. In fact, Judith Jarvis Thomson, whose argument from unplugging the violinist Boonin takes pains to defend, appeals to this parable in her important essay defending abortion.[83] It seems that such values should be considered as possible—even necessary—limits to the value of individual autonomy.[84]

The Royal/Functional View

Middleton discusses how the image of God grounds the sanctity of human life on his view.

> The postfall persistence of the *imago Dei* is assumed also in Jas 3:9, which, like Gen 9:6, undergirds a specific ethical implication, challenging those who would bless God yet curse a person made in the divine "likeness." This NT text echoes the OT

This application of the parable hinges on his functionalist distinction between humans and persons, the same distinction discussed above. Because of the problems with that distinction, Dr. Parker should have considered the other neighbor, the unborn person, as an equal of his/her mother in his ethical decision-making. A good neighbor does not dismember one's unborn neighbor. See Summit Ministries, "Abortion Debate," 38:45—41:42; 45:32—46:17.

83. Her point in appealing to the parable is that a woman should not be morally, let alone legally, obligated to lend the fetus the use of her body to live, even granted that the fetus is a person. See Thomson, "Defense of Abortion," 485–86. One of the fatal flaws of her argument is that it overlooks the vast difference between disallowing someone the use of your body and taking action to kill the other person, in this case usually by dismembering or chemically burning him/her. For this and other criticisms of the violinist argument, see Wagner et al., "De Facto Guardianship and Abortion"; Beckwith, *Defending Life*, 174–99.

84. See DeGrazia et al., *Biomedical Ethics*, 41–48 for a non-theological discussion of autonomy and how it is often accorded such great value among contemporary bioethicists that any infringement must now be thoroughly justified by "liberty limiting principles." Even then, the authors note, bioethicists often argue against many or most of those principles (p. 46). Truly autonomy is the primary value in secular medical ethics today. For an evaluation of autonomy from a Christian perspective, see Rae and Cox, *Bioethics*, 194–216.

wisdom tradition that people somehow represent their maker, so that oppression or kindness shown to the poor and needy are equivalent to insult or honor shown to God (Prov 14:31; 17:5; cf. 22:2). A similar idea lies behind Jesus' claim in the parable of the sheep and the goats (Matt 25:31–46) that whatever works of love a person performs to "one of the least of these" is done to him (Matt. 25:40).[85]

Here it is not the dominion itself that makes a person valuable, but the fact that people represent God in some way. Elsewhere, Middleton says the image is representational in that humans bear some similarity/analogy to God and also that humans represent God functionally in that God appointed people to administer creation and serve as a kingdom of priests.[86] Any similarity to the God who is praiseworthy in every way would seem to ground unique human value, at least before the fall. Similarly, the idea that humans may represent God functionally as the earth's caretakers could give them a certain status. But "human sin/violence has impeded and distorted the calling to be God's image on earth."[87] And, as Kilner points out, people do not all have the same capacity to carry out ruling functions. This seems to make human value vulnerable, especially for those with disabilities.[88] It is possible to hold that God designed people to equally contribute to the creation project and that each will be able to do so in the *eschaton*, however.

It is also possible to embrace a strong functional element and not believe sin tarnishes the image (since the image is Jesus himself) and that the human connection with God is the foundation of human value and also what makes dominion possible. That is the royal family view. The only value to God humanity's dominion might give is usefulness or functional value. As long as this is not confused with any notion that God needs people, it may convey the truth that God wants them to be involved in the creation project. But human sacredness/sanctity/dignity/value is not about usefulness, it is about God valuing people personally apart from what they can do. It seems best to keep these types of value distinct.

Consider another way in which dominion interfaces with human dignity. It was noted in the introduction that Dolores Dunnett defended abortion in certain circumstances using the fact that humans are made in

85. Middleton, "Image of God," 396.

86. Middleton, *Liberating Image*, 1318–50.

87. Middleton, "Image of God," 396.

88. Kilner, *Dignity and Destiny*, 205.

God's image, which stands in stark contrast to the conclusion many other Christians draw from the image of God. How she reasons is of interest.

> We have the right to dominion over everything—including the right to make decisions regarding everything that has the breath of life, as long as it is done in community and for the good of the community (or common good), under the guidance of the Holy Spirit. In terms of the Genesis account mankind has been given dominion (authority) over the rest of God's creation and has been instructed to rule over it and subdue it (1:26–28). Everything is put under our feet (Ps 8:6), not for our own benefit but for God's glory. We are coworkers with God in this earthly task. We are like God in the sense of the responsibility and freedom he has given to us, and this involves our role in caring for and developing and improving a world that will glorify him.[89]

So far, so good. Towards the end of her article, she applies the theology of dominion based on the image of God this way:

> If the woman conceives against her consent through rape or incest and she wants an abortion, her request should be respected. In this case she is more than just a body. She is a person created in God's image, and to deny her this is to deny her personhood.
>
> The third instance of a permissible abortion is when a child will be born with grave physical or mental defects. This option again affirms our responsibility in considering or being concerned with life after birth as well as life before birth. A friend of mine recently had to sacrifice a Down Syndrome child in the hope of having a normal healthy child. The malformed child would not have made the bearing of a healthy child possible because of the medical expenses that would have resulted from the birth of the former. The decision was made to abort the malformed fetus. This proved to be a wise decision, because another fetus was conceived and turned out to be a healthy, beautiful child. The sacrifice was worth it.
>
> This is a good example of using the authority given to us by God to control and rule our lives rather than letting a bad situation develop and ruin several lives. To be responsible coworkers with God helps us care for and develop the world God has made for us in the quality of people we can produce to live in this world to glorify him.[90]

89. Dunnett, "Evangelicals," 216.
90. Dunnett, "Evangelicals," 224–25.

These are heart-wrenching situations that are far easier to write about theoretically than to actually go through. To disagree with Dunnett may sound uncompassionate, particularly in cases of rape and incest. But Christian ethicists must bring the tools of biblical theology to bear on real-world situations and the correct conclusions may be difficult to enact. An appeal to the rape victim's being made in God's image explains why she has the right not to be raped and why the perpetrator should be prosecuted in a manner commensurate with the seriousness of the crime, an outcome that is too often not achieved. But it does not, biblically speaking, ground a woman's right to do harm to an innocent human being, as would happen if she aborted the fetus. The fetus is a human being and a person with her own rights, including the right not to be killed by any means, let alone using methods as brutal as dismemberment or being chemically burned.[91] People do not even use such cruel methods when putting dogs to sleep. Nor should they. In this scenario, it would not be the expectant mother's personhood being denied by pro-life laws, but the fetus's personhood being denied. This notion that women are being treated as less than persons or less than men if they are not allowed by law to have abortions makes no sense. Pro-life arguments are designed to show that there is no morally relevant difference between killing innocent persons after birth and killing innocent persons before birth, and the pre-born are persons. People, including men, are not allowed to kill innocent people after birth. Yet this limitation is not deemed to be treating them as less than persons. So why would it be treating women as less than persons to disallow them from killing unborn persons?

Genesis 4 speaks of the innocent blood of Abel crying out to God from the ground. The flood was occasioned in part by all the violence people were perpetrating against one another (Gen 6:11). And Genesis 9 authorizes governments to punish murder because those murdered are made in God's image. These passages develop the thought about the image of God in people revealed in Genesis 1, applying this truth to the issue of how they must be treated. A right that governments must protect is based on the work of God. Reading the redemptive-historical

91. It is vital that anyone who argues for abortion choice face up to the reality of the act they are defending rather than avoiding that reality with euphemisms like reproductive choice, health care, terminating pregnancy, and so forth. For video explanations of some common abortion procedures by an experienced former abortionist, Dr. Anthony Levatino, see "Aspiration Abortion" and other videos at https://www.abortionprocedures.com. For images of what fetuses look like after these procedures, see "This Is Abortion."

development of the image of God shows that Dunnett's particular application of it is antithetical to the Divine Author's application of it. She justifies violence using the image of God whereas Scripture condemns violence using the image of God.

Dunnett makes her argument in favor of allowing the abortion of a malformed fetus from the idea that human responsibility to rule involves them in making decisions about "the quality of people we can produce to live in this world to glorify him." Logically, this argument could be made for genetically enhancing children to measure up to one's idea of quality people, a problematic issue for many reasons, not least the motives of parents and criteria of what makes for quality people. She is not here making an argument for genetic alterations or eugenics, but the logic can certainly be used that way. Further, the biblical way parents are to ensure the quality of their offspring is by raising them properly, training them to behave justly (Gen 18:17–19; Deut 6; Ps 78). And how accurately can Dunnett or an expecting mother or anyone predict the outcome of the lives of those involved? How much weight should a moral argument put on such a notoriously difficult procedure as future prediction?

In addition, should one assume that the proper reasoning process of rulers of creation includes the ends-justifies-the-means ethic Dunnett uses? She says that sacrificing the Down Syndrome child was worth it to produce a healthy child. Paul specifically condemns doing evil so that good may result in Romans 3:8. And historically, much that is evil has been justified in the name of the ends.[92] In fact, David DeGrazia, Thomas Mappes, and Jeffrey Brand-Ballard point out that such utilitarianism seems unable to coexist with the notion of rights.[93] One of the common arguments for enhanced interrogation at Guantanamo Bay was that the methods used could potentially save many lives. This is a utilitarian argument that many reject because prisoners have rights as human beings. By the same reasoning, one could justify killing an older, unhappy couple in order to release them from their unhappiness.[94] Or one could frame an innocent person on a capital offense to avoid deadly rioting.[95] Surely such actions cannot be justified.

---

92. E.g., slavery, ethnic cleansing, the Final Solution, the many people killed at the hands of Communists over the last century, etc.

93. DeGrazia et al., *Biomedical Ethics*, 12.

94. DeGrazia et al., *Biomedical Ethics*, 12.

95. Wolf-Devine and Devine, "Abortion: A Communitarian Pro-Life Perspective," 71.

Robert George and Christopher Tollefsen explain why it is that rights cannot coexist with any utilitarian or consequentialist ethic:

> Within any such ethic, there will always be human beings who are dispensable, who must be sacrificed for the greater good. Utilitarianism fails in a radical way to respect the dignity and rights of individual human beings. For it treats the greater good, a mere aggregate of all the interests or pleasures or preferences of individuals, as the good of supreme worth and value, and it demands that nothing stand in the way of its pursuit. The utilitarian thus cannot believe, except as a convenient fiction, in human rights or in actions that may never be done to people, regardless of the consequences.[96]

When God gave humans dominion, it was within certain limits, and one of those limits is clearly another person's right to life. This limits human autonomy. And it is not denying anyone's status as a person made in God's image to disallow them from murdering someone, including oneself in suicide, assisted or otherwise. This shows how autonomy must take a subordinate position in a biblical ethic, well behind the sacredness of human life.

Concluding Reflections

The royal family view combines a relational view that is based on the filial relationship between God and his children with a royal/functional view that begins with the insight that God's first stated purpose for creating humans in his image was that they may exercise dominion under him and over the earth and its animals. It is not the dominion purpose that grounds the objective value of human beings, for the potential to exercise dominion in all humans' various ways gives them more of an instrumental value. Rather, it is the filial/relational nature of the image of God that makes humans so very valuable. At a basic level, anyone doing anything intentionally implies that action's value to the person. When a good God creates something, that implies its value to him. And God repeatedly declared what he made good in the beginning. When he made humans male and female in his image and likeness, this implied representation and relationship that suggested greater value than the other things and beings in creation. In giving people dominion, their higher status seemed

---

96. George and Tollefsen, *Embryo*, 1420.

to be confirmed. Then God called everything he had made, which now included humans, very good. Jesus later said people were worth more than many sparrows, confirming the surpassing value of human beings. At no point do the biblical authors ever say or imply that there is any such thing as a human who is not a person, a being made in God's image, or a neighbor. Nor does it say or imply that there are degrees of humanity, personhood, or being God's offspring. It is presumptuous for humans to arrogate such a prerogative to themselves. It is also presumptuous for humans to arrogate to themselves the prerogative of bestowing value upon (some) humans, a usurping of God's own prerogative as Creator. No, it is God who values and thus makes people objectively valuable. Humans must value one another because God values each one and will hold them accountable for their treatment of others. In a fallen world where there is so much selfishness and where human beings are not getting less violent, malicious, or selfish, both the principle of human sacredness and the incentive to uphold it are needed to restrain evil. Far from being redundant, stupid, or useless, human sacredness is a distinct, wise, and vital principle for civil society in general and bioethics in particular.

Conclusion

I RECENTLY READ A sermon on the image of God I preached seventeen years ago. In it, I set forth a broad structural view of the image of God. The image of God meant every way in which humans resemble God. Know God's communicable attributes and you will know what God's image is all about. I was struck by how much my view had changed. I hope this change was the result of an open-minded study of Scripture combined with a greater appreciation for the implications of the doctrine.

Let us review where we have been. The three types of analysis in this book have offered three general tests for a doctrine of the image of God. The first type was a redemptive-historical analysis, which tests the doctrine exegetically within each of the texts and then checks how the doctrine unfolds within the redemptive narrative in Scripture. This was the task of chapters 1 and 2. In particular, a doctrine of the image must make sense of not only a text like Genesis 1:26–28, but also its use in Psalm 8 and Hebrews 2, along with all the other allusions to the image and likeness. The story told in the doctrine must be an integral part of the story told in the Bible as it unfolds diachronically. Of course, there is not just one biblical theology on offer. But the view of redemptive history within which the image of God story has been told here can be evaluated exegetically, historically, and systematically.

The image concept began with a pattern for humans that was God himself, later specified as God the Son, Jesus. Sonship itself was thus set at the heart of the image concept, at least as it pertains to the paradigm, Jesus. In the New Testament, every person is said to be God's offspring, an allusion to the image of God. But since the fall, there is a further sense in which one can be a son or daughter of God, namely being a willing part of his family. The sonship/daughtership of every Christian comes to the forefront, along with our brotherhood and sisterhood within the church, the new humanity that participates in the reconciling of all things to God in the wake of the fall. And that filial relationship with God comes into play in some image texts. The sonship of Jesus is mirrored in the sonship/daughtership of believers, albeit without a Divine nature in believers' case. Yet Jesus shares some of his kingdom authority with his brothers and sisters. Proper human rule in creation had faltered but is now being put back on track until it is fully restored in the *eschaton*. In order for humans to exercise dominion in the manner in which God wants them to (in imitation of his righteous character and behavior), they must be transformed by God's power, an ongoing process until its completion at the resurrection. These are the broad brushstrokes of the story.

The second type of analysis was systematic theology. On the basis of the exegetical and redemptive-historical work in chapters 1 and 2 and a consideration of other systematic theologies of the image, chapter 3 concluded that Jesus himself defines God's image. He is the Son of God (albeit in a Divine sense unlike human sonship/daughtership) and the moral paradigm for their character and behavior. *A human being made in God's image is a royal son/daughter by nature who is meant to enjoy relationships with God and his family and reflect his virtuous character while sharing dominion in creation with God's family.* This royal family view is both relational and functional at the same time, with a moral dimension. All of this presupposes certain capacities of human nature without defining them as what it means to be made in God's image. Yet only beings with such a personal nature with its basic capacities are made in God's image.

Since the fall, everyone fails to measure up to the paradigm and everyone rebels against their Father. His plan of salvation extends the opportunity and enablement to accept his forgiveness, power to change, and fatherly love. This results in peace with God and adoption in the sense of becoming a *willing* part of his family. It seems that this understanding of the image is both consistent with the biblical texts and internally consistent, though the reader can judge those claims.

The third type of analysis was in the area of ethics. Specifically, the question of chapter 4 was whether or not the various views of the image could provide a solid basis for human value, thus giving the world a reason to treat everyone with proper respect and refrain from harming them (and self). In particular, could the relational view (of which the royal family view is one variety) serve as such a basis? The answer was yes, as was acknowledged even by the pro-choice philosopher David Boonin. It is not hard to see why. When God intentionally creates anything, it has value. God is the determiner of what matters and has objective value. His determination of value obligates everyone to value what he values or else face the consequences. But it is not only a matter of authority and punishment, it is a matter of perceiving what is good. Since God is good, what he makes is good. Anyone with a properly functioning goodness-detector will perceive the goodness of what God makes and value it as God does. That is to say, subjective value should follow objective value. This applies to everything God made: the earth, sun, moon, stars, planets, mountains, trees, seas, grass, fish, birds, animals, everything. And it includes human beings. Yet human beings are valued for reasons beyond the fact that God intentionally made them. And humans are valuable for reasons beyond some practical utility. Humans are especially valuable because God made them to be his children. He made them according to the pattern of his divine Son, who was himself not made. He has always existed as God's Son. But they were made to have a filial relationship with the Father and to participate in his dominion over creation in accord with his generous, loving, industrious, creative nature. The character of the Father is seen in the Son whose incarnation gave them opportunity to learn of God in a vivid and direct way. That moral character is the paradigm for humans' moral character and behavior. Whatever deficiencies any person may have in moral character, mental capacities, or any other human/personal capacities does not make someone anything other than a human being, a person, one made in God's image, a son or daughter of God. Though such a person may have to live in such a condition this side of the resurrection, all capacities of his people will be better than new once Jesus raises the dead to live in the new heavens and new earth. Human personhood and value are not determined by what one is like at a given point in time in a fallen world, but by God's love and purposes that transcend time and space. God values each and every person. One's own conformity with the loving paradigm that is Jesus Christ can be tested by how one treats those with diminished capacities or those who have not yet developed their capacities. It is too easy to think one is testing another person when God may be testing him/her using the other person. In any case, the royal family view, with its relational foundations, does ground the value of every human being/person. Again, let the reader decide.

We started with a litany of challenges to human dignity in the world today that included human trafficking, genocides, religious persecution, wars, nuclear proliferation, abortion, assisted suicide, and enhanced interrogation. We brought other issues into the discussion along the way that included sexism, racism, statism, idolatry, justice, world peace, and body-self dualism's denigration of the body in determining personal identity. These are only some of the issues addressed by a theology of God's image. One could easily add issues of poverty, health care, self-esteem, and family. Lives both now and in the eternal future are at stake in the debate over human nature. Many do not believe there is any such thing as human nature at all, cutting off one of the richest sources of common ground with which we might unite humanity. As important as all these issues are, it was not possible to apply our findings to all of them in any thorough way here. And it was not possible to address all the implications of the royal family view of the image to the practical questions of discipleship. It is important for the church to make disciples of Christ that resemble Christ in moral character. How to inculcate Jesus's virtues in his followers remains one of the most important challenges the church faces in a culture that both picks and chooses which Christian virtues to affirm and often fails to practice even the preferred virtues. Christians too often conform more to the pattern of the world than to the pattern of Christ. Short of fully addressing these issues, this book at least set out to put humanity into the proper narrative framework within which the church can effectively fulfill its mission.

Bibliography

"Abortion Statistics: United States Data and Trends." http://www.nrlc.org/uploads/factsheets/FS01AbortionintheUS.pdf.

Akin, Daniel L. *1, 2, 3 John*. The New American Commentary. Nashville: Broadman & Holman, 2001.

Alexander, T. Desmond, and Brian S. Rosner, eds. *New Dictionary of Biblical Theology*. Downers Grove, IL: InterVarsity, 2000.

Allen, David L. *Hebrews*. The New American Commentary. Nashville: Broadman & Holman, 2010.

Allen, Ronald B. "עָפָר." In *Theological Wordbook of the Old Testament*, edited by R. Laird Harris et al., 687. Chicago: Moody, 1999.

Anderson, Ryan T. *When Harry Became Sally: Responding to the Transgender Moment*. New York: Encounter, 2019.

Aquinas, Thomas. *Summa Theologica*. Vols. 17–18. Great Books of the Western World. Chicago: Encyclopaedia Britannica, 1990.

Archer, Gleason L., Jr. "Daniel." In *Expositor's Bible Commentary*. Grand Rapids, MI: Zondervan, 1976. Pradis CD-ROM.

———. *A Survey of Old Testament Introduction*. 3rd ed. Chicago: Moody, 1994.

"Aspiration Abortion." https://www.abortionprocedures.com/aspiration/.

Balla, Peter. "2 Corinthians." In *Commentary on the New Testament Use of the Old Testament*, 753–82. Grand Rapids, MI: Baker Academic, 2007.

Barrett, C. K. *The Epistle to the Romans*. Rev. ed. Black's New Testament Commentary. London: Continuum, 1991.

———. *The First Epistle to the Corinthians*. Black's New Testament Commentary. London: Continuum, 1968.

Barth, Karl. *Church Dogmatics*. Edited by Thomas Forsyth Torrance. Translated by Geoffrey W. Bromiley. Vol. III/1–2. London: T. & T. Clark International, 2004.

Bassler, Jouette M. "1 Corinthians." In *Women's Bible Commentary*, 557–65. Rev. ed. Louisville: Westminster John Knox, 2012.

Beale, G. K. *The Book of Revelation: A Commentary on the Greek Text*. New International Greek Testament Commentary. Grand Rapids, MI: Eerdmans, 1999.

———. "Colossians." In *Commentary on the New Testament Use of the Old Testament*, 841–69. Grand Rapids, MI: Baker Academic, 2007.

———. "Eden, the Temple, and the Church's Mission in the New Creation." *Journal of the Evangelical Theological Society* 48.1 (2005) 5–31.

———. *A New Testament Biblical Theology: The Unfolding of the Old Testament in the New*. Grand Rapids, MI: Baker, 2011.

———. *The Temple and the Church's Mission: A Biblical Theology of the Dwelling Place of God.* New Studies in Biblical Theology. Downers Grove, IL: InterVarsity, 2004.

———. *We Become What We Worship: A Biblical Theology of Idolatry.* New Studies in Biblical Theology. Downers Grove, IL: IVP Academic, 2009.

Beale, G. K., and D. A. Carson. *Commentary on the New Testament Use of the Old Testament.* Grand Rapids, MI: Baker Academic, 2007.

Beckwith, Francis J. *Defending Life: A Moral and Legal Case against Abortion Choice.* Cambridge: Cambridge University Press, 2007.

———. *Politically Correct Death: Answering the Arguments for Abortion Rights.* Grand Rapids, MI: Baker, 1993.

Behr, John. "The Promise of the Image." In *Imago Dei: Human Dignity in Ecumenical Perspective*, edited by Thomas A. Howard, 15–37. Washington, DC: Catholic University of America Press, 2013.

Berkhof, Louis. *Systematic Theology.* Grand Rapids, MI: Eerdmans, 1938.

Bird, Phyllis A. "'Male and Female He Created Them': Gen 1:27b in the Context of the Priestly Account of Creation." *Harvard Theological Review* 74.2 (April 1981) 129–59.

Black, C. Clifton. "God's Promise for Humans in the New Testament." In *God and Human Dignity*, edited by R. Kendall Soulen and Linda Woodhead, 2352–553. Grand Rapids, MI: Eerdmans, 2006. Kindle edition.

Blomberg, Craig L. *Matthew.* The New American Commentary. Nashville: Broadman & Holman, 1992.

Bonhoeffer, Dietrich. *Creation and Fall: A Theological Exposition of Genesis 1–3.* Translated by Douglas Stephen Bax. Minneapolis: Fortress, 2004.

———. *Ethics.* Translated by Neville Horton Smith. New York: Macmillan, 1965.

Boonin, David. *A Defense of Abortion.* Cambridge University Press, 2003.

Borg, Marcus J., and N. T. Wright. *The Meaning of Jesus: Two Visions.* San Francisco: HarperSanFrancisco, 1999.

Borresen, Kari Elisabeth. "The Imago Dei: Two Historical Contexts." *Mid-Stream* 21.3 (July 1982) 359–65.

Botman, H. Russel. "Integrating Three Contemporary Discourses of Human Dignity." In *God and Human Dignity*, edited by R. Kendall Soulen and Linda Woodhead, 1027–201. Grand Rapids, MI: Eerdmans, 2006. Kindle edition.

Boxall, Ian. *The Revelation of Saint John.* Black's New Testament Commentary. London: Continuum, 2006.

Brannan, Rick, et al., eds. *The Lexham English Septuagint.* Bellingham, WA: Lexham, 2012.

Bratcher, Robert G., and William David Reyburn. *A Translator's Handbook on the Book of Psalms.* UBS Handbook Series. New York: United Bible Societies, 1991.

Browning, Don S. "Human Dignity, Human Complexity, and Human Goods." In *God and Human Dignity*, edited by R. Kendall Soulen and Linda Woodhead, 3844–4054. Grand Rapids, MI: Eerdmans, 2006. Kindle edition.

Bruce, F. F. *The Book of the Acts.* Revised edition. New International Commentary on the New Testament. Grand Rapids, MI: Eerdmans, 1988.

Brueggemann, Walter. *Theology of the Old Testament: Testimony, Dispute, Advocacy.* Minneapolis: Fortress, 1997.

Brunner, Emil. *Man in Revolt: A Christian Anthropology.* Translated by Olive Wyan. London: Lutterworth, 1939.

Büchsel, Friedrich. "Ἀλλάσσω, Ἀντάλλαγμα, Ἀπ-, Δι-, Καταλλάσσω, Καταλλαγή, Ἀποκατ-, Μεταλλάσσω." In *TDNT* 1:251–59.

————. "Ἀντί." In *TDNT* 1:372–73.

————. "Γένος." In *TDNT* 1:684–85.

————. "Γίνομαι." In *TDNT* 1:681–89.

Budziszewski, J. *On the Meaning of Sex*. Wilmington, DE: Intercollegiate Studies Institute, 2014. Kindle edition.

————. *What We Can't Not Know: A Guide*. San Francisco: Ignatius, 2011.

Calmes, Jackie. "Planned Parenthood Videos Were Altered, Analysis Finds." *New York Times*, August 27, 2015. http://www.nytimes.com/2015/08/28/us/abortion-planned-parenthood-videos.html?nytmobile=0.

Calvin, John. *Commentaries on the Epistles of Paul the Apostle to the Philippians, Colossians, and Thessalonians*. Translated by John Pringle. Bellingham, WA: Logos Bible Software, 2010.

————. *Commentaries on the Four Last Books of Moses Arranged in the Form of a Harmony*. Translated by Charles William Bingham. 4 vols. Bellingham, WA: Logos Bible Software, 2010.

————. *Commentary on the Book of Psalms*. Translated by James Anderson. Bellingham, WA: Logos Bible Software, 2010.

————. *Commentary on the Book of the Prophet Daniel*. Translated by Thomas Myers. 2 vols. Bellingham, WA: Logos Bible Software, 2010.

————. *Commentary on the First Book of Moses Called Genesis*. Translated by John King. Bellingham, WA: Logos Bible Software, 2010.

————. *Institutes of the Christian Religion*. Edited by John T. McNeill. Translated by Ford Lewis Battles. 2 vols. The Library of Christian Classics 1. Louisville: Westminster John Knox, 2011.

Cameron, Nigel M. de S. *The New Medicine: Life and Death after Hippocrates*. Wheaton, IL: Crossway, 1991.

Carson, D. A. "Current Issues in Biblical Theology: A New Testament Perspective." *Bulletin for Biblical Research* 5 (January 1, 1995) 17–41.

————. "Domesticating the Gospel: A Review of Grenz's Renewing the Center." In *Reclaiming the Center: Confronting Evangelical Accommodation in Postmodern Times*, edited by Millard J. Erickson, 33–55. Wheaton, IL: Crossway, 2004.

————. "Matthew." In *Expositor's Bible Commentary: Matthew, Mark, and Luke*, 8:3–599. Grand Rapids, MI: Zondervan, 1984.

Carson, D. A., et al. *An Introduction to the New Testament*. Grand Rapids, MI: Zondervan, 1992.

Childs, Brevard S. *Isaiah: A Commentary*. The Old Testament Library. Louisville: Westminster John Knox, 2001.

Ciampa, Roy E. "Adoption." In *New Dictionary of Biblical Theology*, edited by T. Desmond Alexander and Brian S. Rosner, 376–78. Downers Grove, IL: InterVarsity, 2000.

Ciampa, Roy E., and Brian S. Rosner. "1 Corinthians." In *Commentary on the New Testament Use of the Old Testament*, 695–749. Grand Rapids, MI: Baker Academic, 2007.

————. *The First Letter to the Corinthians*. The Pillar New Testament Commentary. Grand Rapids, MI: Eerdmans, 2010.

Clines, David J. A. "The Image of God in Man." *Tyndale Bulletin* 19 (1968) 53–103.

Cohen, Jeremy. *Be Fertile and Increase, Fill the Earth and Master It: The Ancient and Medieval Career of a Biblical Text*. Ithaca, NY: Cornell University Press, 1989.

Cohen, Shaye J. D. *From the Maccabees to the Mishnah*. Library of Early Christianity. Philadelphia: Westminster, 1987.

Condic, Maureen L. "The Origin of Human Life at Fertilization: Quotes Compiled from Medical Textbooks and Peer-Reviewed Scientific Literature." http://bdfund.org/wp-content/uploads/2016/05/Condic-Sources-Embryology.pdf.

Copan, Paul. "The Moral Argument." In *Christian Apologetics: An Anthology of Primary Sources*, edited by Khaldoun A. Sweis and Chad V. Meister, 174–90. Grand Rapids, MI: Zondervan, 2012.

Coppes, Leonard J. "אדם." In *Theological Wordbook of the Old Testament*, edited by R. Laird Harris et al., 10–11. Chicago: Moody, 1999.

Cortez, Marc. *Christological Anthropology in Historical Perspective: Ancient and Contemporary Approaches to Theological Anthropology*. Grand Rapids, MI: Zondervan, 2016.

Craig, William L. "Middle Knowledge, A Calvinist-Arminian Rapprochement?" In *The Grace of God and the Will of Man*, edited by Clark H. Pinnock, 141–64. Minneapolis: Bethany, 1989.

Craigie, Peter C., and Marvin E. Tate. *Psalms 1–50*. 2nd ed. Word Biblical Commentary. Nashville: Nelson, 2004.

Cross, Frank Leslie, and Elizabeth A. Livingstone, eds. "Deification." In *The Oxford Dictionary of the Christian Church*, 467. 3rd ed. New York: Oxford University Press, 2005.

Dallas, Joe. "The Transsexual Dilemma." http://www.equip.org/article/the-transsexual-dilemma/.

Davids, Peter H. *The Epistle of James: A Commentary on the Greek Text*. New International Greek Testament Commentary. Grand Rapids, MI: Eerdmans, 1982.

Davis, John Jefferson. *Evangelical Ethics: Issues Facing the Church Today*. 2nd ed. Phillipsburg, NJ: Presbyterian & Reformed, 1993.

DeClaissé-Walford, Nancy, et al. *The Book of Psalms*. New International Commentary on the Old Testament. Grand Rapids, MI: Eerdmans, 2014.

"Debate: Enhanced Interrogation Techniques." http://debatepedia.idebate.org/en/index.php/Debate:_Enhanced_interrogation_techniques.

DeGrazia, David, et al. *Biomedical Ethics*. 7th ed. New York: McGraw-Hill Education, 2010.

Delling, Gerhard. "Τελειόω." In *TDNT* 8:79–84.

Dempster, Stephen G. *Dominion and Dynasty: A Biblical Theology of the Hebrew Bible*. New Studies in Biblical Theology. Downers Grove, IL: InterVarsity, 2003.

Denizet-Lewis, Benoit. "Friends, Friends with Benefits and the Benefits of the Local Mall." *The New York Times Magazine*, May 30, 2004. https://www.nytimes.com/2004/05/30/magazine/friends-friends-with-benefits-and-the-benefits-of-the-local-mall.html.

Derickson, Gary W. *First, Second, and Third John*. Evangelical Exegetical Commentary. Bellingham, WA: Lexham, 2012.

Duguid, Iain M. *Daniel*. Reformed Expository Commentary. Phillipsburg, NJ: Presbyterian & Reformed, 2008.

———. "Exile." In *New Dictionary of Biblical Theology*, edited by T. Desmond Alexander and Brian S. Rosner, 475–78. Downers Grove, IL: InterVarsity, 2000.

Dumbrell, William. *Covenant and Creation*. 2nd ed. Milton Keynes: Paternoster, 2013.

———. *The End of the Beginning*. Eugene, OR: Wipf & Stock, 2001.

Dunn, James D. G. *The Epistle to the Galatians*. Black's New Testament Commentary. London: Continuum, 1993.

———. *The Epistles to the Colossians and to Philemon: A Commentary on the Greek Text*. New International Greek Testament Commentary. Grand Rapids, MI: Eerdmans, 1996.

Dunnett, Dolores E. "Evangelicals and Abortion." *Journal of the Evangelical Theological Society* 33.2 (June 1, 1990) 215–25.

Edwards, James R. *The Gospel According to Mark*. Pillar New Testament Commentary. Grand Rapids, MI: Eerdmans, 2002.

Eichler, Johannes. "Inheritance, Lot, Portion." In *The New International Dictionary of New Testament Theology*, edited by Colin Brown, 2:295–303. Grand Rapids, MI: Regency, 1986.

Ellingworth, Paul. *The Epistle to the Hebrews: A Commentary on the Greek Text*. New International Greek Testament Commentary. Grand Rapids, MI: Eerdmans, 1993.

Ellingworth, Paul, and Eugene Albert Nida. *A Handbook on the Letter to the Hebrews*. UBS Handbook Series. New York: United Bible Societies, 1994.

Ellingworth, Paul, and Howard Hatton. *A Handbook on Paul's First Letter to the Corinthians*. UBS Handbook Series. New York: United Bible Societies, 1995.

Erickson, Millard J. *Christian Theology*. Grand Rapids, MI: Baker Academic, 1985.

Fee, Gordon D. *The First Epistle to the Corinthians*. New International Commentary on the New Testament. Grand Rapids, MI: Eerdmans, 1987.

———. *Revelation: A New Covenant Commentary*. New Covenant Commentary Series. Cambridge, UK: Lutterworth, 2013.

Feinberg, John S., and Paul D. Feinberg. *Ethics for a Brave New World*. 2nd ed. Wheaton, IL: Crossway, 2010.

"Fetal Trafficking Under Oath." http://www.centerformedicalprogress.org/fetal-trafficking-under-oath/.

Fitzmyer, Joseph A. *Romans: A New Translation with Introduction and Commentary*. Anchor Yale Bible. New Haven: Yale University Press, 2008.

Flender, Otto. "Εἰκών." In *The New International Dictionary of New Testament Theology*, edited by Colin Brown, 2:286–88. Grand Rapids, MI: Regency, 1986.

Foerster, Werner. "Κτίζω, Κτίσις, Κτίσμα, Κτίστης." In *TDNT* 3:1001–35.

Fowler, Paul B. *Abortion: Toward an Evangelical Consensus*. Portland, OR: Multnomah, 1987.

García, Robert K., and Nathan L. King, eds. *Is Goodness without God Good Enough? A Debate on Faith, Secularism, and Ethics*. Lanham, MD: Rowman & Littlefield, 2009.

Garland, David E. *2 Corinthians*. The New American Commentary. Nashville: Broadman & Holman, 1999.

———. *Mark*. The NIV Application Commentary. Grand Rapids, MI: Zondervan, 1996.

Geisler, Norman L., ed. *Inerrancy*. Grand Rapids, MI: Zondervan, 1980.

Gelernter, David. "The Irreducibly Religious Character of Human Dignity." In *Human Dignity and Bioethics: Essays Commissioned by the President's Council on Bioethics*, edited by Tom Merrill, 387–407. Washington, DC: n.p., 2008. https://repository.library.georgetown.edu/bitstream/handle/10822/559351/human_dignity_and_bioethics.pdf?sequence=1&isAllowed=y.

George, Robert P., and Christopher Tollefsen. *Embryo: A Defense of Human Life*. 2nd ed. New York: Doubleday, 2011. Kindle edition.

Gesenius, Friedrich Wilhelm. *Gesenius' Hebrew Grammar,*. Edited by E. Kautzsch and Arthur Ernest Cowley. 2nd ed. Oxford: Clarendon, 1910.

Gess, Johannes. "Χαρακτήρ." In *The New International Dictionary of New Testament Theology*, edited by Colin Brown, 2:288–89. Grand Rapids, MI: Regency, 1986.

Giblin, C. H. "'The Things of God' in the Question Concerning Tribute to Caesar (Lk 20:25; Mk 12:17; Mt 22:21)." *Catholic Biblical Quarterly* 33 (1971) 510–27.

"Global Conflict Tracker." Last modified July 6, 2017. http://www.cfr.org/global/global-conflict-tracker/p32137#!/.

Goldingay, John. *Psalms*. Baker Commentary on the Old Testament. Grand Rapids, MI: Baker Academic, 2006.

Grenz, Stanley J. *The Social God and the Relational Self: A Trinitarian Theology of the Imago Dei*. Louisville: Westminster John Knox, 2001.

———. *Theology for the Community of God*. Grand Rapids, MI: Eerdmans, 2000.

Grudem, Wayne A. *Systematic Theology: An Introduction to Biblical Doctrine*. Grand Rapids, MI: Zondervan, 1994.

Grundmann, Walter, et al. "Χρίω, Χριστός, Ἀντίχριστος, Χρῖσμα, Χριστιανός." In *TDNT* 493–581.

Gushee, David P. *The Sacredness of Human Life: Why an Ancient Biblical Vision Is Key to the World's Future*. Grand Rapids, MI: Eerdmans, 2013.

Guthrie, George H. "Hebrews." In *Commentary on the New Testament Use of the Old Testament*, 919–93. Grand Rapids, MI: Baker Academic, 2007.

Haas, C., et al. *A Handbook on the First Letter of John*. UBS Handbook Series. New York: United Bible Societies, 1994.

Habermas, Jürgen. *Time of Transitions*. Malden, MA: Polity, 2006.

Hamilton, Victor P. "הוד." In *Theological Wordbook of the Old Testament*, edited by R. Laird Harris et al., 209. Chicago: Moody, 1999.

———. "מָשַׁח." In *Theological Wordbook of the Old Testament*, edited by R. Laird Harris et al., 530–32. Chicago: Moody, 1999.

———. *The Book of Genesis: Chapters 1–17*. New International Commentary on the New Testament. Grand Rapids, MI: Eerdmans, 1990.

Harris, Murray J. *Colossians & Philemon*. Exegetical Guide to the Greek New Testament. Grand Rapids, MI: Eerdmans, 1991.

———. *The Second Epistle to the Corinthians: A Commentary on the Greek Text*. New International Greek Testament Commentary. Grand Rapids, MI: Eerdmans, 2005.

Hays, Richard B. *The Moral Vision of the New Testament: Community, Cross, New Creation: A Contemporary Introduction to New Testament Ethics*. San Francisco: HarperCollins, 1996.

Hill, Andrew E., and John H. Walton. *A Survey of the Old Testament*. 3rd ed. Grand Rapids, MI: Zondervan, 2009.

Hittinger, F. Russell. "Toward an Adequate Anthropology: Social Aspects of *Imago Dei* in Catholic Theology." In *Imago Dei: Human Dignity in Ecumenical Perspective*, edited by Thomas Albert Howard, 35–78. Washington, DC: Catholic University of America Press, 2013.

Hodge, Charles. *Systematic Theology*. 3 vols. Oak Harbor, WA: Logos Research Systems, 1997.

Hoekema, Anthony A. *Created in God's Image*. Grand Rapids, MI: Eerdmans, 1994.

Hoffman, W. Michael. "Business and Environmental Ethics." In *Beyond Integrity: A Judeo-Christian Approach to Business Ethics*, edited by Scott B. Rae and Kenman L. Wong, 394–403. 3rd ed. Grand Rapids, MI: Zondervan, 2012.

Horrell, David G. "Ecological Ethics." In *Dictionary of Scripture and Ethics*, edited by Joel B. Green, 255–60. Grand Rapids, MI: Baker Academic, 2012.

Horton, Stanley M. *Acts*. Rev. ed. Springfield, MO: Logion, 2001.

―――. *Genesis: The Promise of Blessing = [Be-Reshit].* The Complete Biblical Library Commentary. Springfield, MO: World Library, 1996.

Hughes, Philip Edgcumbe. *The True Image: The Origin and Destiny of Man in Christ.* Eugene, OR: Wipf & Stock, 2001.

"Investigative Footage." http://www.centerformedicalprogress.org/cmp/investigative-footage/.

Irenaeus of Lyons. *Against Heresies.* In *The Ante-Nicene Fathers, First Series,* edited by Alexander Roberts et al., 1:315–567. 10 vols. Buffalo, NY: Christian Literature, 1885.

Jaggar, Alison M. "Abortion Rights and Gender Justice Worldwide: An Essay in Political Philosophy." In *Abortion: Three Perspectives,* 120–79. New York: Oxford University Press, 2009.

Jenni, Ernst. "דמה." In *TLOT* 339–42.

Jenson, Robert W. "*Anima Ecclesiastica.*" In *God and Human Dignity,* edited by R. Kendall Soulen and Linda Woodhead, 851–1024. Grand Rapids, MI: Eerdmans, 2006. Kindle edition.

Just, Arthur A., ed. *Luke.* Ancient Christian Commentary on Scripture. Downers Grove, IL: InterVarsity, 2005.

Kaczor, Christopher. *The Ethics of Abortion: Women's Rights, Human Life, and the Question of Justice.* 2nd ed. New York: Routledge, 2015.

Kaposy, Chris. "The Ethical Case for Having a Baby with Down Syndrome." *The New York Times,* April 18, 2018. https://www.nytimes.com/2018/04/16/opinion/down-syndrome-abortion.html.

Keener, Craig S. *The IVP Bible Background Commentary: New Testament.* Downers Grove, IL: InterVarsity, 1993.

Keil, Carl Fredrich, and Franz Delitzsch. *Commentary on the Old Testament.* 10 vols. Peabody, MA: Hendrickson, 1996.

Kilner, John F. *Dignity and Destiny: Humanity in the Image of God.* Grand Rapids, MI: Eerdmans, 2015.

Kittel, Gerhard. "Εἰκών." In *TDNT* 2:381–98.

―――. "Ἔσοπτρον, Κατοπτρίζομαι." In *TDNT* 2:696–97.

Klusendorf, Scott. *The Case for Life: Equipping Christians to Engage the Culture.* Wheaton, IL: Crossway, 2009.

Kruse, Colin G. *The Letters of John.* Pillar New Testament Commentary. Grand Rapids, MI: Eerdmans, 2000.

―――. *Paul's Letter to the Romans.* Pillar New Testament Commentary. Cambridge, UK: Eerdmans, 2012.

Kuhse, Helga, and Peter Singer. "The Moral Status of the Embryo." In *Unsanctifying Human Life: Essays on Ethics,* 181–87. Malden, MA: Blackwell, 2002.

―――. *Should the Baby Live? The Problem of Handicapped Infants.* New York: Oxford, 1985.

LaHaye, Tim. *Revelation Illustrated and Made Plain.* Rev. ed. Grand Rapids, MI: Zondervan, 1975.

Lange, John Peter. *A Commentary on the Holy Scriptures: Genesis.* Edited by Philip Schaff. Translated by A. Gosman and Tayler Lewis. Bellingham, WA: Logos Bible Software, 2008.

Lewis, C. S. *The Last Battle.* The Chronicles of Narnia. New York: HarperCollins, 1984.

―――. *The Magician's Nephew.* The Chronicles of Narnia. New York: HarperCollins, 1983.

Lints, Richard. *Identity and Idolatry: The Image of God and Its Inversion.* New Studies in Biblical Theology. Downers Grove, IL: Intervarsity, 2015.

Loh, I-Jin, and Howard Hatton. *A Handbook on the Letter from James.* UBS Handbook Series. New York: United Bible Societies, 1997.

Macklin, Ruth. "Dignity Is a Useless Concept." *British Medical Journal* 327.7429 (December 20, 2003) 1419–20.

Marshall, I. Howard. "Acts." In *Commentary on the New Testament Use of the Old Testament*, 513–601. Grand Rapids, MI: Baker Academic, 2007.

———. *The Gospel of Luke: A Commentary on the Greek Text.* New International Greek Testament Commentary. Exeter: Paternoster, 1978.

Mathews, Kenneth A. *Genesis 1–11:26.* The New American Commentary. Nashville: Broadman & Holman, 1996.

Mays, James Luther. "The Self in the Psalms and the Image of God." In *God and Human Dignity*, edited by R. Kendall Soulen and Linda Woodhead, 389–617. Grand Rapids, MI: Eerdmans, 2006. Kindle edition.

McRoberts, Kerry D. "The Holy Trinity." In *Systematic Theology*, edited by Stanley M. Horton, 3068–857. Rev. ed. Springfield, MO: Logion, 2012. Kindle edition.

———. *New Age or Old Lie?* Peabody, MA: Hendrickson, 1989.

Melick, Richard R. *Philippians, Colossians, Philemon.* The New American Commentary. Nashville: Broadman & Holman, 1991.

Merritt, Jonathan. "The Downfall of the Ex-Gay Movement." *The Atlantic*, October 6, 2015. https://www.theatlantic.com/politics/archive/2015/10/the-man-who-dismantled-the-ex-gay-ministry/408970/.

Metzger, Bruce A. *A Textual Commentary on the Greek New Testament.* 2nd ed. Stuttgart: United Bible Societies, 1994.

Michaelis, Wilhelm. "Πρῶτος, Πρῶτον, Πρωτοκαθεδρία, Πρωτοκλισία, Πρωτότοκος, Πρωτοτοκεῖα, Πρωτεύω." In *TDNT* 6:865–83.

Michaelson, Jay. "What Does the Bible Teach About Transgender People?" *The Daily Beast*, March 4, 2018. https://www.thedailybeast.com/what-does-the-bible-teach-about-transgender-people.

Middleton, J. Richard. "Image of God." In *Dictionary of Scripture and Ethics*, edited by Joel B. Green et al., 394–97. Grand Rapids, MI: Baker Academic, 2011.

———. *The Liberating Image: The Imago Dei in Genesis 1.* Grand Rapids, MI: Brazos, 2005.

Miley, John. *Systematic Theology.* 2 vols. Peabody, MA: Hendrickson, 1989.

Millard, Alan R., and Pierre Bordreuil. "A Statue from Syria with Assyrian and Aramaic Inscriptions." *Biblical Archeologist* 45.3 (1982) 135–41.

Miller, Stephen R. *Daniel.* The New American Commentary. Nashville: Broadman & Holman, 1994.

Mitchell, C. Ben, et al. *Biotechnology and the Human Good.* Washington, DC: Georgetown University Press, 2007.

"Modern Era Genocides." https://genocideeducation.org/resources/modern-era-genocides/.

Moltmann, Jürgen. *Man: Christian Anthropology in the Conflicts of the Present.* Translated by John Sturdy. Philadelphia: Fortress, 1974.

Montgomery, John Warwick. "The Christian View of the Fetus." In *Jurisprudence: A Book of Readings*, edited by John Warwick Montgomery, 567–87. Strasbourg: International Scholarly, 1974.

———. *Human Rights and Human Dignity.* Dallas: Probe, 1986.

Moo, Douglas J. *The Epistle to the Romans.* New International Commentary on the New Testament. Grand Rapids, MI: Eerdmans, 1996.

———. *The Letter of James.* Pillar New Testament Commentary. Grand Rapids, MI: Eerdmans, 2000.

———. *The Letters to the Colossians and to Philemon.* Pillar New Testament Commentary. Grand Rapids, MI: Eerdmans, 2008.

Moore, Keith L., et al. *The Developing Human: Clinically Oriented Embryology.* 10th ed. Philadelphia: Elsevier, 2016.

Motyer, J. Alec. *The Prophecy of Isaiah.* Downers Grove, IL: InterVarsity, 1993.

Mounce, Robert H. *The Book of Revelation.* New International Commentary on the New Testament. Grand Rapids, MI: Eerdmans, 1977.

———. *Romans.* New American Commentary. Nashville: Broadman & Holman, 1995.

Moyers, Bill. *Genesis: A Living Conversation.* New York: Doubleday, 1996.

Nathanson, Bernard. *The Silent Scream.* Anaheim, CA: American Portrait Films, 1984.

Neusner, Jacob. "The Restoration of Israel: Soteriology in Rabbinic Judaism." In *This World and the World to Come,* edited by Daniel M. Gurtner, 285–96. New York: T. & T. Clark, 2011.

"New ILO Global Estimate of Forced Labour: 20.9 Million Victims." *International Labor Organization,* June 1, 2012. https://www.ilo.org/global/topics/forced-labour/news/WCMS_182109/lang--en/index.htm.

Nickelsburg, George W. E. *Resurrection, Immortality, and Eternal Life in Intertestamental Judaism.* Harvard University Press, 1972.

———. "Salvation Among the Jews: Some Comments and Observations." In *This World and the World to Come,* edited by Daniel M. Gurtner, 299–314. New York: T. & T. Clark, 2011.

Niditch, Susan. "Genesis." In *Women's Bible Commentary.* Rev. ed. Louisville: Westminster John Knox, 2012.

Niebuhr, Reinhold. *The Nature and Destiny of Man: A Christian Interpretation.* 2nd ed. 2 vols. New York: Scribner's, 1964.

Nolland, John. *The Gospel of Matthew: A Commentary on the Greek Text.* New International Greek Testament Commentary. Grand Rapids, MI: Eerdmans, 2005.

"Nuclear Weapons: Who Has What?" *CNN,* January 6, 2017. http://www.cnn.com/interactive/2013/03/world/nuclear-weapon-states/.

Nunnally, Wave. *The Book of Acts: An Independent-Study Textbook.* Springfield, MO: Global University, 2007.

O'Brien, Peter T. *The Letter to the Ephesians.* Pillar New Testament Commentary. Grand Rapids, MI: Eerdmans, 1999.

———. *The Letter to the Hebrews.* Pillar New Testament Commentary. Grand Rapids, MI: Eerdmans, 2010.

O'Mathuna, Donal. "The Bible and Abortion: What of the 'Image of God.'" In *Bioethics and the Future of Medicine,* edited by J. F. Kilner et al., 199–211. Grand Rapids, MI: Eerdmans, 1995.

O'Rahilly, Ronan R., and Fabiola Müller. *Human Embryology & Teratology.* 3rd ed. New York: Wiley-Liss, 2001.

Ortlund, Raymond C., Jr. *Whoredom: God's Unfaithful Wife in Biblical Theology.* New Studies in Biblical Theology. Grand Rapids, MI: Eerdmans, 1996.

Osborne, Grant R. *The Hermeneutical Spiral: A Comprehensive Introduction to Biblical Interpretation.* Downers Grove, IL: InterVarsity, 1991.

Oss, Douglas A. "Canon as Context: The Function of *Sensus Plenior* in Evangelical Hermeneutics." *Grace Theological Journal* 9 (1988) 105–27.

Oswalt, John N. "בָּרַךְ." In *Theological Wordbook of the Old Testament*, edited by R. Laird Harris et al., 132–33. Chicago: Moody, 1999.

Packer, J. I. *Knowing God*. Downers Grove, IL: InterVarsity, 1973.

———. *Knowing Man*. Westchester, IL: Crossway, 1979.

Panné, Jean-Louis, et al. *The Black Book of Communism: Crimes, Terror, Repression*. Edited by Mark Kramer. Translated by Jonathan Murphy. Cambridge, MA: Harvard University Press, 1999.

Pannenberg, Wolfhart. *Systematic Theology*. Translated by Geoffrey W. Bromiley. 3 vols. Grand Rapids, MI: Eerdmans, 1991.

Pao, David W. *Acts and the Isaianic New Exodus*. Vol. 2. 130th ed. Wissenschaftliche Untersuchungen Zum Neuen Testament. Tübingen: Mohr Siebeck, 2000.

Pao, David W., and Eckhard J. Schnabel. "Luke." In *Commentary on the New Testament Use of the Old Testament*, 251–403. Grand Rapids, MI: Baker Academic, 2007.

Patterson, Paige. *Revelation*. New American Commentary. Nashville: Broadman & Holman, 2012.

Pearcey, Nancy R. *Love Thy Body: Answering Hard Questions about Life and Sexuality*. Grand Rapids, MI: Baker, 2018.

Peterson, David G. *The Acts of the Apostles*. The Pillar New Testament Commentary. Grand Rapids, MI: Eerdmans, 2009.

Philo of Alexandria. *The Works of Philo: Complete and Unabridged*. Edited by Charles Duke Yonge. Peabody, MA: Hendrickson, 1995.

"Physician-Assisted Suicide Fast Facts." *CNN*, June 11, 2020. https://www.cnn.com/2014/11/26/us/physician-assisted-suicide-fast-facts/index.html.

Pinker, Steven. "The Moral Instinct." *The New York Times Magazine*, January 13, 2008. https://www.nytimes.com/2008/01/13/magazine/13Psychology-t.html.

———. "The Stupidity of Dignity." *The New Republic*, May 27, 2008. https://newrepublic.com/article/64674/the-stupidity-dignity.

Piper, John. "The Image of God: An Approach from Biblical and Systematic Theology." *Desiring God* (blog), September 14, 2015. http://www.desiringgod.org/articles/the-image-of-god.

———. "The Image of God: An Approach from Biblical and Systematic Theology." *Studia Biblica et Theologica* no. 1 (1971) 15–32.

Plato. *Plato: In Twelve Volumes*. Translated by Harold North Fowler. Cambridge, MA: Harvard University Press, 1921.

Polhill, John B. *Acts*. The New American Commentary. Nashville: Broadman & Holman, 1992.

Polkinghorne, John. "Anthropology in an Evolutionary Context." In *God and Human Dignity*, edited by R. Kendall Soulen and Linda Woodhead, 1210–1400. Grand Rapids, MI: Eerdmans, 2006. Kindle edition.

Pope, William Burt. *A Compendium of Christian Theology: Being Analytical Outlines of a Course of Theological Study, Biblical, Dogmatic, Historical, Volumes I–III*. London: Beveridge, 1879.

Poythress, Vern S. "Kinds of Biblical Theology." *Westminster Theological Journal* 70.1 (March 1, 2008) 129–42.

Rad, Gerhard von. *Genesis: A Commentary*. Translated by John H. Marks. Rev. ed. The Old Testament Library. Philadelphia: Westminster, 1972.

Rad, Gerhard von, et al. "Εἰκών." In *TDNT* 2:381–98.

Rae, Scott B., and Paul M. Cox. *Bioethics: A Christian Approach in a Pluralistic Age.* Grand Rapids, MI: Eerdmans, 1999.

Rahner, Karl, and Herbert Vorgrimler. *Dictionary of Theology.* 2nd ed. New York: Crossroad, 1981.

Reinders, Hans S. "Human Dignity in the Absence of Agency." In *God and Human Dignity,* edited by R. Kendall Soulen and Linda Woodhead, 1632–847. Grand Rapids, MI: Eerdmans, 2006. Kindle edition.

Richardson, Kurt A. *James.* The New American Commentary. Nashville: Broadman & Holman, 1997.

Ross, Allen P. *Creation and Blessing: A Guide to the Study and Exposition of Genesis.* Grand Rapids, MI: Baker, 1998.

Sadler, T. W. *Langman's Medical Embryology.* 3rd ed. New York: Wiley-Liss, 2001.

Sartre, Jean-Paul. "Existentialism." In *The Great Ideas Today 1963,* edited by Robert M. Hutchins and Mortimer J. Adler, 447–61. Translated by Bernard Frechtman. Chicago: Encyclopaedia Britannica, 1963.

Sasse, Hermann. "Αἰών, Αἰώνιος." In *TDNT* 1:197–209. Grand Rapids, MI: Eerdmans, 1964.

Schaeffer, Francis A. "Pollution and the Death of Man." In *The Complete Works of Francis A. Schaeffer: A Christian Worldview: A Christian View of the West,* 5:1–76. 5 vols. Westchester, IL: Crossway, 1982.

Schaeffer, Francis A., and C. Everett Koop. "Whatever Happened to the Human Race?" In *The Complete Works of Francis A. Schaeffer: A Christian Worldview: A Christian View of the West,* 5:279–410. 5 vols. Westchester, IL: Crossway, 1982.

Schmidt, W. H. "אֱלֹהִים." In *TLOT* 115–26.

Schweizer, Eduard. "Χοϊκός." In *TDNT* 9:472–79.

Schweizer, Eduard, et al. "Ψυχή, Ψυχικός, Ἀνάψυξις, Ἀναψύχω, Δίψυχος, Ὀλιγόψυχος." In *TDNT* 9:608–66.

Schwöbel, Christoph. "Recovering Human Dignity." In *God and Human Dignity,* edited by R. Kendall Soulen and Linda Woodhead, 629–838. Grand Rapids, MI: Eerdmans, 2006. Kindle edition.

Scott, Jack B. "אלה." In *Theological Wordbook of the Old Testament,* edited by R. Laird Harris et al., 41–45. Chicago: Moody, 1999.

Self, Charlie. *Flourishing Churches and Communities: A Pentecostal Primer on Faith, Work, and Economics for Spirit-Empowered Discipleship.* Grand Rapids, MI: Christian's Library, 2012. Kindle edition.

Shead, A. G. "Sabbath." In *New Dictionary of Biblical Theology,* edited by T. Desmond Alexander and Brian S. Rosner, 745–50. Downers Grove, IL: InterVarsity, 2000.

Simpson, E. K., and F. F. Bruce. *Commentary on the Epistles to the Ephesians and the Colossians.* New International Commentary on the New Testament. Grand Rapids, MI: Eerdmans, 1957.

Smith, Gary V. *Isaiah 1–39.* The New American Commentary. Nashville: Broadman & Holman, 2007.

Snodgrass, Klyne. "The Use of the Old Testament in the New." In *New Testament Criticism and Interpretation,* edited by David Alan Black and David S. Dockery, 409–34. Grand Rapids, MI: Zondervan, 1991.

Speiser, E. A. *Genesis.* The Anchor Bible 1. Garden City, NY: Doubleday, 1964.

Spicq, Ceslas. "δόξα." In *TLNT* 1:362–79.

Spong, John Shelby. *Resurrection: Myth or Reality?* San Francisco: HarperSanFrancisco, 1994.

"Status of Global Christianity 2017." https://web.archive.org/web/20170215105830/
http://www.gordonconwell.edu/ockenga/research/documents/
StatusofGlobalChristianity2017.pdf.

Stein, Robert H. *Luke.* The New American Commentary. Nashville: Broadman &
Holman, 1992.

Stonehouse, Ned B. "The Areopagus Address." In *Paul before the Areopagus and Other
New Testament Studies,* 1–40. Grand Rapids, MI: Eerdmans, 1957.

Stuart, Douglas K. *Exodus.* New American Commentary. Nashville: Broadman &
Holman, 2006.

Sulmasy, Daniel P. "Dignity and Bioethics: History, Theory, and Selected Applications."
In *Human Dignity and Bioethics: Essays Commissioned by the President's Council
on Bioethics,* edited by Tom Merrill, 469–501. Washington, DC: n.p., 2008.

Summit Ministries. "The Abortion Debate—Dr. Willie Parker vs. Dr. Mike Adams."
YouTube, February 27, 2019. https://www.youtube.com/watch?v=lTIpSmzlMwo.

Thielman, Frank S. "Ephesians." In *Commentary on the New Testament Use of the Old
Testament,* 813–33. Grand Rapids, MI: Baker Academic, 2007.

Thiessen, Henry Clarence. *Lectures in Systematic Theology.* Grand Rapids, MI:
Eerdmans, 1949.

Thiselton, Anthony C. *The First Epistle to the Corinthians: A Commentary on the Greek
Text.* New International Greek Testament Commentary. Grand Rapids, MI:
Eerdmans, 2000.

"This Is Abortion." http://caseforlife.com/.

Thomson, Judith Jarvis. "A Defense of Abortion." In *Biomedical Ethics,* edited by David
DeGrazia et al., 479–86. 7th ed. New York: McGraw-Hill, 2011.

Tooley, Michael. *Abortion and Infanticide.* New York: Oxford, 1983.

———. "Abortion: Why a Liberal View Is Correct." In *Abortion: Three Perspectives,*
3–64. New York: Oxford University Press, 2009.

Ukpong, Justin S. "Tribute to Caesar, Mark 12:13–17 (Mt 22:15–22; Lk 20:20–26)."
Neotestamentica 33.2 (1999) 433–44.

VanGemeren, Willem. *The Progress of Redemption: The Story of Salvation from Creation
to the New Jerusalem.* Grand Rapids, MI: Zondervan, 1988.

———. *Psalms.* Rev. ed. The Expositor's Bible Commentary. Grand Rapids, MI:
Zondervan, 2008.

Vorländer, Herwart, and Colin Brown. "Reconciliation." In *The New International
Dictionary of New Testament Theology,* edited by Colin Brown, 145–76. Grand
Rapids, MI: Regency, 1986.

Vos, Geerhardus. *Biblical Theology: Old and New Testaments.* Edinburgh: Banner of
Truth Trust, 1975.

Wagner, Stephen, et al. "De Facto Guardianship and Abortion: A Response to the
Strongest Violinist." *Justice for All* (blog), April 13, 2013. http://doc.jfaweb.org/
Training/DeFactoGuardian-v03.pdf.

Waltke, Bruce K. "נֶפֶשׁ." In *Theological Wordbook of the Old Testament,* edited by R.
Laird Harris et al., 587–91. Chicago: Moody, 1999.

Walvoord, John F. *The Revelation of Jesus Christ: A Commentary.* Chicago: Moody, 1966.

Warren, Mary Anne. "On the Moral and Legal Status of Abortion." In *Biomedical
Ethics,* edited by David DeGrazia et al., 468–75. 7th ed. New York: McGraw-Hill
Education, 2011.

Watts, Fraser. "Human Dignity: Concepts and Experiences." In *God and Human
Dignity,* edited by R. Kendall Soulen and Linda Woodhead, 3198–400. Grand
Rapids, MI: Eerdmans, 2006. Kindle edition.

Wenham, Gordon J. *Genesis 1–15*. Word Biblical Commentary. Waco, TX: Word, 1987.

Westermann, Claus. *Genesis 1–11: A Continental Commentary*. Translated by John J. Scallion. Minneapolis: Fortress, 1994.

White, Lynn, Jr. "The Future of Compassion." *The Ecumenical Review* 30.2 (April 1978) 99–109.

———. "The Historical Roots of Our Ecologic Crisis." *Science* no. 155 (March 10, 1967) 1203–7.

Wilckens, Ulrich. "Χαρακτήρ." In *TDNT* 9:418–23.

Wildberger, Hans. "צֶלֶם." In *TLOT* 1080–85.

Williams, J. Rodman. *Renewal Theology: Systematic Theology from a Charismatic Perspective*. 3 vols. Grand Rapids, MI: Zondervan, 1988.

Witherington, Ben, III. *The Acts of the Apostles: A Socio-Rhetorical Commentary*. Grand Rapids, MI: Eerdmans, 1998.

———. *Conflict and Community in Corinth: A Socio-Rhetorical Commentary on 1 and 2 Corinthians*. Grand Rapids, MI: Eerdmans, 1995.

———. *The Gospel of Mark: A Socio-Rhetorical Commentary*. Grand Rapids, MI: Eerdmans, 2001.

———. *The Letters to Philemon, the Colossians, and the Ephesians: A Socio-Rhetorical Commentary on the Captivity Epistles*. Grand Rapids, MI: Eerdmans, 2007.

Witherington, Ben, III, and Darlene Hyatt. *Paul's Letter to the Romans: A Socio-Rhetorical Commentary*. Grand Rapids, MI: Eerdmans, 2004.

Wolf, Naomi. "Our Bodies, Our Souls." *The New Republic*, October 16, 1995.

Wolf-Devine, Celia, and Philip E. Devine. "Abortion: A Communitarian Pro-Life Perspective." In *Abortion: Three Perspectives*, 65–119. New York: Oxford University Press, 2009.

Woodhead, Linda. "Apophatic Anthropology." In *God and Human Dignity*, edited by R. Kendall Soulen and Linda Woodhead, 3006–185. Grand Rapids, MI: Eerdmans, 2006. Kindle edition.

Wright, Christopher J. H. *The Mission of God: Unlocking the Bible's Grand Narrative*. Downers Grove, IL: InterVarsity Press, 2006.

———. *Old Testament Ethics for the People of God*. Grand Rapids, MI: IVP Academic, 2013.

Wright, N. T. *Acts for Everyone, Part 2: Chapters 13–28*. London: SPCK, 2008.

———. *After You Believe: Why Christian Character Matters*. New York: HarperOne, 2010.

———. *The Climax of the Covenant: Christ and the Law in Pauline Theology*. Edinburgh: T. & T. Clark, 1991.

———. *Jesus and the Victory of God*. Minneapolis: Fortress, 1996.

———. *Luke for Everyone*. London: SPCK, 2004.

———. *The New Testament and the People of God*. Minneapolis: Fortress, 1992.

———. *Paul and the Faithfulness of God*. 2 vols. Minneapolis: Fortress, 2013.

———. *The Resurrection of the Son of God*. Minneapolis: Fortress, 2003.

Index of Modern Authors

Index of Ancient Documents

Ezekiel (*cont.*)

11:19–20	105
20:39	48
23:3–21	43
23:14–15	19
23:14	7
28:13	32
36–37	74
36:26–28	106
36:26	127
36:27	118
36:35	17
37	5
38–39	34
38:16	76
40–48	34
44:14	12
47:1–12	17

Daniel

2	59, 60, 63, 151
2:21	58
2:31–45	54–55
2:34	58
2:35	xix, 54, 56, 185, 186
2:37–38	56
2:38	55
2:39–40	55
2:40–41	56
2:44–45	58
2:44	56
2:47	58
3	148, 149, 151
3:1–3	58
3:1	xix, 54, 186
3:4–7	148
3:5	58
3:7	58, 59
3:12	58, 148
3:15	58, 59
3:16–18	148
3:17–18	59
3:18	58
3:25	59
3:28–30	59

4	59, 151, 193
4:25	59
4:30	56, 59
4:33	59
7	59–60, 63, 140, 144, 145, 151, 166, 193
7:2–3	145
7:4	59
7:5–7	59
7:7	150
7:8	59
7:9–13	150
7:9–12	59
7:13–14	60
7:13	61
7:17–18	60
7:17	145
7:18	150
7:21	145
7:22	150
7:27	35, 150
9:11–13	1
9:27	54
10:13–14	53, 135
11:31	54
12:1	53, 135
12:11	54

Hosea

1:2	43
1:10	185
4:16–18	45
6:4	32
6:7	31–32
6:8	32
6:9	32
9:9	114
11	143
11:1	73, 126
11:3–4	126
11:5–7	179
11:8–9	126
11:8	31, 179
11:10–11	179
11:10	179

2 Corinthians

CPSIA information can be obtained
at www.ICGtesting.com
Printed in the USA
FSHW020020090421
80226FS

9 781725 277182